Siauw Giok Tjhan

To my mother, Tan Gien Hwa

Siauw Giok Tjhan

Bicultural leader in emerging Indonesia

Siauw Tiong Djin

© Copyright 2018 Siauw Tiong Djin

All rights reserved. Apart from any uses permitted by Australia's Copyright Act 1968, no part of this book may be reproduced by any process without prior written permission from the copyright owners. Inquiries should be directed to the publisher.

Monash University Publishing
Matheson Library and Information Services Building
40 Exhibition Walk
Monash University
Clayton, Victoria 3800, Australia
www.publishing.monash.edu

Monash University Publishing brings to the world publications which advance the best traditions of humane and enlightened thought.

Monash University Publishing titles pass through a rigorous process of independent peer review.

www.publishing.monash.edu/books/sgt-9781925523362.html

Series: Herb Feith Translation Series

Series Editor: Jemma Purdey

Design: Les Thomas

Cover image: Siauw Giok Tjhan as he appeared on this Indonesian Parliamentarian ID card, 1955. From the personal collection of Siauw Tiong Djin.

Cover quotes:
　Charles A. Coppel: from the 'Foreword' to this book, p. ix.
　Daniel S. Lev, 'Becoming an *Orang Indonesia Sejati*: The Political Journey of
　　Yap Thiam Hien': *Indonesia*, Special Issue, July 1991, p. 102.

National Library of Australia Cataloguing-in-Publication entry:
Creator:	Siauw, Tiong Djin - author.
Title:	Siauw Giok Tjhan : bicultural leader in emerging Indonesia / Siauw Tiong Djin.
ISBN:	9781925523362 (paperback)
Subjects:	Siauw, Giok Tjhan.
	Chinese--Indonesia--Biography.
	Nationalists--Indonesia--Biography.
	Chinese--Indonesia--Politics and government.
	Political activists--Indonesia--Biography.
	Chinese--Cultural assimilation--Indonesia--History.
	Indonesia--Politics and government--20th century.

Printed in Australia by Griffin Press an Accredited ISO AS/NZS 14001:2004 Environmental Management System printer.

CONTENTS

About the author...vi
Foreword..vii
      By Charles A. Coppel
Preface..xi
Introduction..xix

PART I: 1914–1946 1
1. Childhood and formative years 3
2. The Japanese occupation and early months of independence.....29

PART II: 1946–1954 45
3. Partai Sosialis, Badan Pekerja and Yogyakarta 47
4. Journalism and politics in Jakarta 77

PART III: 1954–1965 101
5. Baperki...103
6. Baperki in the 1955 elections.............................123
7. Citizenship and dual nationality 146
8. Siauw's economic platform.................................167
9. Transition to Guided Democracy 184
10. The period of Guided Democracy 208
11. Baperki's educational, cultural and youth programs 236
12. The assimilation–integration debate 251

PART IV: 1965–1981 273
13. Baperki's last months....................................275
14. Imprisonment and release 299
15. A highly successful Chinese leader 306

Glossary..323
Select bibliography 333
Index...341
About the Herb Feith Translation Series 349

ABOUT THE AUTHOR

Siauw Tiong Djin is the son of Siauw Giok Tjhan. He was nine years old when his father was arrested by General Soeharto in November 1965. Like millions of other children in Indonesia whose parents were purged during the New Order period (1965 to 1998), Tiong Djin grew up with the stigma that his father had committed treason. Between 1969 and 1973, while his father was in detention, Tiong Djin visited him frequently and they had long discussions about his father's political journey and political aspirations. These discussions inspired Tiong Djin to restore his father's name and reputation.

Tiong Djin has a Bachelor of Engineering (1979), Master of Engineering (1982) and Master of Business Administration (1990) from RMIT University. While working as an engineer he embarked on his PhD in Political Science at Monash University, completing it in 1999.

FOREWORD

Siauw Giok Tjhan (SGT) was the most influential Chinese Indonesian politician in the two decades after 1945. During the Indonesian struggle for independence he was a member of the KNIP (Central Indonesian National Committee) and its Badan Pekerja (Working Committee) and was an Indonesian cabinet minister. As the chairman of Baperki, the largest organisation of Chinese Indonesians, from 1954 to 1965, he had widespread support from *peranakan* and *totok* Chinese. His radical left political sympathies and status as a Chinese community leader made him a controversial figure, especially among anti-communists and advocates of assimilation. They also led to his arrest and subsequent internment without trial for twelve years. Although he died in 1981, it was not until after the fall of President Soeharto in 1998 that his place in modern Indonesian history could be properly recognised.

Siauw Tiong Djin (Djin), the author of this biography, was only nine years old when his father was arrested and interned in November 1965. When Djin left Indonesia at the end of 1973 to make a new life in Australia, SGT was still in prison. He would only have two brief reunions with his father, each lasting a mere two weeks; one in Jakarta in early 1978 (when SGT was released from prison but still under house arrest), and the other in Europe in early 1980 (when SGT was in political exile in the Netherlands). Notwithstanding this separation, Djin kept in regular contact with his father through exchange of letters.

SGT spent most of the early years after his arrest in Salemba prison, where the family could only visit him once a month for about 15 minutes in the presence and within the hearing of several guards. In June 1970 he was moved first to a concentration camp in Kebayoran Lama and then to a military prison in Lapangan Banteng. In both places he was intensively interrogated and was under severe psychological stress but, unlike others, was not physically tortured. In August 1972 he was moved again to Nirbaya where he was interned with other prominent civilian and military political prisoners, before being returned to Salemba in July 1973.

Paradoxically at these other locations, unlike Salemba, family members could visit him for an hour each week and the visits were made in a more relaxed atmosphere and were less strictly supervised. In visits during this three-year period, Djin asked him questions about Baperki and his political role. Prompted by the pervasive New Order propaganda, his questions ironically mimicked the interrogation that his father was undergoing. Rather than add to the father's stress, the teenage son's questioning gave SGT the opportunity to give more relaxed answers to a trusted confidant. Entrusted with his father's confidences and with tasks on his behalf, Djin in return provided him with an element of 'psychological therapy'.

This crucial period of his life is the key to Djin's determination to rehabilitate his father's name in Indonesian history, especially in Indonesia. Encouraged by Herb Feith and Dan Lev, and notwithstanding that his academic background and profession were in the field of electrical engineering, he embarked on a PhD at Monash University in which his dissertation was to be a biography of his father.

He could only work on it part-time and by the time it was nearing completion events were changing rapidly in Indonesia. From July 1996 there were outbreaks of anti-Chinese violence, a severe economic crisis and rising opposition to the New Order which culminated in the resignation of Soeharto in May 1998. Djin responded by forming the Committee Against Racism in Indonesia (CARI). An early version of the dissertation was submitted for examination in late 1998 and by March 1999 it was published in Indonesian translation (*Siauw Giok Tjhan: Riwajat perjuangan seorang patriot membangun nasion Indonesia dan masyarakat Bhineka Tunggal Ika*, Jakarta: Hasta Mitra 1999). The new Reformasi era gave many opportunities to those wishing to 'straighten' the historical record (*meluruskan sejarah*). For Djin it was a chance to clear his father's name and he grasped it energetically. In May 2000 a book on the contribution of SGT and Baperki to Indonesian history appeared, edited by Djin with Oey Hay Djoen (*Sumbangsih Siauw Giok Tjhan dan Baperki dalam Sejarah Indonesia*, Jakarta: Hasta Mitra 2000).

After his release from prison, SGT had made several attempts to tell his own story. His book *Lima Jaman: Perwujudan Integrasi Wajar* was published by Yayasan Teratai in Amsterdam and Jakarta in 1981 (the year of his death) and appeared in Chinese translation in 1982. Another version of his memoirs confusingly appeared in two volumes in the monograph series published by the Southeast Asian Studies Centre of the James Cook University of North Queensland in Townsville (Bob Hering (ed.), *Siauw Giok Tjhan Remembers: A Peranakan-Chinese and the Quest for Indonesian Nationhood*, 1982 and Peter Burns (ed.), *Siauw Giok Tjhan Remembers: A Chinese Peranakan in Independent Indonesia*, 1984). Djin went on to undertake the major task of editing and combining these versions and the result

Foreword

was published in Jakarta by Lembaga Kajian Sinergi Indonesia in 2010 under the title *Renungan Seorang Patriot Indonesia: Siauw Giok Tjhan*.

The present volume is the revised version of Djin's doctoral dissertation. His dedication to the rehabilitation of his father can, I have suggested, be traced psychologically to his teenage experience with his father in prison. It can also be understood culturally as an expression of the classic Confucian precepts of filial piety (*xiao*, or *hauw* in the Hokkien form, frequently referred to in Chinese Malay didactic texts and novels). Djin has indeed proved himself to be an 'ideal man' in the Confucian tradition, a *junzi* (or *koentjoe*).

At last an English-speaking public can read an easily accessible account of the life of this ethnic Chinese who was a patriotic Indonesian and played an important role in Indonesia's modern history.

Charles A. Coppel
School of Historical and
Philosophical Studies
The University of Melbourne

PREFACE

This book is concerned with the political biography of my father, Siauw Giok Tjhan, an Indonesian–Chinese leader in the period of 1945 to 1965. It is largely derived from my thesis submitted, in November 1998, for the degree of Doctor of Philosophy at Monash University, Melbourne, Victoria. I was conferred with the PhD degree in 1999.

In the process of revising the thesis I completed an Indonesian version which was published as a book by Hasta Mitra in May 1999. That book, *Siauw Giok Tjhan: Riwajat perjuangan seorang patriot membangun nasion Indonesia dan masyarakat Bhineka Tunggal Ika (Siauw Giok Tjhan: A patriot's struggle to develop the Indonesian nation and a Bhineka Tunggal Ika society)*, is also largely based on the PhD thesis. (Bhineka Tunggal Ika is Indonesia's national motto and an Old Javanese phrase that means 'unity in diversity'.)

In 2010, I edited the book and Lembaga Kajian Sinergi Indonesia republished it with a new title: *Siauw Giok Tjhan dalam pembangunan nasion Indonesia (Siauw Giok Tjhan in the emerging Indonesian nation)* in May 2010.

My decision to write about my father was based in good part on the unusual opportunities I had to interact with him when he was in jail. It was also partly prompted by a meeting I had with Dan Lev and Herb Feith in Melbourne in 1988 in which aspects of his political biography were discussed. Go Gien Tjwan also urged me to write and I am grateful to all three of them for their encouragement to carry out detailed research on my father's political activities.

How does one write in a scholarly way about one's own father? The idea of writing this book arose out of admiration for my father's leadership and achievements, a situation which could clearly give rise to problems of imbalance in telling his story. In this sense, my obstacles are distinctly different to those faced by such biographers as John Legge (on Soekarno) and David Hill (on Mochtar Lubis).

Legge's passages on Soekarno's personal qualities clearly reflect his lack of sympathy for Soekarno. Clearly preferring Sjahrir's intellectualism to that of Soekarno, Legge writes:

> Though the world of thoughts was important to Soekarno he was by nature not analytical. Ideas in the round moved him: he was gripped by them and he used them for their evocative power, but his speeches and writings showed little analysis, little reflection, no expressions of

hesitation or doubt ... He was not, in brief, an intellectual's intellectual ... he was not concerned, as was Sjahrir, with the validity of an argument (and he was not torn, as was Sjahrir, by a sense of conflict between the sophistication of his western learning and the cultural heritage of his homeland).

In stronger personal terms Legge says:

> His role as Javanese ruler, the central actor of the Theatre State, had its corrupting effect on Soekarno ... But beyond these characteristics was a growing insensitivity to his own deficiencies of leadership, a hardening of his attitude to opponents and the quickening of a potentate's temper.[1]

In some cases it is the process of conducting research that leads to an ambivalent author–subject relationship. Hill reveals that while completing his doctoral thesis, a biography of Mochtar Lubis, he acquired information which had significantly changed his opinion of Mochtar Lubis. He says:

> The level of criticism, even from those generally sympathetic to him and his political views, was considerable... As I acquired more material about his attitudes, behavior and activities, as various informants provided their particular views of the man, I was increasingly challenged to think critically about his reputation and his life-myth.[2]

In my own case the experience was almost the opposite. In conducting my research, I deliberately sought comments from those who had opposed Siauw's position. While confirming their opposition to his political views, their comments on his personal qualities were uniformly positive. Junus Jahja, leader of the LPKB (Lembaga Pembina Kesatuan Bangsa – Institute for the Promotion of National Unity) and a man with strong commitment to realising assimilation, was a long-time opponent of Siauw's approach to minority problems. He has often blamed Siauw for the hardships experienced

---

[1] J.D. Legge, *Sukarno: A Political Biography*, Allen & Unwin, Sydney, 1984, pp. 37–38. Also see Angus McIntyre, 'Foreign Biographical Studies of Indonesian Subjects' in Angus McIntyre (ed.), *Indonesian Political Biography – In search of Cross-Cultural Understanding*, Monash Papers on Southeast Asia – No. 28, Monash University, 1993, pp. 312–313 for a detailed account of Legge's position on Soekarno.

[2] David T. Hill: 'The Objectification of Mochtar Lubis' in Angus McIntyre (ed.), *Indonesian Political Biography*, p. 271.

Preface

by the Chinese in Indonesia following the defeat of the G30S[3] movement (Gerakan 30 September – 30th September Movement) in 1965. Yet, in an interview in Melbourne in 1989, he stated:

> Siauw was a national hero. I was fortunate that I never met him as he was known to have the ability to convince people to accept his political views. A few of my colleagues met him and after these meetings, they changed their position on assimilation.[4]

Yap Thiam Hien, well known for his opposition to Siauw's left-wing political orientation, stated in December 1988:

> I highly respect Siauw for his dedication. He had a correct vision for Indonesia. It was indeed a pleasure to work closely with him in the 1950s... My resignation from Baperki's vice-presidency was not caused by my disagreement with Siauw. It was caused by my frustration that Siauw had let leftists take control of the Baperki leadership. I had no alternative but to publicly criticise him.'[5]

I have taken note of Angus McIntyre's warning that biographers should be careful in investigating and exploiting the biographer–subject relationship. McIntyre states:

> It is in the overlap or (in a loose sense of the word) identification between biographer and subject that the promises and perils of the biographical project principally reside. Whether this overlap is envisaged in terms of placing oneself in the subject's shoes, or projecting onto the person concerned "some unlived portions" of the self, or discovering that person (or some aspect thereof) in oneself, the principal promise remains genuine insight and an understanding uncluttered by moralism and the principal peril a recasting of the subject according to one's own image or desires.

---

[3] The 30th of September Movement (Indonesian: Gerakan 30 September, abbreviated as G30S, also known by the acronym Gestapu for Gerakan September Tiga Puluh or sometimes called Gestok, for *Gerakan Satu Oktober*, First of October Movement) was a self-proclaimed organisation of Indonesian national armed forces members who, in the early hours of 1 October 1965, assassinated six Indonesian Army generals.

[4] Interview with Junus Jahja, Melbourne, July 1989.

[5] Interview with Yap Thiam Hien, Melbourne, December 1988.

Furthermore, he says, 'Two other possibilities are also undesirable: identification leading not so much to understanding as to obtuse advocacy, and the refusal of identification accompanied by uncomprehending criticism.'[6]

In this case, McIntyre criticises Rose (Hatta's biographer) and Penders and Sundhaussen (Nasution's biographers) for siding with their subjects so that they take their subject's words without critically evaluating them.[7] By contrast he sees both Legge and Penders and Sundhaussen as excessively critical of Soekarno.[8]

My admiration for Siauw obviously stops me from condemning him. Furthermore, the special relationship I have with him enables me to not only understand the subject but also to exploit the biographer–subject relationship. Whenever possible, I have tried to put myself in his shoes as well as critically evaluate his statements or accounts. I have also attempted to distance myself from my subject. But I would not claim to be free from subjectivity.

I have tried to reduce the subjectivity by adopting a strategy which involved consulting as widely as possible with other people associated with events described and checking my father's accounts of events and written materials. I am grateful to all the people who have helped me with this daunting task, in particular my supervisors Dr Barbara Hatley and Dr Herbert Feith.

A major problem I faced in constructing Siauw Giok Tjhan's political life story was concerned with Siauw's reluctance to write about himself. Unlike Soe Hok Gie who diligently wrote detailed accounts of his activities in his diary – largely used by John Maxwell in his doctoral thesis on his biography[9] – Siauw hardly detailed his activities, let alone his achievements, in his writings. Even his *Lima Jaman (Five Periods)*, which was intended to be his autobiography, is sketchy on many aspects of his political journey. The situation led Go Gien Tjwan to write a long introduction to Bob Hering's *Siauw Giok Tjhan Remembers*. He writes 'The purpose of this introduction is to place the figure Siauw Giok Tjhan within the political, social and cultural framework of his time and also to provide more data concerning the political career of Siauw which, due to his personal modesty, have been

---

[6] Angus McIntyre, 'Foreign Biographical Studies of Indonesian Subjects', pp. 307–308.

[7] Ibid., pp. 309–311.

[8] Ibid., pp. 311–314.

[9] John R. Maxwell, *Soe Hok Gie – A Biography of a Young Indonesian Intellectual*, unpublished PhD thesis, Australian National University, Canberra, June, 1997.

understated or scarcely mentioned in the two books written by himself.'[10] Accordingly, many aspects of his political journey detailed in this book are based on Siauw's own accounts conveyed to me by various means between 1971 and 1981.

Unlike Soe Hok Gie, who had a short span of political life, Siauw's 49 years in politics covered a wide range of activities including involvement in a number of organisations, membership of various governmental bodies and offices and participation in major political events.

This story of Siauw Giok Tjhan's life has been structured in four parts. The first two, which relate to his life before he became a leader of a mass organisation in 1954, are largely narrative. The second two are more thematic, discussing various areas in which he exercised political leadership after that year.

I was nine years old when Siauw was arrested in November 1965. I never lived with him after that. In December 1973 I left Indonesia for Australia. Prior to this, I met him in various prisons in Jakarta. In the first six years Siauw was detained mainly in Salemba prison. In that period meetings with him were limited to no more than 15 minutes once a month and were often closely supervised by prison guards.

From late 1971 to late 1973 Siauw was jailed in the Rumah Tahanan Militer (Military Prison) and at Nirbaya (a camp specially established to detain former ministers and senior military officers), both in Jakarta. In this period, my meetings with him were more frequent – once a week – and unsupervised.

In these two years my relationship with my father developed new dimensions. At that time, I was a teenager and a student in a Christian secondary school in Jakarta. At school, I was taught that the PKI (Partai Komunis Indonesia – Indonesian Communist Party) and its supporters were traitors who had nearly destroyed the country, that the PKI and its G30S movement were responsible for the killing of the six army generals in 1965, that the PKI members in jail were dangers to the country and that their ideas had to be completely eliminated.

Teachers and friends at the school knew my background. Fortunately, most of them were sympathetic and were understanding. However, whenever issues relevant to the G30S movement and the PKI were raised, I felt

---

[10] Bob Hering (ed.), *Siauw Giok Tjhan Remembers: A Peranakan Chinese and the Quest for Indonesian Nationhood*, South East Asia Monograph 11, James Cook University of North Queensland, Queensland, 1982.

uncomfortable and threatened. Although I never accepted the assertion that my father was a traitor, and hence bad for the country, questions about what he was committed to and how he was involved in the G30S movement continued to haunt me. Discussions of these issues, which could not be raised during the short meetings in the Salemba prison, could now take place freely. And I used these times extensively.

So I started interrogating my father on his political activities and what he stood for. At home, I started reading his speeches and Baperki documents. These weekly one-hour meetings then turned into sessions in which he conveyed reflections on his political activities and his interactions with prominent figures in Indonesia, Holland and China. Although the discussions were not structured in an interview format and no notes were taken, I remember many of his accounts vividly. I believe my father, himself, found these sessions therapeutic and therefore relieving. He was under pressure not to express his thoughts and frustration to his interrogators. He often told me the questions his interrogators posed to him and the answers he gave. And he talked to me about how he would have answered those questions if he had been in a position to speak freely.

I was always keen to meet my father in prison, not least because it made me feel important. My father assigned me to listen to news broadcasts from the BBC, ABC, Peking Radio and Moscow Radio. I was then to summarise the contents of these broadcasts and verbally convey them to him. In addition, I was assigned to collect clippings from various Indonesian newspapers and such foreign publications as *Newsweek*, *Time* and *The Far Eastern Economic Review*. I remember that I was always nervous when I had to quickly transfer small bundles of clippings from my trousers pocket to his.

As these weekly family meetings were held in a large hall in which people were free to mingle, my father often asked me to sit with other political prisoners who were keen to hear the summaries of news I had memorised. This situation enabled me to hear their comments about my father's political activities and his qualities as a political figure. Outside the prison, I also began to see friends of my father, who helped to financially support my family, to find out about what he stood for and what he had done for the Chinese community. To my pleasant surprise, everyone I talked to had only high regard for and positive words to say about him.

I believe I was most fortunate to be able to talk to Siauw while he was in jail. Through these meetings, I had the opportunity to hear him at his most reflective, having gone through interrogations and being together with a large number of political prisoners who had nothing to do but share their political experiences. His accounts were enriched with reflections on and reminiscences about various political events.

After my father was released from jail, I had the opportunity to be with him for three weeks in Indonesia, in 1978, and two weeks in Holland, in 1980. Many of the accounts he conveyed while in prison were repeated in these meetings. But at these times, my father was in a better position to describe important events and experiences because he had recently completed the manuscripts of his memoirs.

My relationship with my father continued to be special. We exchanged letters weekly, and his letters to me were mainly political. These letters were like editorials in political publications, providing detailed analyses on what was happening in the world and particularly in Indonesia. I do, however, regret that I did not begin writing his biography while he was still alive, as most of the interviews conducted with him were not structured and no notes were taken.

Writing about one's father in a scholarly manner is a difficult task. I am grateful to those who have helped me with it, particularly to Herb Feith and Barbara Hatley who thoroughly and patiently supervised and guided me for more than eight years between 1991 and 1999. Herb's detailed knowledge of the political environments to which my father was exposed helped me understand the complexities of his political work. Barbara provided me with her wealth of experience in analysing the cultural and social aspects of my father's life and helped me address the strengths and weaknesses of his political decisions.

I am indebted to Charles Coppel and Mary Somers Heidhues who provided valuable input and corrections to the thesis.

I have been fortunate to be able to meet and interview a large number of people in Indonesia, Australia, Holland, Germany, France, China and Hong Kong who had either worked closely with my father or dealt with his policies. I have discussed various aspects of my father's work and his leadership with some of them on numerous occasions. I am particularly grateful for the assistance rendered by the following people: my mother Tan Gien Hwa, the late Siauw Giok Bie, Go Gien Tjwan, Lee Nyan Hoo, the late Oei Tjoe Tat, the late Yap Thiam Hien, the late Phoa Thoan Hian, Oey Hay Djoen, Tan Hwie Kiat, the late Tan Tjin Siang, the late Wim Wertheim, Jusuf Adjitorop, the late Tjoa Sik Ien, the late Ernst Utrecht, Soemarsono, Jusuf Isak, Andrew Gunawan, the late Tan Soen Houw, Dan Lev, Ong Hok Ham, Mohamad Isa, Lie Xie Thian, Wong Ian,

Oei Him Hwie, Mrs Utami Suryadarma, Soetomo, Bambang Soemardjo, Hardojo, Francisca Fanggidaej, Arief Budiman, Karlina Leksono-Supelli and numerous others who cannot be named.

I am particularly indebted to my mother who carefully looked after most of the primary sources I used in this study. Her determination to save these important documents considered dangerous by the military authorities in the late 1960s is most admirable.

In addition to the people listed above, I have also received generous assistance from my brothers, sisters and cousins. My children, Thania Hoong-Sian Siauw and Tharee Kim-Hai Siauw have given indirect encouragement to complete the book. I wish to thank them for their continuing support and encouragement.

I wish to thank Ian Sutherland and Eleanor Tan for editing and reformatting the book.

I am also grateful to the Herb Feith Foundation for the generous assistance in making the publication of this book possible.

Finally my special thanks go to my wife, Leony Siauw whose support and encouragement has been indispensable.

I am solely responsible for all mistakes and deficiencies found in this book.

INTRODUCTION

This study examines how Siauw emerged as a bicultural leader, how he confronted and overcame political obstacles and the implications of his policies on the position of the Indonesian Chinese.

Siauw was born in Indonesia in 1914. When he turned 18, he joined the world of Indonesia-oriented politics led by Liem Koen Hian. This enabled him to meet and liaise with many nationalist leaders like Soetomo, Tjipto Mangunkusumo, Soekarno and Amir Sjarifuddin. Siauw thus turned his back on the largest two currents of opinion among the Indies Chinese who were oriented to China and the Dutch colonial system. Also, his participation in politics set him apart from the majority of Chinese who were stereotyped as non-political and business-minded.

Siauw was a prominent leader of the Indonesian Chinese in the first two decades of Indonesian independence. He began his working life in the 1930s as a journalist, on newspapers written for Chinese readers in the Dutch colony, and was active in organisations that tried to persuade the Indonesian Chinese to identify with Indonesia and its nationalist movement.

When Indonesian independence was declared in 1945, Siauw faced an uphill battle in convincing the Indonesian Chinese to support the new Republic of Indonesia. Most Indonesian Chinese, due to excesses during the revolution, had no confidence in Indonesia and preferred to align themselves either with China or the Netherlands.

Closely associated with many prominent leaders during the late colonial and revolutionary periods, Siauw was able to receive support for his political activities and maintain his membership of Indonesia's legislative institutions –the Badan Pekerja (Working Committee of the Central National Committee of Indonesia, or KNIP) during the revolutionary years from 1946 to 1949 and national parliament from 1950 to 1965. Siauw's role as a political leader in Jakarta was helped by the personal capital he brought with him, which included his circle of close associates from the Semarang, Surabaya and Malang groups, his ability to call on financial support from a range of Chinese businessmen and his friendships with Indigenous politicians from a wide range of positions, especially dating from his periods in the Badan Pekerja.

The most important part of his political career was his leadership of Baperki (Badan Permusyawaratan Kewarganegaraan Indonesia – Consultative Body for Indonesian Citizenship), whose members were largely people of Chinese descent. Baperki is the largest Indonesian Chinese organisation in the history of Indonesia. Siauw helped found Baperki in March 1954 and led the organisation from 1954 to 1965.

Siauw was a socialist. He saw socialism as providing answers both to the problems of Indonesia's Chinese and to the problems of Indonesian society as a whole. His commitment to Indonesian nationalism was combined with a socialist internationalism which led him to identify with progressive and anti-racist causes in other countries.

In the Indonesian nationalism of the 1945–65 period, there was persistent tension between two main themes. The first theme was 'we want to build a modern state in which there is justice, prosperity and no discrimination'. The second theme was 'we want to right the structural wrongs of the colonial rule in which the Dutch were on top, the natives at the bottom and the Chinese in the middle'. Siauw associated himself actively with the first theme, but was up against formidable opposition from various Indigenous groups because of the second.

Through Baperki he succeeded in providing political education to the Chinese in Indonesia and in ensuring that government regulations and laws were introduced to protect the interests of the Chinese minority. His main contributions were related to Indonesian citizenship and the propagation of a solution to the problems ethnic minorities faced, which he defined as the integration approach.

Siauw was one of the very few Indonesian Chinese politicians who was widely accepted and respected in the political elite of 1945–65. He was on close terms with such prominent national leaders as Soekarno, Mohamad Yamin, Sartono, Aruji Kartawinata, Adam Malik and many others.

He was particularly successful during the later part of the Guided Democracy period due to his closeness with President Soekarno and other left-wing forces, especially the PKI (Partai Komunis Indonesia – The Indonesian Communist Party). But this close alliance put him and Baperki in a camp opposing the right-wing forces represented by the army and anti-communist organisations. When the balance of power tilted to the right after October 1965, the political demise of Soekarno and members of the left-wing political organisations marked the end of Siauw's political career as a member of parliament and other high level government institutions. Siauw was arrested on 4 November 1965 and jailed without trial for 12 years. His organisation, Baperki, was officially banned in March 1966 and many members of the organisation became political prisoners.

Siauw was finally released from imprisonment in Jakarta on 1 May 1978. By then his health had deteriorated. He had suffered several heart attacks in prison and had lost vision from his left eye. Thanks to help from then Vice-President Adam Malik, a long time friend, he was permitted to go to the Netherlands for medical treatment. He and his wife arrived in Amsterdam on 18 September 1978.

However, Siauw failed to follow his doctors' advice to rest. Soon after his arrival in Holland, he began to campaign for the release of political prisoners in Indonesia and for funds to assist the political prisoners who had been released and their families. He also frequently gave lectures to students and exiled Indonesians in various European cities.

On 20 November 1981, a few minutes before he was to deliver a speech about the failure of Indonesian democracy before a group of Indonesianists at the University of Leiden, Siauw collapsed suddenly and died of a heart attack.

Many authors on Indonesian politics refer to Siauw as a communist or communist sympathiser. This book will show that Siauw was a Marxist and was sympathetic to many communist ideas. However, when it came to defending the Chinese interests in Indonesia, Siauw was very flexible in his Marxism and actively supported the enhancement of domestic capital for the construction of the national economy. In areas involving the Chinese and racism, Siauw often expressed views at odds with those of the PKI.

Siauw's life was intensely political. He lived a great deal of it in the public arena. Like many other political leaders, he gave his immediate family much less time than they craved. But this is a dimension of his life which I see as beyond the scope of this book.

This book details how Siauw Giok Tjhan emerged as a bicultural political figure and how he carried out his political programs in the various phases of Indonesian politics.

It shows that Chinese participation in politics coupled with a mass organisation that voiced the Chinese interests could prove to be effective and powerful in defending Chinese rights. This combination, reflected in Siauw Giok Tjhan's political journey, would have achieved a lot more if the political situation in 1965 had not dramatically changed. The political implications of this change for the Chinese community, the following chapters will show, were not totally dependent upon Baperki's political orientation or Siauw's political convictions.

This book will also address why Siauw's endeavor to combat racism was met with widespread resistance, and what impact Siauw and his policies had on the position of the Indonesian Chinese. A number of writers, including such academics as Charles Coppel, Mary Somers Heidhues, Dan Lev, Go Gien Tjwan and Leo Suryadinata, and such political actors as Oei Tjoe Tat, Yap Thiam Hien, Junus Jahja and Kristoforus Sindhunatha have expressed their views on Siauw Giok Tjhan. The book evaluates these views and compares them with my research findings and conclusions.

Siauw and Baperki fiercely fought for the outlawing of racism, and this was achieved. The 1945 Constitution had been amended to the extent that a non-native Indonesian could now become president of Indonesia. Previously, the constitution gave a justification for continuing to differentiate between Indigenous and non-Indigenous Indonesians. This was of concern to Siauw because, to him, it was destructive to nation building.

Siauw was right. The elimination of racism was indeed conducive to nation building. Many Chinese, particularly those of the young generation today have no qualms about treating Indonesia as their homeland. Many Chinese are involved in politics and social organisations. As Baperki encouraged in the 1960s, many are actively involved in politics, most notably Ahok (Basuki Tjahaja Purnama), who was governor of Jakarta at the time of writing.

While the Chinese today no longer face legal discrimination, one can argue that racism and anti-Chinese feelings remain in existence in social circles.

The upheavals against Basuki Tjahaja Purnama (Ahok), which reflect anti-Chinese sentiments, are the manifestations of the situation that Siauw repeatedly stated: '…menghilangkan rasialisme adalah sebuah perjuangan yang akan memakan waktu panjang…' (the elimination of racism is a long term struggle).

Sources

A large part of this study is based on written materials in the form of Siauw's speeches, articles, books, unpublished manuscripts and letters (particularly those written to me between 1975 and 1981).

Siauw had completed three manuscripts. All three were completed during his home detention period (1975–1978). The first manuscript called *Suatu Renungan* (*A Reflection*) is a detailed account of Indonesian modern history and the involvement of the Chinese in it. It was published in

Chinese in Hong Kong in 1981. The second, *Lima Jaman (Five Periods)* was intended to be a detailed account of Siauw's own involvement in Indonesian politics from the Dutch colonial period to the New Order period. Much of the material presented in *Suatu Renungan* was incorporated in *Lima Jaman*. This was published in Indonesian in Holland in 1981; however, it has failed to become Siauw's autobiography. Like *Suatu Renungan*, it is more a detailed analysis of political developments in Indonesia than an autobiography. *Lima Jaman*, incorporating small sections of *Suatu Renungan*, was translated into English in 1981. The first two chapters of the translated *Lima Jaman*, covering the periods of Dutch colonialism, Japanese occupation and early months of independence, were edited by Bob Hering and published as a monograph by James Cook University, Queensland in 1982. The monograph is titled *Siauw Giok Tjhan Remembers*. Parts of Chapter 3, covering the parliamentary democracy period and formation of Baperki, and parts of Chapter 5, the New Order period, of *Lima Jaman*, and incorporating small sections of *Suatu Renungan*, were later edited by Peter Burns and published by the same university as a monograph with the same title in 1984.[1]

The third manuscript, *For A Brighter Future*, was written in English. In this manuscript, Siauw provided details of the G30S movement (Gerakan 30 September – 30ᵗʰ September Movement) of 1965, his political imprisonment and his solutions to the problems faced by Indonesians in the late 1970s. It was translated into Chinese in 1989 and published in Hong Kong in 1996.

Siauw delivered numerous speeches in his public life. Many of these speeches were not published. Most of those delivered at Baperki functions were printed and circulated to Baperki members. Some were published as Baperki booklets.

As a journalist, Siauw wrote numerous articles in various newspapers and journals. Some of these articles were published using his pen names, which included Sakidjan, Tiong Ho and Tiong Djin. Siauw typed all of his speeches and articles himself. Many of these are available to me. However,

---

[1] This situation has created misunderstanding. Some people believe that the monograph series called *Siauw Giok Tjhan Remembers* are a full translation of *Lima Jaman*. Others believe that they are different from *Lima Jaman*. In reality because of the translation and substantial editing, the monograph series are slightly different from *Lima Jaman*. In this book, where the materials are derived from parts of *Lima Jaman* or *Suatu Renungan* which are also covered in the monograph series, the footnotes will refer to both publications. Otherwise, only *Lima Jaman* or *Suatu Renungan* will be noted.

many of them do not have dates and, as such, references to them will not detail the dates. I also used the minutes of numerous Baperki meetings. Most of these minutes were not widely circulated. Moreover, I have relied on structured interviews with a large number of people in Indonesia, China, Holland, Germany and Australia conducted over eight years. Although Siauw had written so much throughout his political career, many details of his experiences and his personal expectations were never reflected in his writings. I have accordingly also used the accounts conveyed to me during my meetings with Siauw, including the ones in jail.

Along with these, I have used materials from various Indonesian newspapers, journals and publications. Materials on the Indonesian Chinese from such scholars as Mary Somers Heidhues, Charles Coppel, Jamie Mackie, Go Gien Tjwan and Leo Suryadinata are also widely used in the book, along with materials on Indonesian politics from the 1940s to the 1960s written by Benedict Anderson, George Kahin, Herbert Feith, Daniel Lev, Rex Mortimer, Harold Crouch and others.

Historical perspectives

To understand Siauw's political commitments and his role in the political development of Indonesia, one needs to analyse the political, social and legal position of the Indonesian Chinese community, of which Siauw was a member. Set out below, therefore, is a brief summary of the history of the Chinese in Indonesia.

Chinese trade with the Indonesian archipelago goes back a very long way. There are reports of Chinese settlements there in the 7th century. There was a lot of Chinese migration in the 15th century, and when the Dutch East India Company first arrived there in the early 17th century they found sizeable numbers of Chinese merchants in most towns of Java. Most of the people who went to Indonesia from China were of the Hokkien dialect.[2]

In the second half of the 19th century, Chinese migration to Indonesia became more intensive for both 'push' and 'pull' reasons. Migrants were escaping poor economic conditions and general political disorder caused by the Tai Ping rebellion in the southern part of China. They were attracted by the significant economic growth in the Indies, especially after 1870, when there was a big expansion of Dutch private investment in plantations

---

[2] Collection of details of Chinese migration which was cited by Marilyn W. Clark, *Overseas Chinese Education in Indonesia*, US Government Printing Office, 1965, p. 2.

and mines, particularly in Sumatra and Kalimantan. The newcomers to Indonesia were mainly of Hakka and Teochiu language groups.[3] Migration from China receded sharply in 1930, when the colonial government introduced a law to deal with the Great Depression prohibiting the importation of labour from overseas.

Peranakan and totok communities

The great majority of the people described in the initial waves of migration were of the Hokkien speech group, and most of them settled in Java. The great majority of these migrants were also males who went on to marry Indigenous women. As this group grew, and there was intermarriage within it, it became a separate grouping within the Indonesian community. This group came to be called the peranakan Chinese (Chinese of mixed ancestry). The peranakans tend to speak local languages and have been heavily influenced by Indonesian cultures.

Many of the Chinese men who came in the later part of the 19th century and in the beginning of the 20th century brought their China-born wives to the country. These newcomers, largely of Hakka and Cantonese origin, were called 'sin keh' (newcomers). They tended to maintain their Chinese tradition and culture and did not assimilate and acculturate to the local societies. This group of people is called the totok Chinese (literally, 'pure Chinese'). The totoks tend to speak either Mandarin (Kuo You) and/or one of the Chinese dialects.

As a general rule, a Chinese who is born in China and whose daily spoken language is one of the Chinese dialects is called a totok Chinese. On the other hand, a Chinese born in Indonesia who does not speak any Chinese language, is a peranakan Chinese. But the distinction between peranakan and totok goes beyond the birth locations and the spoken languages.

Coppel says the distinction between the two terms has three aspects:

> It is likely that the original distinction was a racial one; a totok Chinese was a genuine, pure Chinese, whereas a peranakan was one of mixed ancestry. A secondary meaning followed from the first: since Chinese immigration to Indonesia before the 20th century was almost exclusively by males, it followed that a totok Chinese was China-born, and that any Chinese born in Indonesia was a peranakan. Among the locally rooted Chinese communities in Indonesia, there were some

---

[3] Victor Purcell, *The Chinese in South East Asia*, Oxford, Singapore, 1980, pp. 411–412.

(especially in Java) which developed a distinctive culture, which was heavily influenced by the culture of the particular Indonesian society in whose midst they had settled. One hallmark of these communities (which have come to be labelled peranakan) is the use by their members in daily speech of the Indonesian language (formerly Malay) or of some regional Indonesian language (or even, in the present century, of Dutch) rather than one or other of the various Chinese dialects spoken by Chinese immigrants on their arrival (principally Hokkien, Hakka, Cantonese and Teochiu) or in modern times, the national language, Kuo Yu (Mandarin). Thus a third sense in which these terms have been used is a sociocultural one, rather than one based upon race or birthplace.[4]

Somers offers a simpler definition. Peranakans, for her are 'persons of Chinese descent born in Indonesia who are neither assimilated to Indigenous Indonesian society nor culturally Chinese'. Furthermore, she suggests 'the most important characteristic of peranakan is considered to be the use of Indonesian (including Malay, from which modern Indonesian derived) or an Indonesian language as their mother tongue. She further says, 'local-born persons are not called peranakans if their mother tongue is a Chinese language, no matter in what other ways they may be acculturated to the Indigenous way of life'.[5]

Skinner emphasises that there is a significant variation from one locally rooted Chinese community to the other. The variation, he argues, depends largely on the length of the Chinese settlement and the cultural influence on the Chinese of the Indigenous population among which they settled. The Chinese communities in Java have been more heavily influenced by local cultures and hence have fewer emotional ties to China than the Chinese communities in the outer islands, who tend to maintain their Chineseness even after several generations of settlement and have not acculturated to the local societies. Skinner sees the Chinese who are more China-oriented (in terms of culture and spoken languages) as totoks, regardless of their origins or birthplaces. While the peranakans outnumber the totoks in Java, there

---

[4] Charles Coppel, *Indonesian Chinese in Crisis*, Oxford University Press, Kuala Lumpur, 1983, pp. 9–10.

[5] Mary F.A.Somers, *Peranakan Chinese Politics in Indonesia*, unpublished PhD Thesis, Cornell University, 1965, p. 4.

are by far more totoks in the outer islands.[6] Skinner's 1963 estimates, based on the 1930 census, suggest that out of the 1.25 million Chinese 750 000 belonged to the peranakan group. Out of these, 500 000 had fathers who were born in Indonesia. Most of the peranakans, about 420 000, lived in Java and Madura, while most of the totoks lived in Sumatra and Kalimantan.[7]

As this book is concerned with the political outlook and convictions of a large group of Chinese in Indonesia, the distinction has an important political dimension. In many parts of Indonesia, peranakan and totok communities are clearly distinct, with intermarriage unusual. But this distinctness has waxed and waned over time. For instance the rise of Chinese nationalism in China itself in the first two decades of the 20th century had important effects in Indonesia, causing many peranakans to become more China-oriented. One aspect of this was that many peranakans, including people of mixed ancestry, sent their children to Chinese schools where Mandarin was the language of instruction or where they spent many hours a week learning Mandarin.

In this book, the term totok is used to refer to a Chinese person, either China-born or Indonesia-born, who continues to maintain Chinese culture and tradition in their way of life, including the daily use of a Chinese language, and has an active interest in events in China. Thus, even a person of mixed ancestry will be referred to as a totok if their cultural and political outlook is predominantly China oriented.

On the other hand, I shall use the term peranakan to refer to an Indonesia-born Chinese of mixed ancestry who has little interest in following events in China and has become significantly acculturated into a local society. Such a person is more interested in local politics and identifies with Indonesia. The group defined as peranakan thus includes people who speak a Chinese language.

Siauw Giok Tjhan himself was a product of a mixed marriage. His father, born in Surabaya in 1880, was a peranakan of Hokkien origin. He did not speak Mandarin or any other Chinese dialects. Siauw's mother, on the other hand, came from a totok family of Hakka origin. She spoke Hakka and Mandarin. As we will see later, although she had a strong totok background, she adopted a peranakan lifestyle and followed rituals which were normally conducted by Indigenous women.

---

[6] G. William Skinner, 'The Chinese Minority', in Ruth T. McVey (ed.), *Indonesia*, New Haven, Conn., 1963, pp. 105–106.

[7] Victor Purcell, *The Chinese in Southeast Asia*, p. 386.

The Chinese position during the colonial period

The Dutch found the Chinese useful in the East Indies. When the Dutch arrived in the region in the 16th century, they found that Chinese merchants had already established effective marketing networks in Java. These networks enabled the Chinese merchants to trade goods imported from China and other places. The VOC (Vereenigde Oost-Indische Compagnie, or Dutch East India Company) quickly displaced the Chinese position in international trade but saw the advantages of maintaining their presence in local trade networks. The first Governor General, JP Coen, introduced a policy encouraging the growth of a Chinese retail industry which was responsible for large numbers of the Chinese, mainly peranakans, being present in commerce, industry and agriculture in Batavia (later to become Jakarta) in the 17th century.[8] The VOC provided economic protection to the Chinese that enabled them to enjoy certain financial privileges in the form of preferential custom tariffs and interest-free loans.[9]

This situation created a small group of wealthy peranakans in Java. From this small group, the Dutch nominated community leaders who were ranked military-style as Lieutenants, Captains and Majors. The Chinese officers were to act as intermediaries between the Chinese and Dutch communities. In this capacity, they had to interpret various rules and regulations and convey these to the Chinese communities. Their advice on Chinese matters could also influence the authorities' decision-making processes and their outcomes. Although they received no salaries, these leaders enjoyed privileges including the holding of various government licenses, monopolies of certain materials, tax concessions and Dutch education for their children. Because of this, their loyalties to the Dutch were unquestioned and, like their native counterparts, the regents (and the larger group of aristocrats called priyais), they often did little to fight for the interests of their communities. These Chinese officers were the core element of the Dutch-oriented group of peranakans until the Chinese Officer system was abolished in the early 1930s.

The overwhelming majority of the Chinese in the East Indies were labourers, petty traders, and craftsmen. They were rarely in much conflict with the Indigenous population. This situation contributed to the establishment

---

[8] W.J. Cator, *The Economic Position of the Chinese in the Netherlands Indies*, The University of Chicago Press, 1936, pp. 7–9.

[9] Ibid., pp. 18–20.

of good relations between the two groups, especially in Java. There was a lot of Chinese assimilation into Javanese society.[10]

However, after 1830 when the culture system or forced cultivation system was introduced, peranakan business in opium, sugar, gambling, money lending and transportation began to threaten the position of the Dutch, especially on the north coast of Java. This led to the introduction of various discriminatory measures against the Chinese. By the end of the 19th century, Chinese traders had not only lost the economic protection they had enjoyed for almost two centuries, but had begun to be severely discriminated against by the colonial government.

In 1863, the Dutch introduced 'pass and zoning' systems to confine the Chinese into Chinese quarters (pecinans). Travel without a permit between these pecinans was prohibited.[11] Other laws separated the Chinese from other racial groups by prohibiting the Chinese to wear western dress or cut off their pigtails and by creating schools exclusively for the Chinese.[12]

The Ethical Policy introduced in 1901 to protect the Indigenous population had some anti-Chinese overtones and created additional financial burdens for the Chinese. Its implementation required a massive financial injection, which was funded partly by increased tax contributions from the Chinese population. Taxes imposed on Chinese were significantly higher than those imposed on Europeans.[13]

The Chinese, particularly educated peranakans, resented this racial discrimination. This, coupled with the rise of nationalism in China as a result of Sun Yat Sen's revolutionary movement, induced a new political awareness among the peranakan community. In March 1900, a group of educated peranakans in Jakarta formed the THHK (Tiong Hoa Hwee Kwan – Chinese Association) and within a short time branches of this association were formed in other cities in Java and some in the outer islands. Although the new organisation's leadership was dominated by educated peranakans, a number of totok community leaders participated. It was the first organisation to attempt to unite the two groups.

The THHK's main program was to reintroduce Confucianism to revitalise Chinese culture and identity. Thus was born a social movement, referred

---

[10] Th. Pigeaud, *Javanese Volksvertoningen*, Batavia, 1938, p. 141.
[11] Lea Williams, *Overseas Chinese Nationalism*, The Free Press, 1961, pp. 27–33.
[12] Leo Suryadinata, *Peranakan Chinese Politics in Java*, Singapore University Press, Singapore, 1981, p. 3.
[13] Ibid., pp. 29–31.

to by such scholars as Fromberg and Lea Williams as the Chinese movement or Pan-Chinese movement.

One important THHK activity was running schools in which Mandarin was the medium of instruction, rather than Hokkien or Hakka. The educational programs were based on modern teachings derived from Japan. In these schools, in which teachers from China and Singapore taught, Chinese nationalism was promulgated to the students.[14] Within a few years, THHK schools were established in all capital cities in Java and in some cities in the outer islands. Most of these schools offered only a primary level of education, but the boost they gave to Mandarin improved communication and cooperation within totok groups and between totoks and peranakans. Impressed by the quality of education in the THHK schools and imbued by Chinese nationalism, many peranakans withdrew their children from Dutch schools and sent them to THHK schools.[15]

The new Chinese nationalism was also expressed by the formation of Tiong Hwa Siang Hwees (Chinese Chambers of Commerce) in 1906 and of the Soe Poe Sia (Chinese Reading Club) in 1909. The latter was active in producing and disseminating reading materials on Chinese nationalism. The Chinese Chambers of Commerce and Chinese Reading Club were heavily dominated by the totoks, but some peranakans were active in them.

Also important was the founding, in 1909 and 1910, of various new newspapers which were published in Malay or Sino–Malay for Chinese readers and carried a lot of news of developments in China. These included *Hoak Tok Po* in Batavia, *Djawa Kong Po* in Semarang, *Han Boen Sin Po* in Sumatra and *Sin Po* in Batavia.[16] *Sin Po* was to survive until the late 1950s and was a principal voice of the China-oriented Chinese, both peranakans and totoks. This China-oriented group was later known as the *Sin Po* group. The programs of the group included the stimulation of Chinese nationalism within the peranakan community to unite the peranakan and totok groups, the encouragement of the use of Mandarin among the peranakans, encouragement for peranakans to be involved in Chinese politics and the organisation of funds and resources to assist various groups in China.

Partly because of the diminished role of the Chinese officers, the China-oriented group became very influential, not least within the peranakan community. It encouraged Chinese in the Indies to reject Dutch nationality

---

[14] Lea Williams, *Overseas Chinese Nationalism*, pp. 42–45.
[15] Ibid., pp. 83–93.
[16] Leo Suryadinata, *Peranakan Chinese Politics*, p. 12–20.

and opt for Chinese nationality. In 1917 the group held a conference in Semarang – attended by some 700 delegates, mostly peranakans – to reject the proposal that Chinese be represented in the Volksraad (People's Council), a new representative body which had been promised by the colonial government. The argument was that involvement in local politics would not improve the Chinese status as a minority group and that participation in the Volksraad would be an act of accepting Dutch nationality.[17]

The growing influence of the *Sin Po* group concerned the Dutch, partly due to the potential strength the Chinese were showing and partly due to the implications of the decline of Chinese support for the colonial government. The group's campaigns and criticisms yielded results. In 1908 Dutch-language Chinese schools of a standard comparable to that of European schools were established. In 1909 restrictions on the Chinese entering Malay-language schools were lifted. In 1910, in response to the rejection of Dutch nationality by the group, the Dutch government passed a Nationality Law that made all Indies-born Chinese Dutch subjects. Restrictions on residence and travel were relaxed and in 1919 they were finally lifted. In 1918, the government introduced provisions for Chinese representation in the Volksraad. The Chinese could fill five out of the sixty-one Volksraad seats.

Siauw Giok Tjhan was born in 1914, at a time when Chinese nationalism was the dominant orientation among the Indies Chinese. The Dutch-oriented Chinese did not actively oppose this but the wind changed as it became obvious that China had failed to evolve into a powerful nation which could improve the situation of the Chinese in the Indies. By 1927, it was clear that a lot of peranakans were disillusioned by the China path and had become more positive in their orientation towards the Dutch. A new organisation, the Chung Hua Hui (Chinese Association) was formed. Unlike the THHK, the Chung Hua Hui was a political party in that it advocated political involvement and representation of the Chinese in the Volksraad.

In 1932, the year Siauw turned 18, a third group of peranakans emerged whose principal orientation was neither Chinese nor Dutch. This group was represented by the PTI (Partai Tionghoa Indonesia – Indonesian Chinese Party) and advocated Indonesia-oriented politics. This group of peranakans identified themselves with Indonesians and was sympathetic towards the struggle to achieve a free Indonesia. Leaders of the PTI were close to

---

[17] Leo Suryadinata, *Peranakan Chinese Politics*, pp. 96–97.

nationalist activists like Soetomo, Soekarno, Hatta and Mohamad Yamin. Siauw was a founding member of this party.

Outline

Siauw's political journey, covered in this book, can be divided into four main segments. The first segment is the training phase (1932–1946). In this phase, Siauw received his political training from his peranakan mentors (Liem Koen Hian, Kwee Hing Tjiat and Tan Ling Djie) and Indigenous leaders (Soetomo, Tjipto Mangunkusumo and Soekarno). In the second segment (1946–1954), Siauw used the political skills and experiences gained in the first phase of his career in carrying out his political activities as a parliamentarian and editor of various daily newspapers. The third segment was the most important one. In this phase (1954–1965), Siauw built and led Baperki, a large political organisation whose political life ended with the collapse of Soekarno's regime. Siauw spent a large part of the last segment of his career (1965–1981) as a political prisoner. He was in Holland as a political refugee for three years before he died in November 1981.

Chapter 1 details how Siauw as a wealthy businessman's son received his Dutch education and how he was influenced by his Western-oriented father, peranakanised mother and his China-oriented maternal grandfather. This chapter also details how three peranakan mentors, Liem Koen Hian, Kwee Hing Tjiat and Tan Ling Djie, shaped Siauw's political orientation and led him to the world of such Indonesian nationalists as Tjipto Mangunkusumo, Soekarno and Amir Sjarifuddin. Siauw's early career as a journalist is also an important part of this chapter.

Chapter 2 discusses the experience Siauw gained during the Japanese occupation as a community leader in Malang. His activity in Malang and its surrounding areas enabled him to establish contacts with leaders of Pemuda organisations.[18] Soon after independence, he joined the Partai Sosialis (Socialist Party) and this led to his appointment to the legislative body, then called KNIP (Komite Nasional Indonesia Pusat – Central National Committee of Indonesia).

Chapter 3 provides details of Siauw's various roles in the Partai Sosialis, the KNIP and its Badan Pekerja, and in Amir Sjarifuddin's cabinets as well as how he developed relationships with figures of differing political views.

---

[18] Pemuda literally means youth. But during the Indonesian revolution, the word Pemuda meant young Indonesian fighters looking to achieve and maintain independence. Pemuda organisations were organised armed youths.

The chapter covers the period between 1946 and 1949 in which Siauw was largely in Yogyakarta.

Chapter 4 details Siauw's activities as a parliamentarian and editor-in-chief of a number of journals and newspapers in Jakarta between 1950 and 1954. The emphasis is on how Siauw used the friendships he built in his Yogyakarta days to achieve his political goals. Central to the discussion in this chapter is the way Siauw formed and led a fairly influential faction in parliament, the Fraksi Nasional Progresif (National Progressive Faction, sometimes called Naspro), which included such prominent figures as Mohamad Yamin, Iwa Kusumasumantri and Djody Gondokusumo.

Chapter 5 describes Siauw's role in opposing the introduction of a bill designed to nullify the Indonesian citizenship of a large number of Indonesian citizens of Chinese descent. It also discusses his role in the formation of Baperki in March 1954.

Chapter 6 describes how Baperki developed between 1954 and 1957 and its achievements in the 1955 elections. In this period, a number of prominent Chinese figures – mainly those associated with the PSI (Partai Sosialis Indonesia – Indonesian Socialist Party) and Partai Katolik (Catholic Party) – who had helped found Baperki, left the organisation.

Chapter 7 details the problems faced by the Indonesian Chinese with regard to Indonesian citizenship. Siauw became the most outspoken parliamentarian against the plans to replace the existing 'passive' citizenship law with that of the 'active' one. The adoption of an 'active' system would force a large number of Indonesian Chinese to be foreign citizens, not because they did not want to be Indonesian citizens but because of their inability to provide proof of their own and their parents' birth places. The chapter also discusses Siauw's role in the debates on citizenship and issues related to dual nationality between 1954 and 1958.

Chapter 8 provides details on how Siauw developed his economic formulations and how he fought against the advocates of indigenisation of the Indonesian economy.

Chapter 9 details Siauw's responses to the decline of parliamentary democracy and the imminent arrival of Guided Democracy between 1957 and 1959. It also describes his involvement in the Konstituante (Constituent Assembly) debates on the new constitution.

Chapter 10 describes Siauw's ability to capitalise on his close relationship with Soekarno for the benefit of Baperki and the Chinese population during the Guided Democracy period (1960–1965). In this period, many of Baperki's programs were officially endorsed by Soekarno and some of

Siauw's economic formulations were incorporated into various government guidelines and regulations. The chapter also outlines Siauw's decision to rely on Soekarno and become a figure in the left-wing camp, opposing the right-wing political forces led by leaders of the army and anti-communist parties.

Chapter 11 details Baperki's activities as an education provider between 1957 and 1965. It also describes how Baperki 'peranakanised' the totok students and motivated students to participate in national politics.

Chapter 12 discusses the debates on assimilation versus integration, which emerged in the early 1960s. It also details how the army-supported LPKB (Lembaga Pembinaan Kesatuan Bangsa – Institution for the Promotion of National Unity) challenged Baperki which was supported by Soekarno and left-wing organisations.

Chapter 13 describes the last months of Baperki's life in 1965 and the dilemma faced by Siauw in containing the drive to make Baperki more closely aligned to the PKI. It also describes how Baperki was attacked and finally dismantled by military authorities after the abortive coup of 30 September 1965.

Chapter 14 provides some details of Siauw's imprisonment between 1965 and 1978 and his last years in Jakarta and Holland.

Chapter 15 summarises Siauw's political career, his involvement in Baperki and his efforts to combat racism and resolve the citizenship issues.

PART I

1914–1946

Chapter 1

CHILDHOOD AND FORMATIVE YEARS

Siauw Giok Tjhan was born in Surabaya, East Java, on 23 March 1914. He was the first child of Siauw Gwan Swie who had been born in Surabaya in 1880.

Siauw Gwan Swie belonged to the peranakan Chinese community in Kapasan, a pecinan (Chinese quarter) in Surabaya. Kapasan, like other pecinan, had been set up by the Dutch to accommodate the Chinese in Surabaya. Most of the inhabitants in Kapasan were peranakans of Hokkien origin.[1]

Siauw Gwan Swie's parents were poor and lived in a poor area of Kapasan. Siauw Gwan Sie lost his parents when he was only 12 and, being the oldest of the five children, had to abandon his studies in order to support his younger brother and sisters. He used to sell cakes in the Kapasan market from 4 am to 8 am and worked as a shop assistant in a nearby shopping centre. It is not clear what type of education Siauw Gwan Sie received or what type of schools he went to in his early years but when he was in his early 20s he became a qualified English teacher, teaching English at a school and giving private tuition to rich peranakans in Surabaya.[2]

Siauw Gwan Swie's ability to speak English enabled him to have contact with Western merchants and become a successful businessman. By around 1910 he was a partner in a Dutch-owned business called Schmidt & Co.

---

[1] The information on Siauw Giok Tjhan's family detailed in this section was largely derived from Siauw's own accounts conveyed to the author; Siauw, *Lima Jaman*, pp. 11–33 and Bob Hering (ed.), *Siauw Giok Tjhan Remembers: A Peranakan Chinese and the Quest for Indonesian Nationhood*, James Cook University of North Queensland, Queensland, 1982, pp. 1–18.

[2] Siauw might have gone to the Yale Institute, established in 1902 by Tiong Hoa Hwee Kwan (THHK), to provide English lessons to peranakans. It was also possible that he taught English at the institute. Siauw Giok Tjhan recalled that his father could not speak Dutch.

which was involved in sugar trading. Improved financial status enabled him to move from the lower-class part of the Kapasan to its elite side, the main Kapasan road, where he occupied a large house. Siauw was quite proud of this achievement and later often reminded his two sons that they too had to work hard so that they could reach the level of the Europeans who tended to look down on the peranakans and treat them insultingly.

Although Siauw Gwan Sie studied English and was influenced by Western culture, he, like many Chinese in that period, was heavily influenced by the movement in China, led by Kang Yu Wei, Liang Chi Chiao and Sun Yat Sen. Because of his connections with publishers of the peranakan dailies in Surabaya, he was well informed of the developments in China.

Siauw Gwan Sie was also a close friend of The Ping Oen, the director of a peranakan daily called *Pewarta Surabaya* (*Surabaya News*) which was established in 1902. *Pewarta Surabaya*, like many other peranakan newspapers published at the beginning of the century, was established by its founders to promote Chinese nationalism. The Ping Oen's office was located next to a grocery shop owned by a totok businessman of Hakka origin, Kwan Sie Liep. The Ping Oen and Kwan Sie Liep shared the desire to promote Chinese nationalism among the Indies Chinese and became good friends.

In the years after 1910, Siauw Gwan Sie, then in his early 30s, visited The's office frequently and became acquainted with Kwan's daughter, Kwan Tjian Nio, who was in her early 20s. Interested in marrying her, Siauw Gwan Sie went to see Kwan to propose. But Kwan initially refused, as Siauw was a peranakan and could not even speak Chinese. Kwan indicated that he would not let his daughter marry any non-Hakka person.

Kwan Sie Liep had arrived in the Indies towards the end of the nineteenth century. Unlike most of the Chinese who migrated to Indonesia in that period, Kwan came with his wife. Siauw Giok Tjhan remembered her, his grandmother, as a small lady with bound feet.[3] Imbued by Chinese nationalism, which developed in Java in the first few years of the century, Kwan became a leader of Surabaya's Tiong Hoa Siang Hwee (Chinese Chamber of Commerce) formed in 1907. He was also actively involved in running a THHK (Tiong Hoa Hwee Kwan – Chinese Association) school located within the Kapasan area.

---

[3] In China, in the old days, the feet of Chinese women were bound. They would not be able to walk or run properly.

Although his daughter, Tjian Nio, was born in the Indies, Kwan was keen for her to marry a person of Hakka origin – a common attitude of most totoks, particularly those of Hakka origin. Kwan was therefore adamant that he would not allow his daughter to marry Siauw Gwan Sie.

However, Siauw Gwan Sie refused to give up. He asked The Ping Oen to convince Kwan that although he was a peranakan, he was a Chinese nationalist and highly valued Chinese culture.[4] The Ping Oen agreed to help and after repeated attempts Kwan finally agreed to the marriage, on condition that their first child would be Chinese-educated. Chinese people, according to Kwan, should be able to speak Chinese and should accordingly understand and appreciate Chinese culture. Siauw Gwan Sie and Kwan Tjian Nio were finally married in 1913. Siauw Giok Tjhan, born on 23 March 1914, was thus a product of a mixed marriage.

Primary schooling and home culture

When Siauw Giok Tjhan turned four and was ready to go to school, Kwan demanded that Siauw Gwan Swie honour his earlier agreement. Kwan himself took the young Siauw to enrol at the THHK school, which he helped run. Siauw Gwan Swie reluctantly let his father-in-law implement the condition of his marriage, though he believed that his son would have a better chance to succeed in life if he were Dutch educated.

Chinese pupils in Java in that period went to THHK schools if their parents preferred a Chinese education and to HCS (Hollandsch Chineesche School – Dutch Chinese School) if their parents preferred a Dutch education. The first HCS had been established in Batavia in 1908 and others were opened in major cities in the following years. Their establishment was a response to complaints that the colonial government ignored the need to provide modern education for the Chinese.[5] It also reflected the

---

[4] Although Siauw Gwan Swie did not understand or speak Chinese, he enjoyed Chinese opera.

[5] The Dutch had in 1901, as a result of the introduction of the Ethical Policy, established two types of schools designed to accommodate Indigenous students. The children of the priyais and well-to-do Indigenous people were accommodated in the first-class schools while the second-class schools accommodated the children of the Indigenous population in general. Chinese students were not permitted to enter the second-class schools. The colonial government was, in part, responding to pressure from the liberal community in Holland, but its main motivation in providing education to the Indigenous population was to produce cheap clerical and technical personnel for the government itself and Dutch private firms which began to flourish at the beginning of the 20th century.

government's fear of Chinese nationalism being spread through the THHK schools.

The opening of the HCS schools in Java quickly polarised the peranakan community. Many of the peranakans could not relate well to the curricula used by the THHK. They found these to be strongly oriented towards China and impractical as far as preparing the students for local employment was concerned. On the other hand, many believed HCS education equipped the students for local employment and provided better professional career opportunities in Indonesia. This encouraged many wealthy peranakans, including THHK leaders, to send their children to HCS schools.[6] The percentage of Chinese primary school students who were educated in Dutch increased from 33 per cent (8060 in Dutch and 16 499 in Chinese) in 1915 to nearly 50 per cent (27 802 in Dutch and 32 688 in Chinese) in 1926.[7]

The Dutch had earlier established ELSs (Europese Lagere Schools – European Elementary Schools). These schools were opened to accommodate only Dutch children but a small number of Indigenous and Chinese students, children of priyais (aristocratic officials) and Chinese officers or wealthy Chinese, were permitted to enter. The standard of ELS was much higher than that of HCS and HIS (Hollandsch-Inlandsche School – school for the native Indonesians).

In 1920, Kwan Sie Liep decided to return to China for good. By now he had a large block of land in his hometown in China and wished to retire there and enjoy the fruits of his hard work in the Indies. Although Siauw Gwan Swie was the more able and experienced businessman, Kwan did not trust his Western outlook and preferred to hand over the management of the shop to his totok son-in-law before he and his wife left for China in the same year.

Siauw Gwan Swie took his father-in-law's departure as a signal that he was free from the obligation to please him in regard to his son's schooling. He moved Siauw Giok Tjhan initially to the Buys Instituut, an expensive private school for both Dutch and non-Dutch students, and a few months later to the prestigious Surabaya ELS. When Siauw entered this school in 1920 a small number of Chinese and Indigenous students were also enrolled in this school. Siauw's younger brother, Giok Bie, did not have to go through the complicated school arrangement. When he began his schooling in 1924, he went straight to the ELS.

---

[6] Leo Suryadinata, *The Chinese Minority in Indonesia, Seven Papers*, Chopmen, 1978, p. 10.
[7] Ibid., pp. 8–9.

Although the young Siauws went to a Dutch school, they were brought up in a typically peranakan way. Their mother could converse well in Hakka and Mandarin, but the young Siauws were not taught either. Instead, they spoke Sino–Malay at home and Javanese with their friends. Because their father preferred Javanese food to Chinese, there was a strong Javanese influence in the food their mother prepared.

Siauw's mother, having been brought up in a totok family, was familiar with Confucianism and Chinese tradition. However, she became very interested in local rituals. Instead of visiting the Boen Bio (Confucian Temple), located in front of their house in Kapasan, she went to burn incense on Mondays and Thursdays at the Cungkup (a holy Muslim grave) located next to the Boen Bio. Kwan Tjian Nio also often took her sons to pray at other Javanese sacred places in Mount Kawi and Mount Giri.

At home, the family often discussed matters concerning religious rituals and the holding of ceremonies that required the presence of a Modin to recite verses of the Koran. However, despite Kwan Tjian Nio's attraction to local rituals and beliefs, she did not convert to Islam but remained a Confucian. When Siauw Giok Tjhan was very sick at the age of five, she readily accepted the advice of her father to offer him to a toapekong (shrine god) as his adopted son. From then, Siauw had to call his parents uncle and aunt.

While Siauw's mother appeared to be more interested in local rituals, Siauw's father, who had no knowledge of Chinese languages, was attracted to many aspects of Chinese culture. He enjoyed Chinese opera and was quite disciplined in celebrating Chinese special days like the Chinese New Year and the Cap Go Meh (the fifteenth day after the New Year). Interestingly, he celebrated these days by inviting peranakan friends to his house to watch wayang kulit (shadow puppet) performances in Javanese. These performances were conducted in his front garden and so they also attracted Indigenous audiences including people from outside the Kapasan area.

All of Siauw Gwan Swie's relatives lived in Kapasan and none of them were Chinese-educated. The ladies, including his wife, like many other peranakan women in the period, wore Javanese style blouses (kebaya) which had batik patterns specifically designed to suit peranakan taste. Siauw Gwan Swie's sisters and cousins had Indonesian-sounding nicknames such as Datang, Tambah and Talen. Some of them also enjoyed chewing betel nut, which was more an Indonesian than a Chinese practice.

This upbringing had an important influence on how Siauw Giok Tjhan identified himself in the following years. Heavily influenced by his mother, he was certainly more a peranakan child than a totok one.

Secondary schooling and early organisational experience

In 1926, Siauw's totok uncle who been given charge of Kwan Sie Liep's business died suddenly, leaving no-one who was able to look after the shop. So Kwan Sie Liep had no choice but to return from China to Surabaya to run the business. His arrival in 1926 coincided with Siauw's last year at the ELS.

When Kwan met Siauw Giok Tjhan, he was shocked to learn that after eight years of Chinese education his grandson was not able to communicate with him in Mandarin. Kwan became very angry to learn that his grandson had, in fact, been Dutch-educated and had no knowledge of Chinese. Siauw Gwan Swie was quick to formulate a compromise, with Siauw Giok Tjhan working in Kwan's shop as his assistant after school. Siauw Gwan Sie believed that by being close to Kwan this way, the young Siauw would be exposed to Chinese culture and business practices and hence would fulfill Kwan's conditions. For the next five years, Siauw was to run the shop from 2 pm to 5 pm while his grandfather had his afternoon nap.

With this compromise, Siauw Giok Tjhan was able to continue his studies at the prestigious Surabaya HBS (Hogere Burgerschool – Dutch Secondary School) in 1927. The HBS, like the ELS, was mainly established to accommodate Dutch students. But graduates from HIS and HCS who had outstanding academic results and the ability to pay the high school fees could also enrol. Roeslan Abdulgani and Tjoa Sie Hwie were among Siauw's non-European school friends.[8]

Siauw's younger brother, Giok Bie, did not obtain sufficiently high marks to be admitted to the HBS. Like most Dutch-educated peranakans, he went to the lower standard secondary school, MULO (Meer Uitgebreid Lager Onderwijs – Dutch Junior Secondary School) instead. As for Siauw, he was one of the privileged peranakans who obtained a thorough western education and this equipped him with a sound academic foundation for his career.

Siauw found his Dutch fellow pupils arrogant, but his resentment of their attitudes strengthened his determination to excel academically. Siauw was one of the best students in this school throughout the HBS program. However, his academic achievements were not sufficient to deter his Dutch school friends from physically bullying Siauw and his non-European

---

[8] Roeslan Abdulgani later played an important role in the Soekarno era. Tjoa Sie Hwie was a member of parliament representing the PNI in the 1950s. President Soekarno had attended the same school.

friends. From time to time, he could not avoid becoming involved in physical fights with the Dutch students. As he had mastered Kung Fu, learnt from his grandfather and other Kung Fu masters in Kapasan, Siauw was able to repel those who insulted him.[9] When he was outnumbered, he was able to rely on the support of his peranakan friends who studied at the THHK and HCS schools.

Siauw's life as a secondary student was comfortable. His house was large and was full of expensive furniture and paintings. His father had two luxury cars to take the young Siauws to school and their mother shopping. His father often rewarded his outstanding academic performance at school with what were considered luxurious items at that time. After he did well in one exam, his father gave him a motorbike. He was also able to purchase books at will and to develop and maintain an expensive photography hobby. But the family was better known in the Kapasan area because of his mother's beauty and generous nature. She often invited friends to come to their house, helped them financially when they were in trouble or gave them things they could use.[10]

Kwan Tjian Nio had a strong influence on her sons. Siauw's friends at Kapasan remembered him and his younger brother, Giok Bie, as humble and unassuming young men who preferred to befriend those who lived in the alleys of Kapasan and appeared to have distanced themselves from the very rich Dutch-educated peranakan children. They also remembered them as friends who were always willing to help others in need.[11]

Siauw's daily interactions with his grandfather were responsible for their special relationship. By managing the shop, Siauw also was able to meet people from various walks of life. Many of the traders who dealt with his grandfather were Chinese and Arabs from the outer islands. As Kwan was a prominent leader of the Surabaya Chinese Chamber of Commerce and their meetings were often held in the shop, Siauw got to know many totok businessmen. From these contacts and interactions, Siauw learned a great deal of the totoks' world and their concern with events in China. When the Japanese army attacked China in 1931, Kwan Sie Liep played an active

---

[9] Kwan, famous for his martial arts, taught Siauw and later enrolled him in one of the Kung Fu clubs in Surabaya, which was attended by many peranakan youths of the THHK School. Siauw was able to reach a high enough level such that he was often requested to perform in various martial art functions. Later in 1932, he briefly earned a living as a part-time Kung Fu instructor.

[10] Interview with Mrs Njoo Soen Hian, Amsterdam, December 1996.

[11] Interviews with Tjoa Sik Ien and Njoo Soen Hian, Amsterdam, November 1981.

role in staging a boycott against Japanese goods. He refused to buy and sell Japanese goods even though that meant a loss of income. Siauw remembered that traders who dared to offer Japanese goods to Kwan's shop were quickly told to leave.

Siauw Giok Tjhan remembered Kwan as a generous and warm businessman who was highly respected by the Chinese in Surabaya. Unlike Siauw's father who enjoyed living comfortably and wearing expensive Western style clothes, Kwan lived unassumingly and was more interested in politics and organisations than making money. Kwan often told Siauw that one did not have to be rich to win respects from others. Because Siauw was at Kwan's shop every day, Kwan had more influence on the development of his personality and outlook than his own father. Siauw's interest in political and organisational activities was perhaps first implanted by his grandfather. Siauw also followed his grandfather's casual attire.

His grandfather's influence encouraged Siauw to mix more with THHK Chinese-educated students than with friends from his own school. Instead of joining the Chung Hsioh Hsing Hui, a youth organisation of Dutch school peranakan students, he joined the HCTNH (Hua Chiao Tsing Nien Hui – Chinese Youth Organisation) that was affiliated with the THHK school located in Kapasan. While members of the HCTNH spoke Sino–Malay, members of the Chung Hsioh used Dutch as their medium. The main dividing line between these two organisations was the difference in the socioeconomic status. Those who joined Chung Hsioh tended to be wealthier. Also unlike his fellow Dutch-educated peranakan students, Siauw preferred to maintain his Chinese name rather than using his Dutch name, Freddy.

Siauw's interests in being involved in and leading organisations began to emerge in his secondary school days. Soon after joining the HCTNH, he became a leader of that organisation. He was also active in the organisation's boy scouts.

Within Kapasan, Siauw was known as studious. Playing soccer as a goalkeeper, he is said to have sometimes read books while waiting for the ball to approach the goal. Unlike his brother, Giok Bie, who was notorious for his love of streetfights, Siauw was known to have a temperament that tended towards conciliation. When streetfights between groups of friends occurred, he often intervened to stop them.[12]

---

[12] Interviews with Njoo Soen Hian, Amsterdam, November 1981 and Siauw Giok Bie, Melbourne, July 1990.

The HBS education equipped Siauw with four foreign languages – Dutch, English, German and French – and he enjoyed reading adventure and detective stories in these languages. Although he was never formally taught to speak and read Sino–Malay, like most peranakans at that time, he was able to master the language well. The ability to read Sino–Malay, also known as 'low Malay', was enhanced by the wide circulation of peranakan newspapers and journals which first emerged in 1901 and flourished in Java in the late 1920s. At home, Siauw's father subscribed to a number of English journals and peranakan dailies, including *Sin Tit Po* and *Pewarta Surabaya*. Siauw read these, as well as Chinese literature translated into Sino–Malay. In addition, Siauw was also impressed by the heroic examples presented by various Peking operas and wayang performances of *Mahabharata* and *Ramayana*.

At this stage, Siauw had yet to develop political interests, although he was aware of the Indonesian nationalist movement and the growing popularity of Soekarno. His contacts with Indigenous communities were limited to his Indigenous school friends and customers of his grandfather's shop. His comfortable life in Kapasan did not prompt his political interest either.

However, Siauw's life situation changed dramatically in 1932. By that time, the world depression had severely impacted on business in the Indies, with a large number of companies going bankrupt and their employees losing their jobs. Siauw's father, who relied on raw material trading, also suffered heavy financial losses. His problem was aggravated by the bankruptcy of the Incasso Bank in which most of his savings were deposited. Siauw's grandfather also suffered heavy losses. The economic disaster in the Indies prompted him to leave the country again in 1932 for China where he retired and later died.

Siauw's mother died suddenly in early 1932. Six months later, his father died of a heart attack. Siauw, then 18, was in his last year of HBS. His brother, Giok Bie, then 14, was in his second year of MULO. Siauw quickly learnt a harsher side of life. His father's rich friends avoided the two young boys, afraid of being approached for financial assistance. With the help of his Kapasan friends, Siauw managed to sell a lot of his parents' belongings and used the money to start a three-wheeled taxi business, which was sufficient to cover their living expenses and Giok Bie's school fees. In addition, because of Siauw's outstanding performance at school, a scholarship was organised by a number of his teachers so that he was able to complete his HBS education in 1933. However, he had to abandon his earlier plans to continue his studies in Holland.

An early circumstance leading Siauw to identify with Indonesian society was his grandfather's departure to China and his own difficulty after his parents' death. As he saw it, totok businessmen who had established a second home in China based on the income they had earned while living in the Indies had a fallback position. But the majority of the Chinese, particularly peranakans, were not in the same position. They could rely on no-one in China. Most of them could not speak Chinese and would therefore find it difficult to establish a new life in China.

In 1932, the year of his parents' death, Siauw was introduced to Liem Koen Hian, then 36. Liem was already a well-known peranakan journalist and a pioneer in the fashioning of Indonesia-oriented attitudes among peranakans. He headed the peranakan daily in Surabaya called *Sin Tit Po*.

Encouraged by Liem, Siauw joined the Indonesian Study Club led by Soetomo and Samsi. This club, founded in 1924, was the centre of Indonesian nationalism in Surabaya. Its members included Indonesian nationalist activists who had recently returned from Holland. In this organisation, Siauw met many nationalist figures. He was also introduced to Sun Yat Sen's *San Min Chu I* as well as to the writings of Soekarno and Hatta. Siauw described his involvement in this organisation as his first political training.

In the same year, 1932, Liem Koen Hian formed the PTI (Partai Tionghoa Indonesia – Indonesian Chinese Party). The party's program included the promotion of Indonesia-oriented politics among the Chinese and the effective representation of the peranakan communities in the Volksraad. Siauw was a founding member of the party, one of the youngest. He also came under the influence of the PBI (Partai Bangsa Indonesia – Indonesian Nation Party) headed by Soetomo. The PBI at that time advocated a policy that encouraged individual ethnic groups to take initiatives to solve their own problems. Siauw was attracted to Soetomo's conviction that political activities should not be based on mass agitation, good speeches and political education – the line adopted by Soekarno and his followers before they were jailed and exiled. In Soetomo's view political activities needed to be supported by social and economic activities designed to improve living conditions.

Encouraged by Soetomo, Siauw and his HCTNH colleagues carried out social activities to help the poor Chinese in the Kapasan areas. In 1933, they regularly collected old clothes and household items from richer people and distributed them to poor peranakans in the area. With the help of friends who had recently graduated from THHK and MULO secondary schools, Siauw established an evening school designed to provide education to peranakans who could not afford to go to any existing schools. He was one of the teachers and acted as its principal. Some fifty students were enrolled, using the buildings of the THHK schools. The program was cut short as the Dutch authority regarded the school as illegal and banned it in 1934.[13]

Liem Koen Hian and Indonesian nationalism

In joining the PTI, Siauw was turning his back on the two largest currents of opinion among the Chinese in the Indies, one oriented towards China, the other towards the Dutch colonial system.

The formation of the PTI marked the emergence of a third current of opinion within the Chinese communities. Its emergence in 1932 followed the decline of the China-oriented group's influence on the peranakans and the growth in popularity of the Dutch-oriented group.

The influence of the China-oriented stream, represented by the *Sin Po* group (associated with the Jakarta daily newspaper of the same name), had been greatest between 1917 and 1920. In those years, most peranakan newspapers supported the *Sin Po* political stance and rejected the colonial government's call for the Chinese to be involved in local politics. Concerned with the growth of Chinese nationalism, the colonial government granted the concessions detailed in this book's Introduction. These concessions and the failure of China to become a powerful state helped neutralise the influence of Chinese nationalism within the peranakan communities.

By the late 1920s, China was weakened by continuing civil wars and in no position to defend itself from the militarily superior Japanese or make any effective international representations on behalf of the Indies Chinese. Thus, the belief that a strong China would protect Chinese interests in the Indies, which had helped create close cooperation between the peranakan communities, diminished rapidly in the late 1920s. By then, the number of peranakans who received Dutch education had also increased significantly. This western education had created a group of peranakan intellectuals who had a positive orientation to the colonial system, preferred Dutch culture to Chinese and spoke Dutch among themselves.

At the end of the first decade, a small number of Indigenous and peranakan students went to study in Holland. Just as Indigenous students in

---

[13] Interview with Tjoa Sik Ien, Amsterdam, November 1981.

1908 formed an organisation called the Indies Association, which became the PI (Perhimpunan Indonesia – Indonesian Association), so the peranakan students formed a similar student organisation in 1911 – the CHHN (Chung Hua Hui Netherlands – Chinese Association Netherlands). Although they rejected Chinese nationalism, they preferred to retain their Chinese identity, as the name of the organisation suggests.

When some of these students – notably Han Tiauw Tjong (CHHN president in 1921), Be Tiat Tjong (CHHN president in 1923) and Oei Tjong Houw (son of Oei Tiong Ham, one of the richest officers in Semarang) – went back to the Indies, they initiated the formation of a political party called the Chung Hua Hui (Chinese Association) in 1927. Being heavily dominated by Dutch-educated individuals, the party's main emphasis was on the achievement of equality with the Europeans and on trying to gain representation in the Volksraad.[14]

The chairman of the party was Kan Hok Hoei, a successful businessman and experienced politician. Kan was already a member of the Volksraad when he was chosen as the party's chairman. While he supported the colonial government, he was also an active member of the Chinese Chamber of Commerce and thus maintained a good relationship with totok business circles and Chinese government representatives. He was personally related to the consul-general of China in Batavia.[15] When the Federated Chinese Chambers of Commerce formed in 1934, Kan was elected its first chairman. Under Kan, the Chung Hua Hui adopted a right-wing, anti-Marxist political direction. The Chung Hua Hui was opposed to the abolition of the repressive penal code and exorbitant laws which were proposed by Dutch socialists in the Volksraad in 1932.[16]

These collaborative policies towards the Dutch irritated many Chinese nationalists and Indonesian nationalists. Some western-educated peranakans were also disillusioned with the Chung Hua Hui and began to turn away from the organisation in 1932. This situation accelerated the process of the establishment of Indonesia-oriented political thinking among the peranakans.

In the first two decades of the 20th century, most of the Chinese in the Indies had remained uninterested in Indonesian nationalism. Of the nationalist organisations formed in this period, only one, the Indische

---

[14] Leo Suryadinata, *Peranakan Chinese Politics*, pp. 39–63.
[15] Ibid., p. 125.
[16] Ibid., p. 77.

Partij (Indies Party), allowed the inclusion of Chinese as members. Serikat Dagang Islam (Islamic Trade Union), formed in 1911, was a byproduct of anti-Chinese movements in Java. Its larger successor, the Serikat Islam (Islamic Association), formed in 1912, had no anti-Chinese policies in its platform but made no effort to bring Chinese into its membership.[17]

The Indische Partij, under the leadership of Douwes Dekker, Ki Hadjar Dewantara and Tjipto Mangunkusumo, promoted the concept of cooperation of all ethnic groups in the Indies. In 1913 Douwes Dekker had indicated his desire that the Chinese should unite with other groups in the Indies in the struggle to achieve a free Indonesia. Tjipto Mangunkusumo went further. In 1917 he formulated his idea on an Indies nation, which should incorporate all persons who considered Indonesia their motherland. But these calls for wide-ranging inter-racial cooperation were made in a period in which most Chinese who had political interests were strongly oriented to Chinese nationalism. In this period, the Chinese were excited by the Chinese revolution and were strongly urged by their community leaders to identify themselves with China. However, a small number of Chinese did join the Indische Partij. These included Liem Koen Hian, who was to introduce Siauw Giok Tjhan to politics in 1932.[18]

Born in Banjarmasin, Kalimantan in 1896, Liem started his career as a journalist with strong China-oriented convictions. By 1921 he had developed into an anti-colonial activist. He frequently challenged and ridiculed people who advocated pro-Dutch policies. He moved to Surabaya in 1925 and joined the followers of Soetomo who had formed the Indonesian Study Club in Surabaya in 1924.

Between 1925 and 1929 Liem edited the *Soeara Publiek*, a peranakan daily in Surabaya. Influenced by Tjipto Mangunkusumo's Indies Nation concept, he actively promoted a concept of Indisch Burgerschap (Indies Citizenship) which was based on the conviction that Indies was the home for all peranakans. In 1929, by which time the term 'Indonesia' had become widely used, he converted his Indisch Burgerschap to Indonesierschap (Indonesianess). In this context, he urged the peranakans to work together

---

[17] By 1914, the organisation's paper, *Oetoesan Hindia*, was almost solely dependent upon the advertisement fees paid by Chinese merchants. As a result of this, Serikat Islam dropped all its anti-Chinese slogans and propaganda. See R. van Niel, *The Emergence of the Modern Indonesian Elite*, The Hague–Bandung, 1960, p. 120.

[18] Mary Somers, *Peranakan Chinese Politics in Indonesia*, Cornell University, 1965, p. 93; Interview with Siauw Giok Tjhan in Holland in 1980.

with other Indonesians to achieve a free Indonesia. In 1930 he became the editor-in-chief of another Surabaya peranakan daily, *Sin Tit Po*.

Liem's formulation on Indonesianness was further clarified in a series of articles published in that daily in April 1930. He asserted that peranakans should orient themselves to the aspirations of the Indonesian nation. They would not need to abandon their cultural heritage, as the future Indonesian nation would have room to accommodate various cultural differences.[19]

Against the China-oriented group represented by *Sin Po*, Liem argued that it was unwise for the Chinese in the Indies to embrace Chinese nationalism as this was only useful if they were in China. Chinese nationalism, he argued, would not change the situation in Indonesia and had made it difficult for the Chinese to be accepted in the Indies. But Liem's views were rejected by most of the peranakans in that period.

While the Indische Partij had invited the participation of all ethnic groups, the PNI (Partai Nasional Indonesia – Indonesian National Party), founded by Soekarno in 1927, limited its membership to Indigenous people. Chinese, Arabs and Eurasians could only become associate members. However, the party did attract some peranakan individuals. Dr Kwa Tjoan Sioe, a personal friend of Soekarno played a leading role in the publication and running of the party's publication, Soeloeh Indonesia Moeda, in 1932.[20] Kwee Tjing Hong, ignoring the party's membership policy, founded the local branch of the PNI in Palembang in 1934.[21]

Journalism and politics

Let us return to Siauw's early exposure to political life. The emergence of the Indonesia-oriented peranakans in the early 1930s coincided with the dramatic end of Siauw Giok Tjhan's comfortable life. After completing his HBS, Siauw realised that due to his limited financial resources, his earlier plans to continue his studies in Holland had to be abandoned.

As a HBS graduate who had learned four foreign languages, Dutch, English, German and French, it would have been easy for Siauw to get a well-paid job in a Dutch-run company. However, impressed by Liem Koen Hian's ability to influence others through his powerful articles published in newspapers, Siauw decided to follow Liem's footsteps and in 1933 he joined

---

[19] Leo Suryadinata, *The Chinese Minority*, pp. 85–86.
[20] Ibid., p. 94.
[21] Suryadinata, Peranakan Chinese Politics, p. 153.

Sin Tit Po. Kwee Hing Tjiat, a famous and controversial pro-PTI journalist, had recently established a peranakan daily in Semarang called *Mata Hari (The Sun)*. Liem was instrumental in introducing Kwee, a Kapasan peranakan, to Siauw. Kwee recruited Siauw to his paper. So, towards the end of 1934, Siauw, aged 20, left Surabaya for Semarang where he began his career as a journalist and a political activist.

The move to Semarang meant that Siauw was now under the mentorship of Kwee Hing Tjiat. Kwee was born in Surabaya in 1891[22] and after becoming editor of a number of peranakan publications in Surabaya and Yogyakarta, became editor-in-chief of the Batavia daily *Sin Po* between 1916 and 1918. From 1918 to 1923 he was in Europe for business but continued to write for *Sin Po*. In this period, Kwee also published a book in Berlin, called *Doea Kepala Batoe (Two Stubborn Men)*, which provided details of his views on Chinese nationalism and the situation of the Indies Chinese.

In 1923 Kwee returned to the Indies but was refused entry to Jakarta port because of his strong Chinese nationalism and anti-Dutch attitudes. For the next ten years, he lived in China as a businessman. While in China, he was influenced by Western-educated Chinese who believed that Confucianism was responsible for the backwardness of the Chinese. At the beginning of 1926 Kwee wrote a controversial article in the peranakan weekly, *Hua Kiao*, in which he condemned Confucianism (and Islam and Christianity also) and encouraged the Chinese in the Indies to abandon religion. His opinion on Confucianism had an impact on the THHK movement, and by 1928 THHK schools had significantly modified their educational programs and reduced their emphasis on Confucianism.

By the early 1930s Kwee felt convinced that as a peranakan he could not live in China happily. He found that his inability to speak Chinese and his unwillingness to fully accept and understand Chinese culture had hampered his intention of becoming a true Chinese nationalist. He had therefore concluded that the Indies was his home and wanted to return there.

Although he lived in China for a long time, Kwee maintained close contacts with peranakan businessmen, in particular Oei Tjong Houw, the son of Oei Tiong Ham of Semarang. Oei, a well-known tycoon, was instrumental in getting the Dutch authorities to allow Kwee to return to the

---

[22] Materials on Kwee presented in this section are derived largely from Leo Suryadinata, *Mencari Identitas Nasional, Dari Tjoe Bou San Sampai Yap Thiam Hien*, LP3ES, Jakarta, 1990 and Siauw Giok Tjhan's unpublished memoir, *Suatu Renungan*, pp. 20–21.

Indies in 1933. Furthermore, Oei agreed to fund Kwee's plan to establish a peranakan daily in Semarang.

By the time Kwee returned to the Indies, the PTI had been established. Kwee was quickly attracted to the party's Indonesia-oriented programs and planned to propagate PTI's Indonesia-oriented politics in his newly established daily. Kwee's initial plan was to call the daily *Merdika* (*Freedom*), but the Dutch authorities forced him to drop the name. He then decided to call it *Mata Hari* (*The Sun*).

In the first few editions of *Mata Hari*, Kwee published a series of articles in which he advocated a concept that went beyond what the PTI had promoted. He urged the peranakans not only to side with Indigenous Indonesians but also to become real Indonesians by treating Indonesia as their only home. The series of articles sparked a major debate. Leaders of the *Sin Po* and the Chung Hua Hui groups joined forces in ridiculing Kwee as wanting to Indonesianise the Chinese and hence lower their status.

The staff of Kwee's paper included three members of the PTI, The Boen Liang, vice-chairman of the PTI, Tjoa Tjie Liang, secretary of the PTI, and Siauw Giok Tjhan. Among its Indigenous Indonesian journalists was Sudarjo Tjokrosisworo, who was to play a major role in the PWI (Persatuan Wartawan Indonesia – Association of Indonesian Journalists) in the 1940s and 1950s. An Arabic journalist, AR Baswedan, chairman of the PAI (Partai Arab Indonesia – Indonesian Arab Party), was also employed by Kwee.

Kwee urged his journalists to report on the independence movement and write stories on nationalist leaders. He also urged nationalist leaders to contribute articles. Kwee assigned Siauw to correspond with exiled nationalists like Soekarno and Tjipto Mangunkusumo to persuade them to write for *Mata Hari*. This provided Siauw with a good opportunity to get to know Soekarno and Tjipto well, and developed his respect and admiration for the two leaders.

In 1976 Siauw wrote:

> I was indeed fortunate to have the opportunity to know Dr Tjipto Mangunkusumo and Soekarno so well when they were exiled. Through many letters, their views on Indonesia and politics were conveyed to me. They inspired me and convinced me that their cause was right. I was particularly impressed by Dr Tjipto for his vision on the way Indonesia was to be established and developed. In Dr Tjipto's view, all Indonesian citizens, including those of Chinese descent, should have the same rights and responsibilities. There should not

be racial prejudice. I truly admire Dr Tjipto and will always consider him my very fine political mentor.[23]

Thus, by the mid-1930s Siauw well and truly belonged to the world of Liem Koen Hian, the small world of peranakans who were trying to convince the great majority of peranakans who did not believe that the Indonesian nationalists had much hope in achieving independence or that the Chinese should actively participate in the process of achieving it. Siauw was willing to pursue this line even at the expense of being ridiculed by many of his peranakan relatives and friends.

Kwee was apparently pleased with Siauw's performance and Siauw quickly became his favorite assistant and was promoted to a position on the editorial staff.[24] In 1937, after the Pacific War started, the Chinese in Indonesia mobilised a movement called the Tjin Tjay Hwee to collect funds to send to assist China to fight against the Japanese. Keen to expand the circulation of *Mata Hari* in Surabaya and to expand Tjin Tjay Hwee activity there, Kwee sent Siauw, then 23, to establish a *Mata Hari* branch in Surabaya.

By the time Siauw reached Surabaya in 1937, radical Dutch-trained peranakans Tan Ling Djie and Tjoa Sik Ien had returned from Holland and taken over the leadership of PTI and *Sin Tit Po*. Tjoa Sik Ien, then 32, was elected chairman of the PTI, replacing Liem Koen Hian who had left for Batavia earlier that year to commence a law course. Tan Ling Djie, who was 36, took over the leadership of *Sin Tit Po* from Liem. Siauw was greatly influenced by both of them, especially Tan Ling Djie. Both of the men turned their thinking in Marxist directions.

Tan and Tjoa were part of a group, born in Surabaya, who had been prominent leaders of the CHHN in the late 1920s. They were attracted to Marxism and were close to leaders of the PI – Hatta, Singgih, Subardjo and Abdulmadjid. An attraction to Marxism was a common phenomenon among students who studied in Holland in that period. Hatta, who was to become an anti-communist vice-president and prime minister, was then an active member of the League Against Imperialism which was closely associated with the Comintern and whose members were mostly Marxists.[25]

---

[23] Siauw's letter to the author, 7 July 1976.

[24] Interview with Oey Hoo Tong, *Mata Hari's* administration manager, Hong Kong, January 1989.

[25] Ruth McVey, *The Development of the Indonesian Communist Party*, Center for International Studies, MIT, 1954, pp. 15–16.

Somers states that in 1929, Tan Ling Djie, Tjoa Sik Ien and Teng Tjin Leng had formed the SPTI (Sarekat Peranakan Tionghoa Indonesia – Union of Peranakan Chinese of Indonesia). Tjoa Sik Ien was elected chairman and under the leadership of these three peranakans, the SPTI frequently held meetings with the PI. Cooperation between these two groups was as much based on a common left-wing ideology as shared Indonesian nationalist sentiment.[26] Go Gien Tjwan, however, believes that Tio Oen Bik, a man from Surabaya and also a founder of the SPTI, was most influential in the group.

In Holland Tan, Tjoa and Tio worked closely with Musso, Alimin, Sardjono and Roestam Effendi. They were all prominent Indonesian members of the Dutch Communist Party and candidates of the party in the 1934 elections to Dutch parliament but only Roestam Effendi was elected.[27] This association was an important factor in establishing a link between the illegal PKI (Partai Komunis Indonesia – Indonesian Communist Party), which was established in 1935, and peranakan activists in the Indies.

The leaders of the SPTI remained active members of the CHHN until 1932. Having failed to convince the majority of the CHHN members to endorse their Indonesia-oriented inclination, they decided to leave the CHHN. But their support remained small and the group was disbanded when Tan and Tjoa returned to the Indies in the middle of 1930s.

Back in Surabaya, Tan Ling Djie and Tjoa Sik Ien were quick to establish contact with Liem Koen Hian in Surabaya. Tan had previously been European correspondent for Liem's *Sin Tit Po*. Liem and Tan clearly influenced each other and it is not easy to establish which flow of influence was the more dominant. The two worked well together and shared many ideas, though Liem did not become much influenced by Marxism.

A parallel can be drawn between the relationship of Liem and Tan and that of Soekarno and Hatta. Liem, like Soekarno, never studied abroad. They both received their political education in the Indies and each developed skills in leading mass organisations. Liem too was a good orator. Tan, like Hatta, had studied in Holland. Although Tan did not complete his law studies at Leiden (he failed to submit his final year thesis before returning to the Indies in 1935), he knew a lot about law, especially international law. He was very much a theoretician, a backroom leader and a strict teacher.

---

[26] Mary Somers, *Peranakan Chinese Politics*, p. 96.

[27] Ruth McVey, *The Development of the Indonesian Communist Party*, p. 17.

Like Hatta, he emphasised political education and relied heavily on cadre development programs. He was a dry and monotonous speaker.

Tan had spent most of his student life in Holland in political study groups, meetings and activities. He was also highly respected by the nationalist activists in Holland for his analytical approach and his commitment.[28] He joined the Netherlands Communist Party in the early 1930s and soon after went to Moscow, living there until 1935 when he returned to Holland. In 1936, without submitting his final year thesis, Tan went to Surabaya to help expand the illegal PKI which had been established by Musso a year earlier.

Tjoa Sik Ien was another important figure in Siauw's life. Tjoa was born in Surabaya to a rich peranakan family. He was Siauw's neighbor in the main street of Kapasan, and their parents were friends. Tjoa studied medicine in Holland, completing his medical course in 1930. He worked closely with Tan Ling Djie and shared many of his political ideas. Like Tan, Tjoa was attracted to communism and became heavily involved in Indonesia-oriented politics and the independence movement. When he returned to Surabaya in 1936, he bought the *Sin Tit Po* printing company and became the director of its publication. As chairman of the SPTI in Holland, he had been a keen supporter of Liem Koen Hian and remained so after he returned to the Indies.

Tan was instrumental in expanding the illegal PKI in East Java. Activists like Amir Sjarifuddin and Oei Gee Hwat were recruited and became Tan's assistants. When Musso left the Indies, Tan took over the leadership of the party and was instrumental in determining the party's anti-Japan and pro-China communist policies. Following the Dimitrov doctrine on popular fronts, by which communist parties were instructed to prioritise opposing fascism, many of the party members joined Indonesian nationalist parties of actively anti-fascist outlook like Gerindo (Gerakan Rakyat Indonesia – Indonesian People's Movement) and some, like Amir Sjarifuddin, became leaders of these parties.

As an admirer of Mao Tse Tung, Tan attempted to stimulate Chinese interest in Mao Tse Tung's leadership through the publications of articles in *Sin Tit Po* that covered the Chinese communist activities and their successes in China. So under the leadership of Tan Ling Djie and Tjoa Sik Ien, the PTI and its mouthpiece, *Sin Tit Po* became much more radical, strongly anti-Japanese and pro-communist. Tan and Tjoa were quick to

---

[28] Z. Yasni, *Bung Hatta Menjawab*, Gunung Agung, 1978, pp. 14–15.

convince Siauw to support them. Under their guidance, particularly that of Tan, Siauw became a Marxist and an admirer of Mao Tse Tung's leadership in China. In 1938 Siauw translated into Indonesian Edgar Snow's *Red Star over China*, a book that detailed the successes of the Chinese communists under Mao Tse Tung. He had intended to publish this in *Mata Hari* but was prevented from doing so because its communist sympathies conflicted with Oei Tiong Ham's commercial interests. Parts of the translated work were published in *Sin Tit Po* until the paper was instructed by the colonial government to stop.[29]

At the urging of Tan Ling Djie, Siauw began to devote a great deal of his working time to the Tjin Tjay Hwee movement. His understanding of the totok world enabled him to be instrumental in linking the PTI with radical totok organisations represented by the *Sin Po* and Soe Poe Sia groups. These PTI initiatives enabled a brief political union between the peranakans and totoks in Surabaya. Even leaders of the Chung Hua Hui were sympathetic towards the efforts to collect funds for China. Such a union, however, did not last long. When the Japanese arrived in 1942, this informal alliance ceased to exist.

While the Tjin Tjay Hwee chapters in other cities like Semarang and Batavia limited their activities to collecting funds and medicine, the Surabaya Tjin Tjay Hwee, dominated by the PTI and the Surabaya Chinese Chamber of Commerce, was more politically oriented. It sent a medical team to China complete with ambulance facilities. The team, which was led by a Malang peranakan doctor, Go In Tjhan, left for China in 1937. In the same year, a number of peranakans left East Java for China to participate in the war against Japan. These included Siauw's younger brother, Giok Bie.

Although Tjin Tjay Hwee activities were based on a political alliance, they did not include boycotts against Japanese goods. This was largely due to the fact that many of the Tjin Tjay Hwee's supporters were businessmen. To boycott Japanese goods would significantly reduce their incomes. The responses from peranakan newspapers in Java were not uniform. Most reflected their anti-Japanese stand but some, like *Sin Tit Po* and *Sin Po*, did not contain advertisements for Japanese goods whereas others like *Mata Hari*, which was funded by the Oei Tiong Ham business, continued to carry advertisements designed to promote Japanese goods.[30] Hence, one

---

[29] Mary Somers, *Peranakan Chinese Politics*, p. 100.
[30] Leo Suryadinata, *Peranakan Chinese Politics*, p. 118; Bob Hering (ed.), *Siauw Giok Tjhan Remembers*, pp. 32–33; Siauw, *Lima Jaman*, p. 62.

can see the irony of the commercial constraints on political activities. Some of the money made from the trade with the Japanese, which supported their military operations, was used to support China in combating their aggression.

Apart from being active in the Tjin Tjay Hwee movement, Siauw helped Tan and Tjoa promote Indonesia-oriented politics in the Chinese community in Java. *Sin Tit Po* and *Mata Hari* were largely in tune in supporting the nationalist movement and in disseminating pro-independence views to their readers. *Mata Hari* was commercially a success, but neither it nor *Sin Tit Po* had much success in convincing the Chinese in the Indies to be Indonesia-oriented. The PTI remained small and was ineffective outside East Java and Central Java.

Somewhat disappointed by their lack of achievement in this regard, Siauw said:

> The peranakan community on the whole was apolitical… Although columns of *Mata Hari* and *Sin Tit Po* and the propaganda of the PTI advised the peranakan to call themselves true Indonesians, a number of them hesitated before declaring their stand openly in this way. Although they would not deny that their roots were firmly set in Indonesia they could not help feeling that to call themselves Indonesians would be lowering their status. They were unable to appreciate that the first step towards uniting themselves with the mass of Indonesians in the struggle to oppose colonial policies, which had brought about the inferior status of Indonesians, was to declare themselves openly as one with the Indonesian people.[31]

Although the PTI failed to gain popular support from the apolitical peranakan community, its prominent leaders sought to maintain good relations with nationalist leaders. In 1936 the PTI representative in the Volksraad, Ko Kwat Tiong, went against members of the Chung Hua Hui in supporting the petition moved by his fellow member Soetardjo which called for self-government in the Indies. The petition was rejected, but it gave grounds for the pro-independence members to carry out further discussions on the topic.[32]

---

[31] Bob Hering (ed.), *Siauw Giok Tjhan Remembers*, p. 35; Siauw, *Lima Jaman*, p. 56.

[32] Leo Suryadinata, *Peranakan Chinese Politics*, p. 143; Siauw, *Suatu Renungan*, p. 21; Siauw *For a Brighter Future*, unpublished manuscript, p. 22.

Following the formation of Gerindo in May 1937, Oei Gee Hwat, secretary general of the PTI, joined the organisation. Liem Koen Hian followed suit in 1939. Gerindo, led by such leaders as Amir Sjarifuddin, Sartono and Mohamad Yamin, was seen by leaders of the PTI as an organisation sympathetic towards the Chinese. Siauw said, 'Gerindo was the first nationalist organisation since the Indische Partij to accept foreign born Indonesians as members'.[33]

Somers, Coppel and Suryadinata have discussed the problem faced by the PTI in gaining full membership of GAPI (Gabungan Partai-Partai Indonesia – Federation of Indonesian Political Parties) in 1939. As it turned out, the PTI failed to get full GAPI membership.[34] Their discussion centres around the fact that the majority of the nationalist leaders were reluctant to accept members who were not Indigenous Indonesians (Asli) into their organisations. Siauw tended to ignore this opposition. His writings show that he was supportive of GAPI and endorsed their position on a single type of Indonesian citizenship which would include all people of the Indies. To Siauw, GAPI's position marked the beginning of a national commitment to bringing people of foreign descent together in achieving common political goals.[35]

By 1939 the momentum of the Tjin Tjay Hwee movement had begun to decline because of disenchantment with the failure of the Kuo Min Tang (Chinese Nationalist Party) government to effectively lead the resistance against the Japanese invaders. Kwee Hing Tjiat was one of many who believed that much of the collected funds fell into corrupt hands. His scepticism over this prompted him to close the Surabaya branch of *Mata Hari* and recall Siauw back to Semarang in 1939.

Siauw's presence in Surabaya and his close association with Tan Ling Djie has aroused the suspicion of many that he was a member of the illegal PKI.[36] Suryadinata states in a number of his books that Siauw was probably a member of the illegal party. Siauw himself denied this allegation

---

[33] Siauw, *Suatu Renungan*, p. 22.

[34] Charles Coppel, 'Patterns of Chinese Political Activity In Indonesia' in J.A.C. Mackie (ed.), *The Chinese in Indonesia*, The Australian Institute of International Affairs, 1976, p. 35; Somers, *Peranakan Chinese Politics*, p. 101; Suryadinata, *Peranakan Chinese Politics in Java*, p. 143.

[35] Siauw, *For a Brighter Future*, pp. 22–23; Siauw, *Suatu Renungan*, p. 22; Siauw Giok Tjhan's lecture notes, Universitas Respublica, unpublished, 1960(?).

[36] Interview with Oei Tjoe Tat in Jakarta in July 1994; Oei Tjoe Tat, Memoar Oei Tjoe Tat – Pembantu Presiden Soekarno, Hasta Mitra, April 1995, p. 21.

whenever it was raised. However, being close to its prominent members like Tan and Amir Sjarifuddin, he was probably involved in some of the party's meetings and activities.[37]

While Siauw denied that he had ever been a PKI member, he had made no secret of his attraction to Marxism or of his admiration for Mao Tse Tung. As a participant in the independence movement of the 1930s, it is not surprising that Siauw was attracted to Marxism. As discussed earlier, Hatta and others who later became anti-communist leaders also embraced Marxism in that period.

Not long after Siauw returned to Semarang, Kwee Hing Tjiat died suddenly of a heart attack. Siauw, then 25, took over the leadership of *Mata Hari* and became its editor-in-chief. Under Siauw, *Mata Hari* followed the style of *Sin Tit Po* and became more strongly anti-Japanese. *Mata Hari* also provided a continuing source of sympathetic information on the communist movement in China. Siauw himself wrote numerous articles supporting the Indonesian nationalist movement in Indonesia. Because of these articles, Siauw frequently had to face the Dutch authorities to explain and justify himself politically.

Back in Semarang, Siauw lived in a boarding house that accommodated a number of young peranakan men and students. He frequently typed his editorials and articles at home and therefore had many opportunities to discuss the political situation and PTI's activities with his fellow boarders. This group of young boarders whom he interested in Indonesia-oriented politics included Oei Tjoe Tat and Lie Tjwan Hie who later became his close associates in the 1950s and 60s.[38]

One of Siauw's fellow boarders was a young HBS girl, Tan Gien Hwa. Siauw and Tan developed a special relationship and were married in 1940. Tan Gien Hwa, born on 22 June 1921, was the daughter of Tan Ping Hoat, a fairly successful peranakan businessman in the Central Java town of Pemalang. After their marriage, they moved to a small house in Semarang not far from the *Mata Hari* office.

Soon after they were married, Tan Gien Hwa's mother died suddenly, and within six months, her father also died. As well as an elder brother, Tan had five younger siblings, four younger brothers and a sister whose

---

[37] Leo Suryadinata, *Peranakan Chinese Politics*, pp. 166–167; Leo Suryadinata, *Pribumi Indonesians, the Chinese Minority and China*, Heinemann Educational Books (Asia), Kuala Lumpur, 1978, p. 102.

[38] Interview with Oei Tjoe Tat in Jakarta in July 1994; Oei Tjoe Tat, *Memoar Oei Tjoe Tat – Pembantu Presiden Soekarno*, Hasta Mitra, April 1995, p. 21.

ages ranged from fourteen down to two years. From then, the young couple was left with the responsibility of bringing up and educating five orphans. Siauw's salary was fortunately sufficient to support the whole family, although their existence was comparatively modest.

When the Japanese invaded the Indies in 1942, all anti-Japanese peranakan newspapers were banned and their journalists purged and arrested. When they entered Semarang, they quickly seized the *Mata Hari* office and arrested a number of the journalists and office workers. Siauw happened to be out of the office and managed to escape arrest. In the same year, Siauw went back to Surabaya with his large family, and then on to Malang where he stayed throughout the Japanese occupation period.

Political outlook

Having been brought up in both the peranakan and totok worlds, Siauw had a good understanding of the aspirations of each of these communities. Although he was Dutch-educated and came from a rich family, he mixed mainly with peranakans who were Chinese-educated. Instead of joining a student organisation established to accommodate Dutch-educated peranakans he joined organisations frequented by Chinese-educated students. His experience of dealing with Chinese-educated peranakans on the one hand and totoks on the other hand proved useful in his political activities, especially with the Tjin Tjay Hwee movement in Surabaya between 1937 and 1939.

One thing that set Siauw apart from the great majority of peranakans in the pre-war period was his early exposure to the world of Liem Koen Hian. In Liem's world, Siauw learned to challenge the positions of those who belonged both to the China-oriented and Dutch-oriented political streams. Through working as a journalist in *Mata Hari*, he was further convinced that the only solution for the Chinese in the Indies was to work closely with the Indonesians to achieve independence. The majority of the Chinese in that period did not consider independence a likelihood. They saw no point in identifying with the Indigenous group, whose status was considered lower than their own during the colonial period. The Chinese, they believed, would be better off aligning with the Dutch community or maintaining their Chinese citizenship status.

Most Chinese would be unwilling to jeopardise their lives and incomes by being involved in politics. Again, Siauw turned his back on this custom. Not only did he choose a career which did not generate a handsome income, he also threw himself into political activities, considered by most Chinese as 'ong hiam' (dangerous). By entering the world of Liem Koen Hian and Kwee Hing Tjiat, he gained contacts with many prominent nationalist activists like Soetomo, Soekarno and Tjipto Mangunkusumo who further enhanced his commitment to Indonesia-oriented political thinking. After 1937, when Siauw came under the influence of Tan Ling Djie and Tjoa Sik Ien in Surabaya, his attraction to the idea of Indonesian independence became coloured by Marxism. As he saw it then, the struggle for Indonesian independence might have to be armed, like Mao Tse Tung's movement in China, and that might help to create a socialistic society.[39]

From Liem Koen Hian, Siauw learned how to lead a political party and how to convince readers to accept certain political views. But Siauw regarded Liem as too emotional and rigid to attract a large mass following.

Kwee Hing Tjiat trained Siauw in how to manage newspapers. Kwee liked and trusted Siauw. Major responsibility for running *Mata Hari* were assigned to Siauw and, more importantly for Siauw's future political career, he was assigned as the contact point for prominent national leaders who were in exile. Siauw highly respected Kwee and treated him like his elder brother. However, he found him to be controversial and learned that his attitudes did not win him many supporters within the peranakan community.

Tjoa Sik Ien was also influential in the shaping of Siauw's political thinking. Tjoa, also a rigid personality, was not one who could readily accept different ideas or criticism and tended to isolate his political opponents. Ko Kwat Tiong, PTI's representative in the Volksraad, left the organisation because of his inability to reach a compromise with Tjoa in 1938. Tjoa's circle within the peranakan community was therefore limited and under his leadership the PTI was unable to expand. Later, in the 1950s, Tjoa and Siauw had different opinions on how the Chinese interests should be defended but their personal relationship remained close and special until the death of Siauw in 1981.

The most influential of all of Siauw's mentors was Tan Ling Djie. Siauw found Tan to be the best of the four mentors for theoretical analysis and explanations. Siauw learned from Tan the discipline of understanding the details of political environments when analysing political situations and deriving political strategies. Siauw admired the way in which Tan forced his

---

[39] A large part of this section is based on Siauw's reflections conveyed to the author in 1972.

assistants to go to markets to check prices of eggs, salt and other commodities before attempting to analyse economic situations. Under Tan's guidance, Siauw read a lot of material about general politics and economics that covered liberalism, capitalism and communism. From this reading, Siauw also developed a strong interest in law, particularly to do with citizenship. Siauw remained very close to Tan and treated Tan like his own brother. When Tan lived with Siauw between 1951 and 1965, Siauw's children called him 'empek' (father's older brother).

By 1942, having been trained in politics and journalism by Liem Koen Hian, Kwee Hing Tjiat and Tan Ling Djie, and having participated in the Indonesian nationalist movement, Siauw was ready to play a greater role in the PTI. However, the arrival of the Japanese changed the situation dramatically.

Chapter 2

THE JAPANESE OCCUPATION AND EARLY MONTHS OF INDEPENDENCE

To the bewilderment of many Indonesians, the Japanese managed to defeat the Dutch military forces within eight days after the first attack was launched on 24 February 1942.

As soon as the Japanese arrived in Indonesia, they quickly dismantled anti-Japanese organisations and, as outlined in Chapter 1, peranakan newspapers were one of their targets. Peranakan newspaper editors and journalists were rounded up and many sent to military camps. Siauw Giok Tjhan managed to escape arrest and lived in Malang for most of the occupation period.

The Japanese waged an intensive campaign to win support from Indonesian nationalists from the late 1930s. Some nationalist leaders like Soetomo and Thamrin were sympathetic to the Japanese and hoped that they would one day help liberate them from colonial rule. Other nationalist leaders like Tjipto Mangunkusumo were always sceptical and suspicious of the real motives of the Japanese. However, Tjipto's views were not widely supported. Many nationalist activists felt the involvement of the Japanese would assist them in expediting the transfer of power from colonial rule to that of the independence fighters.

Siauw Giok Tjhan had always been on Tjipto's side. Having been heavily involved in the anti-Japanese Tjin Tjay Hwee movement, Siauw did not expect the Japanese to help Indonesia to achieve independence. He was convinced that their arrival in Indonesia would be part of their expansionary drive and that they intended to displace the Dutch as the new coloniser of Indonesia. Siauw's articles in *Mata Hari* reflected this conviction.

The spreading of Djojobojo's popular myth before the Japanese' arrival, that one day Indonesia would be liberated from white people's domination by a yellow race, further helped the justification of the pro-Japanese leaders.[1] When the Japanese finally arrived, many Indonesians greeted them with enthusiasm. In the first phase of the Japanese occupation, there was a high expectation that the Japanese would deliver on their promises.

The Japanese initially permitted the flying of the Indonesian national flag and the singing of 'Indonesia Raya' on public occasions. They also put large numbers of Dutch and Eurasian officials into prison camps, creating vacancies which were filled by Indonesians. The top positions in the administration body (Hodohan), the military administrative body (Kenetsu Han) and the semi-official body to coordinate the press (Djawa Shinbukai) were held by Japanese officials, but Indonesians were promoted to perform many day to day duties.[2]

The Japanese released all nationalist leaders who were either jailed or exiled by the Dutch – most notable of these were Soekarno, Hatta and Sjahrir. They also introduced the 'Three-As' movement (Japan as leader, protector and light of Asia) as an attempt to justify their military presence and material exploitation.[3]

But the phase of warm acceptance by the Indonesians was short-lived. The Japanese did not wait long to show their intention to become the new masters of the country. Not long after consolidating their military control, they prohibited political assemblies and demonstrations and forbade the display of the Indonesian flag. They also banned discussion, speculation or propaganda regarding the political organisation or administration of the country.[4]

Thus, by the end of 1942, the second phase of the occupation began, in which decrees were introduced to drastically suppress all formal nationalist movements, and the general populace experienced harsh treatments. People were obliged to bow deeply in the direction of the Imperial Palace in Tokyo, which offended Muslims because of their practice of facing Mecca when praying. Demands for the population to produce and deliver agricultural products to the Japanese with little or no compensation induced alarming famines in many parts of Indonesia.[5]

---

[1] Bernard Dahm, *History of Indonesia in the Twentieth Century*, Pall Mall Press, London, 1971, pp. 77–81.
[2] J.K. Ray, *Transfer of Power in Indonesia (1942–1949)*, Manaktals, Bombay, 1967, pp. 31–32.
[3] Ibid., p. 32.
[4] Bernard Dahm, *History of Indonesia*, p. 82.
[5] Ibid., p. 83; Ray, *Transfer of Power in Indonesia*, pp. 32–33.

The Japanese were especially harsh on the Chinese. They quickly rounded up many Chinese people who had been involved in anti-Japanese movements prior to their arrival. About five hundred Chinese, both peranakans and totoks, including those who worked as journalists, were interned together with thousands of European internees, mainly Dutch, in a prison camp in Tjimahi, West Java.[6] However, a number of peranakan leaders managed to escape arrest and were able to live freely throughout the occupation period. Tjoa Sik Ien was able to live and practice his medicine in Surabaya. Tan Ling Djie lived in Tanggerang for much of the occupation. Liem Koen Hian was arrested but soon afterwards freed after Soekarno's personal intervention with the Japanese authorities.[7]

Moving to Malang

A few days before the Japanese arrived in Semarang, Siauw arranged for his wife, his daughter and his wife's siblings to leave Semarang for Pemalang to seek refuge at a friend's place. He himself stayed in Semarang working at *Mata Hari* for a few more days. When the Japanese arrived in Semarang in March, Siauw left on a pushbike for Pemalang. With the help of his brother, Giok Bie, Siauw and his family moved to Surabaya. Other members of the *Mata Hari* editorial board and journalists were not as lucky – Tjioe Kiem Swie and Tjoa Tjie Liang, together with *Mata Hari* proofreaders, Han Tjiong Djien and Yap Ping Tjwie, were sent to Tjimahi and released only after the Japanese surrendered in 1945.[8]

Having failed to locate Siauw in Semarang, the Japanese did not search for Siauw outside the city, even though a peranakan whose husband had been arrested demanded that Siauw, who was her husband's superior at *Mata Hari*, be arrested instead of her husband.[9]

In Surabaya, Siauw lived with his uncle, Siauw Gwan Hok who owned a shop selling electrical goods. The uncle had no children of his own and was pleased to have Siauw's help in the shop. In fact he hoped Siauw would inherit the business. But when he died a few months after Siauw's arrival in Surabaya, his widow's family wanted to take over his properties. Unwilling to fight over the business and properties, Siauw decided to relinquish all his

---

[6] Mary Somers, *Peranakan Chinese Politics in Indonesia*, p. 105.
[7] Siauw, *Lima Jaman*, p. 70; Bob Hering (ed.), *Siauw Giok Tjhan Remembers*, p. 42.
[8] Tjoa Tjie Liang's letter to the author, October 1991.
[9] Siauw, *Lima Jaman*, p. 71.

inheritance rights to the widow and her family. So, in 1943, Siauw took his family from Surabaya to the smaller town of Malang.

In Malang, Siauw set up a small general store, which he called the 'Tjwan-Tjwan-an' ('Profitable Venture'). The choice of its name, to a degree, indicated that Siauw did not treat the business seriously. 'Tjwan-Tjwan-an' had the connotation of being a game rather than a real business. The shop sold a wide range of goods including rubber products and locally produced confectionaries. However, Siauw failed to run the business profitably. He was too flexible in his business dealings with the suppliers, reluctant to bargain and too ready to agree to prices set. When the quality of the goods was unacceptable to his customers, he rarely demanded refunds from his suppliers. When Siauw's suppliers were late in delivering their products, he did not push them. Once, a Japanese soldier was very angry with him for his failure to deliver a jacket as promised. As a result of this, Siauw received numerous beatings from the soldier. The soldier stopped beating him only when Siauw's 11-year-old brother-in-law cried violently out of fear.[10]

Siauw was often more interested in talking to his customer friends about politics than selling things. He frequently gave things away and was careless about recording cash flows. His shop did not attract many customers but it attracted peranakans interested in discussions, and generated friendship. Three frequent visitors were Han Kang Hoen, a widely respected Chinese community leader in Malang; Han Tik Djien, a close friend of Siauw who was roughly the same age, and Go Gien Tjwan, some six years younger than Siauw. Those who visited the shop from further away included Liem Koen Hian, from Jakarta, and Tjoa Sik Ien, from Surabaya. Go Gien Tjwan recalls that Siauw argued that the Chinese should participate in the movements mobilised by Soekarno and his associates and not allow the Japanese to use them as a buffer.[11] When Siauw got a lot more involved in political discussions and other activities, the shop work was often left to his younger brothers-in-law, Tan Soen Eng and Tan Soen Houw, who, in 1943 were, 11 and 7 years old.[12]

Siauw's brother, Giok Bie, and his wife lived with the family for much of the occupation period and the extended family got by largely because Siauw

---

[10] Interview with Tan Soen Eng, Jakarta, July 1996.
[11] Interview with Go Gien Tjwan, Amsterdam, December 1991.
[12] Interviews with Tan Soen Eng, Jakarta, July 1995 and Tan Soen Houw, Melbourne, August 1995.

Giok Bie's wife ran a food stall and a hair salon. By 1945, four adults and nine children were living together in the small house.[13]

Towards the end of 1942 the Japanese formed various organisations led by popular nationalist leaders including Soekarno and Hatta. The largest of these was Putera (Pusat Tenaga Rakyat – Centre of People's Power), of which Soekarno was appointed leader.

In 1943, following an announcement in the Japanese Diet that the Indonesians were to be invited to cooperate in the government, a central advisory committee (Tjuo Sangi-In) was formed in Jakarta and similar bodies (Sangi-Kai) in the provinces. The Tjuo Sangi-In was led by Soekarno and accommodated many nationalist leaders. Its main function was to provide information and proposals to the Japanese government.[14]

Recognising the importance of the Chinese business domination in Indonesia, the Japanese were also keen to maximise support from the Chinese population. They attempted to defuse Chinese support for the Chiang Kai Shek government and campaigned for the Chinese to support the Japanese-established government in Nanking under Wang Ching Wei, a shift in direction from earlier policy.[15]

In July 1942, the Japanese formed the Kakyo Shokai (Hua Chiao Tsung Hui or Overseas Chinese Federation) for persons of Chinese descent. Within months, Kakyo Shokais were formed in all major cities.

The Kakyo Shokai leaders were elected by the Chinese communities but had to be approved by the Japanese. Unlike the pre-war organisations, whose leaders were largely wealthy Chinese businessmen, Kakyo Shokai leaders were mostly recognised community leaders. In Solo, Ong Siang Tjun, a cigarette manufacturer, was elected. In Bandung, Yap Tjwan Bing, a pharmacist, was nominated. In Malang, the Chinese community elected Han Kang Hoen, a peranakan businessman who was skilful in liaising with groups outside the community.[16] Most of those who became leaders in this way were peranakans partly because there were more peranakans with higher education than totoks. These organisations represented both the peranakan and totok communities and contributed to cooperation between them, but they also accentuated their isolation from the Indigenous population.

---

[13] By then Siauw had four children and Siauw Giok Bie two children. Three brothers and one sister of Siauw's wife were also brought up by Siauw.

[14] J.K. Ray, *Transfer of Power in Indonesia*, pp. 89–91.

[15] Mary Somers, *Peranakan Chinese Politics*, pp. 104–105.

[16] Siauw, *Lima Jaman*, p. 72; Bob Hering (ed.), *Siauw Giok Tjhan Remembers*, p. 43.

The Japanese encouraged the Chinese to learn more about their ancestral background. They were urged to write their names in Chinese characters. Their shops were to have Chinese characters. Dutch language was forbidden and Dutch-sounding names were to be dropped. Because Dutch schools were closed, most peranakans were forced to send their children to Chinese schools. THHK schools, which were initially closed, were reopened in July 1942, and new Chinese language schools were established under the coordination of the Kakyo Shokais.[17]

Although the Kakyo Shokais were denied the right to engage in political activities, the organisations developed enough authority to be useful to the Japanese war effort. Like the Indonesian leaders in Putera, the Chinese community leaders were given unpleasant tasks. They had to raise funds from Chinese business circles for Japanese government agencies and later to collect jewellery and other expensive items from the Chinese communities. However, the Kakyo Shokai leaders, unlike their Putera counterparts, did not have to carry out the much-hated task of recruiting *romusha* (forced labour workers).[18]

Like the Putera leaders, Kakyo Shokai leaders were able to extract concessions for the Chinese communities, which reduced their hardships. Yap Tjwan Bing, the Bandung Kakyo Shokai leader, for example, was able to help improve the living conditions of Chinese in the Tjimahi prison.[19]

When the Tjuo Sangi Kai (Council of Advisers), a representative body led by Soekarno and consisting mainly of well-known nationalist leaders, was formed in 1943, a number of prominent peranakans were included among its members, including Oei Tjong Houw (owner of the Oei Tiong Ham business), Oei Tiang Tjoe (a journalist who was allowed to publish a daily called *Hong Po* throughout the occupation period), Yap Tjwan Bing (Bandung's Kakyo Shokai leader) and Liem Koen Hian. From this organisation, members of the Independence Preparatory Committee were selected in April 1945, including two peranakans, Yap Tjwan Bing and Liem Koen Hian[20].

In Malang, Han Kang Hoen was the main leader of the Kakyo Shokai. However, Siauw Giok Tjhan, who was about fifteen years younger than

---

[17] Siauw, *Lima Jaman*, pp. 71–72; Bob Hering (ed.), *Siauw Giok Tjhan Remembers*, p. 43; Mary Somers, *Peranakan Chinese Politics*, p. 108.

[18] Siauw, *Lima Jaman*, p. 73; Bob Hering (ed.), *Siauw Giok Tjhan Remembers*, p. 44.

[19] Siauw, *Lima Jaman*, p. 72; Bob Hering (ed.), *Siauw Giok Tjhan Remembers*, p. 44.

[20] Siauw, *Lima Jaman*, p. 73; Mary Somers, *Peranakan Chinese Politics*, p. 109.

Han, played a major role in determining the organisation's policies and strategies and running its meetings. Siauw was more experienced than Han in community organising due to his involvement in the Tjin Tjay Hwee movement in Surabaya in the late 1930s. Through this, members of the Chinese community in Malang recognised Siauw's ability to lead.[21]

The Kebotai and preparations for independence

In 1943 the Japanese began to form paramilitary units called the Seinendan (Youth Corps) and Keibodan (Vigilance Corps). Members of the Seinendan were aged from 14 to 25 and were primarily involved in carrying out propaganda activities for the Japanese as well as performing some local security tasks. Perhaps because Seinendan had some political duties, the Chinese were not allowed to participate. On the other hand, Keibodan, an auxiliary police force with members aged from 20 to 35, included Chinese among its members.[22]

In 1944, following the establishment of an auxiliary army for Indigenous Indonesians in Java called Peta (Pembela Tanah Air – Defenders of the Motherland), Kakyo Shokai leaders were instructed to form Kebotai (Chinese Vigilance Corps) which were provided with some firearms. Many Chinese initially welcomed this because it was seen as a means of protecting their safety against violent outbreaks against the Chinese.[23] The Chinese often suffered harassment from members of the Japanese-established paramilitary youth groups like the Seinendan and Keibodan and also from the Islamic Hizbullah and hoped the Kebotai troops would be able to protect their lives and properties.

In Malang, Han Kang Hoen, as the Kakyo Shokai head, chose Thio Kong An as commander of the local Kebotai and Siauw as his deputy. Each had extensive experience in the peranakan scout movement, Thio in Malang and Siauw in Surabaya. Thio was a few years older than Siauw, but had had less political experience.[24] Both Thio and Siauw were sent to Tanggerang, in West Java for intensive military training but, after a few months, Thio,

---

21 Interviews with Siauw Giok Bie, Melbourne, May 1989, Go Gien Tjwan, Amsterdam, December 1991 and Oey Hay Djoen, Jakarta, November 1997.
22 Benedict Anderson, *Java, In Time of Revolution*, Cornell University Press, 1972, pp. 26–27.
23 Siauw, *Lima Jaman*, p. 74; Bob Hering (ed.), *Siauw Giok Tjhan Remembers*, p. 45.
24 Interviews with Siauw Giok Bie, Melbourne, May 1989, Go Gien Tjwan, Amsterdam, December 1991 and Tan Hwie Kiat, Amsterdam, December 1991.

who was concerned with the potential danger of the position to his personal safety, resigned from the leadership. Han then appointed Siauw as Thio's replacement.[25] The fact that Siauw was once a Japanese fugitive in Semarang did not seem to concern the Japanese. It is possible that General Matsuda, stationed in Malang, who had married a neighbour of Siauw's wife in Pemalang, played a role in protecting Siauw's personal safety.

All Chinese between the ages of 20 and 35 were forced to join the physical training conducted by the Kebotai which consisted of two to three weeks of military type training and self-defence exercises conducted in one of the large schools in Malang. After completing the program, the trainees were to exercise for two to three hours every day. After physical exercises, the members were often requested to gather for political indoctrination sessions.

While playing leadership roles in Japanese-established organisations, Siauw established contacts with radical anti-Japanese totok groups in Malang and Surabaya. His previous involvement in the Tjin Tjay Hwee movement meant that these groups trusted him. The totok groups had links with anti-Japanese movements in Malaya and Singapore, which in turn had connections with the Chinese Communist Party. Through this group, Siauw was in touch with Tan Kah Kee who was hiding in Batu, a small town just outside Malang.

Tan Kah Kee, who was 55 years old in 1943, was one of the most widely respected overseas Chinese in Southeast Asia. Prior to the Japanese occupation of the region, he had been a prominent leader of the anti-Japanese organisations in Singapore and Malaya. He also had connections with leaders of the Chinese Communist Party. He later became a member of the Central People's Committee when the communist government was formed on 1 October 1949.[26]

Siauw shared Tan's admiration for the Chinese communists in Yenan and frequently met with him in Batu. In these meetings, Tan urged Siauw to work hard to protect Chinese interests and ensure that clashes between the Chinese and Indigenous units be avoided at all cost. Both men agreed that it was the Japanese intention to use the Chinese communities and their youth corps as buffers against a potential armed uprising, supported by

---

[25] Siauw, *Lima Jaman*, p. 76; Interview with Oey Hay Djoen, Jakarta, October 1997.

[26] For details of Tan Kah Kee's retreat in Indonesia, refer to C.F. Yong *Tan Kah Kee, The Making of an Overseas Chinese Legend*, Singapore Oxford University Press, 1987, pp. 280–291.

the Seinendan, Keibodan and other paramilitary units. Influenced by Tan, Siauw took initiatives in contacting leaders of the Indigenous paramilitary units in Malang.[27]

Together with his close associates, Siauw approached leaders of these organisations in Malang and Surabaya to ensure that full understanding between the Chinese and Indonesian organisations was achieved. They also agreed to assist each other and proposed that if necessary Kebotai could be subordinated to Keibodan. Because this was against what the Japanese intended, the discussions were held in secret.[28] Siauw's Indigenous contacts in East Java included Mustopo, Soedisman, Soemarsono and Roeslan Abdulgani. These leaders were willing to undertake to not attack the Chinese communities.[29]

By the middle of 1944 Siauw was convinced that the Japanese would lose the war, and that the Kebotai leaders were to promote the idea that the Chinese should side with Indonesians in working for independence. Siauw also began discussions with his close associates about what sort of state Indonesia should become.

Siauw was in touch with underground groups led by Amir Sjarifuddin and also the totok groups.[30] During the occupation period, Siauw also played a major role as a mediator, a role closely connected with his outlook seeking to fuse Chinese community interests with a left-wing version of Indonesian nationalism.

Meanwhile, as the Allied forces grew in strength and the Japanese lost various battles, the Japanese escalated activities which showed that they were serious in providing the Indonesians with the opportunity to achieve early independence. This was first promised in an announcement by Premier Koiso on 7 September 1944 in Japan.

In May 1945 the Japanese formed the Panitia Persiapan Kemerdekaan Indonesia (Preparatory Committee for Indonesian Independence or BPKI). The committee, led by Soekarno and Hatta, consisted of 63 members, nominated from all classes of the population and including four Chinese, one Arab and one Eurasian. The Chinese representatives included Liem Koen Hian and Yap Tjwan Bing.

---

27 Siauw, *Lima Jaman*, p. 75; Bob Hering (ed.), *Siauw Giok Tjhan Remembers*, pp. 45–46.
28 Siauw, *Lima Jaman*, p. 74; Bob Hering (ed.), *Siauw Giok Tjhan Remembers*, pp. 45–46.
29 Interviews with Go Gien Tjwan, Amsterdam, December 1991 and Soemarsono, Sydney, January 1992.
30 Siauw's own account in December 1980; Interview with Oey hay Djoen, Jakarta, October 1997.

Liem Koen Hian was active in contacting his political associates, particularly those who were leaders of the PTI. Prior to the BPKI's first meeting (28 May–1 June 1945), Liem Koen Hian went to Surabaya from Jakarta several times to have meetings at Tjoa Sik Ien's house in Surabaya with Tan Ling Djie, who resided in Tanggerang, and Siauw, from Malang. These meetings were held to formulate positions to be presented in the committee.

According to Siauw, these meetings reached the following conclusions:[31]

1. Indonesian nationalism should not be developed towards chauvinism.
2. There would be a single type of Indonesian citizenship and assurance that all Indonesian citizens have equal rights. Racial discrimination should therefore be eliminated.
3. A constitution should be drawn up guaranteeing a system in which the government places the people's interests above anything else.
4. The Chinese should not form ethnic political organisations but be encouraged to participate in politics through national organisations.
5. Their political participation and social integration should not require them to betray their cultural heritage. In relation to the use of Sino–Malay in peranakan publications, peranakan publications should be encouraged to use formal Indonesian language ('high Malay').

These conclusions were the basis of Liem Koen Hian's speech delivered at the PPKI's conference on 28 May 1945. Soekarno, in his 1 June 1945 speech formulating the PancaSila (Five Principles), made particular references to Liem's requests.

After independence

Following the proclamation of Indonesia's independence on 17 August 1945, Han Kang Hoen and Siauw Giok Tjhan tried to mobilise the Chinese groups to welcome and support independence. However, they found this a very difficult task.

The Japanese occupation had resulted in desperately bad conditions and, in some regions, disastrous famines were experienced. Large numbers of

---

[31] Siauw, *Lima Jaman*, pp. 81–88.

people were poor and hungry. During the three-and-a-half-year occupation, the Japanese, like their predecessors, had segregated the society on ethnic grounds.

With the collapse of the Japanese authority, the Pemudas (Indonesian youths trained in the Japanese-established military units like Peta and paramilitary organisations, Seinendan and Keibodan) played major roles in running the country. Armed Pemuda dominated local administrations for many months and in some areas for years. Many of them were ill-disciplined, as well as excitable and hungry, and vented their anger on groups of the population like the Chinese who were perceived to be responsible for the people's suffering.

In the first few months of the revolution, many hundreds of Chinese were killed in Java, accused of being Dutch spies. Many others were kidnapped and robbed. Their properties were looted or confiscated by the armed Pemudas. Some Muslim groups deliberately targeted the Chinese.[32]

As well as facing the armed Pemudas who were carrying out violence against the Chinese, leaders of the Chinese communities in Surabaya and Malang were confronted with the task of countering the activities of an underground movement called San Min Chu I Ching Nien Thoan (Youths of San Min Chu I). This organisation was formed primarily to fight against the Japanese and its leaders were young totok radicals. After the Japanese surrendered, these youths created a blacklist of Chinese people perceived to have collaborated with the Japanese during the occupation period. People who had led the Kakyo Shokai and Kebotai were included in their lists. In Surabaya, members of this organisation kidnapped leaders of the Kakyo Shokai and tortured them. Han Kang Hoen and Siauw were able to influence leaders of San Min Chu I Ching Nien Thoan in Malang so that no-one in Malang and its surrounding areas was harmed.[33]

Soon after the proclamation of independence, the Kakyo Shokais were dissolved. In September 1945, in Malang, Han Kang Hoen and Siauw formed a body called Hua Chiao Tse An Hui (Security Body for Overseas Chinese) to represent the Chinese interests and defend their rights in the chaotic situation.

By October 1945, Dutch troops were returning to Indonesia, and many Chinese in Java expected the independence Soekarno and Hatta had

---

[32] Mary Somers, *Peranakan Chinese Politics*, p. 112; Siauw, *Lima Jaman*, p. 78; Bob Hering (ed.), *Siauw Giok Tjhan Remembers*, p. 55.

[33] Siauw, *Lima Jaman*, pp. 76–77; Interview with Oey Hay Djoen, Jakarta, November 1997.

proclaimed would be short-lived and that the Dutch would again be the undisputed rulers. Having experienced harsh treatment from the armed Pemudas and chaotic conditions they had very little confidence in the new republic. Siauw was concerned that a perception would soon be formed among the Pemudas that the Chinese were either pro-Dutch or inclined to sit on the fence.

In September 1945, Siauw initiated the formation of the AMT (Angkatan Muda Tionghoa – Chinese Youth Movement), a peranakan youth organisation, to show the people, in particular the Pemudas, that the Chinese 'did not merely sit on the fence'. He asked his brother Giok Bie to act as its chairman because Giok Bie had had military training in China in the 1930s and had the physical stature to deal with the Pemudas. Siauw himself provided the group with political direction and handled the liaison with leaders of other Pemuda organisations.[34]

As the AMT was being formed, a decision had to be made about whether or not the organisation was to be armed. Siauw Giok Bie, supported by most members of the AMT, initially preferred to arm all members of the organisation. By then, he himself had acquired a pistol. He argued that the tasks of the AMT would be more effectively performed if his members were appropriately armed. But Siauw Giok Tjhan did not agree. His view was that the primary tasks of the AMT were to provide political education to the Chinese and convince the Pemuda organisations not to attack the Chinese. Clashes between the AMT and Pemuda units should be avoided at all costs because they would only result in more widespread physical violence against the Chinese. Siauw's view eventually prevailed.[35]

With the support from BKR (Badan Keamanan Rakyat – Body for People's Security), a forerunner of the Indonesian army, the AMT was able to ensure smooth Chinese refugee traffic between Malang and Surabaya. Its leaders negotiated with leaders of Pemuda bands to head off robberies and kidnappings of Chinese and it was able to release many Chinese prisoners suspected of being Dutch or Japanese spies from camps in Malang and Surabaya.[36]

---

[34] Interviews with Go Gien Tjwan, Amsterdam, December 1992 and Siauw Giok Bie, Melbourne, May 1989.

[35] Interview with Siauw Giok Bie, Melbourne, May 1989.

[36] Siauw, *Lima Jaman*, pp. 77–78; Bob Hering (ed.), *Siauw Giok Tjhan Remembers*, p. 54; Interview with Siauw Giok Bie, Melbourne, May 1989.

In October 1945, Soetomo, the 27-year-old leader of the BPRI (Barisan Pembrontak Rakyat Indonesia – Insurgent Corps of the Indonesian People) and better known as Bung Tomo, rose to great prominence in East Java. His fiery radio speeches were highly effective in mobilising the Pemudas to fight against the Allied British and Dutch forces. However, they contained anti-Chinese overtones.

These anti-Chinese themes of Bung Tomo's nationalism presented Siauw and his group with difficult challenges. How could they persuade Chinese people to support the nationalism of the new republic if its local manifestations were anti-Chinese? In order to minimise the negative impacts of Bung Tomo's speeches, Siauw instructed Go Gien Tjwan to regularly broadcast the AMT's voice. Go therefore broadcast his speeches, on Wednesdays in Malang, 15 minutes before Bung Tomo's. In these speeches, Go highlighted the efforts made by the Chinese Pemudas in East Java in working together with other Indonesians to defend Indonesian independence. Siauw, together with Giok Bie and Go Gien Tjwan, also met with Bung Tomo several times to convince him to reduce his anti-Chinese overtones. While admitting that he had high regard for Siauw and his AMT group, Bung Tomo could not be convinced that the majority of the Chinese were of the same commitment.[37]

Late in October 1945, Siauw led a delegation of peranakan activists to meet with Bung Tomo, as well as his associates of the BPRI, and Soemarsono and Soedisman of the Pesindo (Pemuda Sosialis Indonesia – Indonesian Socialist Youths) in Nangka Jajar, a small town between Malang and Surabaya. In this meeting, Siauw re-emphasised the importance of effective cooperation between the Pemuda groups and the need to eliminate racial prejudices so that spiritual and material support for the new republic from the Chinese population could be guaranteed. Siauw also made a commitment that the AMT would not be armed and that individual peranakans who were willing to actively participate in the defence of independence would be encouraged to join existing armed Pemuda organisations.[38] As a result of these initiatives, a number of Chinese joined BPRI and Pesindo, most notably Gam Hian Tjong and Auwyang Tjoe Tek. The latter was reportedly the Chinese-looking man holding a Kuo Min Tang flag

---

[37] Interviews with Siauw Giok Bie, Melbourne, May 1989 and Go Gien Tjwan, Amsterdam, December 1992.

[38] Interview with Siauw Giok Bie, Melbourne, May 1989.

who appeared in a widely published photo of the 10 November battle in Surabaya.[39]

Siauw's authority as a mediator also enabled him to take initiatives to save the lives of Dutch women and children who were interned in a camp in Malang. The local BPRI had decided to block food supplies to this camp but Siauw met with its leaders and convinced them that the blocking of food supplies to Dutch internees would damage the new republic's international reputation. He was also able to work with the mayor of Malang, Sunarko, who instructed the AMT to deliver food and medicine collected by its members to the internees.[40]

In this same period, Siauw formed a paramedical team, which he called the Palang Biru (Blue Cross). Tan Sie Liep was appointed its leader. Most of its members were people who had been trained in Kebotai and were also members of the AMT. Palang Biru members were trained to give first aid treatment to wounded fighters. They also collected medicine and distributed them to the fighting groups. Late in 1945, Siauw Giok Bie, who was actively involved in obtaining medicine from the International Red Cross, was invited by Soekarno to Jakarta to be commended for a job well done.[41]

Following the death of British General Mallaby in Surabaya on 29 October 1945 and the issuing of an ultimatum by Major General Mansergh on 9 November 1945, it was widely expected that there would be heavy fighting in Surabaya the next day. Siauw mobilised members of the AMT and Palang Biru to be prepared for the battle in Surabaya. The Siauw brothers, accompanied by a group of peranakans from these two organisations, left for Surabaya in the evening of November 9. They were physically involved in the fighting on the next day as well as providing medical treatment to some of the wounded fighters.[42]

In order to consolidate their political influence among the Chinese in East Java, Siauw, together with Go Gien Tjwan, The Tjing Djien and Tjoa Kian Bo (all members of the AMT), organised a Chinese youth conference. The conference, held in Selecta, near Malang, took place in January 1946. It was attended by 74 participants from 23 cities and towns in East Java. The conference considered how Chinese youth could make

---

[39] Siauw, Lima Jaman, pp. 79–80; Bob Hering (ed.), Siauw Giok Tjhan Remembers, p. 55; Interview with Siauw Giok Bie, Melbourne, May 1989.

[40] Interview with Go Gien Tjwan, Amsterdam, December 1992.

[41] Interview with Siauw Giok Bie, Melbourne, May 1989.

[42] Interviews with Siauw Giok Bie, Melbourne, May 1989 and Go Gien Tjwan, Amsterdam, December 1992.

effective contributions to the establishment of a new society in Indonesia. It heard speeches from well-known peranakan leaders such as Oei Yong Tjioe, a Malang lawyer; Yap Hong Po, leader of the Chung Hua Hui in Yogyakarta; Kwa Tjoan Sioe, a well-known figure from Jakarta who was highly regarded by Indonesian nationalist leaders for his political and financial contributions, and the Chinese vice-consul, Lin Chi Ming.

The main achievement of this meeting was the formation of the Chung Hua Tsing Nien Hui (Federation of Chinese Youth) of East Java. Liem Chong An and Siauw Giok Tjhan were elected chairman and vice-chairman, respectively, and Malang was nominated as its headquarters. Although the organisation was predominantly led by peranakans, its establishment constituted an attempt to unite the peranakan and totok groups to perform various tasks, namely, the establishment of schools for poor Chinese people, the recruiting of first aid teams to help war casualties and the formation of boy scout units and study clubs.[43] The organisation, however, was short-lived. Siauw became much more involved in national politics and, in 1947, he moved to Yogyakarta. With this move, the organisation ceased to exist.[44]

Siauw's interest in promoting Indonesia-oriented politics among the Chinese in Indonesia prompted him to engage in journalistic work again. In January 1946, he established a weekly journal called *Pemoeda* (*The Youth*) with the assistance of his close friends, Go Gien Tjwan, Han Tik Djien and The Siauw Giap, who had supported him throughout the Japanese occupation period.

In the same year, he was also persuaded by the owner of Paragon Press to edit another weekly journal called *Liberty*. While *Pemoeda* was primarily aimed at young Chinese, *Liberty* was for general peranakan consumption. Siauw wrote articles for both publications. Frequently, he emphasised the need for Chinese 'political assimilation'. On other occasions, he discussed Marxism, San Min Chu I and the progress of the Chinese revolution. Articles by Indigenous writers such as Alimin, Sudarjo Tjokrosisworo, Idroes and DN Aidit, as well as appropriate quotations from republican leaders, were featured prominently in both publications. Such a stand was not popular in the East Java Chinese community with its apolitical tradition and its experience of violence in the early months of the republic. As

---

[43] *Pemoeda*, Malang, April 1946.
[44] Interview with Siauw Giok Bie, Melbourne, June 1989.

such, the circulation of these journals, which were led by Siauw until mid 1947, was limited.[45]

Siauw's participation in politics as a community leader in Malang enabled him to establish good relationships with leaders of Pemuda organisations and leaders of the newly formed government. His organisational skills and the respect of the Chinese community for his leadership were recognised by leaders of the newly formed Partai Sosialis (Socialist Party).

It was now time for Siauw to be more involved in national politics. In December 1945, he joined the Partai Sosialis which had become the ruling party of the government. This decision marked the beginning of his involvement in national politics.

---

[45] Siauw's own account, conveyed to the author in December 1980.

PART II

1946–1954

Chapter 3

PARTAI SOSIALIS, BADAN PEKERJA AND YOGYAKARTA

In the first years of the revolution there was a lot of physical violence against the Chinese carried out by gangs of armed youths. The young government's inability to contain these racial outbursts and the success of the Dutch in offering minorities protection in areas it controlled discouraged the majority of the Chinese from supporting the republic.

The Chinese continued to be divided. Of those who had substantial Dutch education, most believed that their interests would be better protected if the Dutch were victorious in their contest with the Soekarno–Hatta republic. Most of those who had a Chinese education remained oriented towards China. Though they were troubled by the new intensity of conflict between the Nationalist Government of China and its communist opposition, they still hoped that a strong China would eventually protect their interests.

Siauw, as one of the small group of Indonesia-minded Chinese, was isolated from both of these segments of the Chinese community. His active involvement in the political life of the new Republic of Indonesia was sometimes ridiculed by them.

By joining the Partai Sosialis in December 1945, Siauw hoped that he could influence the Indigenous activists to change their attitudes towards the Chinese community in Indonesia and play a role in devising policy to protect the Chinese. His active involvement in national politics, his close association with principal leaders of the Partai Sosialis and his organising abilities rapidly brought him to important positions within the party, the KNIP (Komite Nasional Indonesia Pusat – Central National Committee of Indonesia), its Badan Pekerja (Working Committee) and subsequently in Amir Sjarifuddin's two cabinets. This chapter outlines Siauw's activities in these institutions between 1945 and 1950.

Joining the Partai Sosialis

The Proclamation of Independence on 17 August 1945 was followed by the formation of a presidential cabinet, headed by Soekarno, which largely consisted of people who had led the organisations formed by the Japanese during the occupation. Its critics called it the 'Bucho' cabinet because it was dominated by Buchos (heads of ministerial departments). The Java Hokokai, the only Japanese-sanctioned political organisation in the later occupation period, was refashioned as a single party for the nation, under the name Partai Nasional Indonesia (PNI). In the following months, this structure and people who headed it came under fire from a group of leaders who had taken no part in the various organisations created by the Japanese during the occupation period. These men, especially Sjahrir and Amir Sjarifuddin, were keen to replace the governmental and political structure with a more democratic one free from Japanese influence.

The formation of the KNIP on 22 August 1945 gave representation to a large number of Pemuda leaders sympathetic to the ideas of Sjahrir and Amir Sjarifuddin. They were eventually successful in convincing leaders of the government to accept the KNIP as a body with full legislative powers.

On 17 October a Badan Pekerja was formed to carry out the daily work of the KNIP. It was envisaged that the Badan Pekerja, dominated by Sjahrir and Amir Sjarifuddin, would act as parliament and the KNIP as the larger consultative assembly provided for in the constitution.

Keen to dismantle the one-party system, the Sjahrir group persuaded Vice-President Hatta to issue a decree allowing the free formation of parties. This decree was issued on 3 November 1945 after which numerous political parties were formed, the major ones being the PNI, Partai Sosialis and the Islamic Masyumi Party (Council of Indonesian Islamic Associations) which dominated the Badan Pekerja.

On 11 November 1945, Soekarno agreed to appoint Sjahrir and Amir Sjarifuddin to form a parliamentary cabinet and this was achieved on 14 November, with Sjahrir as Prime Minister and Amir as Minister for Defence and Information. The recently formed major political parties were represented in the cabinet.

The introduction of the 3 November Decree resulted in the formation of numerous political parties in November 1945. Among them were the PKI, led by Mohamad Yusuf; the Partai Buruh (Labour Party), led by Njono; Masyumi, led by Sukiman Wirjosandjojo; the Partai Rakyat Jelata (Party for Poor People), led by Sutan Dewanis; Paras (Partai Rakyat Sosialis – Socialist People's Party), led by Sutan Sjahrir, and the PSI, led by Amir Sjarifuddin.

Amir's PSI was officially founded on 12 November 1945 in Yogyakarta. Its nucleus was made up of Amir's close associates of the pre-war Gerindo. Its main programs were based on socialistic ideals.[1]

On 19 November 1945, Sjahrir's supporters formed Paras in Tjirebon as a kind of revival of the pre-war Pendidikan Nasional Indonesia, headed by Hatta and Sjahrir.[2]

A fusion of these two parties was achieved at a congress in Tjirebon on 16 and 17 December 1945. The new party, Partai Sosialis,[3] became a powerful political force, dominating the governments of the next two years. But the divisions between the Amir and Sjahrir groups remained apparent and somewhat divisive.

The party was divided into three main groups[4] led by Amir, Sjahrir and Abdulmadjid. Amir's group was heavily dominated by people from Surabaya and included peranakan figures. Some of these people, like Tan Ling Djie and Oei Gee Hwat, had been members of the illegal PKI set up by Musso in Surabaya in 1935. Many of these people were not highly educated. Anderson asserts that many of Amir's supporters:

> had suffered severely under Japanese repression. Its political ancestry lay, like that of Amir himself, in the family of mass-oriented parties of the pre-war period: the PKI of the twenties, Soekarno's PNI, Partindo (Partai Indonesia – Indonesian Party) and the Gerindo. In the main, its members had humbler origins and less western education than the followers did of Sjahrir. Its Marxism was less sophisticated and less academic and at the same time more populist and tinged with apocalyptic romanticism. Its radicalism was more experienced than read about.[5]

---

[1] Anderson, *Java in a Time of Revolution*, p. 202.
[2] Ibid. p. 202.
[3] Ibid. p. 203.
[4] I prefer to divide the party into three groups rather than five as suggested by Anderson. The five groups outlined by Anderson are the groups of Surabaya, Yogya, Tjirebon, Jakarta and recent returnees from Holland.
[5] Anderson, *Java In a Time of Revolution*, p. 206.

Within Amir's group, Tan Ling Djie provided behind the scenes leadership. Tan was neither an organiser nor a speaker but was highly respected for his detailed political knowledge and his familiarity with international politics.[6]

Sjahrir's group, on the other hand, was dominated by highly Westerneducated politicians of more elite origins. Many were former leaders of the Pendidikan Nasional Indonesia, which had emphasised the training of cadres rather than mass agitation or the propagation of populist nationalism. Others were university students whom Sjahrir had recruited to his following in the years of the Japanese occupation.

The two groups reflected the temperaments of their leaders. Amir, like Soekarno, emphasised organising mass support, while Sjahrir concentrated on educating cadres to influence political developments. These temperaments were reflected in the party's organisational structure. Amir's men dominated the leadership, secretariat and communication committees while Sjahrir's men dominated the information and education committees.[7]

A third component, small in number, was a group recently returned from Holland who had been members or sympathisers of the Dutch Communist Party. This group, led by Abdulmadjid, a member of the Dutch Communist Party, was influential in shaping the party's view of the outside world and in creating its identity as an organisation committed to a worldwide struggle against fascism. This group was a particularly strong advocate of negotiation with the Dutch, arguing that it was necessary to influence public opinion in Holland.[8] Some of its members looked to Tan Ling Djie for leadership.

It was Tan who persuaded Siauw Giok Tjhan, then still in Malang, to join the party in December 1945. Siauw, who had maintained contacts with underground movements during the Japanese occupation and in the lead-up to the events of 10 November in Surabaya, was working with the Surabaya leaders who dominated Amir's group. He would have experienced these leaders' positive attitudes in welcoming the participation of Indonesian Chinese in their political activities. The presence of Tan Ling Djie and Oei Gee Hwat on the party's board of leadership would have

---

[6] Siauw's account conveyed to the author in prison in 1972. Interview with Soemarsono, then a leader of the Pesindo and the Badan Kongres Pemuda Republik Indonesia (Congress of the Organisation of Youth of the Republic of Indonesia), in Sydney in 1995; Z. Yasni, *Bung Hatta Menjawab*, Gunung Agung, 1978, pp. 14–15. Frederiek Djara Wellem, *Amir Sjarifoeddin – Pergumulan Imannya Dalam Perjuanan Kemerdekaan*, Penerbit Sinar Harapan, 1984, pp. 224.

[7] Anderson, *Java In a Time of Revolution*, p. 208.

[8] Ibid. p. 209.

further convinced him that the party would be based on policies which were against racism. Thus, to Siauw, the Partai Sosialis, resembling the pre-war Gerindo, would become a vehicle to encourage the Chinese in Indonesia to adopt Indonesia-oriented attitudes. He was also convinced that the party would enable him to influence the Pemudas and their leaders to provide protection to the Chinese. Go Gien Tjwan, one of his close associates from Malang, also joined the party at about the same time.

Siauw never occupied high positions in the party's formal leadership, unlike Tan Ling Djie and Oei Gee Hwat. But to Amir's group, Tan and Siauw, though not formally qualified, were their 'jagoan intelek', intellectuals in the same league as the prestigious intellectuals of Sjahrir's group.[9]

I have not been able to establish when Siauw first met Amir; however, it was probably in Surabaya sometime between 1935 and 1942. Amir had spent a lot of time in Surabaya in the 1930s and had worked closely with peranakan lawyers and journalists there, including various PTI leaders[10]. By 1945 Siauw and Amir knew each other well and had developed mutual respect[11]. Siauw later described Amir as an emotional leader who often acted without consulting his associates. Nonetheless, Siauw admired his dedication and commitment and respected his leadership.[12]

Siauw, then 31, was appointed a member of the executive Information Committee as soon as he joined the Partai Sosialis in December 1945.[13] Many party documents about its office bearers do not include his name, though he was present at many of the important politburo meetings.[14]

Though clearly part of Amir's group, Siauw was also able to work closely with a number of people in Sjahrir's group. He was particularly close to Djohan Sjahroezah, and claimed to have got on well with Sjahrir.[15]

---

[9] Soemarsono recalls that Siauw was often found together with Amir in Yogyakarta. In his opinion, Amir, whose knowledge of political ideologies was limited, relied heavily on people like Tan Ling Djie and Siauw for theoretical input.

[10] Interview with Jaques Leclerc, Paris, January 1995. The information on Amir's association with peranakan leaders was obtained from Siauw and Leclerc summarised this in his 'Amir Sjarifuddin, Between The State and The Revolution', in Angus McIntyre (ed.), *In Search of Cross-cultural Understanding*, pp. 12–13.

[11] Interview with Soemarsono, Sydney, July 1992.

[12] Siauw's account conveyed to the author in Jakarta, January 1978.

[13] Interviews with Soemarsono, Sydney, July 1992 and Go Gien Tjwan, Amsterdam, January 1990.

[14] Interviews with Soemarsono, Gondo Pratomo, Jaques Leclerc and Go Gien Tjwan.

[15] Siauw's own account; Interview with Soemarsono, who at that time lived together with Djohan Sjahroezah. Sjahroezah, Soemarsono recalls, admired Siauw's qualities.

Soemarsono also recalls that because of his special relationship with Sjahroezah, some of Sjahrir's men regarded Siauw as a member of their own group. Siauw and Sjahroezah worked together as members of the Information Committee of the Partai Sosialis. They shared an interest in applying Marxist theories to practical organisational activities, particularly in the journalistic field. John Legge describes Sjahroezah as one of the most important leaders of the PSI.

> His practical political organisation went along with an interest in revolutionary theory. Some of Sjahrir's student followers saw him as the leader most steeped in Marxist theory. He was the most doctrinaire of those about Sjahrir, said one… Others stressed his role as strategist and tactician, as against Sjahrir's role as a politica thinker.[16]

In early 1946, Siauw also became responsible for coordinating cooperation between the party and its youth affiliate, Pesindo, formed on 10 November 1945 in Surabaya. Pesindo itself was a fusion of seven armed youth groups including API of Jakarta, Gerpri of Yogyakarta, AMRI of Semarang, PRI of Surabaya, Angkatan Muda Kereta Api, Angkatan Muda Gas dan Listrik and Angkatan Muda Pos, Telegrap dan Telepon. Siauw was also close to leaders of the BKPRI (Badan Kongres Pemuda Republik Indonesia – Congress of the Organisation of Youth of the Republic of Indonesia), a loose federation of Pesindo and 21 other youth organisations formed in Surabaya and led by Soemarsono.[17]

Siauw's contacts with the youth leaders from East Java and particularly from Surabaya, who dominated both the Pesindo and BKPRI, encouraged Amir and Tan to make him their link with them. He also became a political adviser to both Soemarsono of the BKPRI and Setiadi of Pesindo.[18]

The KNIP and its Badan Pekerja

The formation of the KNIP on 22 August 1945 in Jakarta was quickly followed by the formation of its regional committees. Siauw Giok Tjhan was elected as a member of the Malang committee in October 1945. Siauw's

---

[16] J.D. Legge, *Intellectuals and Nationalism in Indonesia – A Study of the Following Recruited by Sutan Sjahrir in Occupation Jakarta*, Cornell Modern Indonesia Project, 1988, p. 64.

[17] For detailed account on the formation of Pesindo and BKPRI, see Benedict Anderson, *Java in a Time of Revolution*, pp. 255–257.

[18] Interview with Soemarsono, Sydney, December 1990.

elevation to the central committee in Jakarta in 1946 and later to its Badan Pekerja in 1947 was related to the political changes which took place in the revolutionary period, which in turn was linked to the attempts made by the Dutch to regain their colonial power.

The central line of cleavage throughout the period of revolution was between governments that negotiated with the Dutch and opposition groups that criticised them for making too many concessions. The Sjahrir cabinet, formed in November 1945, adopted the negotiating stance and this was supported by Soekarno, Hatta and Amir Sjarifuddin. They believed that Indonesia's full independence and its recognition could be achieved through negotiations with the Dutch. They also believed that the safest approach to defending the republic was by appealing to Britain and the United States of America (USA) to press the Dutch to adopt a reasonable attitude towards it. The Partai Sosialis, which dominated the cabinet and Badan Pekerja, also endorsed this pro-diplomacy stance.

There were two main reasons for this. Firstly, leaders of the Partai Sosialis were in office. They had no option but to conduct formal negotiations with the Dutch who had succeeded in reoccupying many urban centres. They did not want to provoke military actions from the British and Dutch troops who occupied and controlled many parts of Indonesia. Secondly, they believed in the importance of a united front against fascism and saw the European left as an ally. Siauw recalled that leaders of the Partai Sosialis were heavily influenced by developments in China and Vietnam. In 1946 peaceful negotiations between Vietnam, led by Ho Chi Minh, and France had resulted in the signing of the Fontainebleu Agreement. And Mao Tse Tung had been encouraged by Stalin to cease hostilities against Chiang Kai Shek and work towards a compromise with him.

Reflecting on all this in 1980, Siauw saw this pro-diplomacy stance as mistaken, believing that it was erroneous to follow directions given by international leaders who were not familiar with the political environment of Indonesia nor committed to national interests. Siauw claimed that he had always had some sympathy for the opposition groups' more radical stand against the Dutch.[19]

The opposition was led by Tan Malaka. Older generation politicians in its leadership included Iwa Kusumasumantri, Buntaran and Yamin. The younger leaders included Sukarni, Chaerul Saleh and Adam Malik. They fought for Indonesia's full independence and the nationalisation of

---

[19] Siauw's account, conveyed to the author in Amsterdam in 1980.

all foreign, particularly Dutch, companies. They believed that negotiations with the Dutch should take place only after the Dutch recognised Indonesia's independence.

Tan Malaka, a communist leader in the 1920s, had returned to Indonesia in 1942 after spending long periods in Holland and a number of Asian countries. He had been a representative of the Comintern for Southeast Asia but then had broken away from it. After the proclamation of independence, he emerged as a powerful critic of Soekarno, Hatta, Sjahrir and Amir.

Tan Malaka's vision and leadership style attracted a large number of militant youths and intellectuals. His supporters were successful in assembling leaders of 133 parties and Pemuda organisations and senior military figures like Commander-in-Chief Sudirman at a conference in Surakarta in January 1946. This conference resulted in the formation of the Persatuan Perdjuangan (Union of Struggle).

Many members of the Partai Sosialis and Pesindo, including Siauw Giok Tjhan and Soemarsono, initially sympathised with the new organisation. But they abandoned their support when it became apparent that Tan Malaka and his supporters were attempting to overthrow the Sjahrir government.[20] People from the left side of politics at that time were heavily influenced by Moscow's anti-fascist line. As the Dutch were considered anti-fascist, leaders of the Partai Sosialis were encouraged to adopt a policy involving negotiations with them. Siauw, along with many other Partai Sosialis and Pesindo members who would have preferred a tougher stand against the Dutch, was obliged to accept their party leaders' direction and hence opposed the non-negotiation programs proposed by the Persatuan Perjuangan. But Siauw obviously respected the Persatuan Perjuangan's tough stand. Many of the Persatuan Perjuangan leaders, including Mohamad Yamin, Iwa Kusumasumantri and Ibnu Parna, became his close friends in the years to come.

The pressure from Persatuan Perjuangan also resulted in the increase of the KNIP membership in February 1946. The reason for this is detailed below. Representation for the Chinese was increased from four to five. Siauw Giok Tjhan was appointed by Soekarno to fill the fifth position, in addition to Liem Koen Hian, Yap Tjwan Bing, Tan Ling Djie and Injo Beng Goat.

---

[20] Interview with Soemarsono, Sydney, July 1992.

Late 1945 and early 1946 was a period when British and Dutch troops were expanding the areas under their control, and there was violence against the Chinese in many parts of Java. The worsening situation forced the government to move the republic's capital from Jakarta to Yogyakarta on 4 January 1946. Sjahrir as Prime Minister, foreign minister, and chief negotiator, remained in Jakarta but Soekarno, Hatta and Amir Sjarifuddin moved to Yogyakarta. Yogyakarta, being away from the occupied areas and closer to the locations of armed units of youths, developed as the city which supported armed resistance, while Dutch-occupied Jakarta became the main centre of support for the diplomacy policy.[21]

In response to pressure from the PNI and other components of the Persatuan Perdjuangan, Sjahrir resigned on 28 February 1946. For a time, the Persatuan Perdjuangan appeared to have triumphed. But when Soekarno gave them the mandate to form a new cabinet they failed to settle major differences within the group. The interests of anti-Marxist Muslims, conservative bureaucrats, nationalist communists and competing personal ambitions could not be contained to form a workable cabinet. Soekarno was compelled to ask Sjahrir to form a new cabinet. The second Sjahrir cabinet was formed in March 1946, larger but still heavily dominated by Sjahrir and Amir Sjarifuddin.[22]

Having failed to achieve structural changes in the KNIP, Badan Pekerja and cabinet in March 1946, leaders of the Persatuan Perdjuangan in Madiun threatened to overthrow the government by force. The government responded by sending troops to Madiun and arresting the chief leaders of the organisation, including Tan Malaka, Chaerul Saleh, Sukarni and Mohamad Yamin. In July 1946, other leaders of the organisation attempted to stage a coup but failed. As a result, Persatuan Perdjuangan was banned and many of its leaders jailed.

Indonesian citizenship

One of the major issues debated in the Badan Pekerja, particularly in April 1946, was that of Indonesian citizenship. Tan Ling Djie, supported by the Partai Sosialis, argued that anyone born in Indonesia prior to Independence should be an Indonesian citizen. This, he argued, would minimise the

---

21 Anderson, *Java in a Time of Revolution*, pp. 300–301.
22 George McTurnan Kahin, *Nationalism and Revolution in Indonesia*, Cornell University Press, New York, 1955, pp. 176–177.

number of foreigners in Indonesia and would secure maximum support for the republic from people of foreign descent.

Lukman Hakim of the PNI argued against this, saying that people of Chinese, Arab or European origin should have the right to opt for Indonesian citizenship but not be accorded it automatically. They believed that this method would be more democratic. The debate was won by Tan Ling Djie. Under the Citizenship Bill, which became law on 10 April 1946, all people born in Indonesia would be Indonesian citizens unless they repudiated this before 10 April 1947.

The representatives of the People's Republic of China strongly objected to this new citizenship law and requested that its principle be altered from that of a passive system, where people of foreign descent who were born in Indonesia were declared Indonesian citizens, to one incorporating an active system, where people of foreign descent wishing to be Indonesian citizens were obliged to apply for Indonesian citizenship. As a result of this objection, the period for opting for foreign citizenship was extended from one year (1946–1947) to two years (1947–1949). In 1949 it was again extended to expire in December 1951.[23]

The government viewed this law as an important tool in convincing the Chinese to support the republic. Siauw Giok Tjhan and Tan Po Goan, a Jakarta lawyer four years older than Siauw[24], were charged with publicising it. In April and May 1946 Siauw and Tan travelled to all the major urban centres of East Java, visiting Chinese communities to explain the implications of the new law and to campaign for support for the republic and the Partai Sosialis.

But Siauw found the task difficult. Most Chinese people saw no advantages in becoming Indonesian citizens, and those who were victims of violence by Indonesian Pemudas found it difficult to see why Chinese should work for a republic. Many feared that as Indonesian citizens they would be forced to marry Indigenous people and that their property, particularly their land, would be confiscated. Many also believed that by becoming Indonesian citizens they would lower their status. Siauw believed that much of the anxieties were also caused by a *Sin Po* article of 10 December 1946. Many people referred to this article stating that it would be foolish to reject Chinese citizenship as the People's Republic of China was one of

---

[23] Siauw, *For a Brighter Future*, pp. 70–71.

[24] Tan Po Goan was by then a well-known Jakarta lawyer. It was Tan Ling Djie who introduced him to the Partai Sosialis and encouraged him to work closely with Siauw.

the big five countries in the United Nations (UN) while Indonesia was still struggling for international recognition.[25]

As a result of this working relationship, Tan Po Goan joined the Partai Sosialis and later became a member of KNIP.[26]

Evidence of the strength of Chinese opposition to the republic led its leaders to consider establishing a ministry specifically charged with minority affairs. When Sjahrir was forced to restructure his cabinet a second time in October 1946, he decided to act on this idea. Siauw was initially the candidate for the ministry, but Tan Ling Djie decided to propose that Tan Po Goan become minister of state for minority affairs, the first Chinese to be a minister. Tan Ling Djie did this to secure more support from the Chinese of West Java.[27]

The new KNIP and Badan Pekerja

Protracted negotiations between the Dutch and Indonesian governments led, in November 1946, to the Linggadjati Agreement. In this, the Dutch government recognised the republic as the de facto authority in Java and Sumatra. The two parties agreed to establish the United States of Indonesia by 1 January 1949 to include the Republic of Indonesia, consisting of Java and Sumatra and two other states, the Great East and Borneo. They also agreed to co-operate in the formation of a Netherlands–Indonesia Union, consisting of the Kingdom of the Netherlands and the United States of Indonesia, with the Queen of the Netherlands as its head. Within the republic, the Linggadjati Agreement was supported by government parties but strongly opposed by the Persatuan Perdjuangan.

To secure KNIP endorsement of the agreement, President Soekarno issued a decree on 29 December 1946 increasing the membership of the KNIP from 200 to 515. This decree was initially rejected but finally accepted after a dramatic speech by Hatta in the KNIP which warned that Soekarno would resign if KNIP rejected the decree. Thus a new, enlarged KNIP was formed on 2 March 1947. It included two additional peranakan members, Oei Hway Kim and Tan Boen An, representing Chinese minority groups. Two other peranakan members were elected, not as representatives of the

---

[25] Hering (ed.), *Siauw Giok Tjhan Remembers*, p. 61.
[26] Siauw, *Lima Jaman*, pp. 92–93; Interview with Go Gien Tjwan, Amsterdam, December 1992.
[27] Interview with Go Gien Tjwan, Amsterdam, December 1992.

minority groups, but as representatives of the Partai Sosialis (Oei Gee Hwat) and the PKI (Lauw King Ho).

On 3 March 1947 the old Badan Pekerdja was dismissed by the KNIP and a new one formed. The new Badan Pekerdja had 47 members, 40 of whom were elected from the KNIP. Siauw Giok Tjhan was elected as a representative of the Chinese minority. Tan Ling Djie remained a member representing the Partai Sosialis.[28]

The political influence of the Partai Sosialis and the Sayap Kiri (Left Wing) coalition that supported it remained strong in the new KNIP and Badan Pekerja. With the support of a number of non-party members, Christian party members and representatives of the minority groups who were also members of the Partai Sosialis (Siauw Giok Tjhan and Hamid Algadrie), the Sajap Kiri still outnumbered its opposition, which was represented by the PNI, Masyumi and Tan Malaka's supporters. Thus, the Linggadjati Agreement was finally approved by the KNIP on 5 March 1947. It was formally signed on 25 March.[29]

Not long after his election as a member of the Badan Pekerja, Siauw was asked by Sjahrir to join him to attend the first Inter-Asian Relations Conference to be held in New Delhi, in March 1947. The Indonesian delegation was large and included Prime Minister Sjahrir, Agus Salim who was unaligned with any party, Ali Sastroamidjojo of the PNI, Abu Hanifah of Masyumi, Tambunan of the Christian Party, Djohan Sjaroezah of the Partai Sosialis, Maruto Darusman of the PKI, Suripno of the Badan Kongres Pemuda, Yetty Zain of Pesindo and Mrs Subandrio of the Perwari (Persatuan Wanita Republik Indonesia – Union of Indonesian Women).

Siauw was elected secretary of the delegation[30] and played an important role in providing funds for it. The delegation travelled from Indonesia with almost no foreign currency. When they arrived in Singapore and had to wait there for a few days before departing to India, they were desperately short of money. One of those who solved the problem was Tan Kah Kee, a prominent Singaporean leader whom Siauw had met in Malang during the Japanese occupation[31].

---

[28] George McT. Kahin, *Nationalism and Revolution*, pp. 203–205. It is important to note that Kahin recorded that it was Tan Po Goan who was elected to represent the minority groups in Badan Pekerja. This is incorrect. It was definitely Siauw who got elected by the KNIP.

[29] Kahin, *Nationalism and Revolution*, p. 206.

[30] Siauw, *Lima Jaman*, p. 110; Bob Hering (ed.), *Siauw Giok Tjhan Remembers*, p. 67.

[31] Siauw, *Lima Jaman*, p. 113.

Siauw recalled that the Indonesian delegation was given a very warm welcome at the conference, particularly by Nehru who was to become India's prime minister a few months later. In the first few days of their arrival, each delegation member was accompanied by an Indian guide. Siauw's guide was Nehru's daughter, Indira, the future prime minister of India.[32]

Nationalist China was represented by its deputy foreign minister, George Yeh, who disparaged Indonesia by highlighting the republic's failure to protect the lives and property of the Chinese in Indonesia. Ali Sastroamidjojo and Siauw defended the republic's position. Siauw said he was disappointed that China should be ridiculing a newly founded republic which was still in the early stages of nation building. That, he said, was against the San Min Chu I's principles of Dr Sun Yat Sen which promoted international solidarity among developing nations. The racial violence experienced in Indonesia, according to Siauw, was due to a vacuum of power and the divide and rule policy of the Dutch. He was supported in this by KII Pannikar, who later became the first ambassador of India to the People's Republic of China.[33]

Most of the delegation members returned from India via Singapore. Sjahrir went on from there to Jakarta, but most other members wanted to fly directly to Yogyakarta rather than via Dutch-occupied Jakarta. Siauw again used his contacts to help the delegation to overcome their financial problems. They found the cheapest accommodation, and Malay families were asked to accommodate the two female delegation members. Siauw also arranged for them to eat at cheap Chinese noodle shops. To avoid embarrassment, the delegation members were asked to remove their picis (Muslim caps) while eating in these shops. The group eventually returned to Yogyakarta on a plane chartered from India whose pilot was willing to risk being shot down by Dutch military forces.[34] The episode helped Siauw to build personal relationships with various members of the group, especially Ali Sastroamidjojo and Agus Salim.

The Amir Sjarifuddin Cabinet

Soon after the Linggadjati Agreement was signed, the Dutch and Indonesians began to accuse each other of misinterpreting it. The Dutch

---

[32] Siauw's own account, interview in military prison, 1971.
[33] Siauw, *Lima Jaman*, pp. 113–114; Hering (ed.), *Siauw Giok Tjhan Remembers*, pp. 67–68.
[34] Siauw, *Lima Jaman*, pp. 115–116.

interpreted the agreement to mean that they had the right to exercise leadership until the formation of the United States of Indonesia. The Indonesians on the other hand assumed that the agreement called for joint responsibility and mutual consultation in setting up the federation. The disagreement rapidly grew and the parties involved became more antagonistic towards each other.

On 27 May 1947, the Dutch presented the republic with an ultimatum. This called for the Netherlands to have sovereignty over Indonesia until 1 January 1949. Pending that date, Indonesia was to be governed by a Dutch-dominated interim government. This interim government was to design the political structure of the United States of Indonesia and its organs. It was also to control all exports, imports and foreign exchange for all Indonesia. Governor General Van Mook made it clear that if the republic refused to comply, it would mean war.[35]

Committed to avoiding military confrontation with the Dutch, Sjahrir went as far as he could in meeting the Dutch demands, giving concessions which seriously undermined the republic's position. In a proposal he made to the Dutch on 20 June 1947, he agreed to accept the concept of forming an interim government and to allow this interim government to be Dutch-dominated.

According to Kahin these concessions had been endorsed by the Sjahrir cabinet members who resided in Jakarta, namely Gani, Natsir and Abdulmadjid. Kahin further asserts that Amir Sjarifuddin, who visited Jakarta on 20 June, also endorsed the proposal. But when Abjulmadjid visited Yogyakarta to meet other Partai Sosialis leaders to get support for this, Tan Ling Djie and Wikana condemned Sjahrir for agreeing to the concessions. Amir himself later followed suit. When Sjahrir went to Yogyakarta on 26 June 1947 he was attacked by Tan Ling Djie, Abdulmadjid and Amir Sjarifuddin. By now all of the major parties except Masyumi had abandoned Sjahrir and on 27 June he handed his resignation to Soekarno.[36]

The fear of full-scale war breaking out was aggravated by the stance of the United States of America, which backed the Dutch and encouraged the Indonesians to uphold the concessions Sjahrir had made on 20 June 1947. On 30 June, Soekarno asked the four major parties – the PNI, Masyumi, the Partai Sosialis and Partai Buruh – to form a coalition cabinet. After

---

[35] Kahin, *Nationalism and Revolution*, pp. 206–207.
[36] Ibid.

Masyumi tried to form cabinet and failed, Amir Sjarifuddin was asked to form a new cabinet.

On 3 July the Amir Sjarifuddin cabinet was formed, with the support of the Partai Sosialis, the PNI, the Partai Buruh and a newly formed Islamic party, the PSII (Partai Serikat Islam Indonesia – Islamic Association Party of Indonesia). Masyumi refused to support the new cabinet and Sjahrir declined an offer to become a member of it.[37]

Siauw was appointed by Amir to become one of the five state ministers in charge of minority affairs replacing Tan Po Goan. Siauw was not consulted before this appointment. When he was told of it, he said he did not want to accept. Siauw believed that he would be able to contribute more as a full-time member of the Badan Pekerja. He also said that he preferred to hold a legislative position to an executive one. But his reluctance was overridden by Amir and Tan Ling Djie who told him that he had to accept the position.[38] So in early July, Siauw moved to Yogyakarta, leaving his family in Malang.

As no house was available, Siauw initially stayed in various hotels. For a short period, he slept in his ministerial office. When his family came to Yogyakarta three months later, having been smuggled in through Dutch-occupied areas, Siauw's good friend, Liem Ting Tjay, gave Siauw and his family a large house. Liem Ting Tjay had been the chief judge of Yogyakarta but had had to move to Jakarta. Siauw arranged to share it with a Partai Sosialis colleague Dr Tjokronegoro, vice-minister for social security of the Partai Sosialis, and his family. The two families lived together there until the Siauws moved to Jakarta in 1950.

One of the first initiatives Siauw took as minister was to establish radio programs in Mandarin to be broadcast to areas of Indonesia, such as Bagan Siapiapi, where that language was widely spoken.[39]

Amir's cabinet, like those of Sjahrir, was under heavy pressure to give concessions to the Dutch to avoid full-scale war with the Dutch. It eventually offered concessions which went beyond what Sjahrir had proposed on 20 June but these fell short of what the Dutch demanded – joint control of and participation in government in the republican areas.

On 21 July, the Dutch launched what they called a 'police action'. Using the pretext that the Republic of Indonesia was not able to control its own territory, Dutch forces attacked many hitherto republican-controlled areas

---

[37] Kahin, *Nationalism and Revolution*, pp. 209–210.
[38] Siauw's own account conveyed to the author in prison in 1973.
[39] Siauw, *Lima Jaman*, p. 119.

in Java and Sumatra by land, air and sea. Within two weeks, most major towns in West and East Java, as well as many communication links between them, were under Dutch control. In Sumatra, the Dutch had taken control of most of the estate and oil-producing areas.[40]

One consequence of the Dutch attack was a new wave of anti-Chinese violence. As the republic's army encouraged regional armed youths to co-ordinate resistance activities in their own regions, the fate of people in small towns depended largely on the political and military wisdom of the local youth leaders. Unfortunately many of these leaders were hostile towards the Chinese population. Some confiscated Chinese property.

Others engaged in what is now called ethnic cleansing. Using the excuse of protecting the Chinese, they forced large numbers of people from towns in republican-controlled areas to leave their homes and be taken to concentration camps in the hills, most of them hidden from general public. Chinese urban properties were confiscated and looted. In the makeshift concentration camps, they were often robbed and badly treated. Some were killed.

Siauw Giok Tjhan refers to two such mass evictions in his *Lima Jaman*. In Salatiga, the whole Chinese population was forced to leave their properties and the town. After they left their houses, their houses were looted. Those who refused to leave were branded enemies and risked being jailed or killed. The refugees were not given proper accommodation and had to rely on the government's assistance to survive. Siauw, as state minister, responded by approaching the CHTH (Chung Hua Tsung Hui – Chinese General Association) of Solo, who arranged for Chinese school buildings in Solo to accommodate the refugees.

The same treatment was experienced by the Chinese of Kebumen. The whole population of the pecinan of this town were forced to leave their houses and then taken to a remote location. Their houses were looted and vandalised by local inhabitants. The looters, desperate to find hidden property, dug out the rooms and destroyed walls in the vacated houses. The Chinese refugees were sent to a camp far from town and put under strong pressure to convert to Islam.

Siauw, assisted by members of the CHTH and individual Chinese youths who were attached to armed units, worked hard to locate these concentration camps. Due to Siauw's good connections with prominent Pemuda leaders, like Mustopo and Soemarsono, they were able to locate many of

---

[40] Kahin, *Nationalism and Revolution*, pp. 211–213.

them and, in some cases, to get the inmates released. In other cases Siauw was able to provide material help.[41]

On 22 July 1947, Siauw spoke on the republican radio to condemn the Dutch invasion and blamed the Dutch for spreading racial hatred. He stated:

> The Dutch are still employing people and spending a lot of money to cause disturbances and disruptions in day-to-day life in an effort to exploit these as a pretext for their military actions. The Dutch have tried to pull the wool over the eyes of the world by using as an excuse the same grounds the Japanese gave for their attack on China.[42]

On 2 August, parts of a speech Soekarno made on 1 July were rebroadcast to highlight his wish to maintain law and order. In Soekarno's words:

> I can guarantee that all races can work together and earn a living peacefully and securely by investing in the Republic of Indonesia. I can guarantee that the property of all races will be safeguarded and protected and be available for use in the normal ways in a country in which there is peace and security.[43]

On 8 September, Amir Sjarifuddin showed his strong support for the Indonesian Chinese by broadcasting his speech over the radio.

> It appears that the Indonesian people and our Pemuda who are fighting in the front line are deliberately being roused against the Chinese by the Dutch. Chinese mercenaries are deliberately being put in the front line to provoke anti-Chinese feelings among the Indonesians. In turn Chinese feelings of racial hatred are being fomented by Dutch-employed Indonesian mercenaries to loot and burn the shops of Chinese… I therefore condemn most strongly all actions which have been caused by a blind following of passions with the result that the crimes of a small handful of Chinese are being held at the heads of all Chinese. Those Chinese who have lived among us for generations we regard as members of our own family and, indeed, we have declared them to be citizens of Indonesia.[44]

---

[41] Interviews with Siauw Giok Bie, Melbourne, May 1990 and Soemarsono, Sydney, December 1992.

[42] Hering (ed.), *Siauw Giok Tjhan Remembers*, p. 71.

[43] Ibid.

[44] Ibid., p. 72.

Siauw also persuaded Amir and General Sudirman to instruct all military organisations in the country to avoid racial violence. A written instruction to all military units issued in July 1947 by Amir as defence minister and Sudirman as chief of the armed forces authorised the shooting of anyone caught looting and robbing Chinese premises.[45]

To reduce the suffering of the refugees and to make it less necessary for the government to provide meals and clothing for them, Siauw encouraged the refugees to be self-sufficient through production in their camps. He urged them to produce food like beancurd, soya bean cakes and soya sauce.

Siauw faced an uphill battle in convincing the Chinese population to support the republic. The Chinese in republican areas suffered more hardship than those who were in Dutch-occupied areas. The armed youths in many areas were hostile towards them and treated them badly. Despite Siauw's assurances and the commitments of such figures as Soekarno, Amir Sjarifuddin and General Sudirman, these leaders remained powerless to effectively protect Chinese lives and properties.

Although the victims of these anti-Chinese actions had reasons to be grateful to Siauw for what he did to help them, they could not help being resentful towards the people whom Siauw urged them to treat as their local brothers and sisters. The Chinese press did not help Siauw's cause either. The Jakarta dailies *Sin Po* and *Keng Po* reported these incidents unfavourably and ridiculed Siauw as the minister of 'tahu tempeh' (beancurd and soya bean cake).[46]

As the Chinese population often became targets of armed resistance, Siauw was asked by Amir Sjarifuddin to attend strategic meetings on how to fight Dutch military aggression. At these meetings, the main leaders of the armed forces and armed youth units, people like General Urip, Soetomo, Soemarsono and Sakirman, often discussed how 'scorched earth' tactics were to be deployed. Siauw recalls that, in some instances, he was able to convince the meeting to abandon plans to destroy the buildings in main cities that were normally occupied by the Chinese by arguing that such actions would make the defence of cities from major Dutch military attacks less effective.[47]

---

[45] Siauw, *Lima Jaman*, pp. 120–121; Hering (ed.), *Siauw Giok Tjhan Remembers*, p. 73.
[46] Siauw, *Lima Jaman*, p. 120.
[47] Ibid., pp. 125–126.

Though he failed to convince the majority of the Chinese to support the republic, Siauw made it significantly harder for the Dutch to present the republic as racist and unable to maintain public order. In October 1947, the UN's Good Offices Committee, represented by Australia, Belgium and the United States of America, conducted an investigation on how the republic was maintaining order in their territories. The fact that there were now no longer concentration camps and that there was less looting of Chinese premises helped improve the republic's international reputation.[48]

Another important task for Siauw as state minister was related to the citizenship issue. The Kuo Min Tang government representative in Indonesia, Chiang Tsia Tung, went to Yogyakarta late in 1947 to urge the Indonesian government to abandon the passive system of citizenship and replace it with the active system. Siauw was given the task to meet with Chinese government representatives to explain the republican position. These representatives failed to convince the republican government to adopt the active system.[49]

Siauw was also tasked by the Partai Sosialis to run and edit its mouthpiece in Yogyakarta, a daily paper called the *Suara Ibu Kota (Voice of the Capital)*. In this capacity, Siauw was assisted by two young communists, DN Aidit and Njoto. It was reportedly Siauw who introduced Njoto, then in his early 20s, to journalism.[50] Siauw edited the daily until he left Yogyakarta for Jakarta in 1950.

On 11 November Amir reshuffled his cabinet to include members of Masyumi. Siauw Giok Tjhan became minister for minority affairs, an upgrading compared with his earlier position.

International pressure, particularly through the United Nations, forced the Dutch to accept a ceasefire on 4 August 1947. By this time, the republican territories had been much reduced. The republic controlled only central Java and parts of East Java and Sumatra. But the UN's role had been expanded with the formation of a Committee of Good Offices tasked with facilitating negotiations between the two governments. New talks began on 8 December 1947 on the ship *USS Renville*. To show that he remained committed to involving the Chinese in his political activities, Amir Sjarifuddin appointed Tjoa Sik Ien as a member of the Indonesian delegation.[51]

---

[48] Ibid., pp. 122–123.
[49] Ibid., p. 124
[50] Interview with Soemarsono, Sydney, July 1992.
[51] Siauw, *Lima Jaman*, p. 131; Hering (ed.), *Siauw Giok Tjhan Remembers*, p. 75.

After weeks of negotiation and exchanges of proposals from both sides, an agreement known as the American-sponsored Renville Agreement was signed on 17 January 1948. This agreement confirmed Dutch control of the areas seized in the 'police action'. The republic agreed to take its forces out of those areas and to accept Dutch sovereignty in Indonesia until it was transferred to the United States of Indonesia.

Like Sjahrir in June 1947, Amir was put on the spot. He saw the republic as being militarily weak. Reports from the military forces confirmed that the strength of the republic's forces had rapidly declined due to lack of ammunition and funds. Furthermore, the republican government was under a lot of pressure from countries such as the United States of America and Great Britain to achieve settlement through negotiations.

Amir also experienced what Sjahrir went through some six months earlier. Prior to the signing of the agreement, Amir understood that Masyumi and the PNI would endorse the concessions he was about to make on the government's behalf. Siauw recalled that in order to maintain unity, many members of the Sayap Kiri were compelled to endorse Amir's position, even though they disagreed with it.[52] However, after the Renville Agreement was signed, both the PNI and Masyumi declared that they did not endorse the agreement and would pull out from Amir's cabinet.

On 22 January 1948, in a meeting attended by some Sayap Kiri ministers – Abdulmadjid, Tjokronegoro, Hendromartono, Soyas, Setiadi, Siauw Giok Tjhan, Tamzil, Wikana and Maruto Darusman[53] – Amir expressed his disappointment and said that he had been betrayed. He therefore decided to resign. This decision was made without consulting the Sayap Kiri leadership[54] and on 23 January 1948 Amir resigned as prime minister.

Siauw recalled that Soekarno wanted Amir to form a new cabinet, but he refused, apparently without consulting his party leadership. Senior members of the Partai Sosialis were surprised and disappointed by Amir's decision, seeing it as a recipe for disaster. But Amir argued that there was no point dealing with leaders of Masyumi and PNI who had betrayed him. A week or so later, Hatta offered him the position of defence minister but he rejected this too.[55]

---

[52] Siauw, *Lima Jaman*, pp. 132–133, Bob Hering (ed.), *Siauw Giok Tjhan Remembers*, p. 76.
[53] I.N. Soebagijo: *SK Trimurti, Wanita Pengabdi Bangsa*, p. 159.
[54] Siauw, *Lima Jaman*, pp. 132–133.
[55] Ibid.

Amir's decision not to join Hatta's cabinet was probably to do with his hostility to Masyumi's leaders, like Sukiman, who seemed to be working with the USA to topple him. Sukiman was very close to Dr Frank Graham, who was the USA representative on the UN's Committee of Good Offices, and had played a major role in bringing the Dutch and Indonesian governments to accept the Renville Agreement. The Union of Soviet Socialist Republics (USSR) later pointed to the close relationship between Graham and leaders of Masyumi as evidence that the USA had conspired with Masyumi and PNI in masterminding the downfall of Amir's government.[56]

In opposition

With the resignation of Amir and the inability of other leaders to quickly form a new cabinet, Soekarno decided to form a presidential cabinet with Hatta as prime minister. This cabinet, formed on 31 January 1948, was dominated by members of the PNI and Masyumi. For the first time after Sjahrir became prime minister in November 1945, the Sayap Kiri was out of government.

With the formation of the Hatta cabinet, supported by Masyumi and PNI, the same ironical situation developed – the parties had rejected the Renville Agreement and this rejection had led to the downfall of Amir's cabinet; however, they then endorsed a political program based upon the Renville Agreement.

Within the Partai Sosialis, tension between the right and left factions had been rising since the demise of Sjahrir in June 1947. The internal conflict within the party reached a climax when Sjahrir returned from abroad in late January 1948. Sjahrir criticised Amir for signing the Renville Agreement, but he objected to Amir's decision to oppose the Hatta government which supported the implementation of the agreement.

The internal conflict split the party. On 13 February 1948, leaders who supported Sjahrir – like Supeno, Subadio Sastrosatomo, Djohan Sjahroezah and Tan Po Goan – left the Partai Sosialis and formed a new party called the PSI (Partai Sosialis Indonesia – Indonesian Socialist Party). Branches of the Partai Sosialis that were dominated by the Sjahrir group, especially those in West Java, Sumatra and some parts of East Java, quickly moved to the new party.

---

56   Ann Swift, *The Road to Madiun: The Indonesian Communist Uprising of 1948*, Ithaca, NY, Cornell University, 1989, p. 18.

But the great majority of the Partai Sosialis members, including Siauw Giok Tjhan, remained with Amir Sjarifuddin. The departure of Sjahrir and his followers from the Partai Sosialis did not have a serious impact on the structure of the Sayap Kiri. Amir's leadership was still supported and endorsed by most of its member organisations[57] – the Partai Sosialis, with some 30 000 members; the Partai Buruh, with some 1000 members; the paramilitary Pesindo, with some 100 000 members; the PKI, with some 3000 members; the labour organisation SOBSI (Sentral Organisasi Buruh Seluruh Indonesia – Central All-Indonesian Workers Organisation), with some 1 million members, and a small part of the BTI (Barisan Tani Indonesia – Indonesian Peasant Front).

On or about 21 February 1948, the Sayap Kiri held a conference in Solo which decided to rename the coalition the FDR (Front Demokrasi Rakyat – People's Democratic Front). In this meeting, they attacked Masyumi and PNI for betraying Amir Sjarifuddin's cabinet. Although they agreed to support the carrying out of the Renville Agreement, they would oppose the new Hatta cabinet.[58]

The Madiun Affair

The politics of the republic in the beginning of 1948 was centred in three cities: Yogyakarta, Solo and Madiun. Yogyakarta, being the capital of the republic, was where prominent politicians of all major political forces where located. In military terms, however, the city was dominated by forces loyal to the Sultan of Yogyakarta, Hamengkubuwono IX.

Solo was the military headquarters of three armed youth units: the socialist Pesindo, the Barisan Banteng, who supported Tan Malaka, and the Hizbullah, who were affiliated with the PNI and Masyumi. Armed clashes between these three groups and political kidnappings occurred frequently. Wikana, a leader of Pesindo, had been installed by Amir's government as head of the military government of Solo and held that position until May 1948 but he was in no position to secure control over the city.[59]

Madiun was the stronghold of the Sayap Kiri. In this city, the Sayap Kiri established Marx House, in which its cadres were trained and political meetings were held. The Sayap Kiri leadership in this city was represented

---

[57] Swift, *The Road To* Madiun, p. 6.
[58] Ibid., p. 22.
[59] Ibid., p. 15.

by Oei Gee Hwat and Soemarsono. Tan Ling Djie was most dominant in providing political directions. Siauw Giok Tjhan, by now a member of the Partai Sosialis politburo and living in Yogyakarta, was the main point of contact for many of the Pesindo leaders.[60]

In the first few months after the formation of Hatta's cabinet, the FDR carried out their opposition to the government in conventional ways. Their attempts to topple Hatta involved promoting support for their opposition in various government policies within Badan Pekerja and at public meetings. Amir travelled extensively in Java to gain support. President Soekarno tried hard to maintain national unity and in mid-May it almost seemed possible for a new cabinet to be formed that included the FDR. All the parties had issued a joint statement agreeing on the need for national unity but events of late May 1948 dramatically altered the political direction of the FDR and this further widened the rift between it and the government.[61]

One of the Sayap Kiri's representatives abroad, Suripno, managed to hold talks with leaders of the USSR, and on 22 May 1948 signed a document at the Soviet Embassy in Prague detailing the intention of the Russian government to establish diplomatic relations with the Indonesian government. Pressured by the USA and Dutch governments, Hatta's government showed its reluctance to accept the USSR's offer to establish formal relations. Leaders of the FDR, by now frustrated by the Americans who they said had been too pro-Dutch, publicly criticised the government's action and endorsed the idea of establishing formal relations with the USSR.

The arguments on whether or not Indonesia should have a formal relationship with the USSR led to political polarisation. The Hatta government, containing Masyumi and PNI, was forced to support the USA while the FDR publicly condemned the USA's role in supporting the Dutch in Indonesia and sided with the USSR. This political development made it impossible for a national reconciliation. The FDR remained as the government's major opposition.

At the beginning of June 1948, prompted by the controversy surrounding relations with the USSR and frustrated by the government's inability to achieve resolution with the Dutch, the FDR began to mobilise strikes, public demonstrations and agitation within the military forces. At that point, the FDR was still advocating resolution based on the Renville Agreement and their activities were still focused on domestic issues. Arguments about

---

[60] Interview with Soemarsono, Sydney, December 1990.
[61] Swift, *The Road to Madiun*, p. 31; Kahin, *Nationalism and Revolution*, pp. 259–260.

international politics were limited and support for the Soviet bloc was limited to a call for full diplomatic relations with the USSR.[62]

However, the situation dramatically changed with Musso's arrival in Yogyakarta on 11 August of 1948. Within a few days of his arrival, Musso, a respected leader with international and national credentials, was accepted as a leader who brought Moscow's orders with him. He was able to gain control over the PKI, and a few days later, the FDR.

Musso brought a plan, called the Jalan Baru (New Road), which was presumably prepared before he reached Yogyakarta. In this document, he criticised the way in which the communists had led the FDR. He attacked the communist leaders for trusting the national bourgeoisie and for allowing the PKI to play a minor role in the FDR.

He also criticised Amir for giving up power without resistance, allowing right-wing elements to consolidate their power. Finally, he called for the Partai Sosialis and other FDR parties to be merged into the PKI and the formation of a national front under the leadership of the PKI. Musso's presence and the call for the repudiation of the Renville Agreement and for full independence was appealing to many of the FDR members who were becoming frustrated and impatient with the adoption of the pro-diplomacy approach. They found Musso's leadership radical and attractive.

On 31 August 1948, the PKI announced the merger of the Partai Sosialis and Partai Buruh with the PKI and the dissolution of the FDR. To the surprise of many, Amir Sjarifuddin, Tan Ling Djie, Abdulmadjid, Setiadjit and Wikana all declared that they had been members of the underground PKI established by Musso in 1935.

Amir Sjarifuddin's announcement surprised many who believed that he was more nationalist than communist. Kahin describes this belief by arguing:

> Even if Sjarifuddin actually did become a nominal member of the "illegal PKI", the consensus among non-communist Indonesian leaders is that he was certainly never an orthodox Stalinist communist and, to this end, was more a nationalist than a communist. They attribute his final public espousal of a Stalinist position to two principal factors: disillusionment with the United States and political opportunism.[63]

---

[62] Ibid., p. 50.
[63] Kahin, *Nationalism and Revolution*, p. 274; also see Wellem, *Amir Sjarifoeddin*, p. 57.

Siauw confirmed that Amir had indeed been a member of the illegal PKI.[64]

The leaders of the party disclosed that Tan Ling Djie, Abdulmadjid and Setiadjit had been members of the Dutch Communist Party prior to their return to Indonesia. On 1 September 1948, the PKI announced its new politburo, which included leaders of the FDR like Tan Ling Djie and Amir Sjarifuddin. Amir's role had been significantly reduced in the new organisation. Musso had clearly emerged as the principal leader.

It is most unlikely that Tan Ling Djie was wholehearted in his endorsement of Musso's leadership and plan. He had always opposed the idea of a large legal PKI. He preferred the way in which the Partai Sosialis was led, with the PKI being small and effective in the background. He was probably forced, like Amir, to join by the momentum of Musso's leadership.

The merger was not warmly welcomed by all members. Moderates of the Partai Sosialis and PBI as well as the affiliated SOBSI were uneasy about a merger and opposed it. Siauw Giok Tjhan, while maintaining close and good relationships with the leaders of the new PKI, decided not to join the organisation. Siauw later repeatedly stated that the reason for not joining the PKI was that he felt disillusioned with the ability of political parties to defend minority rights and believed that he would be more effective representing the minority groups in parliament as a non-party member. Siauw also believed that if he were a member of the PKI, most of the Chinese who were apolitical and were fearful of being connected to communism would isolate him. Furthermore, he was never happy with the party's discipline. By being a non-party member of the Badan Pekerja, he was hopeful that he would have a degree of freedom in endorsing or challenging various parties' formulations. His decision was endorsed by Tan Ling Djie.[65]

The merger and the way in which members of the FDR parties were admitted to the new PKI was somewhat confusing. Prominent leaders of the FDR who were close to Amir were more often regarded by the PKI's enemies as members of the PKI.[66]

At the beginning of September 1948, Musso, Amir, Setiadjit and Wikana began a two-week tour around the republican areas to promote the new party's political programs. The population responded

---

[64] Interview with Siauw Giok Tjhan, Amsterdam, January 1980.

[65] Siauw's own account in military prison, 1972 and confirmed in an interview with him in Amsterdam 1980.

[66] Interviews with Go Gien Tjwan and Gondo Pratomo, Amsterdam, December 1990. Gondo was a senior leader of the Partai Sosialis who joined the PKI after the merger.

enthusiastically to Musso's call to repudiate the Renville Agreement. This created new problems for the Hatta government which was still trying to achieve resolution with the Dutch by making compromises in order to avoid direct armed clashes.

Meanwhile, Tan Malaka's supporters, who were long-time opponents of negotiation with the Dutch, attempted to match Musso's activities in gaining mass support. Clashes between the PKI's Pesindo and Tan Malaka's Barisan Banteng and kidnappings of the communist leaders in Solo occurred more frequently, resulting in the involvement of regular military units. In Madiun, Soemarsono responded by disarming the Barisan Banteng.

What happened after this is controversial. According to Kahin:

> After consolidating its control over the villages, the Pesindo and other PKI troops seized control of the towns and city of Madiun, thereby bringing to a head the incipient clash with the local republican administration. This militant phase began at 3 am on September 18 in Madiun with Soemarsono and Djokosujono leading the operation.[67]

Kahin refers to a radio announcement made by Soemarsono, reportedly made on the same day, declaring PKI victory and urging other PKI members to follow the example set in Madiun.

Swift is more definitive. Referring to written publications, she describes the incident:

> When Soemarsono units decided to move in Madiun, they did so quickly and effectively. According to the official PKI account, at one o'clock in the morning of Saturday, September 18, PKI troops of Brigade 29 under Colonel Dachlan moved into the city and quickly put down the minimal resistance they met from the Siliwangi and police mobile brigade units stationed in the city. Police and Siliwangi officers were captured and put in detention… At ten in the morning, Soemarsono took to the air on Radio Gelora Pemuda to announce that the people had taken over the government and were establishing a National Front government for the Region of Madiun.[68]

---

[67] Kahin, *Nationalism and Revolution*, p. 291.
[68] Swift, *The Road To Madiun*, pp. 73–74.

Soemarsono himself has a very different version. He admits that he initiated action against the Barisan Banteng in Madiun, but denies that he initiated a military action against police or Siliwangi army units. He says that he did not make any announcement on air regarding the PKI victory. He says no such claim was ever made on radio. He was therefore surprised by the stories which appeared in various national newspapers and had no option but to defend the Pesindo position when attacked by government troops around 19 September. Only when Musso, Amir Sjarifuddin and other leaders arrived in Madiun did they decide to raise arms against the government. This action was preceded with Musso's direct attack on Soekarno and Hatta on 19 September.[69]

As materials presented by most writers do not produce convincing evidence that Soemarsono did take military action and broadcast his announcement on the PKI victory – Swift admits that a copy of Soemarsono's radio address is not available[70] – I tend to adopt Soemarsono's explanation. Siauw, who knew Soemarsono well, also adopted Soemarsono's version and wrote:

> From Soemarsono's account it is clear that the so-called Madiun Affair was engineered by the Hatta government to find justification to crush the PKI and its affiliates. Hatta was desperate to demonstrate to the US that his government was anti-communist and that it was committed to crushing all pro-communist elements in Indonesia.[71]

Musso and Soekarno exchanged bitter attacks in radio broadcasts, which seemed to confirm earlier reports of the communists' intention to topple the government by force. Within the next two months, the PKI and their armed units were crushed by the regular army supported by Hizbullah and Barisan Banteng forces. The PKI forces and their leaders were soon on the run. Musso and other leaders were killed during the armed clashes. The communist resistance finally ended with the arrest of Amir with some 300 of his armed supporters in Purwodadi on 1 December 1948.

Quite unaware of the situation which resulted in the destruction of the PKI, leaders like Tan Ling Djie and Abdulmadjid and many others were arrested in Yogyakarta and other cities around 19 September 1948. Siauw Giok Tjhan, being linked to the FDR, was jailed and held in the Wirogunan prison in Yogyakarta with many other left-wing leaders.

---

69 Interview with Soemarsono, Sydney, July 1992.
70 Swift, *The Road to Madiun*, p. 74.
71 Siauw, *For a Brighter Future*, p. 47.

Siauw recalled that the prison conditions were poor. The government was not able to provide sufficient food to the prisoners. Like most other prisoners, Siauw was neither interrogated nor charged.

The second Dutch military action and its aftermath

Meanwhile, negotiations on the implementation of the Renville Agreement with the Dutch broke down. On 19 December 1948, Dutch forces began a second major attack on republican areas. Yogyakarta fell to them on the next day. Soekarno, Hatta, Sjahrir, Agus Salim and a number of other leaders were arrested and taken to government-controlled areas of Sumatra.

Facing military attacks and fearing the revival of communist forces, the republican military commanders ordered the killing of all political prisoners. Prison guards were ordered to throw hand grenades into every prison cell before they fled the cities. Siauw recalled that in Dampit and Magelang, all prisoners were executed by firing squads. In some major cities, like Yogyakarta, the prison guards did not follow the orders, instead opening the prison gates and letting the political prisoners free. Siauw Giok Tjhan and Tan Ling Djie were fortunate to be among the prisoners set free on 19 December 1948. Many of the prisoners joined the resistance movement led by General Sudirman. Siauw went back to his house the next day but the Dutch rearrested him a few days later.

So Siauw was soon back at the Wirogunan prison, but this time he was jailed together with many of the political opponents of the FDR. His fellow prisoners included Anwar Tjokroaminoto, Abikusno Tjokrosisworo and Aruji Kartawinata of the PSII, Wilopo and Sajuti Melik of the PNI, and Adam Malik and Ibnu Parna of the Partai Murba (Murba Party).

Siauw's flexible approach won him many friends in this group. Together with Sajuti Melik and Anwar Tjokroaminoto, Siauw compiled a handwritten daily bulletin called *Suara Tapa (Voice of the Hermits)*. It contained a summary and analysis of the news the three were able to obtain from radio broadcasts and newspapers smuggled into the prison.

Siauw also initiated and participated in many political discussions in the prison. Some of these discussions resulted in a statement called the Wirogunan Charter, which was handwritten by Siauw and smuggled out of prison. The charter contained a resolution on the formation of a fully independent Indonesia that was to be socialist in nature.

In August, the Dutch moved Siauw and six other prisoners including Achmad Subardjo, Anwar Tjokroaminoto, Aruji Kartawinata, Adam

Malik and S Parman to Ambarawa in Central Java. They were eventually released from there in November 1949.

Siauw's imprisonment at Wirogunan and Ambarawa brought him closer to many of the non-FDR politicians, particularly leaders of Partai Murba and the PNI. These relationships were to help him greatly in his later parliamentary work, enabling him to play a role in bridging the various political groups which were not willing to amicably discuss issues and reach agreements.[72]

After Siauw's release from prison, he immediately condemned the Round Table Conference (RTC) Agreement. In the Badan Pekerja meeting held in December 1949, Siauw strongly argued that the RTC Agreement left Indonesia vulnerable to neo-colonial exploitation via capitalist enterprises. He was also concerned with its citizenship clauses. He supported the RTC formula providing a passive system with respect to Chinese becoming Indonesian citizens, but rejected the provision enabling Dutch people to obtain Indonesian citizenship after living in Indonesia for only six months.

Siauw was also concerned that accepting the burden of Dutch debts and the obligation of making reparations for Dutch losses incurred during the revolution meant saddling the republic with economic problems which would seriously hamper efforts to rebuild the country. Finally, he argued that accepting the delayed settlement on West Irian would endanger the republic's independence.[73] However, Hatta's position was so strong that the KNIP had little choice but to ratify the RTC Agreement. Accordingly the Republik Indonesia Serikat or RIS (Republic of the United States of Indonesia or RUSI) was officially proclaimed in December 1949.

We have seen in this chapter that Siauw was involved in national politics as a member of the Badan Pekerja and the Amir Sjarifuddin cabinet representing the Partai Sosialis. As a minister in Amir Sjarifuddin's cabinet, Siauw was able to rely on the friendships he established with the Pemuda leaders in protecting the positions of the Chinese.

This chapter shows how the Partai Sosialis involved a number of Indonesian Chinese in their political programs. Apart from having them on its board of leadership (Tan Ling Djie, Oei Gee Hwat, Siauw Giok Tjhan and Go Gien Tjwan), some were also entrusted with running ministries in

---

[72] Interviews with Oey Hay Djoen, Jakarta, November 1997 and Soemarsono, Sydney, July 1992.

[73] Siauw's speech delivered at the Badan Pekerja meeting held in December 1949. Exact date was not noted.

Partai Sosialis governments, notably Tan Po Goan, Siauw Giok Tjhan and Ong Eng Die. Another peranakan Chinese, Tjoa Sik Ien was a member of the republic's team in the Renville negotiations. Siauw was able to capitalise on the party's anti-racist lines but faced an uphill battle convincing the Chinese to support the new republic. Having such influence within the party that dominated the government, these peranakans were able to ensure that the Chinese received a measure of government protection. But this protection failed to stop the Chinese from being victimised by armed Pemudas.

When the Partai Sosialis split into two (with Sjahrir leading a new Partai Sosialis Indonesia), Siauw opted to remain with Amir. However, when Amir's Partai Sosialis merged with other forces within the FDR to form a large PKI, Siauw decided not to join.

The revolutionary periods in Yogyakarta and his imprisonment in Wirogunan had enabled Siauw to be personally close to a large number of national leaders from various political backgrounds. Among these were Ali Sastroamidjojo, Iwa Kusumasumantri, Mohamad Yamin, Sartono, Sajuti Melik and Adam Malik. Siauw was able to capitalise on these relationships in achieving his goals in parliament during the parliamentary democracy period. By dint of his former membership of the Badan Pekerja, he was appointed a member of the federal parliament representing the Republic of Indonesia. With this appointment, Siauw moved to Jakarta, the capital of the new federal government, in January 1950.

Chapter 4

JOURNALISM AND POLITICS IN JAKARTA

Soon after his arrival in Jakarta, Siauw resumed the two professions, journalism and parliamentary politics, that he had plied earlier in Surabaya, Semarang, Malang and Yogyakarta.

Although Siauw, as a leader of various publications, played a significant role in journalism and was often to be found in the world of prominent journalists, his career as a journalist was not well known. He was more active in the SPS (Serikat Perusahaan Surat Kabar – Association of Newspaper Enterprises), than in the PWI, and better known for initiating the formation and the running of various publications than as an author of newspaper articles.

Siauw's main political prominence in the early 1950s was within parliament. In 1951 he was successful in forming a fairly large parliamentary faction, Fraksi Nasional Progresif (National Progressive Faction, sometimes called Naspro), whose members were small parties and individuals who, in general, opposed the positions adopted by the PSI and Masyumi.

Siauw's career as a parliamentarian in the parliamentary democracy period began early in January 1950, when he became a member of the parliament of the RIS in Jakarta. Officially formed on 27 December 1949, the RIS was a federation of the RI (Republik Indonesia – Republic of Indonesia) and 15 states the Dutch had formed during their struggle against the republic in the years 1946–1949. These states cooperated with each other through the Dutch-controlled BFO (Bijeenkomst voor Federaal Overleg – Federal Consultative Assembly).

It was clear from the beginning of the RIS that it was going to be heavily dominated by RI leaders. The 16-member RIS cabinet, with Hatta as prime minister, only contained five representatives of the BFO states. Only two of the five were strong supporters of the federal structure, and they did not hold powerful portfolios.[1]

In the RIS Parliament there were a number of Chinese parliamentarians. Apart from Siauw, there were three other peranakan representatives of the republic, namely Yap Tjwan Bing and Tjoa Die Hwie, from PNI, and Tan Boen An, from PSI. There were also two representatives from the BFO group of members, Teng Tjin Leng, from East Indonesia State, and Tjoeng Lin Seng, from West Borneo State.[2]

Most of the political debates in parliament were devoted to the issues of unitarism and federalism. Although most political parties in this period supported the unitarist movement, not all political leaders in parliament were active in promoting unitarism. The most outspoken member against federalism was Mohamad Yamin who was not affiliated with any political parties. It was he, not leaders of the major political parties, who led the debates against federalism and against the existence of BFO states, which he frequently referred to as 'negara boneka' (puppet states). Yamin's main supporters were mainly members of nationalist parties and the national communist Partai Murba. The PKI was at that time weak and disorganised following the killing of its most senior leaders after the Madiun Affair and was not active in the unitarist movement.[3]

Likewise, Masyumi, the largest political party in this period, was not actively promoting unitarism. Here the problem was political motivation. Masyumi and its members were principally for a unitary state, but they preferred to achieve the re-establishment of the unitary republic by way of plebiscites. To them, the best way of securing power in Indonesian politics was to expedite the holding of general elections as they were confident that their party would obtain the largest support from the population. Rapid realisation of a unitary state, they feared, would reduce the urgency of having general elections and delay the process of Masyumi becoming the most powerful party in Indonesia.

Siauw, who admired Yamin, fully supported him in parliament and in this process was drawn closer to the leaders of small nationalist parties and the Partai Murba than to PKI leaders. It was also perhaps one of the reasons

---

[1] Herbert Feith, *The Decline of Constitutional Democracy in Indonesia*, Cornell University Press, Ithaca, 1962, pp. 47–48.

[2] *Kepartaian dan Parlementaria Indonesia*, Departemen Penerangan, 1954, pp. 629–630; Yap Tjwan Bing, *Meretas Jalan Kemerdekaan*, PT Gramedia, Jakarta, p. 42.

[3] Feith, *The Decline of Constitutional Democracy*, p.75

for Siauw's preference to work closely with their representatives throughout the parliamentary democracy period.

In less than two months, resolutions to incorporate all BFO states except East Indonesia into the RI had been passed. Resistance from representatives of East Indonesia against the re-establishment of Indonesia as a unitary state was quite significant.

By early May 1950 political developments inside and outside the parliament forced Hatta to commence proceedings towards the transformation of the RIS into a unitary state. On 19 May Hatta, representing the RIS and Abdul Halim the prime minister of the RI, agreed to form a joint RIS–RI committee to review all requirements for the establishment of a new unitary state. Another committee, of which Siauw was one of 14 members, was formed to work on a draft constitution for the new state. This committee was successful in producing a draft constitution, which restored some segments of the constitution passed in November 1945. While differing from it on other points, in principle the cabinet would be responsible to the legislative assembly, the parliament. Of significance was the reinstatement of the popular Article 33 of the 1945 Constitution[4] which had been omitted from the RIS Constitution.

The draft was completed in July and subsequently ratified on 14 August 1950 after a heated argument over rights to amend by the parliaments of RIS and RI. Thus on 17 August 1950 a new Republic of Indonesia was officially established.

Republik Indonesia Serikat Parliament

The composition of the new unitary state parliament was also based on an agreement between the RIS and RI governments. Its initial composition would consist of all existing members of RIS except those who were initially appointed by the State of Pasundan (a state created by the Dutch in western Java). The RI would be given the opportunity to appoint 19 new members to replace the initial Pasundan members. Also included in the new parliament were 29 members of the RIS Senate, 46 members of the RI

---

[4] Article 33 runs as follows:
1. The economic system is to be organised as a cooperative venture.
2. The means of production which are important to the state and which determine the livelihood of the people are to be controlled by the state.
3. Land, sea and the mineral resources contained within them are to be controlled by the state and exploited for the general welfare of the people.

Badan Pekerja and 13 members of the RI Supreme Advisory Council. The new parliament, called Dewan Perwakilan Rakyat Sementara (Provisional People's Representative Council or DPRS), officially formed on 16 August 1950 and had a total of 236 members.[5]

On 19 August 1950, Sartono was again elected chairman. Tambunan, from Parkindo (Partai Kristen Indonesia – Indonesian Christian Party); Aruji Kartawinata, from the PSII, and Tadjuddin Noor, from the PIR (Persatuan Indonesia Raya – Greater Indonesian Union), were elected deputy chairmen.[6] The parliament was divided into ten sections including economics, finance, foreign affairs, defence, labour and employment. Siauw Giok Tjhan joined the 39-member economic section.[7] He was also chosen to be a member of two important working committees, the Panitia Permusyawaratan (Consultative Committee) and the Panitia Rumah Tangga (Management Committee).

The Consultative Committee was primarily responsible for providing advice to the chairman and determining the parliament's working programs. It was to become the formal link between the government and parliament. The parliamentary chairman was also the chair of the Consultative Committee and appointed its 21 members.

The Management Committee was primarily responsible for the supervision of the day-to-day management of parliament. This committee was therefore responsible for hiring and firing parliamentary staff and also for the welfare of all members of parliament. Again, the parliamentary chairman, was also the chair of this committee and appointed the 13 committee members.[8]

Sartono also appointed Siauw to various other working committees, including the Inquiries Committee. Sartono is said to have respected Siauw for his knowledge of parliamentary procedures and political issues in general. He was often seen with Siauw during session breaks and was known to consult Siauw often about various parliamentary procedures. When Sartono travelled within Indonesia or overseas he often included Siauw in his delegation. These privileges enabled Siauw to visit almost all Indonesian provinces as well as countries such as Vietnam, the USA and China. A

---

5 Departemen Penerangan, *Kepartaian dan parlementaria di Indonesia*, pp. 626–630.
6 Ibid., pp. 619–620.
7 Ibid., pp. 643–644.
8 Ibid., p. 590.

number of PNI members who missed out on the overseas trips and were not included in some powerful committees reportedly complained about the privileges Sartono gave Siauw, a non-party man.[9] Sartono was reported to have said that he needed Siauw's input in the various committee meetings and official trips he made.[10] Their relationship went back to the Yogyakarta period, when both were members of the KNIP Badan Pekerja.

As Sartono's trust in him suggests, Siauw was seen as an insider in the political elite. Feith describes this group as:

> ... steeped in all-Indonesia modern urban culture which had grown up around the nationalist movement, and its members were correspondingly less closely allied to the cultures of their respective groups. Many members of the elite had contracted inter-ethnic marriages and pointed to them with pride. In fact, the political elite had a considerable cultural homogeneity of its own. Its members had a fairly strong sense of constituting a single group, all political divisions notwithstanding.[11]

Siauw and his family often visited or invited people in this group, particularly Yamin, Aruji, Tambunan, Ali Sastroamidjojo, Diapari, Sukarni, Adam Malik and Sartono, for wedding and birthday parties or other social occasions. Personal friendship appears to be more important than political motivations at this time.

In the 1950s Siauw was perhaps the only peranakan politician who belonged comfortably within this group. Tan Ling Djie still retained some stigma from the Madiun involvement and was therefore politically isolated.[12] Tjoa Sik Ien, after being released from the Wirogunan Prison in Yogyakarta in 1949, lived in Surabaya and was not active in national politics. Liem Koen Hian had not been active in national politics since late 1945. Tan Po Goan and Yap Tjwan Bing (PSI and PNI respectively) were

---

[9] In the early 50s, such privileges were normally given to members who not only had political party affiliations but also had the ability to control them.

[10] Siauw, *Lima Jaman*, p. 302; Interview with Tan Hwie Kiat, Amsterdam, December 1992, who in that period worked for *Sunday Courier* and observed parliamentary sessions in progress; Interview with Sidik Kertapati, then member of parliament, Amsterdam, December 1989.

[11] Feith, *The Decline of Constitutional Democracy*, p. 109.

[12] Although Tan lived in Siauw's house, he rarely joined Siauw's social activities within this group.

members of parliament, but they were not active outside the spheres of their political parties.[13]

The Fraksi Nasional Progresif

The elements of politics in the 1950s were complex. Political deals and decisions were often based on personal connections and ambitions rather than political ideologies. Furthermore, party politics were largely driven by party leaders and the roles these leaders played in parliament and cabinets. Both the discipline and organisational structure of the parties, with the exception of the PKI, were poor. People from small parties would often betray their party goals for their individual advancement.

Many politicians and political parties of that period opposed each other, not because of ideological differences, but more because of the fact that people belonged to opposite camps. In the early 1950s there were two main political camps – that of the ruling parties, mainly the PNI and Masyumi, and that of the opposition, mainly represented by the small nationalist parties, Partai Murba and the PKI.

In the new parliament, Siauw was listed as a member of the SKI (Serikat Kerakyatan Indonesia – Indonesian People's Association) faction, led by DS Diapari, a Batak doctor. Siauw was not a member of the SKI party, but it was possible to be a member of a faction without being a member of the party after which it was named.

The SKI had been founded in January 1946, in Banjarmasin, South Kalimantan, by DS Diapari, A Sinaga and A Rivai. Like many other political parties of that period, the SKI did not have a strong and identifiable political ideology. Its leaders were western-educated nationalists of broadly PNI or Partai Murba outlook.

Early in 1951, realising the political weakness of small political parties and individuals in parliament, Siauw took the initiative in assembling likeminded members to form a larger faction. The basis of the faction's unity was nationalism with a strong tendency towards socialism. The groups and individuals assembled by Siauw were largely nationalists from the pre-war period and people who had been clear-cut republicans in the revolutionary period. These included the SKI, Partai Murba, Fraksi Persatuan Progresip (Progressive Union Faction), PRN (Partai Rakyat Nasional – National

---

[13] Yap Tjwan Bing's memoir, *Meretas Jalan Kemerdekaan* shows that his contacts with figures out side the PNI were limited.

People's Party), PIR, Front Buruh (Labour Front), Fraksi Kedaulatan Rakyat (People Sovereignty Faction), Golongan Tani (Peasant Group) and non-party members like Mohamad Yamin. It was agreed that the expanded faction would be called the Fraksi Nasional Progresif (National Progressive Faction), and Siauw was elected chairman. The majority of the new faction's members were non-Javanese.[14]

The PIR was the largest and perhaps the most conservative of the parties assembled by Siauw in the new faction. The party, led by Wongsonegoro, was considered a party of higher Javanese aristocrats as it was supported by a considerable number of Pamong Praja (Civil Service Police Unit) leaders both in and outside Java.[15] The leaders of this party tended to dislike radical leaders of the PNI. The party had 20 members in parliament, with one of them a peranakan, Tio Kiang Sun, a community leader from West Kalimantan.

The PRN was led by Djody Gondokusumo and had nine members in parliament. Leaders from this party were formerly members of the PNI. They left that party partly in protest against the victory of Sidik Djojosukarto and his associates in the leadership battle in the PNI in late 1950. The PRN leaders were branded as right wing and capitalistic by the Sidik group, but their political positions did not deviate from that of the PNI's radical nationalism. Siauw was particularly close to Djody Gondokusumo.

Among the non-party members who joined Siauw's new faction, Mohamad Yamin was the most prominent. Yamin was a highly respected politician who, like Siauw, refused to join any political party. To Masyumi and the PSI, Yamin was considered left wing, as his political outlook was close to that of the Partai Murba. Yamin was very close to Siauw. He regularly visited Siauw's place in Jakarta and they were often seen together in parliament.[16]

The election of Siauw, a peranakan, as the leader of the new faction greatly consolidated his position in national politics. He was the first peranakan parliamentarian to lead a faction and had proved to himself, and to a large extent to many others, that it was possible to achieve an effective political integration where peranakan and Indigenous politicians worked together for common goals. This position also gave Siauw useful experience

---

14   Interview with Sidik Kertapati, Amsterdam, January 1989.
15   Feith, *The Decline of Constitutional Democracy in Indonesia*, pp. 143–144.
16   Siauw's admiration on Yamin is clearly expressed in his *Lima Jaman*, p. 299, and confirmed in interviews with Oei Tjoe Tat, Go Gien Tjwan, Tan Hwie Kiat and Yap Thiam Hien; also see Oei Tjoe Tat, *Memoar Oei Tjoe Tat*, p. 26.

in leading a group of politicians with differing political opinions. Although Iwa Kusumasumantri, Yamin and Djody Gondokusumo were all known as stubborn individuals, Siauw was often able to settle major differences so that the faction presented positions that were acceptable to all its members.[17]

Many of the faction's members were well known for their skills and political knowledge, and played influential roles in the parliamentary committees. Although many were highly trained professionals, they were critical of political approaches that emphasised professionalism. Most of the faction members were what Feith called 'solidarity makers'. Their political prominence was based largely on their skills as articulators of political goals. Because of this, they often met with strong opposition from the PSI supporters who were, in Feith's terms, 'administrators', people who relied on their professional and technical skills.[18]

As the new republic was dominated by 'administrators' at the beginning of its life, members of Siauw's faction (with the exception of Wongsonegoro and H Johanes who were in the PIR) were not invited to participate in Natsir's government of September 1950 to April 1951, which was dominated by Masyumi and PSI leaders and their sympathisers. The same situation was repeated when Sukiman's cabinet was formed in April 1951 (although Yamin became justice minister for a few months). Hence, Siauw's faction remained in opposition until the political balance changed in 1953, with the formation of Ali Sastroamidjojo's cabinet in which quite a number of the faction members were given influential portfolios.

After the 1955 general elections, the faction was further expanded to include Acoma (Angkatan Communis Muda – Communist Youth League), Partindo, Baperki and a number of other non-party members. The faction continued to exist until the end of the parliamentary democracy period but it also lost a lot of members.

Siauw the journalist

In the immediate post-war period, as in the pre-war period, there were three streams within the Indonesian press, namely Indonesian, Chinese and Dutch newspapers. Jakarta, being the new capital city, became the place where most of the major newspapers were published. In 1950 the total

---

[17] Interview with Sidik Kertapati, Amsterdam, January 1989; Siauw, *Lima Jaman*, p. 241.

[18] For detailed description and definition of the solidarity makers and administrators, see Feith, *The Decline of Constitutional Democracy in Indonesia*, pp. 113–122.

circulation of all Jakarta dailies was 499 150. The Indonesian language papers represented by far the largest portion (338 300), followed by Dutch (87 200) and Chinese (73 650).[19]

The period from 1945 to 1948 was one of expansion of the Dutch population due to the return of many Dutch civil servants, military people, businessmen and professionals to Indonesia, along with the additional personnel required to run many industrial and agricultural estates. While Dutch newspapers were read by Dutch-educated Indonesians and Chinese, the Dutch population was the main readership. The readership of Chinese language papers was divided into two main groups of totok Chinese – those who preferred to read papers which supported the anti-communist Kuo Min Tang of Taiwan, and those who preferred papers that were sympathetic to the communist Kung Chan Tang of mainland China.

The Indonesian newspapers were read by educated Indonesians who lived in major cities and towns, mainly in Java. It is not clear what proportion of these readers lived in Jakarta in 1950, but by 1954 about 50 per cent of Indonesian newspaper readers were from Jakarta. A significant number of these readers were peranakan Chinese, but their first preference was to read papers or journals which were published specifically for the peranakan readership. The two main peranakan dailies were the predominantly China-oriented *Sin Po*, directed by Ang Jang Goan, and the more right-wing and PSI-oriented *Keng Po*, directed by Injo Beng Goat who also published the popular *Star Weekly*.

As the number of readers was growing, and as neither *Sin Po* nor *Keng Po* was oriented to the ethos of the revolutionary republic, the ethos of Yogyakarta, Siauw saw an opportunity to start an Indonesia-oriented publication for the peranakans. He therefore decided to seek financial support to establish a suitable publication in Jakarta.

While in Yogyakarta, in his capacity as a member of the KNIP Badan Pekerja and briefly as a minister in the Amir Sjarifuddin cabinet, Siauw was in close contact with a number of China-oriented totok businessmen in Jakarta. These businessmen had helped to provide accommodation, food and clothes for the Chinese refugees who had been victims of the military clashes and harsh treatment from various units of armed youths. Siauw was particularly close to a group of people running medium-sized businesses who were sympathetic towards Mao's leadership in the new China. Some of

---

[19] Oey Hong Lee, *Indonesian Government and Press During Guided Democracy*, Hull Monographs on South East Asia, p. 49.

the men whom Siauw frequently contacted were Then Djin Sen, Ang Hok Liem and Lay Dje Hoa.

Some time in December 1949, Siauw approached these three men in Jakarta and discussed the idea of establishing a publication aimed at peranakan readers. Siauw was able to convince them to seek help from other totok businessmen to finance the venture. The plan was finalised in the same month and Siauw and Lay Dje Hoa went to visit Oei Tiang Tjioe, the owner of a printing press which had published a Jakarta peranakan daily, *Hong Po*, before and during the war. They sought to persuade Oei to transfer the printing press to Siauw.[20]

Oei Tiang Tjioe, some twenty years older than Siauw, was well known as the director of the largest peranakan funeral and social service organisation in Jakarta, the Hoo Hap. When *Hong Po* was under Oei's leadership it had employed a number of nationalist journalists like M Gani, and had well-known nationalists like Dr Tjipto Mangunkusumo as regular contributors.[21] Like Siauw's *Mata Hari* in Semarang and Tan Ling Djie's *Sin Tit Po* in Surabaya, *Hong Po* was an Indonesia-oriented publication. However, unlike *Sin Tit Po* and *Mata Hari*, which were anti-Japanese, *Hong Po* was a strong supporter of the Japanese. Because of this, Oei Tiang Tjioe was arrested by the Dutch in 1941.[22]

When the Japanese arrived in 1942, *Hong Po* was, for a short time, the only newspaper allowed in Jakarta. Although it was later banned, some of its journalists were able to maintain their profession throughout the occupation period. *Hong Po* did not re-emerge after 1945, but its printing press continued to operate commercially.

Oei personally disliked Injo Beng Goat, the director of the PSI-oriented *Keng Po* daily and *Star Weekly*. He was allegedly responsible for an incident in which Injo's face was badly slashed with a knife in a brawl in Jakarta some time in the late 1940s.

It is not clear how profitable the *Hong Po* press was, but when Siauw visited him in December 1949, Oei Tiang Tjioe was prepared to sell it at a low price to enable Siauw to publish daily and periodical publications which would outperform Injo Beng Goat's *Keng Po* and *Star Weekly*.[23]

---

[20] Interview with Lay Siao Hoa, Lay Dje Hoa's younger brother, Hong Kong, October 1994.

[21] M. Gani, *Surat kabar Indonesia pada Tiga Zaman*, Departemen Penerangan, 1978, p. 103.

[22] Leo Suryadinata, *Eminent Indonesian Chinese*, Gunung Agung Singapore, 1981, p. 93.

[23] Interview with Lay Siao Hoa, Hong Kong, October 1994.

So, financially backed by a number of totok businessmen, Siauw took over the ownership of the *Hong Po* press, located in Jakarta's Chinatown, and renamed it Persatuan (Unity). He remained as its director until October 1953. It is not clear how commercially motivated these totok businessmen were in supporting Siauw's venture. However, one can assume that they knew Siauw was more politically motivated and that under Siauw, the venture would not be financially successful. This was perhaps the first significant link Siauw had with the world of totoks in achieving his political goals.

Before Siauw took over the business from Oei Tiang Tjioe, the press had printed a peranakan weekly called *Sadar* (*Awake*), edited by Thio Ien Lok and devoted to Chinese culture and sport. The arrival of Siauw as the new director of Persatuan and the decision to discontinue *Sadar* was announced in its last issue in December 1949.

In January 1950 Siauw began to publish and edit a weekly called *Sunday Courier*. The English name was presumably selected to challenge the popularity of *Star Weekly* which had been coming out for a number of years. The new magazine contained many articles on China and Chinese culture, but significant parts of it were devoted to political analysis and economic developments in Indonesia and written largely by Siauw himself. Each week, Siauw wrote a column called 'Serba Serbi Parlemen' ('Parliamentary News').

Siauw spent a lot of time writing and editing articles in every edition, and much of his time was also devoted to managing the business operations and providing political connections that helped his staff to obtain material for the journal. Although its emphasis was on politics, which was thought to be unpopular among peranakan readers, *Sunday Courier* proved to be a profitable venture.[24]

In January 1950, Siauw also began to edit a monthly journal called *Republik*. This was published by Tjoa Sik Ien's *Sin Tit Po* press in Surabaya but its circulation was national. *Republik* was a political publication, containing articles of national interest and a column on political debates in parliament. Siauw's influence in this publication was apparent. Many of its regular contributors were his parliamentary colleagues – IJ Kasimo, leader of Partai Katolik; DS Diapari, leader of the SKI; Aruji Kartawinata, leader of PSII, and Ong Eng Die, from PNI. From a business point of view, this publication was a failure and lasted for less than two years.

---

[24] Interview with Tan Hwie Kiat, Amsterdam, January 1989.

It is worth mentioning Siauw's style in leading these publications. By 1950 peranakan newspapers like *Sin Po* and *Keng Po* had switched from Bahasa Melayu Tionghoa (Sino-Malay), used widely in the pre-war era, to more or less standard Indonesian. Although Siauw was able to write and express himself well in standard Indonesian, he continued with the writing style of a pre-war peranakan journalist which, in general, tended to favour long and repetitive expressions.

Siauw's articles, which were mainly devoted to the analysis of national political development and economic issues, were often long and repetitious. To accommodate his writings in the publications, his editors often had to reduce their length[25]. When criticised, Siauw always indicated that in expressing an opinion or view, there is nothing wrong in repeating and emphasising the essence of this view to avoid misunderstanding. Siauw also adopted this approach in delivering his speeches. Go Gien Tjwan recalls that for people who were close to Siauw and who were familiar with the subjects he addressed, his method was boring. However, Go admits that Siauw related well to his audience and was always able to get his messages across to them, regardless of their education levels. As is evident from his published speeches and books[26], Siauw maintained this style throughout his political career.

In January 1951, Siauw established yet another publication *Suara Rakyat* (*People's Voice*). This was initially a weekly aimed at both Indigenous and peranakan readers. In July of the same year Siauw converted the publication into a daily and the name was changed to *Harian Rakyat* (*People's Daily*).

Most of the journalists Siauw employed to work for *Sunday Courier* also worked for *Harian Rakyat*. But Siauw also recruited new staff including the 26-year-old communist intellectual, Njoto. The other Indigenous journalists employed included Surjono, Supeno and Francisca Fanggidaej, from Pesindo. *Harian Rakyat* was perhaps the first national daily in Indonesia whose editor-in-chief was a peranakan.

As we saw in Chapter 3, Njoto worked under Siauw in editing *Suara Ibu Kota*, the mouthpiece of the Partai Sosialis, in Yogyakarta. Prior to joining *Harian Rakyat*, Njoto was responsible for the production of *Bintang Merah* (*Red Star*), the PKI's new monthly which started in August 1950. Like Aidit and Lukman, Njoto had been elevated to the Central Committee

---

[25] Interviews with Oey Hong Lee and Tan Hwie Kiat who worked for Siauw in the various publications published by Siauw, Amsterdam, January 1989.

[26] Even his memoir, *Lima Jaman*, is a true reflection of his writing style.

and politburo by Musso in 1948. The trio used *Bintang Merah* to discredit the leadership of Tan Ling Djie and Alimin, then in their early fifties, who were the most senior PKI survivors of the Madiun Affair. They claimed that Tan and Alimin were deviating from Musso's 'New Road' direction.

Within a short period of time Aidit, Lukman and Njoto, then aged 27, 30 and 25 respectively, managed to gain widespread support from the leadership of the PKI. The contest between that trio and Tan and Alimin came to a head on 7 January 1951. On that day Aidit replaced Alimin as chairman of the politburo which was dominated by Aidit's men, Lukman, Njoto and Sudisman. Tan and Alimin remained members of the Central Committee for the next few years, but lost control over the party.

Siauw and Tan were close in this period. Tan lived in Siauw's house from July 1951. The actions of Aidit, Lukman and Njoto in displacing Tan from the central leadership in 1951 and then conducting a campaign against 'Tan Ling Djie-ism' which resulted in the removal of Tan from the Central Committee in July 1953 did not impress Siauw. Being a parliamentarian, and having experienced the aftermath of the failed uprising in Madiun, he agreed with Tan who was committed to the idea that the PKI would become a small but reliable cadre party which was capable of developing and leading a popular front consisting of socialist and labour parties and other mass organisations, and that the movement needed to concentrate, maximising effective parliamentary representations.[27]

But as Siauw was not a member of the PKI, his disagreement with the new leadership did not cost him any political points. Despite the political disagreement, Siauw was able to maintain an effective working relationship with Njoto in running *Harian Rakyat*. Njoto's presence in *Harian Rakyat* provided a direct link between it and the PKI but Siauw, who dominated production and editorial activities until October 1953, was able to maintain the paper's independence.[28]

It is not clear how much journalistic work Siauw carried out on *Harian Rakyat* as he was also in charge of the business side. Siauw did, however, closely supervise the generation of articles and chair the daily production meetings. According to a few reports he also wrote almost all of the editorials.[29]

---

[27] Siauw's account conveyed to the author in prison in 1973.
[28] Interview with Surjono, Amsterdam, December 1987.
[29] Interviews with Francisca Fanggidaej and Tan Hwie Kiat, Amsterdam, November 1988.

Siauw was a fast worker. He was able to complete long articles in less than two hours. His routine activities in the morning, before going to his office included the completion of editorials and sometimes one or two long articles for various newspapers. Couriers from *Harian Rakyat* and other newspapers were usually waiting at his house at 7 am to collect what Siauw had written.

As a business venture the *Harian Rakyat* of the period 1951–1953 was not very successful. Tan Hwie Kiat, Surjono and Fransisca Fanggidaej report that it was not viable, or barely so. It was distributed to the major provincial capitals of Java and Sumatra but it is not clear what its daily circulation was. As it was not directly linked to any major political parties it did not have the network needed to distribute the publication widely in the country.[30]

Harian Rakyat may well have depended on subsidies from Siauw's totok business friends. Members of its staff were reportedly often entertained by Siauw's friends who owned small and modest restaurants in Jakarta's Chinatown.[31] The consideration over the commercial viability of the publication might have prompted Siauw to transfer the ownership of the whole venture to someone else. This coincided with the decision of the PKI to have its own daily newspaper.

As Njoto was already very heavily involved in the running of *Harian Rakyat*, the decision to take it over from Siauw became an obvious one. This was agreed upon and finalised in October 1953. It is not clear how the transfer of management was done but it is clear that Siauw's management involvement with *Harian Rakyat* ceased on 31 October 1953. The daily became the PKI's mouthpiece with Njoto as its editor-in-chief. Siauw, however, continued to write articles for the newspaper for some years.

Siauw's involvement with *Harian Rakyat*, and his closeness to Amir Sjarifuddin and Tan Ling Djie, led many to believe that he was a member of the PKI. The transfer of management of the newspaper in October 1953 coincided with the removal of Tan Ling Djie from the PKI Central Committee, which was interpreted by some as meaning that Siauw, as a member of the PKI, had been sacked by Aidit.

However, this was not the case. Siauw was not a PKI member either then or later, though there may well have been a significant connection between his break with *Harian Rakyat* and the purging of Tan. Njoto and Lukman

---

[30] Interview with Tan Hwie Kiat, Amsterdam, January 1990.
[31] Interviews with Tan Hwie Kiat, Amsterdam, January 1990 and Francisca Fanggidaej, Amsterdam, November 1988.

continued to regularly visit Siauw's house after 1953. Aidit and Sakirman, who were never personally close to Siauw, continued to have political discussions with him in parliament.[32]

After his departure from *Harian Rakyat*, Siauw maintained an involvement with the *Sunday Courier* which continued to be published until the middle of 1955. By then, Siauw was already chairman of a mass organisation, Baperki. His commitments in the new organisation were probably too much for him to have enough time to properly manage the continuation of *Sunday Courier*.

In late 1953, after the Persatuan press and *Harian Rakyat* were sold to the PKI, Siauw started yet another publication venture, this one with totoks as its principal target. He established a foundation called Yayasan Kebudajaan Sadar (Foundation of Cultural Awakening). He was the commissioner (penanggung jawab), but the chairman of the foundation was Werdojo, then Siauw's parliamentary colleague and leader of the small and radical nationalist group Persatuan Marhaen Indonesia (Union of Indonesian Marhaens). This foundation, supported by a number of left-wing totok businessmen like Go Gak Cho and Kho Nai Chong, who were both leaders of the Jakarta Chinese Association, published a weekly political journal called *Chiao Xing* (*Sadar* or *Awake*) in Mandarin. This attracted a large number of China-oriented totok readers and proved to be profitable.

The journal contained a large number of translated articles from the *Sunday Courier* and of Siauw's speeches. It also had numerous articles on Chinese politics in praise of Mao Tse Tung's achievements. Many articles were written to persuade the totok communities to accept and treat Indonesia as their homeland. Siauw was assisted by a number of Mandarin-speaking journalists, notably Lie Xie Thian and Tjang Tjing Kuok, who reportedly went to Siauw's place twice a week to discuss the journal's contents.[33]

The Yayasan Kebudajaan Sadar also published a large number of translated novels, mainly from the Chinese language but also some from English. It published a number of dictionaries (Chinese–Indonesian and Indonesian–Chinese). The foundation remained in existence until Siauw was arrested in November 1965, though *Chiao Xing* was banned in 1959.

---

32 Interview with Jusuf Adjitorop, Beijing, October 1994. Adjitorop recalls that whenever major minority issues were discussed, Aidit instructed his subordinates to consult with Siauw.

33 Interview with Lie Xie Thian, Hong Kong, in January 1988.

Siauw's activities in the press also included his membership of SPS. The organisation was initially formed by members of the PWI in June 1946 but only gained a formal structure in 1949, with 33 newspapers from various places in Indonesia registered as its members. The main purposes of this organisation were to ensure that the needs of the national press were taken care of and to create a situation in which national interests were reflected in national newspapers.

The organisation promoted the concept that 60 per cent of national newspaper ownership should be in the hands of Indonesian nationals, and that the decision-making process on the content of these newspapers should be led by Indonesian nationals.[34] Until January 1951, the SPS and PWI organisations were run by the same people and their meetings were called SPS–PWI meetings. In 1951, it was decided that the PWI and SPS would exist independently and have independent management structures. Sudarjo Tjokrosisworo, a good friend of Siauw, became the SPS general secretary.[35]

Siauw, in his capacity as director of *Harian Rakyat* and the *Sunday Courier*, joined the SPS in 1951. He was actively involved in formulating the organisation's positions on parliamentary bills which were concerned with press, publication of newspapers and journals, advertising, limitations on foreign magazines and bans on pornography in newspapers. He was also instrumental in defining terms on pornography for SPS members. As a result of the recommendation of the three-man Committee on Press Ethics (Panitia Susila Pers), of which Siauw was a member, SPS members who allowed pornography in their publications were expelled from the SPS.[36]

In leading journalistic work, Siauw was apparently strict about moral standards. He particularly disliked writing and stories that contained pornography. From about 1954, the *Sunday Courier's* circulation significantly reduced due to Siauw's decision to discontinue the publication of a romance series which, in Siauw's opinion, contained pornography.[37]

Siauw's involvement in the SPS provided him with ample opportunities to associate closely with a large number of prominent national journalists and with other newspaper editors. He was particularly close to Djawoto,

---

[34] Tjokrosisworo, *Sejarah Pers Sebangsa*, SPS, 1958, p. 69.
[35] Tjokrosisworo, *Sejarah Pers Sebangsa*, SPS, 1958, pp. 75–76.
[36] Ibid., pp. 92–93.
[37] Interview with Tan Hwie Kiat, Amsterdam, December 1993, who recalls that some articles from *Sunday Courier* regular contributors had to be rewritten because they failed to comply with Siauw's standard.

the chairman of the PWI from Antara who was sympathetic to the PKI; Adam Malik, who was sympathetic to Partai Murba; M Tabrani, who had been secretary of Siauw's ministry in Amir Sjarifuddin's cabinet and was from the daily *Pemandangan*; Hasyim Rachman, from *Bintang Timur*, and Joesoef Isak, from *Merdeka*. Because of these connections, Siauw was able to have much of his writing on minority issues and Baperki published in a large number of national papers.

In this period, through his writing and published speeches, Siauw became more well known in the political arena. As well as being known for his political convictions, he was also known his personal qualities. Members of Siauw's staff remember him as a modest and unassuming political figure. When people who did not know Siauw visited his office for business reasons, they were often surprised to learn that Siauw was the director of the small corporation. At work, he normally wore old T-shirts and shorts. He rarely wore shoes, preferring sandals. Some said that he dressed more poorly than his staff. Some thought he behaved more like a Chinatown totok shop owner who cared more about making money than impressing potential customers. The way Siauw dressed was often a topic of discussions among his colleagues in parliament.[38] President Soekarno, who was well known for his fussiness about how people dressed, enjoyed making jokes about Siauw's casual appearance. In 1947 he made Siauw a present of three new shirts.[39]

Until the parliamentary housing department found him rented accommodation towards the end of 1951, Siauw converted the Persatuan printing office into a temporary residence for his family of seven which included children aged between two and twelve. During the day, the small office of 20 square metres housed a number of busy journalists and at night the office desks were arranged and used as beds for the seven people. When Siauw and his family moved to the rented accommodation in Menteng, the elite part of Jakarta, some of the young unmarried journalists, like Tan Hwie Kiat and Njoto lived in that same printing office.[40] Apparently Siauw never took the opportunity to purchase the house in Jalan Tosari, which he rented until December 1965, though tenants had the option to buy at

---

[38] Interview with Tan Hwie Kiat and Francisca Fanggidaej, Amsterdam, January 1990.

[39] Interviews with Oei Tjoe Tat, Jakarta, December 1994 and Go Gien Tjwan, Amsterdam, January 1990; Oei, *Memoar Oei Tjoe Tat*, p. 46.

[40] Interviews with Mrs Siauw Giok Tjhan and Tan Hwie Kiat, Amsterdam, January 1992.

a highly subsidised price. This modest middle-class lifestyle was one of Siauw's strongest political assets, not least because it set him apart from rich Chinese.

It is now time to evaluate Siauw's political views and discuss what politicians of the period – friends and foes, academics and others – have said about him.

Analysing Siauw's political conviction and how he identified himself in the multiparty political landscape of the period is a much more difficult task than analysing his position within the political elite.

Most people, particularly Siauw's foes, regarded him as a PKI member. This assertion is usually based on three things: his close relationship with Tan Ling Djie and Amir Sjarifuddin in the Yogyakarta period; his perceived involvement in the Madiun Affair, indicated by his jailing by the Hatta government in 1948; and his directorship of the *Harian Rakyat* between 1951 and 1953, which most people have mistakenly regarded as the PKI's official newspaper from the time it was established.

Lacking definitive details on his association with the PKI, Somers, Coppel, Suryadinata, McVey, Hindley and Lev tend to link Siauw's 'probable' PKI membership to his directorship of the *Harian Rakyat*.[41] Some, like McVey and Somers, appear in agreement with the suspicion that Siauw either resigned from *Harian Rakyat* in response to Aidit's action in expelling Tan Ling Djie from the PKI Central Committee or that he was forced to resign by Aidit because of his closeness to Tan Ling Djie. McVey, for example, has the following description:

> In January 1951, DN Aidit and his allies of the younger generation seized control of the party organisation from Tan and his associates, and at the October 1953 Central Committee that consolidated Aidit's command the older leadership group was denounced for the sin of "Tan Ling Djie-ism". Shortly thereafter Siauw Giok Tjhan, co-editor and founder of the party paper *Harian Rakyat*, resigned from the

---

[41] Mary Somers, *Peranakan Chinese Politics*, p. 144; Coppel, 'Patterns of Chinese Political Activity in Indonesia', pp. 46–47; Leo Suryadinata, *Pribumi Indonesians, The Chinese Minority and China*, Heinemann Educational Books (Asia), Kuala Lumpur, 1978, p. 102; Ruth McVey, 'Indonesian Communism and China' in Tang Tsou (ed.), *China's Policies In Asia And America's Alternatives*, Volume 2, The University of Chicago Press, 1968, pp. 360–361; Daniel Lev, *Becoming An Orang Indonesia Sejati: The Political Journey of Yap Thiam Hien*, Symposium on The Role of the Indonesian Chinese in Shaping Modern Indonesian Life, July 13–15, 1990, Cornell University, p. 105; Donald Hindley, *The Communist Party of Indonesia, 1951–1963*, University of California Press, Berkeley, 1964.

journal along with the only other Chinese member of its editorial staff. Siauw was a friend of Tan Ling Djie, and it is not clear whether his departure was a matter of association with Tan or of a party decision to minimise the number of Indonesian Chinese holding leading public positions in the communist movement. That the latter was possible is indicated by the fact that the new party leadership was intensely nationalistic.[42]

The chronology of the formation of *Harian Rakyat*, its management and its eventual sale to the PKI has been outlined above. After the paper and the Persatuan press business were sold to the PKI, Siauw ceased his organisational involvement with the paper. He did, however, continue writing articles, and sometimes editorials, for it.

The sacking of Tan Ling Djie from the Central Committee could not have pleased Siauw. From the Yogyakarta period, he was more in agreement with Tan with regard to the way the PKI was to play a role in Indonesian politics. However, as a non-member, he had no influence on the party's decision and equally, was not affected by it.

The more important issue for some, like his former Baperki associates Yap Thiam Hien, Auwyong Peng Koen and Injo Beng Goat, is not related to whether or not Siauw was a PKI member but to how Siauw embraced Marxism and communism. Coppel stresses the affinities between Siauw and the PKI, saying:

> Although Siauw Giok Tjhan has never described himself as a communist, his record suggests that he has been in agreement with the PKI's stand on most important issues. His speeches have a Marxist ring to them, even when dealing with race discrimination; his conviction has been that only with the achievement of a socialist Indonesia can discrimination be eliminated, and he has constantly cited the Soviet Union and the Chinese People's Republic as models for the solution of the problems of national minorities… Whether or not Siauw was a member of the PKI, its ideas were quite congenial to his own.[43]

My own preference is for the more qualified position of Lev, who says:

---

[42] McVey, *Indonesian Communism and China*, p. 361.
[43] Coppel, *Patterns of Chinese Political Activity in Indonesia*, pp. 46–47.

Siauw evidently had been attracted to communism since the 1930s, when Tan Ling Djie, to whom he remained quite close, influenced his ideological education. Until 1953, he edited *Harian Rakyat*, after that it had been sold to the PKI. Questions were raised about whether he was a secret member of the party, but in fact he may have resented the Aidit leadership for having ousted Tan Ling Djie, if Siauw thought this was inspired by anti-Chinese animus or too much sensitivity to anti-Chinese sentiments… My point, however, is that Siauw was rather more devoted to the survival of peranakan Chinese than he was to communism.[44]

Coppel is right. Siauw, through his writings and speeches in this period was advocating Marxism, and openly used success in the Soviet Union and later China as models of the society he would like to see develop in Indonesia. The political solutions to the problems or issues he raised were mainly based on providing prosperity and justice to the have-nots. The Siauw of the early 1950s Siauw was very much 'in love' with Marxism and saw himself as a socialist. However, he rarely used the communist theories used by the PKI leaders in their speeches and writings. He hardly quoted Marx or Lenin in analysing political situations. In this sense, his approach was similar to that of the Partai Murba leaders and to radical nationalists in the PNI like Sidik Djojosukarto. He was, as Lev argues, more a nationalist and socialist than a communist.[45]

Siauw was therefore strongly against foreign-based monopolies and multinational capitalism. He was not in favour of Indonesia becoming a dictatorial state. In some of his parliamentary speeches in the early 1950s, he repeatedly suggested that the term 'pemerintah' ('government', but literally a person who orders or instructs) be altered to 'abdi rakyat' (literally 'servants of the people'). To Siauw, democracy was one of the ingredients for a successful socialist state.

Siauw was against policies adopted by the PSI, which tended to use western states as models for providing solutions to the problems faced by

---

[44] Lev, *Political Journey of Yap Thiam Hien*, p. 105. Lev has misinterpreted Siauw's terminology on 'meng-Indonesiakan' (literally 'to Indonesianise') the PKI leadership. By this, Siauw meant that Aidit and company intended to replace the older PKI leadership which included Tan Ling Djie, mostly trained in Holland, with people who developed their political experience in Indonesia. Siauw did not accuse Aidit and company of adopting anti-Chinese attitudes and hence expelling Tan Ling Djie purely on racial grounds.

[45] Ibid.

Indonesia. However, he was friendly with a number of such PSI parliamentarians including Djohan Sjahroezah and Tan Po Goan. He was fairly consistently opposed to the Islamic Masyumi, the largest political party before the 1955 elections. Masyumi's policies were anti-communist, and to a large degree, anti-socialist.

Having a political outlook as described above and being close to people who shared his ideological sentiments, Siauw was perhaps comfortable, and in fact preferred to be identified, as a leftist in the wide and complex political spectrum of that period.

As a politician, Siauw worked well as a 'free agent'. He preferred to work with people who shared his political outlook, particularly with respect to the solutions for minorities in Indonesia, regardless of their overall political ideologies. One was to find that Siauw disliked and ignored disciplines and rules which constrained him from achieving his goals or objectives. He frequently said that the interests of minority groups sometimes differ from those of large political parties. In such a situation, Siauw tended to oppose party positions which undermined minority rights. This political behavior was perhaps the basis of his special relationship with such well-known politicians as Mohamad Yamin, Iwa Kusumasumantri and Sartono.

Finally, Siauw's close association with Partai Murba leaders and figures sympathetic to the Partai Murba, such as Mohamad Yamin and Iwa Kusumasumantri who were political enemies of the PKI, as well as other members of his Fraksi Nasional Progresif, who were mostly known as people who could not be regarded as communists, makes it unlikely that he was a member of a party that had strict organisational disciplines.

Sukiman's anti-communist raid

After the fall of Natsir's cabinet in April 1951, there was some hope that the radical nationalists represented by the PNI, small nationalist parties and the Partai Murba (thus, many members of Siauw's faction in parliament) would have an opportunity to be actively involved in governing the country. But the attempt, initiated by Sartono, to form a cabinet with members of this group failed. Sukiman, a prominent leader of Masyumi, subsequently emerged as prime minister.

With Sukiman acting as prime minister and Masyumi dominating the cabinet, the political outcome became worse for the oppositionists. In order to secure support from the USA, the government quickly developed and implemented anti-communist policies. Part of the motive for moving towards the USA in the Sukiman period was a scheme in which the USA would push the Dutch out of Irian.

By 1951, the USA was keen to contain the influence of communist China whose prestige was on the rise. In June 1950 the Korean War began, with the USA supporting the anti-communist regime in the South and China supporting the communists in the North. In Indonesia, the Chinese government was successful in gaining widespread support from the large totok communities. The political balance within the totok world was in their favour, with the pro-Taiwan group much smaller and isolated. With the displacement of Tan Ling Djie and Alimin from the PKI's leadership in January 1951, the party, under Aidit's leadership, began to expand rapidly.

Meanwhile, between June and early August 1951 there developed a number of industrial strikes, riots and demonstrations in Jakarta and other large cities in Java which were seen to be linked to the PKI. Although the PKI continued to deny their links to these disturbances, Sukiman was convinced that they were involved. In order to demonstrate his opposition to communism, Sukiman arrested a large number of PKI members and their supporters in August 1951. Many of the people arrested were totoks oriented to communist China. By October 1951 the government had declared that as many as 15 000 people had been jailed[46].

Among those arrested were 16 members of parliament, members of the PKI, the Partai Buruh and Golongan Tani factions. The list of the members to be arrested was apparently given to Sartono on the day they were arrested. Siauw's name was not on this list but he too was arrested in the morning of 16 August. He later learned from some of the military officials involved that his name was on a list of leftist Chinese compiled by the pro-Kuo Min Tang (Taiwan–Nationalist) group in Jakarta. Liem Koen Hian and Ang Jang Goan, director of *Sin Po*[47], were also arrested on the basis of that list.

The crackdown was executed inefficiently. A number of members of parliament were wrongly arrested including Abdullah Aidit, the father of Aidit, who was a member of Masyumi. Aidit and Lukman managed to escape arrest, as did Njoto who was living at the *Harian Rakyat* office. Tan Ling Djie was not so lucky. He was arrested along with Siauw, perhaps because he lived in Siauw's house.

---

[46] Feith, *The Decline of Constitutional Democracy in Indonesia*, p. 189.
[47] Siauw, *Lima Jaman*, p. 168.

Sukiman's action generated strong opposition in parliament. The protests were led by the PSI's Tan Po Goan, supported by Tambunan and Iwa Kusumasumantri. Their speeches made specific references to Siauw's jailing and the demand that the political prisoners be released immediately. But Sukiman succeeded in rallying parliamentary support. Tan Po Goan's motion criticising his action was lost and, as a result, the PKI became an isolated party. It became something like an underground party through the life of Sukiman's cabinet.

Siauw, together with many others, was jailed in the Cipinang prison. If his earlier period of imprisonment in Yogya and Ambarawa had enabled him to build personal relationships with a variety of people from Muslim and nationalist parties, this one enabled him to strengthen his ties with radical totoks. The jailing of such a high number of totoks had a dramatic impact on this community's perception of Indonesia. Partly as a result of these mass arrests, the number of Chinese who opted to repudiate Indonesian citizenship by the December 1951 deadline was significantly high (in excess of 300 000).

One tragic consequence of the 1951 arrests was the decision of Liem Koen Hian, one of the early leaders of the pro-Indonesian current in the peranakan community, to repudiate his Indonesian citizenship. He was especially angered because Achmad Subardjo, then foreign minister and Liem's close personal friend whom Liem had helped financially during the Japanese occupation, refused to help expedite his release. Siauw attempted to convince Liem that his action was not wise and could undo much of his political work as the father of Indonesia-oriented politics in the peranakan world. But he failed.

Because of an eye operation and Sukiman's personal intervention, Siauw was allowed to return home in January 1952. He was under formal house arrest but he ignored the government's instruction to stay at home and attended parliamentary sessions and went to his offices as usual.

With the fall of Sukiman's cabinet in February 1952 and the formation of the Wilopo cabinet in April all the political prisoners from the August 1951 raid were released. The formation of the Wilopo cabinet provided the PKI with an opportunity to re-emerge from underground.

In this period, Siauw emerged both as a journalist active in a variety of newspapers and as an independent parliamentarian with many ties to representatives of different groups. His chairmanship of the Fraksi Nasional Progresif gave him the experience of working closely with prominent Indigenous figures. Although he relied heavily on the support of figures who belonged to the leftist group, he was able to work closely with people from various political factions. Because of this electic nature, Siauw was able to gain support for many of his arguments on minority issues.

Siauw's ties with the totoks arising from his activities in the revolution period and in the establishment of newspapers were further enhanced while he was in jail in 1951. These close ties helped Siauw to establish Baperki schools and university in the later part of the parliamentary democracy period.

PART III

1954–1965

Chapter 5

BAPERKI

The birth of Badan Permusyawaratan Kewarganegaraan Indonesia (the Consultative Body of Indonesian Citizenship or Baperki) in 1954 and the election of Siauw as its general chairman marks the beginning of Siauw's career as leader of a large organisation. This chapter details the political developments that prompted a group of peranakan leaders to form this organisation and the role Siauw played in its formation.

After the three short-lived cabinets that preceded it Ali Sastroamidjojo's cabinet, which was dominated by the PNI, the PIR and the NU (Nahdatul Ulama – Religious Scholars League), came into existence in July 1953. The new cabinet's two-year tenure had significant impact on the overall Indonesian political environment and brought a lot of changes that seriously affected the Indonesian Chinese.

For the first time in the post-revolutionary period, the anti-communist and right-wing Masyumi and PSI were not represented in the cabinet. Although their exclusion was not directly attributable to the PKI's efforts,[1] the cabinet's formation and its composition was considered a success by the left-wing forces. The political orientation of Ali's cabinet, and many of its individual ministers, was more acceptable to left-wing political organisations and individuals than its many predecessors. Although the PKI was not directly represented in the cabinet at least two influential ministers were considered sympathetic to its cause, Sadjarwo of the BTI and Iwa Kusumasumantri of the Fraksi Nasional Progresif.[2]

During the period of Ali's cabinet, the stigma of Madiun was significantly reduced and the PKI were able to enhance their activities in

---

1   For a detailed account on the formation of Ali's cabinet, see Feith, *The Decline of Constitutional Democracy*, pp. 330–339 and Deliar Noer, *Partai Islam di Pentas Nasional*, pp. 228–237.
2   Iwa was close to Siauw who led the Fraksi Nasional Progresif. Feith however argues that Iwa was believed to be politically closer to the Partai Murba than the PKI. See Feith, *The Decline of Constitutional Democracy in Indonesia*, p. 339.

promoting their political ideology in the country. Together with the now expanded BTI, the PKI was successful in exerting significant influence in rural areas. The PKI's claimed membership rose dramatically from 165 206 to 500 000 between March 1954 and November 1954.[3] By the end of this cabinet's tenure, the PKI had become a major party. Politicians with a left-wing orientation and the left-wing press also became more acceptable to society in general in this period.

Because of its policies and political orientation, the cabinet received widespread support from organisations of different political spectrums for most of its life, and it enjoyed a parliamentary majority. This cabinet quickly disposed of many bills that could not be passed by its predecessors.[4]

The cabinet adopted foreign policies that, in many respects, reversed what its predecessors had advocated. Its predecessors tended to ally themselves with the USA and thus pursued an anti-communist foreign stance. Ali, as an ex-diplomat, gave foreign policy issues high priority and pioneered a set of new policies in this area. He was particularly keen on developing a good relationship with the People's Republic of China and was willing to stand up to the USA in pursuit of what he saw as a truly independent and non-aligned position.

It was Ali's cabinet that concluded the first trade agreement with the People's Republic of China in December 1953 and worked for its expansion in 1954 and 1955. When the Bandung Conference of Asian and African heads of government was planned in India, Ali Sastroamidjojo supported Prime Minister Nehru's suggestion to invite China. In this period, the Indonesian government was prepared to back the Chinese government on disputes with Taiwan. Activists who supported the Kuo Min Tang were deported from Indonesia in December 1954 and February 1955.[5]

This attitude towards China was understandably supported by the pro-Beijing totok organisations in Indonesia. The political polarisation between the pro-Taiwan and pro-China groups became still more prominent with the declining influence of the pro-Taiwan group.

The Chinese government was able to have more direct access to various Chinese organisations, and from these contacts a major group of totok leaders told the Chinese government about their concerns over the existing passive system of Indonesian citizenship. The general consensus was that

---

[3] Feith, *The Decline of Constitutional Democracy*, p. 407.
[4] Ibid., p. 412.
[5] Ibid., p. 389.

they preferred an active system as they saw it as more democratic. Many of the totok leaders were apparently impressed by the progress the People's Republic of China was making in both the domestic and international arenas, and they indicated their preference to stay Chinese citizens so that when their children, whom they would encourage to become Indonesian citizens, grew up and became independent, they themselves would be able to return to China to retire.[6]

The Chinese population also had other reasons to be pleased with the new cabinet. Two of its ministers were peranakans. Dr Ong Eng Die, a highly trained economist of the PNI, was given the important finance portfolio. Dr Lie Kiat Teng (also known as Mohamad Ali) of the PSII was health minister. This was the first time since 1948 that a cabinet had Chinese ministers. Siauw Giok Tjhan and Ong Eng Die were ministers in the Amir Sjarifuddin cabinet which fell in 1948. It was natural for them to expect that, with the pro-China stance and two prominent peranakan ministers, the cabinet would be able to eliminate most of their concerns in both the political and economic spheres.

Siauw, as leader of the Fraksi Nasional Progresif, also had reason to be pleased with the new cabinet. Four important ministers were members of his faction. Iwa Kusumasumantri was defence minister, Djody Gondokusumo was minister for justice, while Muhamad Yamin and Dr FL Tobing were ministers for education and information respectively. Siauw was also personally close to Prime Minister Ali Sastroamidjojo, Deputy Prime Minister Zainul Arifin of the NU, Ong Eng Die of the PNI, and Aruji Kartawinata and Sudibjo, both of the PSII.[7] Siauw evidently believed that an opportunity to resolve many of the minority issues existed and was hopeful that the Chinese would soon be better off.

However, he was soon to be disappointed.[8]

Citizenship issues

Towards the end of 1953, many Chinese who had been confirmed as Indonesian citizens on 27 December 1951 were facing the serious possibility

---

[6] Interview with Chu Yi, then the People's Republic of China's foreign ministry officer, in Beijing, October 1994.

[7] Interviews with Go Gien Tjwan, Tan Hwie Kiat, Amsterdam, December 1991. Ong Eng Die, like Siauw, had been a member of Amir Sjarifuddin's cabinet in 1947, as finance vice-minister. At that time, Ong was a member of Partai Sosialis.

[8] Siauw, *Lima Jaman*, pp. 191–192.

of losing their citizenship. Foreign Minister Sunario was introducing a draft bill, which would re-open the whole issue of their citizenship.

In order to understand the implications of this bill, it is necessary to review how citizenship issues had been handled by the Indonesian government from 1945 onwards. In 1946, citizenship – in particular that concerning people of foreign descent – was debated in the Badan Pekerja. As the majority of these people were Chinese in descent, the debate was therefore mainly about the Indonesian Chinese. Tan Ling Djie, supported by Siauw Giok Tjhan, argued for a passive system, based on the *jus soli* principle. Under this system, all Chinese born in Indonesia who still resided there would be accepted as citizens except those who made a declaration rejecting Indonesian citizenship. Tan and Siauw argued that a large number of Chinese would remain a permanent part of the population and that adopting the passive system would make more Chinese support the republic against the Dutch. This opinion was backed by many other leaders in the Partai Sosialis camp. Siauw recalled that most leaders of parties represented in the KNIP and its Badan Pekerja were in agreement with the principle that as many as possible of the Chinese, Arabs and Eurasians born in Indonesia should become Indonesian citizens.

The opposition to this group, led by Lukman Hakim of the PNI, advocated an active system. Under this system, Indonesian-born Chinese who wanted to become Indonesian citizens would have to apply for citizenship and make a declaration rejecting Chinese citizenship. They argued that this would guarantee only those who were loyal to the republic could become citizens. They also argued that by making it harder for people of Chinese descent, opportunities would be created for Indigenous Indonesians to improve their position in the economy and the distribution of economic benefits and opportunities would be fairer. Protection against exploitation by foreigners (meaning alien Chinese), they argued, could not be described as racial discrimination.

The debate was concluded with the passing of the Citizenship Act of 1946, which incorporated the passive system. The Act ruled that Chinese who were born in Indonesia and others who had resided there continuously for five years would be citizens of Indonesia unless they chose to reject Indonesian citizenship by August 1947.

The RTC of 1949 confirmed the adoption of the passive system for Indonesian citizenship. Under the RTC agreement, a new two-year option was provided. This would end on 27 December 1951.

When the option period expired on 27 December 1951, a surprisingly large number of Chinese – more than 300 000 – opted to reject Indonesian citizenship. Most of them opted for Chinese citizenship, with a small number choosing to be Dutch citizens. A probable 80 per cent of these were totoks. The high number presumably reflected the high prestige of China after Mao Tse Tung's victory in 1949 as well as bitterness over the harsh treatment many Chinese had endured during the revolution. Resentment towards the policies of Sukiman's cabinet, notorious for its August raid of 1951 which jailed thousands of Chinese, was probably also a contributing factor.

The expiry of the repudiation period in 1951 legally confirmed all peranakans who did not reject Indonesian citizenship as citizens. However, some supporters of the active system refused to accept this situation. One of these was Sunario who had been a key figure in the 1946 debate on citizenship in the Badan Pekerja and had again argued for an active system during the preparation of the republic's position at the RTC.[9]

Asli (Indigenous) businessmen and their political associates – many of the PNI – were keen to displace Chinese businessmen. One quick way of achieving this was to turn as many Chinese businessmen into foreigners as possible. The various policies introduced in the early 1950s forbade the involvement of foreigners in certain business sectors.

Political parties were heavily dependent on financial support from Asli businessmen and the removal of Chinese businessmen from business sectors was hoped to significantly increase the number of Asli businessmen. Sunario's argument for introducing the active system was therefore supported by many party members who were dependent on financial support from Asli businessmen.

Soon after his appointment as foreign minister, Sunario helped to prepare a new citizenship bill. The draft he submitted to cabinet in August 1953 contained provisions that allowed only third-generation residents to apply for Indonesian citizenship. Those applying for citizenship had to prove that their parents were born in Indonesia and had lived in the country continuously for ten years. To many Chinese, this requirement was impossible to fulfill. Most Chinese did not have the necessary documents to prove their birthdates and birthplaces. Also, civil registration in the colonial

---

[9] Again it is not clear who else supported the Active System. See Siauw's *Lima Jaman*, pp. 202, 212–214.

period was poorly managed and many documents had been destroyed during the Japanese occupation and revolution.

There was strong opposition to this bill from the Chinese community. The implementation of this bill would have made many citizens of Chinese descent into aliens. The most outspoken opponent was Siauw Giok Tjhan who, throughout 1953, delivered numerous speeches in parliament and wrote articles which were published in various daily newspapers. Siauw argued that it was unwise to reverse what had legally taken place and that the implementation of the bill would cause confusion about who was actually an Indonesian citizen.[10]

The confusion and unrest due to the issue of citizenship was not the only problem faced by the Indonesian Chinese of the 1950s. The Chinese, particularly those who earned their living from business ventures large or small, experienced the introduction and implementation of various discriminatory measures which seriously affected their existence in the business world. In many respects, the citizenship issues were closely linked to the economic policies adopted by the government.

Anti-Chinese policies

As discussed in the preceding chapter, the economic policies with respect to creating a national economy of the various governments since 1949 tended to discriminate against Chinese business operators. The national economic policies are summarised by Feith as covering three basic goals: one, the diversification of production to reduce extreme dependence on raw material exports; two, economic development and prosperity, and three, the transfer of control and management of economic enterprises from foreign to Indonesian hands. The third goal was often referred to as the Indonesianisation policy. Feith further asserts that, while previous cabinets tended to prioritise the first two economic goals, the policies of Ali's cabinet put special emphasis on Indonesianisation, in effect the Indigenisation, of economic life.[11]

The economic policies of Ali's cabinet were shaped mainly by the PNI, particularly by its minister for economic affairs, Iskaq, until his resignation in November 1954. Within a short time, Iskaq was successful in

---

10   Donald E. Willmott, *The National Status of the Chinese in Indonesia 1900–1958*, Monograph Series, Cornell University, 1961, p. 39.

11   Feith, *The Decline of Constitutional Democracy*, pp. 373–374.

implementing his schemes which provided credits, licences and protection to a large number of Indigenous Indonesian establishments and severely limited business opportunities for the Chinese. Iskaq expanded the protection policies adopted by his predecessors in which the 'economically weak', meaning Indigenous businesses, were to be protected. In these schemes, aliens were to stop operating in the business of importing of certain goods, and the transportation, production and distribution of certain raw materials. The implementation of these schemes also, at times, affected Chinese businessmen who had acquired Indonesian citizenship under existing legislation.

Iskaq's policies provided many politicians with opportunities to enrich themselves as they had the power to grant licenses and credits that were much sought after. The Indigenisation scheme also forced many Chinese business operators to find Indigenous partners with political connections to work with them. It is therefore not surprising that, as a result of this, many ruling party leaders and government officials became involved in various business ventures. Towards the end of 1954 it became public knowledge that various leaders of PNI and PRN were rich businessmen.[12]

However, the economic problems faced by the country were serious enough to give the opposition effective ammunition to attack the government and force the resignation of Iskaq as well as a fairly major cabinet reshuffle in 1954.

The implementation of Iskaq's policies also brought about discussions on Indonesian citizenship in political circles, particularly in parliament. The policies forbidding aliens from operating in these ventures provided the opportunity for officials to demand proof of Indonesian citizenship when they were dealing with businessmen with Chinese names. Many Chinese who did not have clear evidence of their Indonesian citizenship were declared aliens by these officials. This situation encouraged 'Ali Baba' business alliances – Chinese businessmen (the 'Baba') were forced to find Asli partners (the 'Ali'), who often made no real business contributions to the joint ventures, so they could obtain certain business licenses or loans from government banks.

Siauw, who had been outspoken against earlier policy measures to promote Indigenous business, believed that the politicians involved in implementing this scheme saw the business opportunities in Indonesia as an opportunity to have their own slice of the cake. If more Chinese who

---

[12] Sutter, *Indonesianisasi*, pp. 1242–1243.

were operating successfully in various profitable business ventures were made aliens, the Indigenous newcomers to business would get a bigger piece of the cake. Perhaps because of this, Foreign Minister Sunario was able to gain support in the cabinet to endorse his active system citizenship proposals as these would dramatically increase the number of aliens who would be barred from entering certain business fields.

As political parties became more dependent upon the new and emerging Indigenous middle class for their election campaign funds, Sunario's arguments against the passive system of citizenship became more widely accepted within the ruling parties.

Siauw's concerns over the Indigenisation scheme, and particularly the citizenship issues, were shared by many peranakans including members of the PDTI (Partai Demokrat Tionghoa Indonesia – Party of Indonesian Chinese Democrats) and smaller similar organisations outside Jakarta. Sunario's bill was seen as a real threat to the Chinese communities. These organisations were looking for effective means to challenge the proposed bill, but they felt powerless as, since independence, peranakan organisations had not been able to gain widespread support and fight against racial discrimination. Furthermore, they had few contacts with ethnic Indonesian politicians who sympathised with the Chinese. Their feelings of powerlessness helped to create the climate in which Baperki was formed.

Peranakan organisations in the early 1950s

Soon after independence, on 15 October 1945, leaders of the Japanese-sponsored Chinese Federation, Kakyo Shokai, formed the CHTH as an umbrella organisation for all Chinese community associations in Indonesia. In this new form, the organisation included members who were Dutch-oriented during the pre-war period and after independence. Initially the Dutch educated peranakans were more influential, but towards the end of the 1940s a group of totoks came to play a more important role and swayed the organisation towards nationalist China.

In 1948 Thio Thiam Tjong founded and became the chairman of a political party called Partai Persatuan Tionghoa (Chinese Union Party or PT). Thio had a long history of political involvement. In the pre-war era, he was one of the leaders of the Chung Hua Hui. He was interned by the Japanese and because of his influence in the Chinese communities he was appointed adviser to Lieutenant Governor-General Van Mook, along with Injo Beng Goat (editor of *Keng Po*) and Ang Jang Goan (director of *Sin Po*).

The PT was dominated by a group of people who were also members of a peranakan social organisation called the Sin Ming Hui (Association of New Light), which was formed in 1946 in Jakarta and was a member of the CHTH. Sin Ming Hui was a kind of brotherhood and was in existence until 1966. As a social organisation, it provided the Chinese communities in Jakarta with legal, employment, recruitment and vocational training services. With the formation of PT in 1948, Sin Ming Hui broke away from the CHTH and became more Indonesia-oriented.

The PT's leaders included Khoe Woen Sioe (director of *Keng Po*) and Injo Beng Goat, both in their late forties, and Tan Po Goan, the lawyer who had been a minister of state in one of Sjahrir's cabinets in 1946. All three were close to Sjahrir of the PSI. Other important leaders of the party included Ang Jang Goan and Yap Tjwan Bing, a former leader of the Bandung Kakyo Shokai and later a member of parliament representing PNI[13]. The party called for the elimination of racial discrimination and for the safeguarding of the interests of the Indonesian Chinese.

In 1950, soon after the formation of the RIS, the name of the PT was changed to PDTI. Thio Thiam Tjong remained to dominate the party along with other leaders of the PT including peranakan members of parliament who were also members of other political parties – Tjung Tin Yan, from Partai Katolik, Tan Boen An from the PSI, Tjoa Sie Hwie and Yap Tjwan Bing from the PNI.[14] All these had been elected in the Dutch-controlled states. On the other hand the PDTI failed to attract peranakans who were former members of the republican parliament, such as Tan Ling Djie and Siauw Giok Tjhan, or prominent figures like Liem Koen Hian and Tjoa Sik Ien.

It is not clear how many members or branches the PDTI had[15] but the party appeared to have difficulty in attracting support from the wider peranakan communities. Unlike the pre-war Chung Hua Hui, which had been

---

[13] Ang Jang Goan and Yap Tjwan Bing appear to be inactive members of this party. Yap Tjwan Bing made no reference of his involvement in this party in his published memoirs.

[14] Mary Somers, *Peranakan Chinese Politics in Indonesia*, PhD Thesis, Cornell University, p. 137.

[15] Oei Tjoe Tat, who was at that time the party's secretary, recalled that the party had more than 10 000 members and more than 27 branches were formed throughout Indonesia. Interview with Oei Tjoe Tat in Jakarta, July 1993.

able to receive financial and political support from rich and Dutch-educated peranakans, the PDTI failed to gain much support from businessmen. This was partly due to the fact that in the 1950s business newcomers were from the totok groups and they could not see the benefits of supporting organisations such as PDTI.

Another major contributor to the weakness of the PDTI was its leaders' lack of strong nationalist credentials. Thio Thiam Tjong had been close to Van Mook, and none of the PDTI's leaders had clearly sided with the republic. By 1953, its parliamentary representatives no longer openly represented the organisation. Thio felt that the party was ineffective. In the last PDTI newsletter, *Berita PDTI*, published in December 1953, Thio was quoted as saying that the party existed only in name.

Similar peranakan-based organisations had grown up in the early 1950s outide Jakarta. Most were founded as the PDTI had been, by peranakans disillusioned with the CHTH organisations which were dominated by totoks who were principally interested in developments in China and in sponsoring and managing Chinese language schools in Indonesia. In Surabaya, Perwanit (Persatuan Warganegara Indonesian Tionghoa – Union of Chinese of Indonesian Citizenship) was formed; in Kediri, Perwitt (Persatuan Warga Indonesia Turunan Tionghoa – Union of Indonesian Citizens of Chinese Descent) and, in Makassar, Pertip (Perserikatan Tionghoa Peranakan – Union of Indonesian Chinese). While these organisations were politically conscious, they did not have a strong political presence in national politics.[16]

Towards the end of 1953, concerned with the developments over the citizenship issue particularly with respect to the bill, PDTI leaders decided to form a working committee to oppose it. This Panitia Kerja Kewarganegaraan Indonesia (Working Committee on Indonesian Citizenship) was to involve prominent peranakan lawyers who were either members of the PDTI or the Sin Ming Hui, such as Yap Thiam Hien, a non-party Protestant; Auwyong Peng Koen, a Catholic; Liem Koen Seng, Liem Koen Hian's cousin, and Gouw Giok Siong, a law academic. Oei Tjoe Tat, the vice-chairman of the PDTI, also a lawyer, was assigned by PDTI leaders to convene the meeting to form the committee. The committee was also to include all peranakan members of parliament including Siauw Giok Tjhan, chairman of the Fraksi Nasional Progresif; Tjung Tin Yan, of the Partai Katolik; Tan Po Goan, of the PSI, and Lie Po Yoe, of the PNI. The

---

16 Interviews with Oei Tjoe Tat and Phoa Thoan Hian, Jakarta, December 1992.

committee formed in January 1954 and elected Siauw Giok Tjhan as its chairman.[17]

After several meetings in Jakarta, the committee issued a statement attacking the bill. This statement provided a number of legal arguments which challenged the legal existence of the draft. The committee's arguments included the following:[18]

1. It would be unwise and illegal to reverse the effects of legal procedure implementations. The Chinese who did not repudiate Indonesian citizenship by 27 December 1951 had the opportunity to repudiate the citizenship in two separate periods, between 1946 and 1949 and between 1949 and 1951. By law, these people had legally become Indonesian citizens.
2. To allow such a reversal to occur would create uncertainty. It would be difficult for citizens to trust existing laws if they believed that future laws could again make them foreigners.
3. Civil registration of the Chinese began only in 1918 in Java and in 1926 outside Java. Moreover, the majority of the Chinese population were either too poor to pay for the necessary documents or too ignorant of requirements to formally register births and marriages. For a large number of Indonesian Chinese, it would therefore be difficult, if not impossible, to provide the proofs which were required by the proposed bill. The acceptance of the proposed bill would therefore induce a situation where people become foreigners not because they did not want to be Indonesian citizens, but because the law made that impossible.

Due to Siauw's close relationship with Ali Sastroamidjojo and other senior members of the cabinet and the assistance of Ong Eng Die and Lie Kiat Teng, ministers for finance and health respectively, Siauw was able to get the cabinet to withdraw the bill before it was presented to parliament.

---

[17] Oei Tjoe Tat recalled that Siauw dominated the committee meetings. Although Siauw was not a trained lawyer, his knowledge of citizenship issues and the associated legal matters was apparently highly respected by the committee members.

[18] Siauw, *Lima Jaman*, pp. 230–233; Peter Burns (ed.), *Siauw Giok Tjhan Remembers*, Book II, James Cook University of North Queensland, Queensland, 1984, pp. 9–10. The civil registration dates referred to in the document are incorrect. Civil registration came into effect in Java and several places outside Java in 1919 and in the whole of Indies for the first time in March 1925. See Ong Eng Die, *Chineezen in Nederlandsch–Indie: Sociografie van een Indonesiche Bevolkingsgroep*, Assen: van Gorcum, 1943, p. 44.

Siauw's success in having the bill withdrawn could also be due to the persuasive arguments used in his numerous speeches that Indonesianisation should not be the basis for racial discrimination and that the government should be motivated to expand business opportunities by mobilising domestic capital (alien and national) rather than eliminating Chinese capital and commercial expertise from the arena. The government issued a statement to the effect that it was revising changes.[19]

Members of the committee, particularly those from the PDTI, were very pleased with the result and impressed by Siauw's ability to influence cabinet decisions.[20]

The birth of Baperki

Reports of the proposed Citizenship Bill of 1953 had created a new sense of urgency for many peranakan leaders. In a meeting in February 1954 PDTI leaders concluded that their party could no longer provide effective services to the peranakan community. They agreed to approach leaders of similar organisations like Perwitt, Perwanit and Pertip to form a federation. In the same meeting, they also discussed the need for a leader who would be acceptable to national political leaders and who had the ability to influence the legislative processes to protect peranakans' interests.

The group of leaders who participated in these discussions included Thio Thiam Tjong, Khoe Woen Sioe, Injo Beng Goat, Auwyong Peng Koen, Tan Eng Tie and Yap Thiam Hien. All of these leaders were Dutch-educated.

Khoe Woen Sioe, then 49, had helped to found the Sin Ming Hui in 1946 and been elected its first chairman. He had a long career as a journalist, first with *Sin Po* in 1923 then *Keng Po*, which he directed until it ceased publication in 1958. He was known mainly for his active participation in social welfare organisations as a leading member of the Sin Ming Hui. Politically he was close to Sjahrir's PSI. Being one of the oldest in the Sin Ming Hui, he was perhaps regarded by the younger members like Oei Tjoe Tat and Auwyong Peng Koen as their mentor. He appeared to have been even more highly respected in PDTI circles than Chairman Thio Thiam Tjong.[21]

---

[19] Willmott, *National Status of the Chinese in Indonesia*, p. 34.
[20] Interview with Oei Tjoe Tat, Jakarta, December 1992.
[21] Suryadinata, *Eminent Indonesian Chinese*, p. 45; Interview with Oei Tjoe Tat in July 1993.

Injo Beng Goat, then 50, was also a prominent journalist. Being the editor-in-chief of *Keng Po* daily, he was presumably very close to Khoe Woen Sioe. His political orientation would also be that of the PSI. Although well known as an experienced journalist, due to his personal characteristics Injo was not as popular as Khoe Woen Sioe. Nevertheless, he was also an influential member of the PDTI.[22]

Auwyong Peng Koen, then 34, was a lawyer who had graduated from the University of Indonesia in 1950. He was a Catholic and perhaps already a member of the Partai Katolik. He was strongly anti-communist and worked in the same law firm in Jakarta as Tan Po Goan, Oei Tjoe Tat and Yap Thiam Hien.[23]

Tan Eng Tie, then 47, was a skin specialist who had graduated from Holland. He was active in the CHTH and Sin Ming Hui. Like Thio Thiam Tjong, he was a PDTI leader who had no association with other political parties.[24]

Yap Thiam Hien, then 41, was a lawyer who had graduated from Holland in 1947. He was a devout Protestant but not a member of Parkindo. Though anti-communist, he was able to work well with people with a left-wing political orientation.

The last of them, Oei Tjoe Tat, then 32, was also a lawyer. As described above, he played an important role in convening the formation of the PDTI's Working Committee on Indonesian Citizenship that was chaired by Siauw Giok Tjhan. Although close to Khoe Woen Sioe, and sympathetic to some of the PSI's political programs, he was not a member of the PSI. Being young and energetic, he was often asked to draft legal documents for the organisations he was associated with. Of all the PDTI leaders who were involved in the plan for the new organisation, Oei was the only one who knew Siauw well. They had met in Semarang in 1938 as boarders in the same boarding house. At that time, Siauw was a journalist at *Mata Hari* while Oei was still a secondary school student.

Thio Thiam Tjong endorsed the appointment of Oei Tjoe Tat to coordinate meetings which would determine the form the new organisation was to have. The discussions in which senior PDTI leaders took part were

---

[22] Suryadinata, *Eminent Indonesian Chinese*, p. 34; Interviews with Oei Tjoe Tat, Jakarta, July 1993 and Go Gien Tjwan, Amsterdam, December 1993.

[23] Ibid., pp. 99–100; Interviews with Oei Tjoe Tat, Go Gien Tjwan and Yap Thiam Hien in December 1988.

[24] Ibid., p. 127; Interview with Oei Tjoe Tat, Jakarta, July 1993.

held in Jakarta. In order to gain as much support from the peranakan communities as possible, they concluded that the new organisation should not be a political party. The leaders feared that if the new organisation were to become a political party, experienced and influential peranakan politicians who were already members of other political parties would be discouraged from joining. The consensus was to establish a mass organisation of which people could be members while maintaining membership of other political parties.[25]

In order to realise the expectation that other organisations like Pertip, Perwanit and Perwitt could be merged with PDTI, a mass organisation in the form of a federation was considered. The name Baperwatt (Badan Permusyawaratan Warga Negara Turunan Tionghoa – Consultative Body of Citizens of Chinese Descent) was proposed. Permusyawaratan (consultation) was then a popular term in Indonesia, indicating the wish to find consensus outcomes through consultative processes. Oei was assigned to draft the new organisation's constitution.

When I interviewed Oei, he told me of discussions about who should be appointed as chairman of the new organisation. There were people in the PDTI who regarded Khoe Woen Sioe as the most suitable candidate for the chairmanship. Khoe was senior, widely respected and close to all the PDTI leaders. On the other hand, Oei, who regarded Khoe as his mentor, recalled that when the question of who should lead Baperwatt was raised, all concerned, including Khoe Woen Sioe, nominated Siauw Giok Tjhan. Oei said Siauw's political career and his friendships among political figures outside the Chinese community were seen as assets Baperwatt needed. Siauw's recent success in having the bill on citizenship withdrawn by the cabinet reinforced their confidence in him.[26]

How does one explain the fact that the PDTI leaders who were influenced by Sjahrir's PSI, and who were in many cases strongly anti-communist, endorsed Siauw as their new leader, despite his past associations with Amir Sjarifuddin and the FDR? One can assume that they valued Siauw's political reputation and his acceptance in the general political arena more highly than their political differences. Also, as discussed earlier, although many people were still cautious about communism the political environment created by Ali's cabinet had made it easier for pragmatically minded people to accept left-wing orientations. The success of the People's Republic of China in gaining world recognition and support meant that the Chinese

---

[25] Interview with Oei Tjoe Tat, Jakarta, July 1993.
[26] Also see Oei, *Memoar Oei Tjoe Tat*, p. 71.

in Indonesia were more ready to accept Mao Tse Tung's leadership in China than they had been a few years before.

Another aspect of Siauw's leadership ability, which the PDTI leaders presumably appreciated, was his ability to work well with totok leaders. Siauw's success in the campaign against Indigenous protection policies, particularly those related to the transportation and rice-milling enterprises owned by totok business operators, had made him one of a small number of peranakan figures who was highly respected by the totok communities.

The totoks in this period did not seem as disturbed about the citizenship issues as the peranakans. This is the main reason why they did not play any role in the formation of the new organisation. However, they were certainly concerned about the implementation of policies that severely restricted their business operations.

As previously discussed, Siauw was never associated with the PDTI, although its publications had often quoted his speeches and praised him for his defence of the peranakans.[27] His contacts with the organisation were limited to casual personal contacts he had with one or two of its leaders. Because of Oei's relationship with Siauw, he was assigned by other PDTI leaders to meet with Siauw and discuss the party's intention of forming a new federation and Siauw's nomination as its chairman.

Siauw accepted Oei's invitation to meet at the Sin Ming Hui building in Jakarta on 13 March 1954 to discuss the formation of the new body. But he made no commitments regarding his nomination as the chairman.[28] He may well have had hesitations about that because of a long-standing conviction that Indonesian Chinese should not be involved in ethnically specific organisations.

Siauw's involvement in the Partai Sosialis and then in the FDR has been detailed in previous chapters. However, since the dissolution of the FDR in 1948 he had not been a member of any party.

Siauw's speeches in parliament in the 1950s, particularly those related to minority representations in parliament, clearly indicate that he was disillusioned by political parties' lack of interest in solving minority problems, especially those with respect to racial prejudice. He often argued that the agendas of the major political parties, even those whose political platform

---

[27] Somers, *Peranakan Politics*, p. 144.

[28] Oei recalls that he had spoken to Siauw to say that they hoped he would become chairman, and that Siauw had indicated that there might be others who would be more suitable.

would have matched his own, would not necessarily be the same as those who suffered from racial discriminatory practices. This would have been the main reason for him not to join a political party.

Knowing his handicap as a minority representative as described previously, Siauw chose to initially work closely with the SKI faction which was led by the Batak politicians FL Tobing and DS Diapari. Soon after that, he initiated the formation and became chairman of the Fraksi Nasional Progresif. But as far as defending minority rights was concerned, Siauw remained an individual fighter.

A number of Siauw's close associates also encouraged him to form or join a mass organisation.[29] Here he might have faced a political dilemma. On the one hand, he was convinced that his desire to fight against racial discrimination could not be effectively channelled through major political parties as their political agendas would be different from those in need of protection against racial discrimination. On the other hand, he was convinced that fighting discriminatory measures through an explicitly ethnic organisation would not be effective. However, he was probably of the opinion that the proposed new organisation, with a modified political platform, would meet his agenda.

Oei Tjoe Tat played a major role in convening the 13 March 1954 meeting. Thio Thiam Tjong was apparently away overseas when preparations for the formation meetings were being made by leaders of the PDTI.[30] Apart from inviting leaders of the regional organisations Perwanit, Pertip and Perwitt, the PDTI also invited many other peranakans from various walks of life.

Also invited was Go Gien Tjwan, then 35, who was Siauw's close friend, their association going back to Siauw's days in Malang. Go had also been a member of the Partai Sosialis and had worked in the Antara News Agency. He became well known after he was expelled from Holland, where he headed the Antara office, in 1953. He was known as a leftist by the PDTI leaders. Missing from the list of invitees were Tjoa Sik Ien and Tan Ling Djie, both former leaders of the PTI. They were probably left out because they were known to be communists.

---

[29] Perhaps it was coincidental that Oei Tjoe Tat's visit occurred about the same time of the receipt of a number of letters from his sympathisers in Bandung and Surabaya. These letters described Siauw as a general without an army ('panglima tanpa barisan'). The letters were clearly designed to encourage Siauw to join a party or establish a new body.

[30] Baperki meeting minutes, 13 March 1954.

More than 44 participants attended the meeting.[31] They were all peranakans and mostly Dutch-educated. Most were from Java but a number of them were from Sumatra (Padang and Palembang), Borneo (Banjarmasin) and Sulawesi (Makasar).[32] Some, like Thio Thiam Tjong, Dr Thung Sin Nio and Tan Siang Lian, were members of the pre-war Chung Hua Hui. Only a small number had been China-oriented before the war.

The participants could be divided into three main groups. The first group was led by right-wing peranakans who were closely associated with the PSI and Partai Katolik. All of these people disliked communism and some probably supported the Kuo Min Tang. This influential group included people like Khoe Woen Sioe; Tan Po Goan, a former minister in one of Sjahrir's cabinets who was close to Sjahrir; Auwyong Peng Koen and Tan Siang Lian, who had been in the pre-war Chung Hua Hui and was a close friend of Thio Thiam Tjong.

At the other end of the spectrum were people with a relatively radical political outlook. It is unlikely that any of them were members of the PKI, but all of them were socialists impressed by the achievements of Mao Tse Tung in China. The principal members of this group were Siauw Giok Tjhan, Go Gien Tjwan and Ang Jang Goan, director of the China-oriented Jakarta daily *Sin Po*.

Between these two was a third group who were not strongly oriented to any particular political ideology. Principal members of this group were Thio Thiam Tjong, Oei Tjoe Tat, Yap Thiam Hien, Tan Eng Tie as well as Liem Tjiong Hian, a lawyer who lived in Palembang and also a leader of the PDTI, and Liem Koen Seng, a member of the PDTI and a cousin of Liem Koen Hian.

Most of the participants were either professionals or small business operators but Thio Thiam Tjong and Tan Siang Lian were as prosperous as the businessmen who led the pre-war Chung Hua Hui.

The first topic discussed at the 13 March meeting was the idea of forming an organisation that would absorb the existing peranakan organisations – Perwanit, Pertip, Perwitt, Perwari and the PDTI. Both Thio Thiam Tjong,

---

[31] The meeting minutes listed 44 names. But Siauw Giok Tjhan in his *Lima Jaman*, and Oei Tjoe Tat in his *Memoar Oei Tjoe Tat*, referred to names of people like Dr Thung Sin Nio and Tjung Tin Yan who, they said, attended the meeting but whose names were not listed. Presumably these people either did not register their names or only attended the meeting on a part-time basis.

[32] A large part of this section was derived from the meeting minutes of the 13 March meeting.

as chairman of the PDTI, and Oei Tjoe Tat, as the convenor of the meeting, outlined the reasons for the political failure of the PDTI and the need to form a new organisation which would absorb all existing organisations in order to consolidate their strength and fight against racial discrimination.

The design, outlined by Oei Tjoe Tat, was for a mass organisation not a political party. Hence, members of other political parties would be able to join. Siauw, in discussions with some of his close friends during the session breaks, referred to the National Association for the Advancement of Colored People (NAACP) in America as a model. He saw NAACP as militant in combating racism, and free from party politics and ideology.[33]

As previously mentioned, the PDTI leaders led by Yap Thiam Hien and Kwik Hay Gwan, a representative from Semarang, wanted the new organisation to be called Badan Permusyawaratan Warga Negara Turunan Tionghoa (Baperwatt). They argued that it was important to maintain the word 'Tionghoa' so that the organisation would be able to identify itself with the Chinese minority. Without the term Tionghoa, they were concerned that the organisation would not be supported by the Chinese communities.

A second group, led by Siauw Giok Tjhan, argued that to limit the organisation's membership to Chinese members would be interpreted as an act of racial exclusiveness. Siauw further outlined the need to create a stronger sense of citizenship. He believed that nation building should be understood as closely related to the achievement of a sense of equal citizenship.

Based on this principle, he proposed that the name be changed to Badan Permusyawaratan Kewarganegaraan (Consultative Body for Citizenship, or Baperki). He believed the proposed name reflected the intention to educate people on the meaning of citizenship, which would in turn translate into political activities to fight against racial discrimination.

Siauw was able to dominate the meeting. In less than thirty minutes the participants agreed, without the necessity of voting, to adopt the name proposed by Siauw – Baperki. At this point, Siauw was presumably ready to wholeheartedly join the organisation as in its newly defined form it was a national organisation. His success on the matter of the new organisation's name enabled Siauw to feel sure and convince other former PTI leaders that he had remained true to the spirit of the agreement he had reached with other PTI leaders in 1945 in Surabaya. To emphasise the fact that Baperki was a national body, he argued that one of its most important objectives

---

[33] Interview with Go Gien Tjwan, Amsterdam, December 1990.

should be 'to implement national aspirations to ensure that all citizens become genuine and true citizens (warganegera sejati)'. The other two main objectives were formulated to be 'to ensure the upholding of democratic rights and human rights' and 'to ensure the realisation of equal rights and responsibilities as well as opportunities for all citizens regardless of their racial origins, cultural backgrounds and religions'.

Siauw, as the only candidate, was unanimously elected as chairman.

The choice of vice-chairmen was more complex. Thirteen candidates were nominated, including Thio Thiam Tjong, Oei Tjoe Tat, Khoe Woen Sioe, Yap Thiam Hien, Go Gien Tjwan, Liem Tjiong Hian, Tan Siang Lian and The Pek Siong, leader of the Surabaya Perwanit. Votes were then taken to elect four vice-chairmen. Oei Tjoe Tat obtained by far the highest number of votes (83 votes) and the other three chosen were Khoe Woen Sioe (58 votes), The Pek Siong (57 votes) and Thio Thiam Tjong (48 votes).[34]

The nomination of candidates for secretary and treasurer was conducted without voting. Tan Siang Lian, who chaired the meeting, proposed that Go Gien Tjwan and Ang Jang Goan be nominated secretary and treasurer respectively. This proposal was unanimously accepted. The meeting minutes did not detail how this nomination was conducted. Go Gien Tjwan, however, recalls that it was Siauw who recommended him for the position of secretary.

After the elections, the meeting was chaired by Siauw Giok Tjhan. He asked Yap Thiam Hien to outline the resolution adopted by the PDTI's Working Committee on Indonesian Citizenship. Siauw continued the discussion by detailing the historical and political perspectives of the draft bill, which was withdrawn by the cabinet before the end of 1953. The new organisation fully endorsed the committee's resolution. Although much of the information given in the meeting was presumably known by most of the participants, the explanation, given by Yap and Siauw, of the working committee's achievements appeared to have boosted the hope that the new organisation under Siauw and the new leadership team would be far more effective in combating racism than their old organisations.[35]

Within two days, the formation of Baperki was reported by major daily and weekly peranakan journals like *Sin Po*, *Keng Po*, *Sunday Courier* and *Sin Min*. All the reports were sympathetic. In the next few weeks, these newspapers published numerous articles about Baperki and the formation

---

[34] Although there were only 44 participants, representatives from major capital cities were given 6 votes, from other cities 4 votes and individuals 1 vote.

[35] Interviews with Oei Tjoe Tat, Phoa Thoan Hian and Go Gien Tjwan in 1993.

of Baperki's branches. *Sin Min*, an influential daily in Semarang, published Baperki's constitution in full. These reports suggest that there was a feeling of hope that Baperki would become an important peranakan organisation.

Siauw was concerned that Baperki should not be seen as simply another Chinese organisation, a new PDTI. To change this perception, Siauw invited various Asli politicians to accept leadership positions. When Baperki established its first and largest branch, the Jakarta branch, Siauw succeeded in convincing his new Baperki colleagues to endorse Sudarjo Tjokrosisworo as its chairman. Sudarjo Tjokrosisworo had worked with Siauw for *Mata Hari* in Semarang and, after independence, had founded and become the first president of PERDI (Persatuan Jurnalis Indonesia – Indonesian Journalists' Association) which later became the PWI. He was also the founder and head of the SPS.

DS Diapari, a Batak member of parliament and a member of Siauw's Fraksi Nasional Progresif, became deputy chairman of Baperki's Jakarta branch. In Surakarta, Slamet Harto Prodjohartono became the first chairman. In Menado, B Richter, an Indo-European, became one of its committee members. In Bandung, another Dutch Indonesian, JFG Steyn was elected secretary. Support from Javanese members of the community was secured in some parts of Sumatra, presumably because they saw themselves as members of a minority group in Sumatra.

On the 26 March Siauw led a Baperki delegation to meet Prime Minister Ali Sastroamidjojo to explain Baperki's objectives and the reasons for its formation. Prime Minister Ali reportedly expressed support for Baperki's formation and endorsed its program of educating the society on the meaning and essence of Indonesian citizenship.[36]

Siauw's appointment as leader of Baperki represented a new phase in his political career. He now had an organisation and masses he could rely upon. Although leaders of the Baperki intended to make it an organisation with wide-ranging national interests, his chairmanship of Baperki consolidated his ability to represent the Chinese in various arenas, and his involvement in national politics became more focused towards defending the rights of the Chinese.

---

[36] *Sin Min*, 27 March 1954.

Chapter 6

BAPERKI IN THE 1955 ELECTIONS

Plans for holding nationwide general elections in Indonesia were announced by the newly proclaimed Indonesian Government as early as 5 October 1945. However, due to the upheavals experienced by the newly established republic, coupled with a series of military confrontations with the Allied and Dutch forces, these plans were abandoned.

When independence was consolidated in December 1949, and the unitary state of Indonesia was re-established eight months later, promises for nationwide general elections were again made by successive governments. But due to urgent government business, and pressure from parties and individual parliamentarians who expected to lose seats, there was further delay.

The reluctance to endorse the holding of elections was due to a number of reasons. Firstly, a number of major parties feared that the elections would ultimately be won by the major Muslim parties Masyumi and NU. Many feared that this would lead to the creation of an Islamic state. Secondly, many members of parliament who enjoyed privileges and business connections, and hence the generation of individual wealth, were concerned that the elections would unseat them. Thirdly, many non-Javanese members were concerned that the elections would significantly reduce the representation of the outer islands.[1]

General elections did not become an issue of primary political importance until after the crisis of 17 October 1952. On this date a group of high-ranking army officers organised a demonstration backed with artillery, which was directed at both the parliament buildings and the palace. The action was prompted by the officers' resentment of the way in which parliamentarians had criticised the army leadership in the preceding months.

---

[1] Feith, *The Decline of Constitutional Democracy in Indonesia*, pp. 274–277; Herbert Feith, *The Indonesian Elections of* 1955, Interim Reports Series, Southeast Asia Program, Cornell University, pp. 1–2.

The organisers of this action not only failed to get Soekarno's endorsement but were purged by the government not long after the event. In the weeks after 17 October 1952 there were counter-coups in Surabaya, Makassar and Palembang organised by pro-Soekarno elements in the army. These greatly weakened the Wilopo cabinet, a PNI–Masyumi–PSI coalition, but it managed to regain some political initiative by accelerating moves to create an election law.

The Indian elections at the end of 1951 had put pressure on the Indonesian leadership to follow suit. It was widely argued that the existing parliament, which was formed after a compromise arrangement with the Dutch, lacked the support of the people and therefore authority. Many said elections would produce greater political stability.

The Wilopo cabinet's bill was submitted to parliament on 25 November 1952 and on 4 April 1953 it became law. The law provided for direct elections for both the parliament and the Konstituante (Constituent Assembly) based on proportional representation so that every 300 000 Indonesian citizen–residents would be represented by a member of parliament. The country was divided into sixteen electoral districts, most of which corresponded to existing provinces. Each area was to have seats proportional to the number of citizens residing in the area and each area was to have a minimum number of three representatives for the parliament and six for the Konstituante.

Citizen–residents could be represented by political parties or by individuals nominated by more than 200 eligible voters.[2] In addition the Chinese, European and Arab minority groups were to be represented by at least nine, six and three members of parliament respectively. If these numbers were not reached by the process of the election, the government would appoint representatives up to those numbers.[3]

Siauw initially opposed the provision which allowed the government to appoint members to represent the minorities, arguing that such a provision would enable government parties to manipulate numbers in parliament to their political advantage at the expense of fair representation of the minority communities. The government conceded that such appointments would need to be based on the wishes of the minority groups. How

---

[2] Feith, *The Indonesian Elections of 1955*, p. 3; Siauw, *Lima Jaman*, p. 181; Harmaili Ibrahim, *Pemilihan Umum di Indonesia 1955, 1971 dan 1977*, CV Alhidayah, Jakarta, pp. 16–17.

[3] Harmaili Ibrahim, *Pemilihan Umum di Indonesia 1955, 1971 dan 1977*, CV Alhidayah, Jakarta, pp. 18.

such wishes were to be measured, however, was not spelled out and this turned out to be an oversight which caused Baperki to lose parliamentary seats in 1956.

The election law of 1953 gave voting rights to all citizens above 18 years of age, as well as those who were under 18 but married. It also provided for active participation of political parties in the electoral machinery through the multiparty Central Electoral Committee (Panitia Pemilihan Indonesia). But its implementation was slow and, with the fall of the Wilopo cabinet in June 1953 and the inability of Ali Sastroamidjojo's new cabinet to agree on the membership of the Central Electoral Committee till December 1953, the elections were further delayed. They were eventually held in September 1955, by which time the Ali cabinet too had fallen and been replaced by the Masyumi-led cabinet of Burhanuddin Harahap.

Baperki's position on general elections

The political pressure of being involved in general elections prompted Siauw to quickly turn Baperki into a formidable political force. The preparation for the national campaign also provided Siauw and other leaders of Baperki with an effective platform to introduce Baperki and its political programs to the Chinese communities across the nation.

However, soon after its formation Baperki leaders were faced with a number of major political issues. The forthcoming elections were one of Baperki's two principal concerns after its formation in March 1954, the other being citizenship legislation.

Although the subject of elections was not discussed at length during the formation meeting of 13 March 1954, it was resolved that Baperki would participate in general elections. At the end of this meeting, one of the participants, Kwee Hwat Djien, urged the other participants to collect donations to fund Baperki's election activities. At Baperki's first formal meeting on the following day, a general elections committee was set up under the leadership of Kwee Hwat Djien. Its members included Yap Thiam Hien and Auwyong Peng Koen. But controversy on whether or not Baperki should participate in the elections arose later in the month, prompted by questions from Surabaya representatives.

In the first issue of its bulletin *Berita Baperki* (*Baperki News*), published in April 1954, Baperki confirmed its decision to nominate candidates representing the Chinese minority groups for both the parliament and Konstituante.

Siauw justified this decision by stating:

> If the provisions for minority representations are entirely left to the policies of the government and the major political parties, they will be used solely to protect their political interests, and the interests of the minority groups will be jeopardised. Baperki, as an organisation whose members are largely those from the minority groups, needs to nominate candidates for effective representations in the parliament and Konstituante.

Siauw clarified Baperki's intention by stating:

> Baperki is not a political party. It is not Baperki's intention to compete with any political party. Its election objective is not to gain maximum number of seats in parliament to govern. Baperki's candidates who are elected to parliament will be free to express and adopt their political views and ideologies but they will be required to consult each other on citizenship matters.[4]

Baperki's declaration to nominate candidates invited reactions from the PNI, PSI and Partai Katolik. These groups were alarmed by Baperki's success in establishing branches all over the country within the first few months of its formation. In three months, Baperki had established 48 branches and attracted thousands of members.[5]

Sarino Mangunpranoto, in a PNI meeting held on 16 June 1954, declared that it was unwise for the minority groups to nominate their own candidates for the general elections. The groups' interests, he said, would be best served if the provisions for minority representations were left to major political parties. He urged the minority groups to support candidates nominated by parties.[6] In the existing parliament, PNI was represented by Lie Po Yoe, Yap Tjwan Bing, Tjoa Sie Hwie and Tony Wen.

The Partai Katolik's objection was detailed in an article published in *Penabur* on 30 May 1954. The article warned Catholic peranakans that Baperki was dangerous for the Catholics as it was led by communists whose main objective was to support the Peoples' Republic of China. It argued that if representations of the Chinese minority were dominated by Baperki

---

[4] *Berita Baperki*, 26 May 1954.
[5] Ibid.
[6] *Sin Po*, 19 June 1954.

in parliament, the interests of the Catholics would be jeopardised. By encouraging Chinese voters to vote for it rather than for one of the national parties, Baperki was turning the minority it claimed to represent against the Indonesian people.[7] In the existing parliament, Tjung Tin Yan represented the Partai Katolik.

On the other hand, peranakans who were sympathetic to the PSI urged Chinese minority groups through *Keng Po* not to support Baperki's position as they viewed the action as dangerous. They argued that by actively participating in the elections, Baperki would isolate the peranakan groups and would therefore create a small nation within a larger nation.[8] Tan Po Goan, a state minister in Sjahrir's cabinet, represented the PSI in parliament. However, some PSI-sympathising peranakans like Khoe Woen Sioe and Injo Beng Goat joined Baperki, and it appears until October 1954 there was no pressure from the PSI on its peranakan members or sympathisers to leave Baperki.

Siauw rebutted the positions outlined by the PNI and Partai Katolik. He indicated that the PNI's proposal that the minority groups abandon their rights to choose their own representatives was undemocratic. He further asserted that a number of major political parties intended to use minority representation in parliament for their own political advantages and were therefore fearful of Baperki's potential success in ensuring true minority representations.

But the most difficult objection came from within the organisation itself. Baperki leaders from Surabaya, led by one of Siauw's closest political allies, Tjoa Sik Ien, strongly rejected the proposal for active participation in the elections.

Tjoa, a former leader of the PTI, was the most influential peranakan leader in Surabaya. He was able to convince the Surabaya branch leaders to unite against Baperki's decision to independently participate in the elections. Their objections were initially raised at a number of meetings held in Jakarta, through correspondence and direct representations, but they were not able to gain popular support from the leaders of Jakarta and other branches.

It is probable that Tjoa Sik Ien based his argument on the agreement reached by Tan Ling Djie, Liem Koen Hian, Siauw Giok Tjhan and Tjoa himself in Surabaya in August 1945. As detailed earlier, these four agreed

---

[7] *Penabur*, 30 May 1954.
[8] *Sunday Courier*, 27 June 1954.

that they would not re-establish the PTI but rather became active in organisations that were not based on ethnic membership. Tjoa, evidently happy about the formation of Baperki, became a leader of its Surabaya branch. But to him, participating in elections by nominating peranakan candidates represented a violation of the agreement the four men had made.

Knowing Tjoa's disagreement over the election issue, Siauw assigned Go Gien Tjwan to attend the Surabaya branch meeting which was held in July 1954 to specifically discuss the issue. Go was able to convince most of the meeting participants that Baperki should participate in the elections but he failed to change the position of Tjoa Sik Ien and a number of other Surabaya leaders. Tjoa was able to influence the Surabaya members to adopt his position.[9]

The issue was a principal item of debate at Baperki's second congress which was held in Jakarta in early August 1954 and attended by representatives of 58 branches. Surabaya representatives distributed a written statement, prepared by Tjoa Sik Ien.[10] While the criticism was not directed at Siauw personally, it contained harsh words against Baperki's leadership. Their arguments can be summarised as follows.

Firstly, they said that, unlike the PDTI and Perwitt, Baperki was a mass organisation with a national identity. It was not supposed to be an organisation exclusively for the ethnic Chinese. By nominating Chinese candidates to represent the Chinese minority groups, Baperki would violate its own principles and would act in the same way as the PDTI and other ethnic organisations in the past.

Secondly, they argued that, as a mass organisation, Baperki could not adopt a political ideology. If Baperki were successful in the elections, its representatives in parliament would have differing political ideologies and interests. This would induce splits in the organisation and ultimately jeopardise the organisation's political objectives.

Thirdly, they stressed that by nominating its own candidates in the elections Baperki would automatically challenge political parties, including some who would otherwise be Baperki's political allies. Baperki could more effectively achieve its democratic goals by encouraging its members to support

---

[9] Interview with Go Gien Tjwan, Amsterdam, December 1993. Go recalls that he was able to obtain an overwhelming support from the meeting participants. But the minutes of the Baperki congress of August 1954 confirm that Surabaya's official position in the congress was still to object to Baperki's participation in the elections.

[10] Interview with Go Gien Tjwan, Amsterdam, December 1993.

organisations and candidates who were known to be sympathetic to these goals.[11]

Surabaya's position invited reactions from the delegates. However, only delegates from Pasuruan supported Surabaya's arguments. Most delegates refused to endorse Surabaya's position and some even considered it destructive.

The debate on the elections represented the first test for Siauw's leadership in Baperki's early days. Most delegates, former leaders of the PDTI who favoured participation in elections, were convinced that the Surabaya delegates would be easily outnumbered.[12]

Siauw was the last speaker in the session and repeated the arguments he had outlined in a number of Baperki's publications. He argued that as a mass organisation, Baperki would always have members of differing political orientations, either in parliament or in general political arenas, and that Baperki's representation in parliament would enhance Baperki's unity. Encouraging Baperki members to support parties in elections, he said, would create divisions within the organisation.[13]

When a vote was taken after the six-hour debate, Surabaya was decisively outnumbered. Fourteen votes supported Surabaya's position, while 155 accepted the active participation of Baperki in general elections.[14] Tjoa Sik Ien, disappointed by this situation, decided to leave Baperki's leadership immediately after the congress. Although he maintained a good personal relationship with Siauw and kept his membership in the organisation, he remained uninvolved in its management until 1964.[15]

This was the first major test of Siauw's political ability to lead an organisation that had influential members with diverse political views. Siauw's victorious position in this debate showed his political domination in Baperki. He was a pragmatic leader who was willing to depart from certain political principles in order to achieve certain political objectives. It is highly probable that he was in agreement with what Tjoa Sik Ien had

---

[11] To Go Gien Tjwan's surprise, the speech was not delivered by Tjoa Sik Ien who was present in the Congress.

[12] Interview with Oei Tjoe Tat, Jakarta, July 1993.

[13] Baperki Second Congress meeting minutes, 9 August 1954; *Berita Baperki*, 26 August 1954.

[14] Baperki Second Congress meeting minutes, 9 August 1954.

[15] Interviews with Siauw Giok Bie, Melbourne, May 1989 and Go Gien Tjwan, Amsterdam, December 1993.

argued. But to him, accepting Tjoa's demands would mean that minority representations in parliament would be jeopardised.

Dan Lev asserts, 'Politically acute, well-connected with and highly respected by national political leaders, Siauw turned Baperki into the most highly mobilised political organisation ever of the Indonesian Chinese'.[16]

Lev also provides an accurate observation on the characteristics of Baperki's leadership. While there were leaders from various parts of Indonesia, Baperki followed the characteristics of such major political parties as the PNI in that Baperki's central leadership was dominated by leaders from Java, in particular East Java.[17] This was reflected by the fact that Siauw's most loyal supporters continued to be a close political associate from Malang, Go Gien Tjwan; Siauw's younger brother, Siauw Giok Bie, and a number of other leaders who were involved in the activities in Malang and Surabaya prior to independence. Hence while such leaders as Yap Thiam Hien (from Aceh) and Oei Tjoe Tat (from Semarang) played important roles, Siauw remained much closer to his East Javanese associates.

Baperki's list of candidates was worked out after months of debates and negotiations in a large number of meetings at branches and in Jakarta. One early argument was about whether the list should include outsiders, such as non-Chinese people like Sidik Kertapati (leader of Acoma) and S Brata (Partai Murba) who were close allies of Siauw in Parliament. Siauw offered this suggestion but later withdrew it after it failed to receive enthusiastic support. Most Baperki members were concerned that non-Chinese representatives would not be totally committed to defending the interests of the Chinese.

On the other hand, the meeting accepted Siauw's request that one exception be made to the principle that only Baperki members should be listed. He requested the inclusion of his personal friend, Teng Tjin Leng, a Catholic and a prominent lawyer in Makasar, though Baperki had not been established in Makasar and Teng had not joined Baperki.[18] Many years later Siauw indicated that he always preferred to favour the placement of people who were not necessarily members of his inner circle in important positions. He was convinced that this strategy would generate more support

---

[16] Dan Lev, *The Political Journey of Yap Thiam Hien: The Role of the Indonesian Chinese in Shaping Modern Indonesian Life*. Ithaca, N.Y.: Southeast Asia Program Publications, Cornell University, 1991.

[17] Ibid., p.103.

[18] Baperki meeting minutes, 30 July 1954.

from sections of communities that would otherwise be indifferent to his political goals.[19]

The August 1954 Congress finally decided candidates ranked as follows:

1. Siauw Giok Tjhan
2. Go Gien Tjwan
3. Liem Tjiong Hian
4. Teng Tjin Leng
5. Auwyong Peng Koen
6. Tan Kian Lok
7. Oei Tjoe Tat
8. Yap Thiam Hien
9. Tan Hwat Tiang
10. Tan Eng Oen
11. Tan Po Goan
12. Tan Siang Lian[20]

Like the Baperki leadership, the list of candidates reflected the wide range of political spectrums within Baperki. The left political orientation was represented by Siauw and Go. The Catholic group was represented by Teng Tjin Leng and Auwyong Peng Koen. The centre group was represented by Oei Tjoe Tat, Yap Thiam Hien and Liem Tjiong Hian, and the PSI-sympathising group was represented by Tan Po Goan.

For the Konstituante, 24 candidates were nominated, with Siauw as the first candidate, followed by Auwyong Peng Koen, Oei Tjoe Tat, Go Gien Tjwan and Yap Thiam Hien. Again the list showed a gathering of forces from a wide range of political perspectives.[21]

Vote-pooling

The elections law made provision for vote-pooling arrangements between political parties and candidate bodies. Under these provisions it was possible for the surplus votes of a political party or candidate to be allocated

---

[19] Siauw's account, conveyed to the author in prison in 1973.
[20] *Berita Baperki*, 26 August 1954.
[21] Ibid.

to another political party or candidate with whom an agreement to share surplus votes had been made, at either electoral district or national level.[22]

These arrangements forced Baperki to consider a number of options as to how it might relate to other parties and groups. One option, which Baperki rejected early, was to include candidates in the list of political parties who agreed to work closely with Baperki. A second option was for Baperki to arrange to share surplus votes with political parties who agreed to work with it in particular electoral districts. A third option was to enter into nationwide vote-pooling arrangements.[23]

The first party that contacted Baperki to explore cooperation was the PSI. In a meeting, which took place in Jakarta on 29 June 1954, Subadio Sastrosatomo and Major Polak of the PSI met with Baperki, which was represented by Siauw Giok Tjhan, Khoe Woen Sioe, Yap Thiam Hien, Go Gien Tjwan and Auwyong Peng Koen. Subadio indicated that the PSI was willing to work closely with Baperki as none of Baperki's political programs conflicted with those of the PSI. However, Baperki would need to agree to join the PSI faction in parliament. PSI's support would include the supply of the PSI's high calibre peranakan candidates in Baperki's lists.[24]

The PKI was also keen to work closely with Baperki. Like the PSI, the PKI was also willing to supply their candidates in Baperki's lists, and its cooperation was not made conditional upon Baperki's agreement to join the PKI's faction. The PKI merely requested that Baperki guarantee to support the PKI's main political programs in parliament.

The party that indicated the strongest desire to cooperate with Baperki was the PRN. In July 1954, the chairman of the PRN, a close personal friend of Siauw, indicated that the PRN would only have a vote-pooling arrangement with Baperki.[25]

The country was highly polarised at the time the vote-pooling arrangement was being debated within Baperki. The Masyumi–PSI–Catholic coalition, which was not represented in the Ali cabinet, acted in opposition against the PNI-dominated cabinet, which was supported by the PKI. Arguments between these two opposing groups at high levels were intense, and sections of the army leadership were supporting the opposition against

---

[22] Feith, *The Indonesian Elections of 1955*, p. 63.
[23] Baperki meeting minutes, 22 June 1954.
[24] Baperki meeting minutes, 29 June 1954.
[25] Baperki meeting minutes, 23 July 1954. PRN's position was subsequently altered as detailed in Feith, *The Indonesian Elections of 1955*, p. 63.

what it claimed was a communist-leaning and corrupt cabinet. Such a political rift had a serious influence on the political divisions within Baperki which included, on the one hand, members who were from the PSI and Partai Katolik and, on the other, members who were from the PNI and PKI.

Siauw was initially in favour of having some vote-pooling arrangements. However, he finally decided against vote-pooling to avoid internal conflict. When the vote was taken, the advocates of vote-pooling were decisively defeated.[26]

Baperki's election campaign

Having consolidated its position to participate in the elections, Baperki quickly established the organisation's machinery for political campaigns. The organisation's election committee, comprising five members, was formed immediately after Baperki was founded. The committee's chairman was Kwee Hwat Djien, a pharmacist and a prominent member of the Sin Ming Hui. The committee's members included Auwyong Peng Koen, a lawyer and editor of the *Star Weekly* who was sympathetic to the Partai Katolik, and Yap Thiam Hien, also a lawyer. The election committee was assigned to coordinate and implement Baperki's political campaigns for the general elections.

Yap Thiam Hien, as detailed in the preceding chapter, failed to get nominated to the organisation's vice-chairmanship, but in the leadership meetings held in the first few months after Baperki was established played a significant role in the determination of the organisation's plans. It was apparent that Baperki recognised his positive contributions. When The Pek Siong, one of the vice-chairmen, resigned in August 1954 Yap was elected by the August 1954 Congress to replace him.[27] The minutes of the election committee's meetings also confirmed Yap's leadership role, and when Kwee Hwat Djien resigned from Baperki weeks before the elections were held in September 1955, Yap was assigned by Siauw to replace him.[28]

In April 1955 the government-established Central Electoral Committee announced that elections for parliament and the Konstituante were to be

---

[26] Baperki Congress meeting minutes, 9 August 1954.

[27] The Pek Siong was the first leader to leave Baperki. It is not clear what motivated him to leave Baperki so early in the piece. The Congress minutes indicated that he resigned because of health reasons.

[28] Baperki meeting minutes, 26 May 1955.

held on 29 September 1955 and 15 December 1955 respectively. Like all other political organisations that had been preparing for these elections, Baperki quickly developed its election plans and formulated its election guidelines.

Siauw was assigned to generate the election guidelines which were then published in *Berita Baperki* and distributed to all branches in April 1955. Siauw formulated the guidelines as follows.

Firstly, Siauw re-emphasised the importance of highlighting that Baperki was not a political party, and that it was a mass organisation whose members were Indonesian citizens concerned with nation building and realising a society free from racial discrimination. Siauw re-affirmed that, as a mass organisation, Baperki had no political ideology and that it included people of differing political views and commitments. Baperki's main objectives, Siauw emphasised, included the realisation of a democratic state and the elimination of colonialism.

Secondly, Baperki would fight for the citizenship issue to be resolved in a way that enabled as many Indonesians of foreign descent as possible to be Indonesian citizens.

Thirdly, Baperki would fight against racial discrimination and campaign for the passing of a law to enshrine the country's motto, Bhineka Tunggal Ika (Unity in Diversity) in the implementation of government laws and regulations. It would also fight for adherence to the United Nations' Universal Declaration of Human Rights which opposes racial discrimination and prejudice.

With respect to general political issues related to the national economy, women's rights and education, Baperki would also fight for laws and regulations which would guarantee the exploitation of natural resources for the people's benefit, the realisation of social justice, equal rights for women in all fields and the provision of education to all citizens without consideration of ethnic or financial background.

Finally, Siauw confirmed Baperki's intention to provide effective minority representation in both parliament and the Konstituante, a representation which, in Siauw's definition, would be free from any individual party's political agendas.

Equipped with these election programs, Baperki leaders began to actively campaign for the elections in August 1955. The central leaders, including Siauw, Yap Thiam Hien, Go Gien Tjwan, Oei Tjoe Tat and Auwyong Peng Koen, travelled extensively in Java, Sumatra, Sulawesi and Kalimantan. The campaigns were directed at gaining as much support as possible from the peranakan communities in Java and Madura, which were estimated to contain in excess of 600 000 individuals.[29] Although the number of Chinese was probably just as high on other islands, they were mostly aliens and ineligible to vote.

Siauw and Go Gien Tjwan often travelled together when visiting the regencies of Java. They were often surprised to find the enthusiasm of the peranakan communities in remote areas.

Siauw's reputation as a political figure who had defended the peranakans' interests in various fields and his ability to use simple language when detailing the political problems peranakans were facing and what Baperki could offer them prompted a large number people of all ages, who would normally be uninterested in politics, to come to campaign meetings. Old peranakan ladies in their sarongs came from remote areas in trucks and old buses to go to meeting places to listen to speeches by Siauw and the other leaders.[30]

Baperki leaders sought to give the impression that the organisation was politically balanced. During the campaigns, they attempted to mix leaders who were known to be leftists with those who tended to have right-wing sympathies. When Baperki decided to send their Jakarta leaders to Pontianak and other cities in West Kalimantan, Auwyong Peng Koen, Oei Tjoe Tat and Siauw were assigned to the task.[31] In other instances, Go Gien Tjwan was paired with Yap Thiam Hien.[32]

Baperki's emphasis in the elections differed from that of the parties in that it focused its intention on peranakan communities that shared common interests and problems. Hence Baperki's selling points could be easily conveyed to its audience. Other parties needed to differentiate their individual organisations from each other by highlighting political programs that were often difficult for villagers to comprehend.[33]

For most political parties, large attendance at mass meetings in villages or small towns could not be used to measure the amount of support or, more importantly, the number of votes the parties could rely on in the ballot. Most people in small towns and villages tended to come to meetings

---

[29] Somers, *Peranakan Chinese Politics in Indonesia*, p. 147.

[30] Interviews with Go Gien Tjwan, Oei Tjoe Tat and Siauw Giok Bie. Go recalls how people at these meetings were willing to sit quietly and attentively to listen to Siauw's often long and repetitious explanations on citizenship, racial discrimination and Baperki's political platforms.

[31] Oei, *Memoar Oei Tjoe Tat*, pp. 75–78.

[32] Lev, *Political Journey of Yap Thiam Hien*, p. 105.

[33] Feith, *Indonesian Elections of 1955*, p. 18.

out of curiosity or for the festive atmosphere.[34] In Baperki's case, however, when a large number of peranakans came to hear the political speeches, one could safely assume that they were there to get to know an organisation they hoped to be able to turn to for protection. Hence, the size of attendance at Baperki's mass meetings, as proved by the election results later, was a direct measurement of how Baperki would perform.

In the campaigns, Baperki's leaders outlined the disadvantages of relying on political parties to fight for minority rights. Siauw, in particular, was able to refer to specific policies which were either introduced or supported by leaders of some political parties who, at that time, had peranakan members in parliament.

Siauw was particularly critical of the policies of Sumitro Djojohadikusumo of the PSI who, as minister of economic affairs in the Natsir cabinet, had introduced measures that severely limited the involvement of traders of foreign descent in the importation of various goods. Siauw declared that these measures had led to the formation of Ali Baba companies (companies in which Indigenous citizens were merely front men for Chinese traders) which badly affected the country's economy and created unnecessary burdens for Chinese traders. He also accused PSI parliamentarians of creating unnecessary doubts about the loyalty of Indonesian citizens of Chinese descent.

Siauw also criticised the policies of Iskaq, the PNI minister of economic affairs in the first 14 months of the Ali Sastroamidjojo cabinet. Siauw indicated that when Iskaq was minister for economic affairs, he introduced and implemented the Asli policies which seriously jeopardised the Indonesian Chinese traders' opportunities in Indonesia. Other examples of the PNI's anti-Chinese policies, according to Siauw, included regulations that stopped the Chinese from being involved in rice milling and limited the running of public transport companies by people of Chinese descent. These actions, according to Baperki leaders, were taken to maximise opportunities to collect funds for parties and to enrich party leaders.

These examples, Baperki claimed, were the strongest indications that minority rights could not be fought for through party platforms. Baperki also claimed to be free from such political motivations and to be committed to working solely to eliminate the grievances of minorities and fighting for the introduction of policies which would protect the interests of the minority groups.

---

[34] Ibid., p. 22.

The enthusiasm of the peranakan Chinese for Baperki created tension with parties like the PSI and Partai Katolik who had previously had peranakan support. This led to divisions within Baperki's leadership in the month before the 29 September elections.

Baperki enjoyed widespread peranakan support in most places in Java and some places in Sumatra. In South Kalimantan, where most peranakans were Catholics, Baperki had little success. The Partai Katolik was able to convince most of the peranakans in this area not to vote for Baperki, which they declared to be a communist organisation. There was also resentment against Siauw for the deportation from Indonesia of Pastor Wang, a Taiwanese pastor who had worked in the area. The deportation order was issued by Minister for Justice Djody Gondokusumo, known to be a close friend of Siauw.[35]

The PSI also began to urge their peranakan supporters to desert Baperki. Tan Po Goan, a prominent PSI leader and a candidate in Baperki's list was the first one to declare his resignation from Baperki. Tan, however, left without criticising Baperki and remained a good friend of Siauw. He justified his action by confirming his intention to represent only the PSI in the elections.[36] Not long after Tan left Baperki, Khoe Woen Sioe, also a strong PSI supporter and director of *Keng Po*, resigned as one of Baperki's vice-chairmen. Like Tan Po Goan, he left on good terms, and maintained his Baperki membership.[37]

The friendly departures of Tan Po Goan and Khoe Woen Sioe contrasted with that of Injo Beng Goat, editor of *Keng Po*, who was also a PSI candidate for parliament. Injo left Baperki not long before Khoe Woen Sioe resigned from his vice-chairmanship.

In his articles published in *Keng Po* on 9, 13 and 24 September 1955, days before the elections, Injo attacked Siauw and Go Gien Tjwan as communists. Siauw had been close to Amir Sjarifuddin and Tan Ling Djie in 1948, Injo said, and was therefore involved in the Madiun Affair. Injo further warned the communities that after the departure of Tan Po Goan and Khoe Woen Sioe, Baperki was now under the influence of communists and to side with Baperki would therefore be dangerous. The *Keng Po* articles also predicted that without leaders of the calibre of Tan and Khoe, Baperki

---

[35] Siauw, *Lima Jaman*, p. 250.

[36] Interview with Oei Tjoe Tat, who ran a law firm with Tan Po Goan, Jakarta, July 1993.

[37] Interview with Oei Tjoe Tat, Jakarta, July 1993; *Berita Baperki*, 7 October 1955.

would fall apart. Injo further encouraged readers to follow his lead to elect the PSI.[38]

In response to Injo's allegations, Baperki issued a number of articles which were published in *Berita Baperki* and other publications. These articles claimed that Siauw's personal friendship with Amir Sjarifuddin and Tan Ling Djie did not make him a communist. They attacked Injo as an opportunist who had been closer to the Dutch than to the republican government during the revolution. Referring to his personal friendship with the Dutch JD Katz, they alleged that he was against the re-incorporation of West Irian into Indonesia. Baperki requested the PWI to sanction *Keng Po* for misleading the public about Baperki.[39]

Baperki's election campaign up to this point was quite free from attacks on other parties. But Injo's articles and the PSI's apparent support for Injo's position prompted Baperki attacks on the PSI. Baperki alleged that the PSI did nothing in combating racial discrimination policies and that it was supporting Asli policies, which discriminated against citizens of foreign origins.

Right–left tensions within Baperki also came to the fore in the form of arguments about the order in which the group's candidates were listed. Two weeks before the election, the Catholic lawyer, Auwyong Peng Koen, listed as Baperki's fifth candidate, approached Oei Tjoe Tat and Yap Thiam Hien, ranked seventh and eighth in the list respectively, to indicate his dissatisfaction with the list of preferences.[40] Auwyong argued that if Baperki were represented by Siauw and Go, whom he described as leftists, Baperki would not effectively represent the political views of all its members. Auwyong suggested that the second candidate, Go Gien Tjwan, be replaced by someone like himself to balance Siauw's left-wing political orientation.

In response to this, Siauw agreed that the ranking which had been determined in Baperki congress of August 1955 be modified. Go agreed to be dropped from the second ranking but was unwilling to see his seat go to Auwyong. Other possibilities should also be considered, he said, including the Protestant, Yap Thiam Hien, or the Catholic lawyer, Teng Tjin Leng.[41]

---

[38] *Keng Po*, 9, 13, 24 September 1955.

[39] *Berita Baperki* 7 October 1955; *Antara*, 26 September 1955. No action was subsequently taken by PWI against *Keng Po*.

[40] Prior to this, Auwyong left Baperki briefly over his disagreement on Baperki's opposition to the closure of Chinese schools in Indonesia. But he rejoined Baperki.

[41] Interview with Go Gien Tjwan, Amsterdam, December 1993, *Berita Baperki* 7 October 1955.

In a meeting attended by Siauw, Oei, Yap, Go and Auwyong on 16 September 1955, Auwyong was advised that Go Gien Tjwan was willing to let his electoral advantage go to another candidate. Although no commitment was made by the participants of this meeting that Auwyong would definitely replace Go as the second candidate, Auwyong expected that this would happen. Go said that he would announce his willingness to vacate the second position at the Baperki congress to be held on 19 September 1955.[42]

The congress, however, voted not to replace Go, and Auwyong did not openly challenge this decision at the congress.[43] Disappointed by this decision, Auwyong decided to join Injo Beng Goat in attacking Baperki. On 26 September 1955, three days before the election, he published a letter in *Keng Po* declaring his resignation from Baperki. He accused Siauw and Go of being communists and claimed that he had not been fairly treated by the organisation with respect to his candidature for parliament. He warned the readers to be wary of Baperki's political orientation as its communist inclinations would invite unfavourable reactions from Islamic groups against the Chinese communities.[44]

Yap Thiam Hien, Go Gien Tjwan and Oei Tjoe Tat all sent letters to *Keng Po* on 26 September condemning Auwyong Peng Koen for being an opportunist, a liar and unethical. Only Oei's letter was published by *Keng Po*. The letters of Yap and Go were then published in *Berita Baperki* on 7 October 1955.

Siauw himself did not join the others in condemning Auwyong and Injo Beng Goat. His written response, not published by *Keng Po* but contained in *Berita Baperki* of 7 October 1955, did not refer to Auwyong, arguing merely that Baperki would continue to represent a wide range of political views.[45]

The campaign ended on 24 September 1955, and political organisations waited for the results of the 29 September ballot. More than 39 million Indonesians went to the polls, with 37 875 299 votes considered valid. Because of technical and communication problems only 85 per cent of the votes were cast on 29 September, with the remaining votes cast over the next four weeks.[46] On 15 December 1955, the exercise was repeated for the Konstituante.

---

[42] Interviews with Go Gien Tjwan and Oei Tjoe Tat, December1993. Yap Thiam Hien's letter published in *Berita Baperki*, 7 October 1955.

[43] Interviews with Go Gien Tjwan and Oei Tjoe Tat, December 1993.

[44] *Keng Po*, 26 September 1955.

[45] *Berita Baperki* 7 October 1955. Siauw was well known for his conciliatory attitude.

[46] Feith, *Indonesian Elections of* 1955, p. 39.

The election results

Ten days after ballot day, results of the elections began to emerge. The results were surprising and significantly altered the pattern of representation in parliament. In terms of the increased number of parliamentary seats, NU was by far the largest winner, followed by the PKI. The big losers included the PRN, PSI, PIR, Partai Murba and SKI.

Despite the exodus of leaders from Baperki in the last weeks of the campaign, Baperki performed well at the election. Baperki's total votes were 178 887 for parliament and 160 456 for the Konstituante – Table 7.1 shows the votes collected by Baperki.[47] From this table, one can see that about 80 per cent of Baperki's votes were collected in Java. Baperki's results indicate that it was able to secure around 70 per cent of the Chinese votes in Java. Baperki clearly gained more peranakan votes than any other organisation.[48]

In some ballot places, Baperki outperformed major parties. In some cities, like Semarang, Bandung and Cirebon, its votes were among the highest.[49] There were some surprises. The village of Bobotsari, near Purbolinggo in

Provinces	Parliament	Konstituante
East Java	35 489	33 369
Central Java	44 743	44 908
West Java	38 376	33 595
Jakarta	26 944	23 384
South Sumatra	10 178	8496
Central Sumatra	4495	3918
North Sumatra	4674	4044
South Kalimantan	2132	1981
East Kalimantan	536	441
North Sulawesi	2195	2100
South Sulawesi	1462	1165
East Nusa Tenggara	3784	1111
West Nusa Tenggara	3859	1981

Table 7.1: Baperki's votes by province

---

[47] Ibid., p. 65; Somers, *Peranakan Chinese Politics In Indonesia*, p. 146.
[48] Somers, *Peranakan Chinese Politics In Indonesia*, pp. 147–148.
[49] Ibid., p. 148; *Antara* 6 October 1955; *Berita Baperki*, 7 October 1955.

Central Java, had no Chinese inhabitants and yet Baperki received all the votes, apparently because its symbol the lotus flower was seen as a symbol of Kejawen, the religion of Javanese who wanted to emphasise that they were syncretists rather than Muslims.[50]

Baperki's 178 887 votes entitled it to one seat in parliament. Siauw, as the first candidate in Baperki's list, occupied this seat. Because Baperki had no vote-pooling arrangement with other political parties, its surplus of some 43 000 votes, the second largest surplus after that of the PKI, could not be used to add another seat for Baperki. Another peranakan who gained a seat in parliament through the elections was Tjoo Tik Tjoen, a candidate in the PKI's list. Tjoo, then 34, was also a leader of Baperki in Surabaya. At the time of his election to parliament, he was the secretary of its Surabaya branch.

As the electoral laws provided that the Chinese minority should be represented by at least nine members, the government needed to appoint seven others. Clause 136 of the election law stated that appointees representing the Chinese, Arab and Indo-European minorities would be chosen on the basis of the wishes of the minority groups concerned. Siauw, in a statement issued in February 1956, argued that the rights of the minority groups could only be properly defended if the appointees were picked from the lists of representatives submitted by credible minority organisations, not from lists prepared by political parties.[51]

In the same month, Baperki and GIKI (Gabungan Indo untuk Kesatuan Indonesia – Association of Indo-Europeans for Indonesian Unity) issued a joint statement signed by Siauw Giok Tjhan and WRC Meinke requesting the active involvement of President Soekarno in appointing minority representatives to ensure that the representatives nominated by the minority groups were those actually appointed by the government.[52]

Baperki campaigned to become the sole organisation to provide the list of candidates who would represent Chinese minority groups to be considered by the government. Attempts were made to highlight the support the organisation received from the peranakan communities. Baperki collected more than 67 000 signatures confirming the endorsement of Tan Hong Hie, Baperki's treasurer in Semarang; Teng Tjin Leng, a Catholic lawyer

---

[50] Siauw, *Lima Jaman*, p. 265
[51] *Berita Baperki*, 15 March 1856.
[52] Ibid.

in Makasar, and Yap Thiam Hien in Semarang. Yap Thiam Hien's nomination was also supported by peranakan Protestant communities in Jakarta.[53] Several parties followed suit, also producing lists of peranakan candidates and submitting them to the government.

In August 1956, various newspapers published the names of seven Chinese minority representatives to be appointed by the government. Six of these seven men were also members of the parties represented in the post-election Ali Sastroamidjojo cabinet. One was from Parkindo, one from the Partai Katolik, two from the NU and two from the PNI. The government did not confirm or deny these reports.[54]

Siauw responded in the same month with a written question to the prime minister, minister for justice and minister for home affairs. Siauw argued that the suggested appointees had not been involved in the elections as candidates for the minority groups and were therefore unknown to the minority groups.

To the Chinese minority groups, Siauw added, these appointees were not minority representatives but rather party representatives. Siauw demanded that the government adhere to Clause 136 of the electoral laws, which detailed the requirement to satisfy the wishes of the Chinese minority groups.

Baperki's arguments were supported by the PKI and other non-government parties. Sakirman of the PKI criticised the government's action and explained that the PKI did not intend to reduce the number of minority representation by claiming Tjoo Tik Tjoen, elected to parliament using the PKI's ticket, to be one of the minority representatives. Sakirman further added that the appointments should be made from the list of candidates produced by organisations who had the largest surplus of votes.[55]

On 30 October 1956, Siauw questioned the government in his interpellation, which was supported by the PKI's Tjoo Tik Tjoen, independent members Bung Tomo and Imam Sutardjo, and communist parliamentarians Hartojo and Suprapto. Siauw argued that the government had violated the spirit of the electoral law with respect to minority representation and ignored the wishes of the minority groups. If the government wanted to offer representation to the Chinese minority on the basis of the religious outlooks of its members, it should include members of the Sam Kauw

---

[53] *Berita Baperki*, 15 November 1955.
[54] *Berita Baperki*, 15 September 1956.
[55] *Republik*, 6 September 1956.

religious group[56], which he said represented the majority in the Indonesian Chinese communities.

Siauw argued that Tan Hong Hie in Semarang, representing Baperki and the Sam Kauw group, had collected the signatures of 22 000 Chinese; Liem Tjiong Hian in Palembang, representing Baperki and the Sam Kauw group, had collected 16 000 signatures; Yap Thiam Hien, in Jakarta, representing Baperki and Protestants had obtained 17 000. Teng Tjin Leng in Makasar, he said, was endorsed by the Catholic peranakans in Makassar. And Go Gien Tjwan, the second candidate on Baperki's original list, should be given a seat in view of Baperki's 43 000 surplus votes.[57]

In his response, Minister for Justice Muljatno, confirmed that the government intended to appoint seven minority representatives nominated by parties who did not have peranakan members in parliament. He argued that since Baperki and the PKI had won seats in parliament, they would not be given additional seats. He also argued that the allocations of seats would not alter the balance of party representation within parliament.[58]

Dissatisfied with Muljatno's response, Siauw moved a corrective motion. This time, the motion was supported by Tjoo Tik Tjoen, Moh, Yamin, Imam Sutardjo, Hartojo and Suprapto. It demanded the cancellation of the government's appointments for the Chinese minority representation in parliament and the introduction of new government regulations that would guarantee true minority representations in both parliament and the Konstituante. Siauw assembled support from members of his Fraksi Nasional Progresif, the PKI and other non-government political parties.

This brought about a compromise. Muljatno was forced to emphasise that Siauw's motion was not a motion of no confidence, and that he would be prepared to review the list of appointees.[59] Following Mulyatno's public announcement, Siauw withdrew his motion on 14 December 1956.[60]

By late 1956, the Ali cabinet was on the back foot, with attacks coming from various sides. A concession in the area of minority representations was perhaps seen as necessary to reduce further political damage. As part of the compromise, Baperki was granted a second seat in parliament. To everyone's surprise, Siauw decided to nominate Ang Tjiang Liat, a prominent

---

[56] Sam Kauw incorporates elements of Buddhism, Confucianism and Taoism.
[57] *Risalah Parlemen*, 1956.
[58] *Berita Baperki*, 15 December 1956.
[59] Ibid.
[60] *Republik*, 15 December 1955.

judge in Banjarmasin and a member of the Central Electoral Committee, to occupy this additional seat. Ang had not been on Baperki's original list of candidates, but was included in Baperki's list of candidates to be appointed. Siauw was presumably concerned with healing divisions within Baperki. If he had chosen Go Gien Tjwan, the charge would be made that Baperki was represented only by leftists. If he chose the Protestant Yap Thiam Hien, the Catholic groups might be disappointed. Likewise, if Teng Tjin Leng, the Catholic candidate, was appointed, the Protestants would feel aggrieved.[61]

Ang Tjiang Liat took the seat, which was supposed to be occupied by the NU's Ko Kwat Oen, a Protestant, who was initially a Baperki leader in Bandung and was listed as a candidate by Baperki. Ko left Baperki after the elections and joined the NU, who was willing to nominate him as its candidate for government appointment. Ko, who became a Konstituante member representing the NU, was expelled by Baperki in December 1956 for his attacks on the organisation.[62]

For the Konstituante, the compromise significantly increased Baperki's representation. Baperki was able to get two Konstituante seats through the elections. These seats were occupied by Siauw and Oei Tjoe Tat. Three other peranakans were elected, namely Tan Ling Djie and Oey Hay Djoen of the PKI and Tony Wen of the PNI. Under the compromise arrangement, the government agreed to allocate an additional seven seats to Baperki. These seats were occupied by Yap Thiam Hien, Go Gien Tjwan, Liem Koen Seng, Oen Poe Djiang, Jan Ave and CS Richter. The last two were representatives of the European minority groups.[63]

Baperki learned from its mistake in 1955. For the regional elections held in 1957, it decided not to waste any of its surplus votes and therefore decided to enter into vote-pooling arrangements. The most successful vote-pooling arrangements for the organisation were with the PKI; however, it also made similar arrangements with the NU, PNI, Parkindo, Partai Katolik, PIR and PSII, thanks largely to Siauw's close personal relationship with these parties' leaders.

By 1957 Baperki had established itself as the most capable organisation to defend the interests of peranakan Chinese. Using this reputation, Baperki actively campaigned in Java, Sumatra, Sulawesi and Kalimantan.

---

[61] Interviews with Go Gien Tjwan, Amsterdam, December 1993 and Oei Tjoe Tat, Jakarta, July 1993.
[62] Minutes of the Baperki Congress in December 1956.
[63] *Republik*, 21 November 1957.

Baperki's performances in some areas were significantly increased, particularly in East Java where Baperki's votes rose from 35 489 in the 1955 elections to 70 770. Although the total number of votes for Baperki did not significantly increase, due to the decline of votes across all political parties except the PKI Baperki's proportion of the total votes significantly increased.[64]

The decision of which political parties to ally with was left to regional Baperki leaders[65] but the general tendency was to ally with parties expected to perform well. In East Java and Central Java, Baperki tended to ally with the PKI. In West Java, it tended to ally with other parties.[66]

These elections resulted in Baperki having representatives in most regional parliaments. Prominent Baperki leaders like Liem Koen Seng, Tan Eng Tie and Lie Tjwan Sien were elected to the Jakarta regional parliament. In other cities, Baperki was represented by its regional leaders.

Siauw regarded the elections and Baperki's campaigns as effective means to provide political training to a large number of Chinese. Prior to and during the campaigns, a number of Baperki branches were established and many activists were recruited who developed as the organisation's most committed members and helped it grow rapidly. One of Baperki's important achievements was related to its ability to incite Chinese participation and interest in national politics.

Having proved that Baperki received widespread support from the Chinese communities, Siauw focused his attention on issues of great importance for the Chinese – citizenship, economics and education.

---

[64] Mary Somers, *Peranakan Chinese Politics in Indonesia*, p. 158.
[65] Baperki meeting minutes, September 1957.
[66] Mary Somers, *Peranakan Chinese Politics in Indonesia*, p. 159.

Chapter 7

CITIZENSHIP AND DUAL NATIONALITY

As detailed previously, those who founded Baperki in March 1954 wanted to combat moves by certain leaders of the government to reduce the number of Indonesian citizens who were of Chinese descent.

Siauw's success in halting the government's plans to introduce a new citizenship law which would have made many Indonesian citizens of Chinese descent foreigners was short lived. Not long after Baperki was formed in March 1954, the controversial Citizenship Bill was reintroduced to parliament by the government.

Several months after this, the Republic of Indonesia and People's Republic of China commenced discussions on dual-nationality issues which were concluded by a dual nationality treaty signed by Prime Minister Chou En Lai and Foreign Minister Sunario in April 1955. Both the bill and treaty called for a reopening of the question of the citizenship of people of Chinese origin who had opted for Indonesian citizenship under the passive choice arrangements of the RTC Agreement of 1949.

This chapter outlines Siauw's battles against proponents of an active system and the roles he played in relation to the citizenship law of 1958.

The proposed Citizenship Bill, which was withdrawn in March 1954, was reintroduced to parliament with some changes on 15 October 1954. The main changes were related to the definition of who would have dual nationality. Under the revised bill, only those who represented the first generation of immigrants, that is, people whose parents were born in China, would be treated as people who had dual nationality. The timing of the introduction of the bill almost coincided with the commencement of negotiations with China on matters concerning dual nationality.

The article in contention (Article 4) provided that foreigners and people of foreign descent could obtain Indonesian citizenship if they fulfilled all three of the following conditions:

1. They must have been born in Indonesia and must have their residence in Indonesia.
2. Their fathers must have been born in Indonesia and must have resided there continuously for at least ten years before their births.
3. Within one year after reaching eighteen years of age, they must go to the nearest court of justice and make an official declaration requesting Indonesian citizenship and repudiating their other citizenship.

These provisions effectively limited the granting of Indonesian citizenship to third generation residents in Indonesia. Passage of the bill would mean that Chinese who had acquired Indonesian citizenship under the 'passive choice' system of the 1949 RTC Agreement would lose their citizenship unless they could prove that their fathers were born in Indonesia and had resided there for at least ten years continuously before they were born, and they made an official declaration rejecting Chinese citizenship.

The government attempted to justify the bill by indicating that *jus soli* extended only to the first generation gives not the slightest assurance that persons of foreign descent will regard Indonesia as their native land. If such persons have resided there for generations or if they have no country of origin, it may be properly accepted that they regard Indonesia as their own country.[1]

In his speeches in parliament and press statements in October and November 1954, Siauw stated that it was impossible for many of the people concerned to prove that their parents were born in Indonesia and that they had lived in Indonesia for ten years continuously. Civil registration for the Chinese came into effect in Java and several other places outside Java in 1919 and in the whole of the Indies in March 1925.[2] Furthermore, many of these registration records had been destroyed in the revolutionary wars. The passing of this bill in its existing form, he declared, would jeopardise nine years of hard work in generating feelings of true citizenship among citizens of foreign descent.

Depriving large numbers of people of citizenship would be violating the international convention on nationality created at The Hague in 1930, by which one's citizenship could not be arbitrarily cancelled. Persons who had dual nationality, Siauw said, should be regarded as citizens of

---

[1] Willmott, *National Status of the Chinese in Indonesia*, p. 36.
[2] Ong, *Chineezen in Nederlandsch–Indie*, p. 44.

both countries until such time as they rejected the citizenship of one. The Indonesian Chinese who had become Indonesian citizens should remain so. The fact that they also had Chinese nationality, because of the Chinese Government's citizenship law, which was produced and implemented beyond their control, should not change their status as Indonesian citizens.

On 10 November 1954, Baperki asked the government to redraft the bill. It proposed that the articles which provided for the Chinese to prove that their parents had been residents of Indonesia for ten years continuously and the requirement for the Chinese to actively declare their wishes to be Indonesian citizens in courts be dropped altogether. It also counterattacked by asking that special provision be made for people who had rejected Indonesian citizenship between 27 December 1949 and 27 December 1951, giving them an opportunity to reconsider their decision.[3]

We have seen Siauw as a supporter of the Ali Sastroamidjojo cabinet. He knew Prime Minister Ali well. A number of senior ministers in the cabinet were members of his Fraksi Nasional Progresif in parliament, as were two peranakan ministers, Ong Eng Die and Lie Kiat Teng.

Ironically, Djody Gondokusumo, of the PRN, as justice minister presented the Citizenship Bill. Djody was not only a member of Siauw's Fraksi Nasional Progresif but also a close personal friend who frequently visited Siauw's house. Furthermore, Sunario of the PNI, the then minister for foreign affairs, whom Siauw saw as the driving force behind the proposal for an active system, was also a friend of Siauw. Like Djody, he too was often seen at Siauw's place in Jakarta.[4]

This showed that personal association, even political association, at times did not result in full political alliance in parliament. There were party disciplines and interests that went beyond personal relationships. On the other hand, interestingly enough in this period, there were instances whereby personal relationship played a role in getting certain bills supported regardless of parties' official lines.

Although the bill was officially signed by Djody, Siauw never referred it as the document prepared by Djody. He always referred to it as the government's document, or as the document prepared by the Ministry of Justice.

It is likely that the bill was never discussed in cabinet meetings. Dr Lie Kiat Teng, health minister and a member of the PSII, claimed in a press interview that he was not aware of any cabinet discussion of the bill. He

---

[3] *Berita Baperki*, October–November 1954.
[4] Interviews with Go Gien Tjwan and Tan Hwie Kiat, Amsterdam, December 1993.

added that his party would not support it and would continue to support the Citizenship Act of 1946, which incorporated the passive system.[5]

Siauw continued to dominate the debates in parliament opposing the bill. He was supported by spokesmen of the pro-government parties who were mostly members of his Fraksi Nasional Progresif and the PKI. Spokesmen of the opposition parties, Masyumi, PSI, Partai Katolik and Parkindo, also opposed the bill. The opposition to the bill was obviously, in part, politically motivated but most of the arguments presented were along the lines used by Siauw.

Although no party made any official statement supporting the bill, it was generally understood that the PNI (Sunario's party) and PRN (Djody's party) supported it.[6]

In responding to Siauw's questions about the bill in parliament, Djody was willing to consider modifications of it. With regard to the requirement to prove that one's father was born in Indonesia and had lived in Indonesia for ten years continuously before one was born, Djody said that if the necessary documentation was not available, statements supported by a number of witnesses would suffice. The government did not view the bill as final, he said, and would be willing to consider variations which were supported by the majority of members of parliament.[7]

The bill was not discussed in a plenary session of parliament. It was only discussed in a number of parliamentary sections. One section passed a resolution requesting the government to withdraw the bill. Another section proposed that the government postpone discussions on the bill until after discussions with China on dual nationality were concluded. Fearing its defeat in parliament, the government decided to again withdraw the bill in November 1954.

Soon after this, obviously influenced by his personal relationship with Siauw, Djody's position on the matter changed dramatically. From the beginning of 1955 Djody frequently spoke on citizenship issues at functions organised by Baperki. Together with Siauw and other Baperki leaders, he travelled to Semarang, Surabaya, Malang, Yogyakarta and other places outside Java to explain his views. In these talks, he supported Baperki's view that all Chinese residing and born in Indonesia who did not reject Indonesian citizenship on or before 27 December 1951 should remain

---

[5] *Sin Min*, 11 November 1954.
[6] Willmott, *National Status of The Chinese in Indonesia*, p. 39.
[7] *Sin Po*, 1 November 1954.

Indonesian citizens. Although he did not categorically state that the new law would be based on the passive principles embodied in the 1946 legislation and RTC Agreement, he strongly hinted that he would support these principles[8].

Proof of citizenship

While the Citizenship Bill was being debated, the Indonesian Chinese also faced bureaucratic harassment because of a new regulation setting out that people of foreign descent needed to prove that they were Indonesian citizens. The document which was used to provide this proof was generally known as the STKI (Surat Tanda Kewarganegaraan Indonesia – Proof of Indonesian Citizenship), or 'kartu kuning' ('yellow card'), and was introduced in 1954.

The regulation on the proof of citizenship was issued by a body called UPBA (Urusan Peranakan dan Bangsa Asing – Bureau of Minority and Alien Affairs), established in early 1954 within the Ministry of Home Affairs. In May 1954 the bureau issued a plan which required all people of foreign descent to be issued with the STKI. The formulation became public when the head of UPBA, Oetojo, wrote letters to the heads of UPBA regional offices indicating that citizens of foreign descent could only participate in the elections if they could produce an STKI[9].

Siauw quickly disputed the legality of these letters saying the UPBA was not authorised by any law to issue instructions demanding the presentation of STKIs. After Oetojo's letters were issued, Djody, as justice minister, wrote a letter to the Ministry of Home Affairs stating that the instructions were unlawful. Siauw was also able to obtain Djody's confirmation in parliament that no-one should be forced to obtain an STKI to prove their Indonesian citizenship.[10]

But the STKI system remained in existence. While acknowledging that it was not compulsory for people of foreign descent to obtain an STKI, Oetojo said it would be useful for them to have one.[11] These statements appeared to have encouraged various government agencies and officials

---

[8] *Berita Baperki*, 26 February 1955. Interviews with Go Gien Tjwan, Oei Tjoe Tat and Tan Hwie Kiat.

[9] *Berita Baperki*, 26 June 1954.

[10] *Risalah Parlemen* 1954.

[11] *Keng Po*, 5 July 1954.

to use the STKI system to extract bribes and make it harder for people to operate in various fields. Chinese people were forced to produce their STKIs to obtain passports, to enrol their children at schools, to obtain business licences and to borrow money from banks. Without an STKI, they were treated as foreigners.[12]

One of the major problems faced by Siauw was the widespread perception that many Chinese would bribe their way around any law. Siauw argued in parliament that the STKI system would create a minority complex which would be difficult to solve. He also argued that if people could buy STKIs, then the cards did not have acceptable and legitimate value as proof of citizenship.

Based on these arguments, Siauw demanded that the government reconfirm its instruction that no-one was required to obtain an STKI, that Indonesian citizens who did not have an STKI should nevertheless be treated as Indonesian citizens, that the government replace the UPBA within the Ministry of Home Affairs with a committee which consisted of minority representatives and public servants representing the ministries of Justice, Home Affairs, and Economic Affairs, and that this committee be charged with the solution of problems related to ethnic minorities. In July 1954, the contents of Siauw's speeches were summarised in Baperki's memorandum on the STKI and signed by Siauw and Go Gien Tjwan.

In July 1954, the minister of home affairs, Hazairin of the PIR, confirmed in parliament that the STKI was not a condition of Indonesian citizenship, that it was not compulsory to obtain an STKI, that an STKI was only to be issued if it was applied for and that the government would take action regarding proper civil registration for all citizens.[13]

Many of the misapplications of the STKI system were rectified after Baperki's intervention. Instructions were sent from Jakarta to regional offices to ensure that no citizens were registered as aliens. Officials were informed that STKIs were not required to prove Indonesian citizenship and that other documents such as birth certificates supported by a letter from the appropriate court of justice that the bearer had not rejected Indonesian citizenship would suffice. The minister of home affairs finally decreed that no STKI certificates would be issued after 1 March 1956.[14]

---

[12] *Berita Baperki*, 26 July 1954.
[13] *Berita Baperki*, October–November 1954.
[14] Willmott, *National Status of the Chinese in Indonesia*, p. 81

The success of Baperki in combating the STKI system and the unpopular Citizenship Bill significantly helped Baperki's position in the eyes of the peranakans. But many government agencies ignored the ministerial decree and continued to require STKIs before granting licenses and privileges.

After 1 March 1956, the Chinese in Indonesia were not able to obtain STKIs but these certificates were still required to obtain various licenses. Hence, a large number of Chinese who needed STKIs to obtain various business licenses were not able to obtain them. The requirements for STKIs were finally stopped by the introduction of a citizenship decree of 4 June 1957, issued by the army chief of staff under the martial law provisions introduced three months earlier, which required all citizens who needed proof of citizenship to obtain court certificates on citizenship.

The fees for these court certificates were relatively high and were considered too heavy for most Chinese. Siauw strongly criticised the government for introducing the fees and demanded for a significant reduction. In a meeting Siauw had with Prime Minister Djuanda, reported in *Sin Po* and *Keng Po*, Djuanda promised to review the fees and said that the government did not intend to use the system as a means of raising revenue. Before the much-resented regulation was altered in October 1957, many incidents due to the misapplication of the regulation and confusion were reported in newspapers.[15]

In his speeches in parliament, Siauw also demanded that the regulation be better defined and its application be limited solely to situations that required the issuing of court certificates.

The revised regulation issued in October reflected consideration of Siauw's demands. It specified that proof of citizenship was to be pursued only if the government agency concerned was in the process of distinguishing one's citizenship status. Thus, these certificates would be required for persons who needed licenses or permits which were not available to aliens, but not for matters such as driving licenses.

In March 1958, all military decrees issued under the state of emergency expired, including the regulation about court certificates of citizenship. The decree for court certificates was renewed and the fee was reduced from 1000 rupiahs to 60 rupiahs.[16]

---

[15] Ibid., p. 82–83.
[16] Ibid., p. 84.

The problem of dual nationality

The citizenship law of the People's Republic of China, like that of its predecessor the Republic of China, was based on the *jus sanguinis* principle. Therefore, children of Chinese nationals, regardless of their birthplaces, were Chinese citizens under Chinese law. Because of this, there was a considerable number of Chinese in Indonesia who were both Indonesian and Chinese citizens.

The rise of a powerful China had made a number of governments in Southeast Asia concerned about the high number of Chinese residents in their countries who, as Chinese citizens, could play major political and financial roles in assisting China to become more influential in the region. For these reasons, various governments began to propose a resolution to the issue of dual nationality. In Indonesia the government adopted the view that there should be no dual nationality in Indonesia. Thus, the Chinese in Indonesia should either be Indonesian or Chinese citizens. Siauw and his Baperki strongly supported this view which was also endorsed by the majority of the political parties in Indonesia.

It was suggested by a number of scholars and newspaper articles in Indonesia that Indonesia, through Prime Minister Nehru of India, raise the subject with Chou En Lai when he visited India in July 1954. It was reported in New Delhi that Chou assured Nehru that China was ready to give up its claim to the citizenship of overseas Chinese.

Although this report was denied by Chinese authorities in Jakarta, in September 1954 Chou indicated in his report to the National People's Congress that China was willing to urge the overseas Chinese to respect the laws and customs of the countries in which they lived. He further indicated that China was ready to settle nationality issues with Southeast Asian governments in order to improve the status of the overseas Chinese and the relationships between China and the countries concerned.[17]

Nehru appeared to have played an important role in facilitating the Chinese to have a position that would be acceptable to the governments in Southeast Asia. India had previously agreed that its subjects abroad would no longer be able to hold dual nationality.[18]

Preliminary discussions between the Indonesian and Chinese governments commenced on 2 November 1954, in Beijing. The Indonesian

---

[17] Willmott, *The National Status of the Chinese In Indonesia*, pp. 44–45.
[18] Ibid., p. 45.

delegation was led by Sukardjo Wirjopranoto, head of the Asia and Pacific Bureau of the Ministry of Foreign Affairs. Delegation members included Ambassador Arnold Mononutu, Tajib Napis of the Ministry of Justice and Suhardjo, a lawyer. The Chinese were represented by Chang Han Fu, vice-minister of foreign affairs, Huang Chen, ambassador to Indonesia and Consul-General Chao Chung Shi.[19]

The preliminary discussions ended on 23 December. Details of the discussions were not made public but various sources reported that the Chinese were originally willing to abandon claims to the citizenship of all peranakans in Indonesia who had become Indonesian citizens under the Citizenship Act of 1946 or the 1949 RTC Agreement.

However, the Indonesian delegation pushed for a new round of opting according to the active system and the Chinese delegation accepted its demands.[20] Willmott suggests that this position might have been based on a desire to increase the number of Chinese under Chinese jurisdiction.[21]

But this interpretation is not consistent with the statements made by Chou En Lai on a number of occasions in which he declared that the Chinese Government was willing to give up their claims on overseas Chinese. By the time the negotiations took place, the Chinese government had significantly reduced its earlier reliance on financial and political support from Southeast Asian Chinese. As Mozingo wrote in 1965:

> The Chinese communist assumption that the overseas Chinese in Indonesia would send substantial remittances to mainland China and could be used to strengthen the local communist movement led Peking to make a concerted effort after 1949 to arouse this minority's allegiance to the CPR. Remittances from the overseas Chinese, however, fell well below the pre-World War II levels… When the Chinese and Soviet economies became largely interdependent in 1953, and the international communist line shifted to cultivating nationalist regimes, the relative importance of the overseas Chinese to Peking diminished.[22]

---

[19] *Berita Baperki*, 26 February 1955. According to Willmott's account, the delegation included Lie Tjwan Sien, one of Baperki's leaders.

[20] Willmott, *National Status of the Chinese in Indonesia*, pp. 46–47.

[21] Ibid., p. 47.

[22] David Mozingo, *Sino-Indonesian Relations: An Overview, 1955–1965*, United States Air Force Project Rand. Memorandum RM–4641–PR, July 1965, p. 6.

Mozingo's view is in contrast to that of Barnett who, in May 1955, wrote:

> Many of the questions concerning the agreement raised by foreign observers were related to Peking's political motivation and sincerity. The period when the treaty negotiations took place was one in which the Chinese communists actually intensified their appeals to overseas Chinese and gave little real indication of willingness to abandon interest in them. Peking has recently taken steps to encourage investments by overseas Chinese, to attract their children to homeland schools, to facilitate remittances to their native districts... Did the Chinese communists possibly believe that the 'active' choice principle might actually result in a large number of Chinese citizens in Indonesia who, as clear-cut aliens, would rely increasingly on outside support?[23]

But Mozingo suggests that the more decisive motive was to do with the improvement of China–Indonesia relations, by letting the Indonesians decide how the dual nationality issue should be settled. China also wanted to show other Southeast Asian countries that it was willing to be flexible on the nationality of the overseas Chinese.[24]

Siauw, however, was of the view that the communist Chinese government's position on the nationality of overseas Chinese differed from that of the Kuo Min Tang government of the late 1940s. The Kuo Min Tang government had wanted to have the highest possible number of Chinese nationals in Indonesia, hence its strong objections to the 1946 Citizenship Law and the RTC Agreement. The newly established communist government, he thought, did not believe in maintaining the loyalty of overseas Chinese through nationality. Having met Premier Chou En Lai himself and heard accounts of what he said to Chinese leaders in Indonesia (Chou reportedly encouraged the Indonesian Chinese to become Indonesian citizens and help develop Indonesia), Siauw was convinced that the Chinese government was genuine in allowing freedom to foreign-born Chinese to become nationals of Indonesia and other countries.[25] This interpretation is consistent with the view conveyed to me by an official of the Chinese

---

[23] A. Doak Barnett, *A Choice of Nationality: Overseas Chinese in Indonesia–Problems and Issues raised by the Sino-Indonesian Agreement on the Issue of Dual Nationality*, American Universities Field Staff, May 28, 1955, p. 11.

[24] Mozingo, *Sino-Indonesian Relations*, p. 6.

[25] Siauw, *Suatu Renungan*, p. 84.

Ministry of Foreign Affairs who was intimately involved in the negotiation process.[26]

The negotiations were rushed to completion to allow Chou En Lai and Sunario to sign the Dual Nationality Treaty at the time of the Asian–African Conference held in Bandung in April 1955.

This treaty was very similar to the draft bill on citizenship, which the Ali cabinet had submitted to parliament in 1954 and then withdrawn in the same year in response to criticism from Baperki and others. It provided for an active system – that is, it required a new set of active choices by Chinese who had become Indonesian citizens under the passive systems embodied in the Citizenship Act of 1946 and the 1949 RTC Agreement. On the other hand, there would be no new option for people who had rejected the Indonesian citizenship during the opting periods of 1946–1947 and 1949–1951. Nor was a choice offered to people who were born in China and had never been naturalised as Dutch subjects.

The treaty included the following major points:

1. Adults with dual nationality of the two countries would be given two years to choose one of the citizenships. They would have to declare before the appropriate authorities that they repudiate one of the two.
2. Adults who neglected to make such a choice within the two-year period would acquire the nationality of their father.
3. Persons under eighteen years of age would acquire the nationality of their father. They would need to choose a nationality one year after they became eighteen or were married.
4. In future, all children born in Indonesia of alien Chinese parents would acquire Chinese citizenship.

This was a major victory for those who wanted to reopen the question of the citizen status of peranakans who had obtained Indonesian citizenship under the 1946 and 1949 provisions and for those who wanted as few Chinese people as possible to be Indonesian citizens.

The PNI was quick to declare its full support, stating that the treaty 'would remove the basis for the continuing existence of minorities'.[27] *Berita Minggu*, edited by PNI people, published an article supporting the treaty.

---

[26] Interview with Chu Yi, a staff member of the Chinese foreign ministry in the 1950s.
[27] Willmott, *National Status of the Chinese in Indonesia*, p. 48.

It argued that Indonesian citizenship should not be made available to the Chinese too easily and that the treaty should be used as a tool to radically restructure economic power in the villages which, according to these PNI leaders, were dominated by Chinese operators.[28]

The PKI also issued a statement on 17 May 1955 declaring its support, arguing that while the passive system was a simpler method to be adopted, it had failed to eliminate dual nationality problems. The party had therefore decided to generally support the active system.[29] The PKI leadership may have seen Beijing's acceptance of the treaty as giving it freedom to adopt a position close to that of its ally, the PNI.

For Siauw and Baperki, the treaty was a slap in the face and Siauw used the press to voice his objections. While expressing his appreciation for the efforts made by the two governments in settling the dual nationality issues, he indicated grave disappointment over a number of clauses contained in the treaty.

According to Siauw:[30]

> Dual nationality issues in Indonesia are unique because they create sentiments and prejudices as well as perceptions that people who have dual nationality are people who are opportunistic and therefore have dual loyalties. These perceptions and prejudices are used to justify the implementation of discriminatory measures against the Chinese population in Indonesia. Because of this situation, Baperki fully supports the attempts to settle the dual nationality issues so that Indonesian citizens could live without fear of racial prejudices and discriminatory measures.

Siauw further stated:

> Baperki is disappointed by the agreements outlined in the treaty because:
>
> 1. The treaty contains principles embodied by the Citizenship Bill which created confusion and concerns within the communities of Indonesian citizens of foreign descent, particularly those who are of Chinese descent. Some of the treaty conditions have

---

[28] *Berita Baperki*, 26 May 1955.
[29] *Harian Rakyat*, 17 May 1955.
[30] Siauw's speech delivered to Baperki in May 1955.

not been fully accepted by the parliament. The government has failed to define who should be considered as people who have dual nationality.

2. The treaty is supposed to settle dual nationality matters. Under this treaty, however, a woman who has Indonesian citizenship can maintain her Indonesian citizenship after marrying a man with Chinese citizenship. So their family has dual citizenship. The concern is that Indonesia will be faced with ongoing dual nationality problems. It is of great concern that this provision will only be applicable for people who marry Chinese citizens.

3. The treaty appears to be designed to significantly reduce the number of Indonesian citizens of Chinese descent. It replaces the *jus soli* principle with that of *jus sanguinis*. This will create a situation whereby people whose parents are Chinese citizens will always be Chinese citizens even if they represent a group who have been living in Indonesia for a number of generations.

4. The treaty jeopardises the government's efforts which, since 1945, have been made to ensure that Indonesian citizens of foreign descent were encouraged to be good Indonesian citizens.

5. The treaty also jeopardises the legal status of Indonesian citizens, especially after the citizens had two opportunities to opt for Indonesian citizenship in the periods 1946–1948 and 1949–1951.

With respect to which Chinese people should be defined as having dual nationality, Siauw offered a solution based on the following three categories:

1. those who declared themselves to have dual nationality and wished to reject Indonesian citizenship
2. those whom the Indonesian government suspected of having two passports when travelling abroad
3. those who were under 18 in the period from 27 December 1949 to 27 December 1951 and so did not have the opportunity to opt for Indonesian citizenship and whose parents rejected Indonesian citizenship in the same period.

Siauw urged the government to treat people who did not fall into any of the three categories listed above as Indonesian citizens, or as Chinese citizens if they were born in China and had rejected Indonesian citizenship. Siauw also urged the government to treat people who were eligible voters in general elections and who served as cabinet ministers, members of parliament or public servants as Indonesian citizens.

Siauw was not alone in opposing the treaty. The press also reported statements made by other Baperki leaders such as Yap Thiam Hien.[31] But more interestingly, Siauw's views were also shared not only by members of his Fraksi Nasional Progresif, like Diapari of the SKI, Hazairin of the PIR and Sukarni of the Partai Murba, but also by the opposition parties.

Jusuf Wibisono, of Masyumi, objected to the treaty on three separate grounds. Firstly, it was contrary to the Political Manifesto of 1945[32], the Citizenship Act of 1946 and the 1949 RTC Agreement; secondly, it would jeopardise the trust of many Chinese whom Indonesia had considered as friends; and thirdly, it would create tremendous difficulties in the registration of those having to opt for citizenship and encourage corruption.[33]

The PSI was equally strong in opposing the treaty. In its newspaper *Pedoman* the party 'denounced the hardships which the active system would make for Indonesian citizens of Chinese descent. The party feared that increased numbers of aliens would be an invitation to foreign intervention.'[34] The Partai Katolik and Parkindo also issued statements objecting to the treaty.[35]

Willmott suggests that anti-communist politicians were opposing the treaty partly because it would involve the establishment throughout Indonesia of registration offices manned by personnel of the People's Republic of China.

Although the arguments presented in parliament were logical and supportive of Siauw's position, the motivation for these objections was more political than pro-Chinese or pro-Siauw. It is highly probable that the opposition parties intended to make the treaty a parliamentary issue which could ultimately bring down the Ali government.

---

[31] Willmott, *National Status of the Chinese in Indonesia*, p. 52.

[32] This provides that the government is committed to expediting the process of ensuring that Indo-Asians (Chinese, Arabs and Indians) and Indo-Europeans become Indonesian citizens and true Indonesians.

[33] Willmott, *National Status of the Chinese in Indonesia*, pp. 49–50.

[34] *Pedoman*, cited by Somers, *Questions Concerning the Chinese in Indonesia since Chou–Sunario Treaty*, p. 2.

[35] Willmott, *The National Status of the Chinese in Indonesia*, p. 50.

Chou En Lai was reportedly surprised by the negative reactions. He requested Huang Chen, the Chinese ambassador, to invite Siauw to discuss with him the various aspects of the treaty. This discussion took place in the Chinese Embassy in Jakarta towards the end of April 1955. Chou and Siauw began the discussion at 11 pm and concluded it at 4 am the next morning.[36] Siauw had previously consulted Prime Minister Ali and obtained his approval to give a detailed explanation to Chou.[37]

In this meeting Siauw convinced Chou that he had been poorly briefed by his staff and Foreign Minister Sunario, and that if the treaty were implemented in its current form a few hundred thousands of peranakans would lose their citizenship. This, according to Siauw, would worsen their legal status in Indonesia and would be a victory for political leaders who wanted to carry out discriminatory measures.

Siauw was able to convince Chou to issue an Exchange of Notes, which would significantly reduce the impacts of the treaty. On the next day Prime Minister Ali met with Premier Chou and Siauw. It was agreed in that meeting that Baperki would prepare a memorandum which would become the basis of the Exchange of Notes.[38]

Chou was apparently embarrassed by the episode and reportedly scolded some of his staff who had been involved in the negotiations with the Indonesians. He instructed them to consult Siauw before finalising agreements on citizenship issues in the future.[39]

Siauw was quick to prepare the memorandum and submitted it to Prime Minister Ali for his approval. Go Gien Tjwan believes that Prime Minister Ali fully supported Siauw's position when the issue was discussed in cabinet meetings.[40] Furthermore, Baperki issued a memorandum to the government, towards the end of May 1955, reiterating the points addressed by

---

[36] Interview with Go Gak Cho, Hong Kong, December 1990. Go was then general secretary of the Federation of Chinese Associations and acted as Siauw's interpreter in the Chou–Siauw meeting.

[37] Siauw, *Lima Jaman*, p. 220.

[38] Siauw, *Suatu Renungan*, pp. 84–85; Peter Burns (ed.), *Siauw Giok Tjhan Remembers*, p. 38; Interviews with Go Gak Cho, Hong Kong, December 1990, Go Gien Tjwan, Amsterdam, December 1990 and Chu Yi, Beijing, October 1994, then staff of the Chinese foreign ministry.

[39] Interview with Chu Yi, Beijing, October 1994.

[40] Interview with Go Gien Tjwan, Amsterdam, December 1990.

Siauw in various forums.[41] The same memorandum was also sent to Premier Chou En Lai.

Ali went to visit China in the first week of June 1955. In this visit, Chou and Ali had discussions on the finalisation of the dual nationality problem.[42] Both parties agreed to significantly alter the principles embodied in the treaty and so agreed to issue an Exchange of Notes.[43] On 3 June 1955, Chou En Lai issued a formal letter to Ali. This letter, designed to be the Exchange of Notes, contained the issues highlighted by Siauw's memorandum, including:

1. Once the people concerned had chosen their citizenship under the provisions of the treaty, they would not be required to choose again, even after the treaty expired.
2. The two governments agreed that among those considered to have dual citizenship there was a group of people who, according to the Indonesian Government, had, in an implicit manner, renounced Chinese citizenship. This group of people would be treated as Indonesian citizens and would not be required to choose their citizenship under the provisions of the dual nationality treaty.
3. A joint committee would be set up to plan and implement the treaty.
4. The status quo would be maintained for people who had dual nationality until the two-year period in which they had to choose their citizenship expired.

In his response, Ali indicated that he fully accepted Chou's conditions. Thus the Exchange of Notes was formalised. On 7 June 1955, the day parliament reconvened after a one-and-a-half-month recess, Ali returned to

---

[41] *Berita Baperki*, 26 June–July 1955.

[42] Siauw, *Lima Jaman*, p. 221; Siauw, *Suatu Renungan*, p. 85; Peter Burns (ed.), *Siauw Giok Tjhan Remembers*, p. 39. In his *Suatu Renungan* and Burns' *Siauw Giok Tjhan Remembers*, Siauw indicated that in the Ali–Chou meeting, Ali attempted to ignore Siauw's memorandum and wished to maintain the original treaty. This was a change of heart from Ali's side, which might have been prompted by pressure from Sunario and others within the PNI camp. But as outlined in Siauw's *Suatu Renungan* and Burns' *Siauw Giok Tjhan Remembers*, Chou was able to convince Ali to include points highlighted in Baperki's memorandum in the Exchange of Notes.

[43] Interview with Chu Yi, Beijing, October 1994.

Indonesia. He announced that he had successfully negotiated an agreement with Chou to ensure smooth implementation of the treaty.[44]

Obviously pleased with the achievement, Siauw praised the results of the Chou–Ali meetings in China. But an oversight had been made in that he had failed to clearly define what was meant by Article 2 of the notes: '… according to the Indonesian Government, had, in an implicit manner, renounced Chinese citizenship. This group of people would be treated as Indonesian citizens and would not be required to choose their citizenship under the provisions of the dual nationality treaty'.[45]

He foresaw that there could yet be trouble when parliament came to discuss the treaty. In a press interview, he indicated that the Exchange of Notes clarified the group of people who were to be affected by the treaty. In his opinion, shop owners, taxi drivers, farmers and labourers of Chinese descent who had lived in Indonesia for several generations (representing about 80 per cent of all peranakans in Indonesia) should be exempt from choosing their citizenship, because by virtue of their economic status and way of life they could only be treated as Indonesian citizens.

Siauw further argued that members of parliament, cabinet ministers, public servants and members of national political parties and mass organisations like Baperki should also be treated solely as Indonesian citizens. He proposed that the Indonesian parliament when considering the Citizenship Bill should pass an amendment which would guarantee that people who had become Indonesian citizens under the passive system of the 1946 Act and RTC Agreement would be exempt from choosing their citizenship. This, according to Siauw, would simplify the implementation of the treaty and would be in line with the spirit of the Exchange of Notes.[46] Siauw's position on this was supported by opponents of the original treaty, including the PSI and various peranakan newspapers.[47]

Just as Siauw was gaining momentum in parliament in getting support for the ratification of the treaty, the Ali government fell in July 1955. The treaty did not come up for discussion in parliament during the period of its successor the Masyumi-led cabinet of Burhanuddin Harahap. It was

---

[44] Mary Somers, *Questions Concerning The Chinese in Indonesia since the Chou–Sunario Treaty*, April 4, 1960.

[45] This is puzzling. It is highly probable that Siauw's original detailed definition was rejected by Ali who wanted a more generic expression in the exchange of notes.

[46] *Sin Po*, 16 June 1955.

[47] Willmott, *National Status of the Chinese in Indonesia*, p. 56.

briefly discussed in the period of the next cabinet, the second Ali cabinet, but inconclusively.

On December 5 1957, Siauw Giok Tjhan and thirteen other peranakan leaders representing the PNI, the PKI, Baperki, the NU, Masyumi and the Partai Katolik presented a petition to the government urging it to exempt all Chinese who had voted in the 1955 elections from the need to make a further option. Foreign Minister Subandrio said the government supported this proposal. On 17 December of the same year, the treaty was finally ratified.[48]

Not long after that, on 30 December 1957 the Standing Committee of the National People's Congress of the People's Republic of China also ratified the treaty.

There was a further glitch, however, in December 1957, when the Djuanda cabinet refused to confirm that people who had voted in the 1955 elections would be exempt from the need to make a choice under the treaty. In January 1958, Prime Minister Djuanda responded to Siauw's question in parliament about who should be exempt by indicating that the government would consider the matter and that the implementation committee to be set up by the two governments would include peranakan members of parliament.

In April 1958, Indonesia formed the Dual Citizenship Committee to implement the treaty. Siauw was included in this committee. During the committee discussions on who should be exempt from the treaty application, Siauw strongly pushed for his definition of who should be declared Indonesian citizens. As described earlier, among those to be exempt according to Siauw were all Chinese who worked as labourers and farmers, members of parliament and cabinets, public servants and members of the armed forces. At Siauw's suggestion the committee members visited a community of poor farmers of Chinese descent in Tangerang, 30km from Jakarta. They were convinced that the Chinese in Tanggerang lived like poor 'Asli' farmers and that they had no means of keeping all the necessary documents to prove that they were born in Indonesia. As a result of this visit, the committee recommended to the government that all Chinese who worked as farmers in rural areas be regarded as 'anak Pribumi' (Indigenous people).[49]

The committee's recommendations must have included Siauw's other demands that government employees and members of the armed forces be

---

[48] *Sin Po*, 17 December 1957.

[49] Siauw, *Suatu Renungan*, pp. 86–87; Peter Burns (ed.), *Siauw Giok Tjhan Remembers*, pp. 40–41.

included in the list of people declared as Indonesian citizens and so they were exempted from re-opting for Indonesian citizenship under the treaty.

On 26 May 1959, the government issued Regulation 20/1959 which stipulated categories of people considered to have rejected Chinese citizenship already – public servants, members of the armed forces, members of diplomatic offices, people who had represented Indonesia abroad, members of parliament and cabinets, and peasants.[50]

The Exchange of Notes was finally issued on 20 January 1960, two years after the treaty was ratified in parliament, and all those who had voted in the 1955 elections were exempted.

One of Siauw's efforts in parliament was concerned with the passing of a provision which enabled children of people who rejected Indonesian citizenship between 1949 and 1951 to apply for Indonesian citizenship. He was able to get enough support in parliament to have this passed as well. On 1 August 1958, a regulation was passed which enabled these children to apply for Indonesian citizenship if they were of age before 1 August 1959. Supported by the PNI, NU and PKI, Siauw was later able to have this extended to 1 August 1960.[51]

Siauw was therefore successful in achieving three major concessions which were contained in three areas: firstly, the Exchange of Notes; secondly, the regulation on the minors of Indonesia-born Chinese who had rejected Indonesian citizenship between 1949 and 1951; and thirdly, in Regulation 20/1959. These concessions, in theory, would maximise the number of Indonesian citizens of Chinese descent.

The statistical impact of these concessions is hard to assess. Mozingo, Skinner, Willmott and Somers agree that the total number of Chinese in Indonesia in the late 1950s and early 1960s was approximately 2.45 million. Of these, about 1.5 million were considered aliens – between 300 000 and 400 000 of these were Indonesia-born Chinese who had rejected Indonesian citizenship between 1949 and 1951.[52] The remaining 950 000 were therefore considered dual nationals.

---

[50] Somers, *Questions Concerning The Chinese in Indonesia since the Chou–Sunario Treaty*, p. 8.

[51] Siauw, *Suatu Renungan*, p. 86; Peter Burns (ed.), *Siauw Giok Tjhan Remembers*, p. 45.

[52] On the total number of people who had previously rejected Indonesian citizenship, these writers give different estimates. Willmott states that the number is around 300 000. Skinner gives the figure of around 200 000. Mozingo and Somers, citing the estimates released by the Department of Justice in September 1961, estimate it

Mozingo estimates that 400 000 people were affected by concessions 1 and 2 (200 000 were people who had voted in elections and 200 000 were children of Indonesia-born parents who had rejected Indonesia citizenship between 1949 and 1951). He did not specify the number of people affected by concession 3.[53] Somers' estimates of those affected by concessions 1 and 2 closely match those of Mozingo. She estimated the number of people affected by concession 3 to be between 10 and 15 per cent of all people of Chinese descent, the majority of whom would be those classified as farmers.[54] So the effect of these concessions should have been that between 550 000 and 650 000 dual nationals became Indonesian citizens.

However, the treaty's implementation disappointed Siauw – as will become clear in Chapter 10.

Citizenship Law of 1958

As outlined before, the ratification of the Dual Nationality Treaty was delayed partly because there were forces in parliament who demanded that the parliament first passed the citizenship law before ratifying the treaty. The second Ali cabinet introduced a draft citizenship law to parliament but was forced to withdraw it because it became clear that the parties who supported the government were in conflict about it.

In November 1957, the Djuanda cabinet forwarded a bill on citizenship and naturalisation to parliament, which was largely based on the bill prepared by the second Ali government.

This 1957 bill was drafted in a spirit similar to that of the Dual Nationality Treaty, as eventually put into effect, and was different from the spirit of the 1954 bills. It contained a number of conditions which were supported by Siauw and other opponents of the bills of 1954. The major features of the bill were as follows:

1. All people who had become citizens under laws, agreements or regulations which had been promulgated since 17 August 1945 would be treated as Indonesian citizens. The need to choose actively would apply only to people who were dual nationals under the provisions of the Dual Nationality Treaty.

---

to be 400 000. See David Mozingo: 'The Sino-Indonesian Dual Nationality Treaty', *Asian Survey I*, 1961, No 10, p. 25.
[53] Mozingo, 'The Sino-Indonesian Dual Nationality', p. 26.
[54] Somers, *Peranakan Chinese politics*, p. 242.

2. Chinese of foreign descent who had acquired Indonesian citizenship through the 1946 Act or under the RTC Agreement would maintain their citizenship.
3. It would be impossible for anyone to have dual citizenship after the option period provided in the Dual Nationality Treaty expired.
4. There was a two-generation *jus soli* provision. An alien born and residing in Indonesia could apply for Indonesian citizenship providing their father was also born in Indonesia and if they renounced their former citizenship.
5. The proposed Act followed the *jus sanguinis* principle in that one's citizenship was derived from that of one's father.

The Citizenship Act was finally passed on 1 July 1958 without much opposition in parliament. It was a formulation that satisfied Baperki on most of the main issues. The only major provision which disturbed Siauw was related to the two-generation *jus soli* principle. He preferred the previous citizenship law which provided that all persons born in Indonesia were considered Indonesian citizens unless they repudiated the Indonesian citizenship. But he was willing to compromise and hence endorsed the new law.[55]

---

[55] Siauw, *Suatu Renungan*, p. 86.

Siauw's parents: Kwan Tjian Nio (mother) and Siauw Gwan Swie (father). Surabaya, 1931.

Siauw, leader of the Chinese Boy Scouts. Surabaya, 1931.

Siauw, HBS Student, 1932.

Tan Gien Hwa. Semarang, 1939.

Siauw, editor-in-chief, *Mata Hari*. Semarang, 1939.

Siauw (centre) campaigning in Semarang, 1955.

Siauw, Tambunan, unknown, Sartono and Zhou En Lai. Beijing, 1957.

Siauw (third from the left) and fellow MPs. USA, 1957.

Siauw and Soekarno. Jakarta, 1960.

Siauw amongst URECA (Baperki University) students. Medan, 1964.

Siauw (front) with his brother-in-law Tan Soen Eng,
his wife, Tan Gien Hwa, and youngest daughter, Siauw Lee Ming,
in the army hospital. Jakarta, 1974.

Tan Gien Hwa and Siauw under house arrest. Jakarta, 1977.

The author, Tan Gien Hwa and Siauw. Amsterdam, 1979.

Ji Beng Fei, Vice Premier of the People's Republic of China, and Siauw. Beijing, 1981.

Go Gien Tjwan, Siauw and Tjoa Sik Ien. Amsterdam, 1981.

Chapter 8

SIAUW'S ECONOMIC PLATFORM

A key direction in government policy in the 1950s was the Indonesianisation of the economy. All of the cabinets of the period affirmed that the economy should become more national and less colonial, and various of them actively pursued policies intended to lessen the role of Chinese businessmen, including those who were Indonesian citizens as well as aliens.

Dutch capital had been given strong guarantees under the RTC Agreement of December 1949. One of the strengths of Siauw's position was that he was able to argue in a way that resonated with mainstream Indonesian nationalism as far as Dutch economic power was concerned. He was, however, rowing against the current when he defended Chinese business.

One reason for this was that the ideological position of the Chinese was weak. There was strong support in the politically active sections of the population for negative stereotypes of the Chinese – as outsiders, exclusive, a community of rich people who stuck to themselves and thought that they were better than others, who always got their way through bribery, who were politically opportunistic, potentially disloyal, money-minded, stingy and so on.

To many people in the political mainstream the creation of a national economy implied that Asli Indonesians should be favoured at the expense of the Chinese as well as the Dutch.

There was a great deal of pressure from both PNI and Masyumi constituencies for facilities of various kinds to be handed over to Indigenous businessmen to enable them to compete more effectively with better established firms, as well as pressure from party activists for jobs and perks.

We will also see in this chapter that Siauw, in his support for Chinese economic power, did not differentiate between Chinese who were Indonesian citizens and alien Chinese. He also argued against measures introduced against alien Chinese.

Finally, the constituencies that favoured legality, upholding standards set out in the Universal Declaration of Human Rights and not discriminating against one group of citizens, were weak.

Despite these difficulties, Siauw made some achievements in these areas. This chapter will detail how these results were achieved.

The 'Asli policy'

Not long before the RTC of 1949, national leaders commenced discussions on the transition of the colonial economy to a national economy, which would involve nationalisation of foreign investments and capital. An important part of the debate was related to ta policy which was designed to limit the influence of Chinese business operators and to promote the significant growth of Asli business operators. This scheme was widely known as the 'Asli policy', although officially it was called the National Economic Policies.

Siauw resented the application of the term 'Asli' to economic and racial formulations. In all his writings and speeches, he always used quotation marks for the term Asli. No Indonesian, he said, could verify that he had pure Indonesian blood. According to Siauw, the term Asli, as used by politicians, had no legality and should accordingly be eliminated. He further argued that there was no such thing as an Indonesian race. What existed and was established by the founding fathers of Indonesia was the Indonesian nation. The definition of Asli Indonesians, which was more aligned with that of Indonesian race, was therefore not legitimate.

The Asli policy, according to Siauw, was first introduced by Djuanda as the minister for economic affairs in the RIS cabinet in December 1949. The origins of this policy were first debated in the Inter-Indonesian Economic Conference held in Yogyakarta in December 1949.[1] The policy was aimed at protecting the economically weak groups in Indonesia which, in Djuanda's definition, consisted of Indigenous (Asli) Indonesians. The Chinese, according to Djuanda, belonged to the economically strong groups. The policy introduced measures allowing Asli business operators to gain privileges and business concessions and barred Chinese operators from obtaining these privileges and concessions.

Siauw argued that under this policy, a rich Asli businessman would be considered belonging to an economically weak group while a poor Chinese businessman would be treated as an economically strong person.

---

[1] John Sutter, *Indonesianisasi: Politics in a Changing Economy, 1940–1955*, Cornell University, April 1959, p. 1125; *Berita Baperki*, Nomor Istimewa, December 1954, p. 11.

From the time this policy was debated in parliament, Siauw consistently condemned it as a policy that treated the Indonesian Chinese as stepchildren. In his speech in RIS parliament in August 1950, Siauw demanded the government explain the validity of a formulation that determined the weakness or strength of a person's economic position solely on their ethnic background. Siauw's position was supported by Hamid Algadrie, a representative of the Arab community and of the PSI.

In his reply, Prime Minister Hatta confirmed that the definition of the economically weak group was applicable to all citizens and that not all Asli citizens would be considered economically weak. Hatta, however failed to state that the test of economic position should be based purely on real economic status and not on ethnic background.[2]

The changes of government in the republic's early years did not affect the implementation of the Asli policy. Prime Minister Natsir, in his response to Siauw's repeated questions and protests, even promised in October 1950 to make changes in legislation which discriminated between citizens of the same status[3] but these promised changes were never enacted.

When Sukiman took power in 1951, Siauw again joined the opposition group in condemning the continuation of the Asli policy. He continued his insistence that the government drop the policy and demanded that the government differentiate between large alien monopoly capital and small to medium alien capital that was not monopolistic.

He indicated his strong support for the elimination of giant alien monopolistic enterprises – Dutch, British, American and so on – and urged the government to quickly take them over. On the other hand, he urged the government to protect and maximise the utilisation of small and medium capital owned by Chinese business operators, both aliens and Indonesian citizens. Again, like its predecessors, the Sukiman government denied that it carried out discriminatory measures against the Chinese and assured the parliament that it treated all citizens equally.[4]

Basing his arguments on the requirements of speeding up the transition from a colonial economy to a strong national economy, Siauw repeatedly called on the government to avoid measures which would benefit companies of giant capital owned by colonial nations and which would jeopardise small to large domestic capital. He also recommended that companies involved in

---

[2] *Ichtisar Parlemen*, 1950, pp. 353–474.
[3] *Risalah Parlemen*, 1950, pp. 2205–2207.
[4] *Risalah Parlemen*, 1951, pp. 4426–4778.

production train their local employees regardless of ethnic background and minimise the importation of European experts.

Siauw's position on the Asli policy was generally supported by influential members of his faction, namely Iwa Kusumasumantri, Mohamad Yamin and DS Diapari. Occasionally, Sakirman of the PKI, IJ Kasimo of the Partai Katolik, Tambunan of the Christian Party, Subadio Sastrosatomo of the PSI and Snel, a representative of the European community, also supported his arguments in parliament.

Masyumi-dominated governments between 1950 and 1953, whose economic portfolios were held by Hatta, Djuanda, Sjafruddin Prawiranegera and Sumitro, kept denying the discriminatory nature of their Asli policies but they also kept failing to provide a cast-iron guarantee that measures that discriminated against the Chinese in Indonesia would be stopped.

When Iskaq, of the PNI, was minister for economic affairs, the Asli policy was further expanded and his ministry introduced a wide range of measures which severely jeopardised the economic position of the Chinese. In Siauw's speeches and writings, he made it obvious that he resented these measures and made no apologies in strongly condemning Iskaq's policies.

To Siauw, the principle, promoted by Djuanda in the Masyumi-dominated era, of assisting the economically weak citizens and the principle, stressed by Iskaq in the PNI-dominated era, of developing a balanced middle class were not implemented for the interests of all Indonesian citizens. Siauw saw these principles as a means of enriching certain office holders and party officials and resulted in forcing many alien and peranakan business operators to go out of business.

The following sections outline in detail some of the measures, which Siauw opposed in parliament and public arenas.

'Benteng' and national importers

In 1949 Djuanda, who led the Indonesian delegation in the Financial and Economic Affairs Committee at the RTC, formulated a regulation which was designed to protect economically weak groups. His formulation became a government regulation (peraturan pemerintah) when Djuanda became minister for economic affairs in 1949.

In April 1950 Djuanda introduced a further regulation to protect Indigenous importers from competition with foreign importers. The protection was provided by reserving a range of goods, defined as Benteng goods, for Indigenous importers and by providing privileges to Indigenous importers, including credits and granting of licences. This protection scheme was applicable to companies 70 per cent of whose capital came from Indigenous Indonesians.⁵

In response to Siauw's criticism, Djuanda confirmed his intention to protect Asli newcomers to business and indicated that, in his view, the government had the right to protect economically weak groups. While he agreed with Siauw that some Asli individuals were well-to-do, he maintained that the vast majority of the Asli population belonged to economically weak groups who deserved government protection. With this confirmation, Chinese importers were forced to significantly alter their modes of operation.

The Benteng policy was carried out by the next four cabinets. By the end of 1950, national importers numbered 250. By April 1952, when Wilopo took office as prime minister, the number had jumped to 741. But this was still a small fraction of the total 3119 importers, the majority of which were Chinese. Both alien and peranakan Chinese were more experienced and better connected in the international arena and still dominated the field.

When the first Ali cabinet was formed in 1953, with Iskaq Tjokroadisurjo as the minister for economic affairs, there was a rapid intensification of Indonesianisation programs. Indonesianisation could mean the diversification of production to reduce dependence on exports of raw material but its main focus was on the transfer of control and management of economic enterprises from the Western and Chinese firms to Indonesian ones. Under Iskaq, the economic policies emphasised the third goal by severely limiting Chinese business ventures and forcing the rapid creation of Indigenous middle class businessmen.⁶

Iskaq not only continued to implement the Benteng policy but also introduced another policy in the importing arena. Companies involved in importing goods were required to be recognised as national importers. These companies had to have a significant number of Asli partners and operators to be recognised and registered as national importers. Moreover, Iskaq's regulation required that all stockholders had to be Indonesian citizens and those who were of foreign descent had to prove their citizenship.⁷

Before Iskaq took office, national importers received less than 40 per cent of all exchange allocations for imports. By the end of Iskaq's term, some fourteen months later, they were given an estimated 80 to 90 percent. The

---

5   Sutter, *Indonesianisasi*, p. 1018.
6   Feith, *Decline of the Constitutional Democracy in Indonesia*, p. 374.
7   Sutter, *Indonesianisasi*, p. 1022.

number of national importers had increased to at least 2211 and possibly to between 4000 and 5000.[8]

Siauw was quick to condemn this policy. He indicated that it was improper to force existing importers, regardless of their ethnic backgrounds, to form partnerships with Asli businessmen. He argued that even partnership among brothers was often difficult to be harmoniously achieved and asked how one could trust a person one barely knew to be one's business partner.[9]

Supported by Tjung Tin Yan of the Partai Katolik, Siauw was able to force Iskaq to issue a statement on 2 December 1953 that racial discrimination would stop and that companies run by Indonesian citizens, regardless of their origin, would be classified as national importers.[10]

Alien Chinese businessmen who wished to be involved in importing goods had to use Asli contacts' names for business registration purposes. With government credits easily available to Indigenous businessmen with the right connections, many high level public servants and politicians who had little or no commercial experiences became directors of what were called the 'briefcase' firms. The Indigenous partners of these firms appeared in various government offices with briefcases to obtain business licenses and permits only to resell them to Chinese businessmen who had the capital and business experience. Of the thousands of registered national importers in early 1955, only 50 were considered bona fide establishments, with another 200 firms considered borderline.[11]

Siauw repeatedly argued that these arrangements increased operational costs and encouraged corruption. It was alleged in parliament that the corruption in the Central Office of Import Affairs existed in that officials had to be bribed to obtain import licenses and that licence-selling with commissions of up to 200 percent had become common. As a consequence, individuals entitled to receive licences did not get them.[12] Many of the licences went to people who agreed to pay into party funds, especially of the PNI.

This situation resulted in the government debt with the Bank of Indonesia increasing from Rp 1051 million in June 1953 to Rp 3410 million in September 1954. In the same period, foreign exchange reserves

---

[8] Feith, *The Decline of Constitutional Democracy in Indonesia*, pp. 374–375.

[9] Siauw's speech in Parliament, April 1953.

[10] *Ichtisar Parlemen*, 1953, pp. 1172–1173.

[11] Feith, *The Decline of Constitutional Democracy in Indonesia*, p. 375.

[12] Sutter, *Indonesianisasi*, p. 1082.

fell from Rp 1,145 million to minus Rp 20 million. Inflation rose significantly in 1954. Prices for 44 imported items rose by 59.4 percent. Because importers were mainly interested in importing goods which generated large profits, many machine parts that were required to maintain effective manufacturing operations were not imported, severely hampering manufacturing activities.[13]

This situation, coupled with the discovery of Iskaq's corrupt activities, prompted members of parliament to mount strong pressure on the Ali government to force Iskaq to resign. The action was led by Tjikwan of the opposition party, Masyumi, but was also supported by Siauw and others who were members of the government parties. Although Siauw participated in the activities to unseat Iskaq from the cabinet, he criticised Masyumi leaders who, according to Siauw, had also enjoyed the fruits of the implementation of Asli policies carried out by previous Masyumi-dominated cabinets.

Despite Siauw's claims that Masyumi leaders were also involved in discriminating against the Chinese in previous cabinets, Tjikwan of Masyumi, and Assaat, a non-party member, presented arguments which were largely in line with Siauw's position on Asli policies and the conversion of the colonial economy to a national one.

After Tjikwan's motion against Iskaq was lost in April 1954, debate continued for some time and further developed to create serious rifts and unrest within the government parties. Iskaq was finally forced to resign in November 1954 and was replaced by Roosseno of the PIR. This enabled the cabinet to survive a no-confidence motion moved by Masyumi's Wibisono and defeated by a small margin, in December 1954.[14]

Some months before Iskaq's resignation, the non-party member, Margono Djojohadikoesoemo, moved a resolution in parliament demanding investigation into the practices conducted by the Ministry of Economic Affairs from 1950 to October 1954 with the focus on the field of trade and imports. This resolution was finally accepted. An Investigation Commission involving Tjikwan, Margono, Jusuf Muda Dalam and Siauw was established on 28 January 1955.

Although the commission did not complete its assignment, it did submit an interim report which paved the way for an inquiry into corruption set up by the Burhanuddin cabinet which succeeded the Ali cabinet in 1955. Iskaq

---

[13]   Feith, *The Decline of Constitutional Democracy in Indonesia*, p. 376.
[14]   ibid., pp. 379 – 383; Sutter, *Indonesianisasi*, pp. 1078–1080.

left the country for reasons relating to the health of a member of his family before this inquiry was concluded.¹⁵

Bus and truck transportation

The Chinese in Indonesia, both aliens and Indonesian citizens, had dominated bus and truck transportation since the colonial period. Although some Indigenous bus operators existed in the early 1950s, the great majority of operators and owners of transportation companies were Chinese. These businesses were considered lucrative and hence attracted the attention of many influential politicians.

In the early 1950s, Djuanda was the communications minister and bus and truck transportation was part of his ministry's responsibility.

Late in January 1951, a number of members of the parliament's Communications Committee reported that bus companies owned and run by the Chinese, both alien and citizens, in Java and Sumatra were much better equipped and funded than those run by Asli owners. They also indicated that the Chinese bus companies made much larger profits than the Asli ones did. These speakers therefore recommended the introduction and implementation of policies which limited alien Chinese ownership of bus companies and protected the position of Asli operators.¹⁶

Anticipating support from parliament, Djuanda issued a new set of guidelines to all governors for the granting of bus franchises. The guidelines included:¹⁷

1. Franchises for half of the buses required should be granted to Indonesian citizens who had operated the bus routes in question under Dutch rule. The other half should be granted to other Indonesian citizens, with emphasis on giving priority to those considered to belong to economically weak groups.
2. A company would be considered Indonesian if the owner can prove Indonesian citizenship and 75 per cent of the capital stock was held by citizens.
3. The government would not recognise pre-war franchises.

---

15   Sutter, *Indonesianisasi*, p. 1089.
16   Ibid., pp. 907–908.
17   Ibid., p. 911.

The guidelines were included in the proposed Pedoman Baru (New Guidelines Bill) and debate about the bill commenced on 19 June 1951. Siauw argued that the country should maximise the utilisation of experience and capital developed by alien and citizen Chinese for the development of its economy. While he supported the idea of providing protection and assistance to people who were considered economically weak, he demanded that the government stop using racial background as the basis for assessment of whether one was to be considered economically weak or not.

In this debate, Siauw faced strong opposition, including from the PKI. He finally lost the battle, and the Pedoman Baru was accepted at the end of June 1951. The implementation of this policy resulted in the reduction of alien ownership from 64 per cent at the beginning of 1951 to 6.4 per cent at the end of the year.[18]

When the Wilopo cabinet took office in 1952, Djuanda retained his position as the communications minister. Siauw again initiated the debate about the Pedoman Baru. He repeatedly asked Djuanda to confirm that the Pedoman Baru was not designed to implement racial discrimination against the Chinese.

Siauw's protests against the Pedoman Baru were supported by a number of his faction members, like Diapari and Iwa Kusumasumantri, and also by Tan Po Goan of the PSI, who himself was a bus operator. But most of the speakers in the debate, including Sakirman of the PKI, were in favour of Djuanda's bill.

In response to Siauw and his fellow critics, Djuanda told parliament on 12 February 1953 that the Pedoman Baru did not differentiate between Indigenous and non-Indigenous citizens. He also agreed to changes which reduced the number of Chinese operators affected. It is hard to quantify the total number of Chinese bus operators who were affected as many of them found Asli partners to form mixed enterprises, either openly or secretly.[19]

Rice milling

As in the area of transportation, since the colonial period most of the rice mills in Indonesia were owned by the Chinese. After independence, this situation stayed the same. The question was then whether these owners were aliens or Indonesian citizens.

---

[18] *Risalah Parlemen* 1951.
[19] Sutter, *Indonesianisasi*, p. 922.

In this area, the big onslaught began during Iskaq's period as minister for economic affairs. Government Regulation No. 42 (Peraturan No. 42), issued by Iskaq in 1954, contained the following provisions:

1. A rice miller is not allowed to be a citizen other than a citizen of Indonesia.
2. No rights involving a rice milling enterprise may be held by persons who are citizens other than citizens of Indonesia.

Siauw was quick to condemn this new gegulation. As the dual nationality agreement with the People's Republic of China had not been finalised, he argued that the implementation of this regulation would eliminate a significant number of experienced operators and also create 'straw man' situations whereby Asli figures with powerful connections were engaged as non-active business partners.

Siauw also argued that the regulation violated the constitution, as it would arbitrarily confiscate the property of citizens. Siauw ridiculed the situation whereby people of Chinese descent could become cabinet ministers and members of parliament but were not allowed to become rice millers, even though they had been operating in the field for generations and had proven capabilities to perform the roles effectively. Such action, he said, would result in ill feeling within communities. Siauw strongly urged the government to revoke the new regulation.[20]

Siauw's complaints forced Iskaq to say, in late 1954, that the regulation was directed only at foreign citizens who operated in the industry. Dual nationals, Iskaq said in his reply to Siauw's question, would be classified as Indonesian citizens until they rejected Indonesian citizenship. In November, the policy was then altered to reflect this explanation.

Due to these modifications, a significant number of existing rice millers were able to survive. The government extended existing agreements and licences for 12 months until the end of 1955. These licenses were later further extended until the end of 1956.

Siauw's achievement in parliament in forcing the government to back down on the implementation of the regulation was widely recognised by Chinese rice millers. Early in 1955, a group of rice millers decided to collect funds to reward Siauw's hard work. The donation they collected, amounting to a few hundred thousand rupiahs, was delivered to Siauw's home in Jakarta. Siauw requested that it be taken to Baperki's office for the

---

[20] *Ichtisar Parlemen*, 1954.

organisation's use. Yap Thiam Hien was the one who received the donation in Baperki's office.²¹

Siauw's fierce defence of the positions of Chinese businessmen puzzled some anti-communist leaders like Yap Thiam Hien. Dan Lev concluded this was a strong indication that Siauw was compelled to defend and protect thte interests of the Chinese and would readily place their interests well above his political ideology as a Marxist. Lev asserted, 'Much was made about Siauw's communist sympathies, not least by Yap (Yap Thiam Hien), but Siauw's communism came with a lower case "c", and it is likely that the Chinese factor counted for more in his commitments than ideology'.²²

Siauw's economic formulations further confirmed that he could not have been a PKI member as many of his political enemies suggested. Communism of the 1950s would not be in agreement with Siauw's assertion that domestic capitalism (hence including businesses run and operated by the Chinese) should not only be protected but also encouraged to grow.

Baperki's economic platform

It is clear from the references made in this chapter and the preceding ones that Siauw put significant emphasis on economic formulations in his political activities.

Within days of Baperki being formed, Siauw urged the organisation to have a conference on the economy. Its aims, he said in April 1954, should be:

1. to properly define the goal of a national economy
2. to explain the implications of various government economic policies
3. to develop a platform to be adopted by Baperki in combating discriminatory measures.

The Baperki leaders decided to invite peranakan economic experts, mostly people with academic standing, including Oey Beng To and Lo Kim Tjing.²³ Before the conference took place, Siauw himself wrote a number of long articles on economic policies and national economy published in *Berita Baperki*, *Sunday Courier* and *Sin Min*. In these articles, published in the last few months of 1954, he consolidated his economic views as well as his criticism of various government policies and outlined

---

21 Interview with Yap Thiam Hien, Melbourne, December 1988.
22 Lev, *The Political Journey of Yap Thiam Hien*, p. 105.
23 Baperki meeting minutes, October 1954.

his demands for improvement as well as how racial discriminatory measures should be eliminated. The following paragraphs are largely derived from these articles.

Siauw pointed out that the various cabinets of the period 1949–1954 had not only failed to achieve the realisation of a national economy but also lacked the determination to achieve it. Quoting official figures published by a number of government bodies including Bank of Indonesia, Central Indonesia Economic Council (Dewan Ekonomi Indonesia Pusat), Central Institute of Small Industries (Yayasan Pusat Induk Perindustrian Kecil), the Ministry of Industry and the Ministry of Information, Siauw highlighted the economic decline that had occurred, as shown in the number of unemployed, the failure to achieve production targets, the lowering of cash reserves, the significant increases in trade deficits and funds transferred overseas, and the economic control of large foreign corporations.

Siauw criticised the government for failing to undo clauses of the RTC Agreement which protected Dutch economic interests at the expense of Indonesia's economic growth. He highlighted the power of the big Dutch companies, which he described as monopolies, especially in oil extraction, tin mining, shipping, plantations and many areas of trading. To Siauw, this was the continuation of Dutch colonialism in the economic sphere. Siauw indicated that these monopolies had drained the country's resources and had placed the country in a most difficult position to construct the infrastructure necessary for the prosperity of the people.

Creating a national economy should, according to Siauw, be defined as ensuring that the country's resources were used for the benefit of the people. Quoting relevant parts of the constitution, he said a national economy would consist of three types of corporations:

1. government corporations whose charters are to guarantee the prosperity of the people
2. corporations or other bodies which are run by people's cooperatives
3. small to medium private companies.

Corporations involved in fields which had significant impact on the prosperity of people, such as those in oil extraction, tin mining, sugar and rubber plantations, major transportation, utility and major trades, should be owned and controlled by the government, not by foreign monopoly forces. To Siauw, this was the most important feature of a national economy and should accordingly be given the highest priority.

In Siauw's opinion, the government had deliberately delayed the implementation of measures to reduce the power of Dutch and other Western capital and had instead attacked the capital of Chinese operators in various fields. Small to medium private corporations, regardless of who owned and ran them, should be encouraged and assisted to grow healthily. These corporations, he explained, did not transfer their profits out of the country. They represented important domestic capital needed to construct a national economy.

Siauw alleged that some government leaders were motivated by personal greed and were compromised by their connections with foreign corporations. He ridiculed the idea that Indonesians were not ready to take over large corporations from foreign monopolies but were capable enough to replace Chinese businessmen in owning and running their businesses.

Siauw pointed out that large corporations did use Chinese firms as their intermediaries in the distribution network during the colonial period but now had a vested interest in replacing them with Indigenous operators in order to secure political protection. This was, he alleged, the main reason for the long delays in terminating the RTC Agreement and for the highly motivated attempts to displace Chinese businessmen. If leaders of the government persisted with this strategy, he said, Indonesia's economy would continue to be under colonial control.

Baperki's economic conference was held in Jakarta on 27 and 28 of November 1954 and was attended by leaders of Baperki and some forty peranakan businessmen from various parts of Indonesia. Roosseno who had just replaced Iskaq as the minister for economic affairs was one of its speakers. Unlike Iskaq, whom Siauw obviously resented, Roosseno respected Siauw and got on well with him in the social and political spheres.

In his response to Siauw's pledge for the creation of a national economy and for the elimination of racial discriminatory measures, Roosseno confirmed that he was committed to combating racism and to creating regulations to eliminate it. He urged all citizens to work closely together and asked the non-Indigenous citizens to be more willing to assist economic development by providing technical training to Indigenous Indonesians and by investing in industrialisation.[24]

The conference concluded with the acceptance of Siauw's economic programs as Baperki economic policies. A committee chaired by Siauw was

---

[24] Baperki meeting minutes, October 1954.

then established to disseminate these policies to business communities in Indonesia.[25]

Siauw's fight against racially discriminatory measures had won him a lot of friends within the Chinese business communities. Totoks were particularly grateful for Siauw's effective defence of their economic position. Because of this, Siauw's relationship with leaders of various Chinese associations, particularly in Jakarta, grew closer. He was often consulted by these leaders in relation to various business decisions. In return, Siauw was able to rely on these totok businessmen for financial contributions to fund Baperki's activities.

The 'Assaat Movement'

In March 1956, at a meeting of the National Importers' Association in Surabaya, Assaat, who was the chairman of the association, urged the government to introduce policies which excluded Chinese from certain businesses, regardless of their citizenship.

This reflected a dramatic change of position. Assaat, a Masyumi-sympathising member of parliament, had been one of Siauw's supporters in attacking Iskaq's policies in parliament. It became apparent that his opposition to the racially discriminatory measures introduced by Iskaq was politically motivated. The inclusion of Masyumi in the cabinet quickly altered Masyumi's stance on racial discrimination. As Siauw pointed to in the earlier debates, in the pre-PNI era Masyumi leaders initially encouraged the implementation of the measures and had, in fact, benefited from these measures.

Assaat went further than Iskaq in that he linked his call for changes of economic policy with open expressions of racial sentiment against the Chinese. He called the Chinese opportunists, saying they had supported the Dutch during the colonial period, Chiang Kai Shek during Kuo Min Tang rule and Mao Tse Tung after China's nationalist government was toppled in 1949. He also blamed the Chinese for all the financial difficulties Indonesia was facing.[26] Until then, prestigious political figures had been careful to acknowledge the distinction between Chinese of Indonesian citizenship and those of foreign citizenship. Assaat said he regarded the Indonesian Arabs as Indigenous Indonesians.[27]

---

[25] Baperki meeting minutes, 14 October 1954.
[26] Feith, *The Decline of Constitutional Democracy in Indonesia*, pp. 481–482.
[27] Somers, *Peranakan Chinese Politics in Indonesia*, p. 17.

Assaat was a political leader of high standing. He had been acting president of the Republic of Indonesia for the eight months from 1949 to 1950 when it was a member state of RIS so there was something shocking about his open expression of racism.

Assaat's call attracted positive comments from many circles including Masyumi and the PSI. Within a few weeks, Assaat committees were formed in many parts of the country. Such was the level of support for Assaat's proposals that sections of the media began to talk of the 'Assaat Movement'.

Baperki was quick to condemn Assaat's views. In a number of publications, Siauw rebutted Assaat's claims that the Chinese in Indonesia were responsible for the financial difficulties Indonesia was facing. Siauw indicated that the Chinese were not in control of the monopoly businesses which had destroyed the economy and that it was erroneous to assume that the economic position of the Chinese was detrimental to the Indonesian economy.

Siauw urged members of Baperki's economic section to initiate a meeting to be attended by many businessmen from different ethnic backgrounds to discuss the issues raised by Assaat. This meeting took place in Jakarta on 27 June 1956. In this meeting, Siauw called for the formation of national organisations of businessmen of various industries such as rice milling and bus transportation but attempts to have meetings with leaders of the organisations of Asli businessmen failed to be arranged. BR Motik, of the PSI, who was one of the coordinators of the National Business Association, organised a meeting involving Asli businessmen in July 1956. Baperki claimed that no Chinese businessmen were invited to attend the meeting.[28]

In this meeting, the Kongres Ekonomi Nasional Seluruh Indonesia (All Indonesian National Economic Congress or KENSI), Assaat succeeded in securing passage of a resolution urging that all non-Indigenous enterprises be transferred to Indigenous businessmen within the shortest possible time.

Siauw moved to gain support in parliament. He labelled the movement as racist and called for public condemnation. In response to Siauw's call, the PKI claimed that enemies of the Indonesian Chinese, the nationalists and the PKI were enemies of the Indonesian revolution.[29]

Other parties followed suit. A PNI congress held in September 1956 opposed Assaat's proposal. In parliament, supporters of the proposal were

---

28   *Berita Baperki*, 15 October 1956.
29   *Harian Rakyat*, 23 August 1956.

also criticised by speakers of other parties like the NU, Partai Katolik, Parkindo and Partai Murba.[30]

Siauw's success in gaining support to oppose Asli policies and 'Assaatism' was related to bigger contests which came to a head in the years from 1956 to 1958 – contests between a PNI-led coalition of parties and a Masjumi-led one.

In the later part of 1956 and into the following year, the Assaat Movement was eclipsed by other dramatic developments. In October 1956, President Soekarno made the first of his calls for an overall reshaping of the political system towards 'Guided Democracy'. In December 1956 Masjumi and PSI-sympathetic officers in Sumatra seized power from Jakarta-appointed civilian governors, prefiguring a long tussle between the central government and various regions outside Java.

In December 1956, labour organisations under PNI and PKI leadership seized control of Dutch enterprises all over the country. Within a few weeks all Dutch firms had been placed under army control, to be later nationalised. More than 46 000 Dutch nationals fled Indonesia for Holland in the following months. In February 1958, the challenge by Masyumi and PSI-sympathising regional groups came to a head with the proclamation of the Revolutionary Government of the Republic of Indonesia in Padang, West Sumatra. Within a few months, that challenge was defeated by military actions, which meant victory for President Soekarno's ideas of Guided Democracy and a widespread discrediting of Masyumi and PSI.

Assaatism was discredited by these developments not least because Assaat himself joined the Sumatra-based rebellion. Many of the Asli business groups which had previously been trying to expand at the expense of Chinese firms were also able to find opportunities within the huge business empires seized from the Dutch in December 1957.

From this point onward, Siauw began to reinforce his economic program formulation that was largely based on the development of domestic capital – capital that was owned by Chinese businessmen regardless of their citizenship status. In this, Siauw argued that capital that is owned by such businessmen was vital for national economic development and as such should not only be protected but encouraged to grow.

This chapter shows how Siauw was fighting an uphill battle in defending the Chinese economic position. But due to the existence of powerful opposition parties, he initiated moves against various racially discriminatory

---

[30] *Berita Baperki*, 15 October 1956, *Republik*, 23 October 1956.

measures which resulted in changes which were favourable to the Chinese. As Siauw gained positive results in parliament, the support from the Chinese business communities grew and this was particularly helpful to Baperki. But Siauw remained concerned about the vulnerability of the system that enabled powerful figures from various parties in power to introduce new regulations which undermined existing non-discriminatory laws. Quietly, he was hoping for stability which could provide the Chinese with long-term protection. He believed that Soekarno could initiate the realisation of such stability and was eager to support him.

Siauw's involvement in constructing and modifying regulations concerning Indonesian citizenship indicates that parliamentary democracy worked for him. He was able to capitalise on support from his faction and members of the opposition parties to gain significant political mileage. Parliamentary democracy provided him with similar results in his pursuit to defend the position of the Chinese.

Chapter 9

TRANSITION TO GUIDED DEMOCRACY

Siauw had long been an enthusiastic participant in parliamentary politics and after the 1955 elections was hopeful that the position of the Chinese in Indonesia would be better defended in the newly elected parliament and Konstituante. But parliamentary democracy was cut short by the introduction of martial law in 1957 and subsequently by the forced acceptance of Soekarno's Guided Democracy.

Between late 1956 and late 1959, Siauw, like many other politicians in Indonesia, was involved in the debate about the type of democracy that should be adopted. Having experienced the political instability caused by frequent changes in government and the inability of political parties to work together effectively in parliament, Siauw was one of the first politicians to support Soekarno's proposal for Guided Democracy. As a long time opponent of the Masyumi and PSI alliance, Siauw also supported the move towards the return to the 1945 Constitution and hence the realisation of the Guided Democracy infrastructure with Soekarno as the chief leader of the executive government.

This chapter outlines Siauw's involvement in the transformation process from parliamentary democracy to Guided Democracy in both parliament and the Konstituante and the impacts of this involvement to Baperki.

Indonesians were hopeful that, as promised by the political leaders, the 1955 general elections would significantly improve the way in which government would run its political programs and would also significantly reduce, if not eliminate, political instability caused by friction between the political parties.

But political developments after the election greatly disappointed the Indonesians. The big four political parties – PNI, Masyumi, NU and PKI – continued to have differences in the way policies were to be formulated and implemented. Furthermore, the post-election PNI–Masyumi–NU cabinet led by Ali Sastroamidjojo proved to be as ineffective as the pre-election cabinets in resolving major problems faced by the country. Events which developed in the later part of 1956, including abortive coup attempts by Colonel Zulkifli Lubis, uncontrolled large scale smuggling of goods by military commanders in the exporting areas of North Sulawesi and Sumatra – which was later followed by the displacement of Jakarta-controlled administrations with those of the regional military commanders – further undermined the second Ali cabinet, which finally resigned in March 1957.[1]

The political cleavage between Masyumi, supported by PSI, Parkindo and Partai Katolik, on one hand, and PNI, supported by PKI, NU and other nationalist parties, on the other, became sharper after the elections. The tensions between these two main political blocs came to have more of a regional dimension – thanks partly to what the elections had shown. PNI, NU and PKI had been successful in Jakarta, Central Java and East Java during the elections. These parties were therefore identified as the parties of Java, the regions that imported more than they exported, so benefitting from the situation where the rupiah was overvalued. Masyumi and PSI, on the other hand, performed better in the outer islands and West Java. They accordingly identified themselves with the outer islands, the main exporting regions of Indonesia. Partly due to regional identification and partly due to political orientation, PNI and PKI tended to be closer and more accommodating to Soekarno. On the other hand, Masyumi and PSI were supporters of Hatta.[2]

By the end of 1956, there existed three groups of power in Indonesian politics. The first group was represented by Masyumi, PSI and a number of military commanders of the outer regions. They demanded that the Ali cabinet resign and that there be dramatic changes made to the way the government implemented policies, giving the regions more power to run their own affairs. They also demanded the return of Hatta, who had just resigned from the vice-presidency, to the prime ministership. Their increasing demands for autonomy and more representation in government were voiced by a number of army officers of the outer regions. These demands were followed by rebellious movements in Java and Sumatra, which began to spread in 1957 and 1958.

---

[1] Herb Feith, 'Dynamics of Guided Democracy', in Ruth McVey (ed.), *Indonesia*. pp. 316–320.
[2] Ibid., p. 318.

The second group was led by Soekarno himself. Having been kept out of executive roles since November 1945 (and especially since the achievement of internationally recognised independence in December 1949), he was keen to re-emerge as a leader involved in the formulation of policies and in the running of the country. Between the end of 1956 and the beginning of 1957, Soekarno talked about the failure of parliamentary democracy and about the need to dramatically alter the implementation of democratic principles by adopting what he termed Guided Democracy. One key aspect of this was the formation of a cabinet in which all major political parties, including the PKI, were represented. PNI and PKI as well as a number other parties and organisations like Baperki supported Soekarno's formulation.

The third group was the central leadership of the army under the leadership of General Nasution. Their key demand was for increased power for the army. As the regionalists sought to undermine Jakarta's authority through military actions, which came to a head with the formation, in February 1958, of a rebel government in Padang – the PRRI (Pemerintah Revolusioner Republik Indonesia – Indonesian Revolutionary Government) – Soekarno and the government were forced to rely on the army's central leaders to defeat this challenge. The army leaders thus held the balance of power between Soekarno and the regionalists.

When the elected parliament was inaugurated in 1956, Siauw re-formed the Fraksi Nasional Progresif. This faction included the following small political parties and individuals: Baperki, Partai Murba, PRN, Permai, Garindo, SKI, Acoma, Partindo, Mohamad Yamin and Sudjono. Siauw was re-elected chairman.

Siauw was greatly concerned by the increased power of the army. In September 1956 the army chief, Nasution, issued a regulation which severely restricted the freedom of the press. Siauw was quick to condemn the regulation in parliament. Together with Soetomo of the BPRI, Siauw moved an interpellation, questioning Nasution's action, which Siauw described as illegal. Siauw argued that this regulation violated the spirit of Articles 19 and 33 of the 1950 Constitution. Prime Minister Ali defended Nasution's action so as to minimise confusion and instability which could be caused by irresponsible reporting of political events. Ali promised that the regulation would be further supported by a formal bill on how the country was to be run under the state of emergency,[3] but his cabinet fell before that bill was tabled.

---

[3] *Republik*, 24 October 1956; *Republik*, 31 October 1956.

Transition to Guided Democracy

Soekarno first talked about a new political framework for Indonesia in October 1956, soon after he returned from visits to China and the Soviet Union. On 28 October 1956, as part of the celebration of Youth Pledge Day, he said that parliamentary democracy had failed because the country had too many parties who refused to work together in achieving common goals. He said that it was his dream that the youth organisations of the various parties would deliberate together and decide to 'bury the parties'. Two days later, in a function of the Teachers Union, he repeated his call to 'bury the parties' and explained that a Guided Democracy would be more appropriate for Indonesia than it was for Western democracy.[4]

In a speech to the Konstituante on 10 November 1956, Siauw talked of the importance of creating a constitution which was right for Indonesia and that this constitution should not be copied or adapted from other countries. He said, 'Always bear in mind that the constitution to be drawn up is intended for the Indonesian people, and the character, the identity of the Indonesian people, should be reflected in this constitution'.[5]

By now, Siauw had been frustrated by the attitudes of most political parties. The transition to a national economy from the colonial one had not only failed to eliminate racial discrimination but had actually encouraged many political leaders to exercise racial discrimination. He was further frustrated by the delays in settling the dual nationality and citizenship issues and blamed the frequent changes of cabinet for these delays.

Siauw was also happy that Soekarno was impressed by the systems adopted by the Soviet Union and People's Republic of China. He wrote many articles supporting the systems and admiring the political and economic achievements of the two states. He was particularly supportive of Soekarno's judgment that the one party system was better than the multi-party system. Although it was not clear that Siauw would endorse the PKI as the one party to be established, he was in favor of the single party concept.[6]

Siauw would have been supportive of Soekarno's conclusion regarding the system he observed in the Soviet Union. In a speech delivered in 1956, Soekarno said:

---

[4] Siauw, *Lima Jaman*, p. 270; John Legge, *Soekarno*, p. 271, p. 279.
[5] Legge, *Soekarno*, p. 280.
[6] Interviews with Oey Hay Djoen in Jakarta, October 1997 and Go Gien Tjwan, Amsterdam, December 1993.

> In countries with only one party, shaping and reshaping, thinking and rethinking, can proceed easily. For instance in the Soviet Union, brothers and sisters, if it is necessary to reshape, it is very easy; once that single party has managed to change its opinion, it starts the reshaping. So, look at the government in the Soviet Union, brothers and sisters: it is elected from and by the presidium, the presidium is elected by the Supreme Soviet. The Supreme Soviet is elected by the people. The government is then an extension of the community. For that reason things are extremely easy.[7]

In this, Siauw was supported only by some of his Fraksi Nasional Progresif, namely members of Partai Murba. He was in conflict with most of the party leaders, including Aidit, who were not in favor of disbanding their parties.

But Soekarno did not define his strategy on how the 'burial' of political parties was to be achieved, nor did he actively campaign for the achievement of this political dream. By the end of 1956, the formulation of Guided Democracy remained a concept, received with mixed reactions from leaders of the political parties and organisations.

Soekarno's concept only became clearer in February 1957. Soekarno began to actively canvass his ideas with a number of political figures close to him. By then, he no longer spoke of burying political parties but limited the concept to the formation of a gotong royong (mutual assistance) cabinet involving the main political parties, including PKI, and the formation of the Dewan Nasional (National Council). The Dewan Nasional was to act as an advisory body for the formulation of national policies. This body, Soekarno was to later declare, was to reflect a wide representation of the whole nation, including the 'functional groups' (the armed forces, police and organisations of youth, women, labourers, peasants and minority groups) as well as political parties and regions. Leaders of the political parties were invited to hear from Soekarno himself what he meant by Guided Democracy and what the concept included.

Siauw led his Fraksi Nasional Progresif delegation to visit Soekarno on 20 February. Based on Soekarno's explanation, Siauw indicated that his faction fully supported the concept and urged Soekarno to be more determined in implementing the concept. Furthermore, he proposed that in implementing this concept Soekarno should not be constrained by complicated legal

---

[7] Baladas, *Indonesian Politics 1955–59*, p. 96.

and formal regulations.[8] The PKI, whose leaders had also been invited to see Soekarno a day earlier, made a statement supporting the concept.[9]

The concept itself was formally unveiled by Soekarno on 21 February 1957. In a speech delivered to more than 900 guests, Soekarno blamed parliamentary democracy, or 'liberal democracy', for being responsible for the instability and disunity experienced in the first eleven years of independence. He insisted that Western democracy was not in harmony with the Indonesian spirit and personality. He argued that Indonesians highly valued the principle of Gotong Royong. Decisions and directions should, according to Soekarno, be derived through 'musyawarah' ('deliberations') and 'mufakat' ('consensus').

Therefore, political opposition would no longer exist. All parties would cooperate and work together to achieve common goals. Soekarno said:

> The Gotong Royong Cabinet would be the compressed form of parliament. On the other hand, the Dewan Nasional would be the compressed form of the living society, the bustling society. The Dewan Nasional and the cabinet shall stand side by side, it will constitute an immense and strong bridge connecting the government with the living forces.

Soekarno gave the parties a week to consider his concept and requested that by 28 February, they submit and confirm their positions[10].

Within days of the announcement of the concept, parties began to rally their support to either endorse or reject it. Of the major parties, PKI and PNI supported the concept, while Masyumi and NU rejected it.[11]

Member organisations of the Fraksi Nasional Progresif, including Baperki, fully supported the concept. Baperki issued a statement on 25 February 1957 supporting it. In this statement, which was clearly prepared by Siauw, Baperki highlighted four major failures associated with parliamentary democracy.

Firstly, colonial regulations containing racial discrimination had not been replaced by ones which outlawed racial discrimination in every field. Secondly, the system had failed to convert the colonial economy into a national economy in which the utilisation of useful domestic capital for

---

[8] *Republik*, 21 February 1957.
[9] Ibid.
[10] *Republik*, 22 February 1957; Baladas, *Indonesian Politics 1955–59*, pp. 80–81.
[11] Legge, *Sukarno*, pp. 285–286.

the construction of a national economy could be guaranteed. Thirdly, the system had led to political instability, resulting in frequent changes of government. Each change was followed by the arrival of new political figures who were more interested in enriching their own groups and had thus introduced many regulations which harmed the economy and local production capacities. Fourthly, the system had also failed to expedite the finalisation of a citizenship bill and so the state did not have a workable citizenship law.

Baperki was confident that the new system proposed by Soekarno would create national unity and hence political stability. Baperki believed that such a situation would be able to guarantee better living conditions for the minority groups. Accordingly, Baperki fully endorsed the concept.[12]

The debate on the Gotong Royong cabinet proposal was short lived. Early in March 1957, the territorial commander of East Indonesia took over the civil administration of his region by declaring martial law, an act of defiance of central authority similar to those in December 1956 in Sumatra. On 14 March 1957 the Ali cabinet resigned, and Soekarno, in response to pressure from General Nasution, proclaimed a 'state of war and siege' – martial law.

Under martial law, the army leadership became an important rival of the civilian government which was formed in April 1957 and led by Prime Minister Djuanda. Later in 1957 the army forbade strikes in all vital industries. Press freedom was also limited through censorship.

With the weakening position of the political parties and the reduced influence of parliament in politics, the parliamentary democratic systems began to be whittled away. The formation of the Dewan Nasional in May 1957 further reduced the significance of parliament. The Dewan Nasional, headed by the president himself and including the chiefs of the armed services and leaders of major parties, became a highly important deliberative body. This was supposed to serve as an advisory body to the president and cabinet but, instead, became a vehicle for spreading his ideas and influence. In 1958 and 1959 many policies were conceived and debated in the council. Reluctant to challenge the formulations proposed by the council, the Djuanda cabinet tended to accept them.

Early in 1958 the army took control of a vast range of Dutch businesses including trading houses, estates, mines and the country's main shipping companies. Initially seized by a series of workers' actions, apparently instigated

---

[12] *Republik*, 25 February 1957.

by leaders encouraged by President Soekarno, they were then taken over by the army. The army's position was further consolidated when it was able to crush the rebellious PRRI/Permesta movement in 1958, which was supported by Masyumi and PSI. By mid-1958 the army became the most powerful force in Indonesia, gaining a much stronger position in military, political and economic affairs than ever before.

Deliberation and argument

Meanwhile, the Konstituante began its deliberations to form a new constitution. In this process, Siauw was particularly active in the formulation of a 'dasar negara' ('state philosophy') and human rights.

In the Konstituante, Siauw formed two separate factions, the Baperki faction, represented by Siauw, Oei Tjoe Tat, Jan Ave and CS Richter, and the 'five-person faction', represented by Go Gien Tjwan, Yap Thiam Hien, Liem Koen Seng, Ang Pin Hian and Oen Poe Djiang. The two factions were later combined in a group faction called the Fraksi Bhineka Tunggal Ika (Unity in Diversity Faction), under Siauw's chairmanship. Siauw's idea was to maximise support for Baperki's various positions for the new constitution and he believed that by forming two separate factions, in which the members could generate a wide range of political ideas and proposals, Baperki's ultimate objectives could be realised.[13]

Siauw's knowledge of parliamentary rules and procedures led to his inclusion in the 15-member committee specially charged with developing procedures to be adopted by the Konstituante, including one on how the chair and vice-chair were to be elected.[14] Wilopo, of PNI, was finally elected chair. When the elections of vice-chairs took place, Siauw proposed the nomination of Mrs Ratu Aminah Hidayat, leader of the IPKI (Partai Ikatan Pendukung Kemerdekaan Indonesia – League of Supporters of Indonesian Independence), and she was elected as one of the vice-chairs.[15]

Being busy in Jakarta with the daily management of Baperki's activities, the running of the daily, *Republik*, and his parliamentary duties, Siauw appointed Oei Tjoe Tat, Liem Koen Seng, Yap Thiam Hien and Jan Ave to

---

[13] Interviews with Oei Tjoe Tat, Jakarta, July 1993 and Go Gien Tjwan, Amsterdam, December 1993.

[14] *Republik*, 13 November 1956. The committee also included Mohamad Yamin, Zainul Arifin of NU, Leimena of Parkindo and Kasimo of Partai Katolik.

[15] Interviews with Oei Tjoe Tat, Jakarta, July 1993 and Go Gien Tjwan, Amsterdam, December 1993.

represent Baperki in the smaller Konstituante committee, the Committee for the Preparation of the Constitution (Panitia Persiapan Konstitusi). They were required to be present in Bandung on a day-to-day basis for much of the lifetime of the Konstituante (November 1956 to July 1959).[16]

There were two major blocs within the Konstituante and one minor one. The largest of the three was the Pancasila Bloc, consisting of PNI, PKI, PRN, Christian parties, other minor national parties and Baperki. This bloc advocated Pancasila as the foundation of the state. The Islamic bloc was represented by Masyumi, NU, PSII, Perti (Perhimpunan Tarbiyah Islamiyah – Islamic Educators Association) and other small Islamic organisations. Members of this bloc advocated Islam as the basis of the state. The smallest one was the social-economic bloc containing the Partai Buruh, Partai Murba and Acoma. This group advocated a socialist economy.[17]

The debates in the Konstituante were really a sideshow, an easily superseded aspect of the transition period to Guided Democracy. However, Siauw's speeches in these debates reflected his formulations on various principles and were included in this section as highlights of his political expectations in the period concerned.

In a speech delivered in the Konstituante on 25 August 1958, Siauw strongly advocated the inclusion of Article 33 of the 1945 Constitution or Article 38 of the 1950 Constitution in the new constitution. He declared:

> If the government owns and controls land, water and all natural resources contained in the land and utilises and exploits these resources for the benefit of the people, the construction of a just and prosperous Indonesian society can be realised. In such a society, unemployment will not exist and economic crises can be fully overcome. Furthermore, it is paramount that the land, water and resources are not only controlled but fully owned by the government. Foreign monopolies should not be allowed to own any of these vital resources. …the new constitution should therefore have provisions which ensure the establishment of national economy.[18]

---

[16] Oei, *Memoar Oei Tjoe Tat*, p. 87.

[17] Adnan Buyung Nasution, *The Aspiration for Constitutional Government In Indonesia*, Pusataka Sinar Harapan, Jakarta, 1992, pp. 32–34.

[18] *Risalah Perundingan Konstituante*, Departemen Penerangan, 1958, Volume V, pp. 2329–2331.

Siauw urged the Konstituante to formulate provisions which would guarantee appropriate living conditions of public servants. Siauw indicated:

> The adoption of Article 38 of the 1950 constitution means that the country would have a large number of state enterprises which would form the backbone of the national economy. This means our country would have a large number of public servants. Currently the wages of our public servants are low and would not encourage them to work efficiently. This situation must be improved. They have to be encouraged to perform better for the country and the encouragement has to be more than symbolic appreciation. It is also important to dramatically change the attitudes of our public servants. I recommend that the term 'pegawai negeri' [literally 'state officers'] be altered to 'abdi negara' ['servants of the state']. The term will constantly remind them that they need to serve the people.[19]

The Konstituante also spent a great deal of time deliberating and debating human rights issues. Many speakers in the Konstituante considered human rights to be as important as the state philosophy and argued that matters related to human rights should be grouped together in a special chapter within the new constitution.[20] During the debates, it became apparent that there was disagreement about certain rights covering religions, the Indonesian Chinese and private property. But Buyung Nasution asserts:

> The main body of universally recognised human rights had been agreed. This fundamental agreement on human rights may indeed be considered as the most unequivocal outcome of the whole work of the Konstituante. It can be justly be considered as the substantive constitutional norm of the Republic of Indonesia, ranking in importance next to the Declaration of Independence.[21]

In these debates, Baperki was most frequently represented by Oei Tjoe Tat and Siauw Giok Tjhan, with Yap Thiam Hien also delivering a number of speeches. Baperki's representation was not limited to the rights of the Chinese or minority groups but also covered a wide range of general human rights issues. On 11 February 1958, Siauw delivered his main speech on the

---

[19] Ibid., pp. 2935–2936.
[20] Nasution, *Aspirations for Constitutional Democracy in Indonesia*, p. 131.
[21] Ibid., pp. 131–132.

subject in the Konstituante. He explained that he based his arguments on two main principles:

> Firstly human rights need to be upheld in order to ensure that the construction of a just and prosperous society, which is in line with the 1945 spirit, is achieved. Secondly our constitution has to contain proper clauses which guarantee that human rights are protected in Indonesia so that the reputation of our republic which took the initiative in holding the first Asian–African Conference and upholds the Bandung spirit, will be further enhanced.[22]

Siauw argued that the existing 1950 constitution did not provide adequate protection of human rights, particularly with respect to minority groups. He advocated the adoption of a principle contained in the constitution of the Federal Republic of Germany, which stated, 'No-one may be prejudiced because of his sex, descent, race, language, homeland of origin, faith or his religious and political opinions'. Siauw was also attracted to the provisions contained in the constitution of the People's Republic of China which stated, 'All ethnic groups have the freedom to use and develop their own languages and to maintain or change their habits, customs and natural heritage'. He argued that it was paramount for Indonesia, which had a large number of ethnic groups and minority groups, to have such provisions in the new constitution to protect the rights of these groups. Finally he stressed that discrimination against minority groups should be constitutionally prohibited, and furthermore, constitutional protection should be given so that they could speak their language freely and maintain their customs and cultural heritage.

Siauw was also heavily involved in the debates on the constitution's provisions for economic development and controls. He was particularly concerned that parliament should be able to control and monitor the state's budgets. He was keen to include provisions, which enabled the parliament to receive full explanations on the state's income and expenses on a regular basis from relevant ministers. Siauw argued that state budgets had to be approved by parliament and the budget performance had to be checked and calculated by the Body for Financial Audits (Dewan Pengawas Keuangan). Siauw complained that since the formation of parliament, cabinet ministers were never obliged to account for their departments' financial performances and the parliament was powerless in stopping unlawful expenses. The new

---

[22] *Risalah Perundingan, Konstituante*, Volume II, 1958, pp. 1054–1055.

constitution, Siauw urged, should contain provisions, enabling the parliament to correct erroneous policy implementation.[23]

Guided Democracy ideas were not a major focus of debate in the Konstituante. It was in the Dewan Nasional more than in any other body that various proposals were discussed for how the country's political and constitutional system should be changed towards Guided Democracy. The discussions in the Konstituante only echoed debates which took place in the Dewan Nasional.

The collapse of parliamentary democracy

While the Konstituante was at work and achieving progress, changes in other political areas continued to undermine the constitutional processes, changes which ultimately nullified the Konstituante's achievements.

The political climate in this period was one dominated by both co-operation and competition between the army and the president. The rise of the army as the main organisational force in the state had significantly reduced the effectiveness of parliament and cabinet. The emergence of Soekarno as a political force and of the Dewan Nasional, which he chaired, further weakened them.

The army leaders agreed that Indonesia should adopt Guided Democracy as an alternative political framework. But they opposed many of Soekarno's concrete proposals for how it should be given constitutional form. In general they favored a big role for functional groups.

A committee on Guided Democracy within the Dewan Nasional was formed in August 1958, headed by Tumakaka, Siauw's close political associate and a member of Baperki. The committee was assigned to formulate the framework of the Guided Democracy, in particular the simplification of the party system and the improvement of the system of representation.[24] The committee also included other political associates of Siauw's, Iwa Kusumasumantri, Nja Diwan and Tjan Tjoe Som. The last two were also members of Baperki.

This committee failed to deliver a unanimous report on how Guided Democracy was to be implemented. How much representation within the parliament the functional groups should have was the topic of dispute. The

---

[23] *Risalah Perundingan Konstituante*, Volume VI, pp. 2932–2934.
[24] Daniel S. Lev, *The Transition to Guided Democracy*, Cornell University Press, Ithaca, 1966, pp. 220–221.

anti-party group demanded that the functional groups should hold up to 50 per cent of the parliamentary seats. Representatives of the parties, however, could not accept more than a third of the seats. The Dewan Nasional then took a vote in October 1958 and the anti-party group, strongly backed by representatives of the armed forces, convincingly won the battle. The Dewan Nasional then submitted its proposal, which contained the following provisions, to the cabinet: [25]

1. one half of the total membership of the next parliament will represent the functional groups
2. candidacy of the functional groups will be via the Front Nasional[26] (National Front), led by the president
3. the method of election will be based on a double-choice system. The voter will vote once for a party symbol and once again for a functional group symbol.

It was becoming obvious to the public that the political party system was nearing its end, as this proposal would soon force the parties out of the political system. The Functional Group faction, whose members would be independent from the parties and hence could not be influenced by them, would dominate the next parliament. Soekarno, who would lead the Front Nasional, from which membership of the Functional Group would be derived, would also play a much more influential role in running the government.

Representatives of the armed forces, led by Nasution did not stop there. In November 1958, Nasution pushed for a significant (50 per cent) military representation in the Functional Group. Nasution further demanded that military members should be appointed by the president, not elected.[27]

Nasution's demands for greater participation by the army in politics and parliament received strong opposition from the PKI and Baperki. Articles in both *Harian Rakyat* and *Republik*, published on November 14, highlighted their opposition to Nasution's proposals by arguing that politicians and military officers moved in different worlds and had different functions in society. The military personnel should concentrate on military duties and

---

[25] Daniel S. Lev, *The Transition to Guided Democracy*, Cornell University Press, Ithaca, 1966, pp. 221–222.

[26] A body, headed by Soekarno, set up to mobilise the masses and to propagate Soekarno's political ideology.

[27] Ibid., p. 225.

should not interfere with politicians' duties. Likewise, politicians should not be involved in military affairs. They conceded that military leaders should hold high positions in the highest bodies in government but not that they should be represented in parliament.[28]

But the parties were divided in facing the drive towards eliminating them. The PNI and NU were not very strong in rejecting the proposal. Masyumi had suffered as a result of its involvement in the failed attempts to gain power in the outer islands and was not active in either supporting or rejecting it. The PKI, while voicing its opposition, was not totally opposed to army representation in parliament. After several months of debates, open talks and discussions the cabinet remained deadlocked on the involvement of the armed forces.

Return to the 1945 Constitution

Finally, in February 1959 a compromise was reached in cabinet. The compromise was the adoption of the 1945 Constitution. This was initially proposed by Nasution in 1957. Nasution's proposal, according to Lev, was prompted by his desire to minimise the influence of the parties. The return to the 1945 Constitution would eliminate the Konstituante which had become deadlocked on issues around the position of Islam in the constitution. More importantly, the 1945 Constitution included a reference to groups which could be used to legitimise the representation of functional groups. The inclusion of representatives of functional groups in the legislative and executive bodies would, in Nasution's view, legalise the army's active involvement in politics.[29]

Although Soekarno had previously rejected this idea, by early 1959 he finally endorsed it. It was seen as a compromise as it contained provisions to be defined by law on groups to participate in legislative bodies. This provision was seen to allow Soekarno to be involved in defining who should participate in the Functional Group and hence was hoped to eliminate the deadlock on army representation in legislative bodies.[30]

In February 1959, the cabinet finally endorsed the return to the 1945 Constitution and the implementation of Guided Democracy within the framework of the 1945 Constitution. On 20 February, Soekarno formally

---

[28] *Harian Rakyat*, 14 November 1958; *Republik*, 14 November 1958.
[29] Lev, *Transition to Guided Democracy*, pp. 207–208.
[30] Ibid., pp. 240–242.

accepted the cabinet's decision and announced his support in a public function. On 22 April 1959, President Soekarno formally proposed the adoption of the 1945 Constitution by the Konstituante, calling it a constitution which would suit Indonesian culture and embody Indonesia's true ideology.[31]

Under the 1945 Constitution the power of the executive would be strengthened and that of the parliament would be reduced. The president would be accountable not to parliament but to the larger MPR (Majelis Permusyawaratan Rakyat – People's Consultative Assembly) which would determine the state's policy principles.

Though the constitution had no explicit reference to functional groups, it was agreed that they would be given a major role. Soekarno, in his 22 April speech, endorsed the appointment of armed forces representatives in parliament, the MPR and the DPA (Dewan Pertimbangan Agung – Supreme Advisory Council). He agreed to there being 35 armed forces members in parliament. Soekarno also endorsed the cabinet's position that the 1945 Constitution should be adopted without any amendments.[32]

Following Soekarno's speech, the Konstituante began its deliberations on the acceptance of the 1945 Constitution. The majority of the parties and organisations represented in the Konstituante, including Baperki, supported the proposal on the condition that the constitution was to be amended. Only the Partai Murba and the IPKI endorsed the acceptance of the constitution without any amendment. Masyumi, the smaller Islamic parties, the Partai Buruh and the Partai Katolik strongly rejected the 1945 Constitution.[33]

In his speech delivered in the Konstituante on 11 May 1959, Siauw highlighted his concern that Article 6 of the 1945 Constitution could be used by some government bodies or officials as a justification to implement racially discriminatory measures. Article 6, which dictates that the Indonesian president should be an Asli Indonesian, was created, according to Siauw, because the constitution was prepared when the Japanese were still in Indonesia and its drafters were concerned that the Japanese would appoint a Japanese national as the first president of Indonesia.

Siauw further stated that he knew of this fact from Mohamad Yamin, who was involved in drafting the Constitution in 1945, and that he was

---

[31] Lev, *Transition to Guided Democracy*, p. 247.

[32] Nasution, *Aspiration for Constitutional Government*, p. 322.

[33] Ibid., p. 325.

convinced that the drafters had no intention of permitting discrimination against Indonesians of Chinese origin. Apart from Article 6, Siauw believed that the Constitution as a whole reflected the spirit of 1945 and that it would be an effective foundation for the realisation of a just and prosperous society. Accordingly, he declared his support for the readoption of the 1945 Constitution. However he urged that the MPR should remove the word 'Asli' from Article 6.[34]

With regard to greater presidential power contained in the 1945 Constitution, Siauw argued that this greater power was necessary to implement a national economy based on Article 33 of the constitution, in which production would rest on the three pillars of state enterprises, people's cooperative ventures and domestic private firms. Siauw also proposed that the conclusions reached by the Konstituante on human rights, be designated as the official guide (pedoman) in implementing the 1945 Constitution. He argued that this would help persuade the Konstituante to accept the 1945 Constitution with the necessary two-thirds majority.

In response to Siauw's question in parliament regarding Article 6, Djuanda confirmed that Article 6 could not be used as the basis of racially discriminatory practices. He added that the 1945 Constitution was indeed against racial discrimination.[35]

Siauw was one of the main speakers for the Konstituante's resolutions on human rights in the 1945 Constitution's amendments. He was able to get the support of 29 other members from nearly all political parties in the Konstituante. Two other outspoken speakers, Mang Reng Say of the Partai Katolik and Chanafiah of the PKI, argued for similar amendments. As a result of this, the government agreed to amend the 1945 Constitution to include provisions on human rights based on the Konstituante resolutions.[36]

The debates in the Konstituante were, in the end, linked to the question of the Jakarta Charter of August 1945 which included a requirement that Muslims be bound by Islamic law (Sharia). The government's submission to the Konstituante affirmed its recognition of the Jakarta Charter as an important historical document. But this was not enough for the Islamic parties. NU as well as Masyumi insisted that the Charter be included in the preamble of the Constitution. The secular parties and organisations and the two Christian parties rejected this proposal.

---

[34] *Republik*, 12 May 1959.
[35] *Republik*, 21 May 1959.
[36] Nasution, *Aspirations for Constitutional Democracy*, pp. 386–387.

As a result, lacking the support of the Islamic parties, the Konstituante failed to reach the necessary two thirds of the votes in accepting the adoption of 1945 Constitution on three separate occasions: 30 May, 1 June and 2 June 1959.[37]

Following the failure of the Konstituante to reach an agreement, General Nasution issued a decree imposing a ban on all political activities. The decree was also designed to suspend all Konstituante meetings until the return of President Soekarno, who was abroad. The IPKI, representing the army, went further. In the middle of June 1959, they initiated a movement to dissolve the Konstituante. This movement was supported by 17 other political parties belonging to the Front to Defend Pancasila (Front Pembela Pancasila). The PNI and PKI later supported this movement and declared that they would only attend a Konstituante meeting to vote for its dissolution.[38]

A few days later, Aidit, representing the PKI; Suwirjo, representing the PNI, and Djody Gondokusumo representing the Front to Defend Pancasila, urged the president to dissolve the Konstituante and issue a decree to force the adoption of the 1945 Constitution.[39] Siauw too supported this proposal.[40] On 29 June, Soekarno returned to Indonesia and was urged by the army to issue a presidential decree to adopt the 1945 Constitution.[41]

On 5 July 1959 Soekarno acted by issuing a presidential decree which dissolved the Konstituante, affirmed the adoption of the 1945 Constitution as the new constitution without amendment and foreshadowed the early formation of the Provisional People's Consultative Assembly (Majelis Permusyawaratan Rakyat Sementara or MPRS) and the DPA. The era of parliamentary democracy is usually said to have come to an end at this point.

The proponents of the 1945 Constitution immediately praised Soekarno for his decisive action. Siauw, in an article published in Republik, argued that his quick decision would end the political division that had existed for some time. He also praised Soekarno for agreeing to quickly form the MPRS and the DPA so that his role as president could not be described as that of a dictator.[42]

---

[37] Ibid., p. 397.
[38] Lev, *Transition to Guided Democracy*, p. 275.
[39] *Republik*, 4 July 1959.
[40] Ibid.
[41] Daniel S. Lev, *Transition to Guided Democracy* p. 276.
[42] *Republik*, 6 July 1959.

On 6 July 1959, Djuanda returned his mandate to the president and on 8 July 1959 nine parliamentary factions, including the Fraksi Nasional Progresif, declared their support for the decree.[43] On 9 July, the first presidential cabinet was formed, with Soekarno acting as prime minister and Djuanda as first minister.

On 29 July 1959, the new DPA was formed. Soekarno appointed Siauw as a member representing the minority groups (Siauw was the only Chinese on the body). The 46-member DPA also included members of Baperki, namely Utrecht, representing the Eurasian minority group; Tumakaka, representing intellectuals, and Adam Malik, representing the 1945 Generation (Angkatan 45).[44]

In August 1959, a committee of five parliamentarians was formed to formulate new parliamentary procedures and day-to-day management arrangements of parliament in line with requirements of the 1945 Constitution. Recognising Siauw's knowledge of parliamentary procedures, Soekarno and Sartono included Siauw in this committee.[45]

The re-enactment of the 1945 Constitution, the formation of a new presidential cabinet, and the creation of the MPRS, DPA and Depernas (Dewan Perancang Nasional – National Planning Agency), marked the end of the erea of parliamentary democracy. For the next six years, Indonesia was run under the principles of Guided Democracy, where the role of the parties in parliament was significantly reduced and there emerged three strong political forces in Indonesian politics: the army, Soekarno and the PKI.

Why was parliamentary democracy defeated and superseded? On this, scholars can be grouped into four major streams that differ mainly in the factors they emphasise.

Stream 1, represented by Feith, emphasises the political factors. People in this stream believe that the collapse was due to:

1. the high level of political unrest and disappointment over the government's performance
2. political conflicts between a PNI-led coalition of forces, in Java, and Masyumi-led forces, in the outer islands, that had immobilised government – there was a real danger of a civil war

---

[43] *Republik*, 9 July 1959.
[44] *Republik*, 31 July 1959.
[45] *Republik*, 8 August 1959.

3. a perception by most political leaders that the adoption of a different system would lessen the aforementioned problems. The alternative system, Guided Democracy, endorsed by Soekarno, appeared to many politicians to offer advantageous solutions.
4. the leaders, Feith's 'administrators', who had initially endorsed and implemented parliamentary democracy were not strongly committed to upholding this system and eventually prepared to abandon it

Stream 2, represented by Glassburner and Schmitt, links the collapse to the conflict betwen major political forces representing Java and the outer islands which developed due to the government's exchange rate. Specifically:

1. inflation and the undervalued rupiah of the 1950s hurt exporters (mainly in the outer islands) and benefited importers (mainly in Java, in particular Jakarta)
2. Masyumi represented the outer islands, while the PNI–NU–PKI coalition represented Java. Traders supported Masyumi and bureaucrats supported the PNI.
3. the clash between the forces whose main interest was in combating inflation (Masyumi and PSI) and those who were prepared to risk financial stability to rid the economy of Dutch control (PNI, NU and PKI) reached a climax in 1957–1958, resulting in the victory of the latter group who supported Guided Democracy

Stream 3, represented by Benda, challenges Feith's analysis. Benda emphasises the cultural aspects of Indonesia and was convinced that parliamentary democracy would not survive because:

1. parliamentary democracy was not suitable for Indonesian culture and thus went against the grain of Indonesian history
2. Indonesian politicians were not committed to parliamentary democracy and to the values which accompany it

Those in Stream 4 argue that parliamentary democracy did not fail but was killed off by a Soekarno–army coalition. They emphasise the roles of the actors rather than the influence of the political factors. Dan Lev, Oey Hong Lee and Harold Crouch emphasise that it was the army who actually killed off parliamentary democracy. Soekarno was, in their view, the weaker party in the late 1950s, and was accordingly used by the army to realise its ambitions.

I agree with the emphasis of Stream 4 but consider, as Legge does, that Soekarno was the prime mover in changing the system and structure of the Indonesian government and politics in the late 1950s. Without the presence and involvement of Soekarno, the changes which took place in the 1950s, regardless of the environmental factors and cultural characteristics, would not have taken place.

From speeches in parliament and newspaper articles in the period, particularly those of Siauw Giok Tjhan, I believe that widespread support for Guided Democracy was due to:

1. acceptance of Soekarno's logic that there were far too many political parties in Indonesia and that this was responsible for political instability
2. acceptance that many leaders of these political parties were enriching themselves and their parties at the country's expense
3. acceptance of Soekarno's argument that parliamentary democracy was not for Indonesia, on cultural and historical grounds. Many regarded parliamentary democracy as a system copied from the Dutch.
4. acceptance that Soekarno's leadership would be more reliable and have stronger support than that of other political leaders. There was a strong sense of relief that Soekarno took the initiative in dismantling the existing system which was perceived to be destroying the state.

Speaking much later, Siauw admitted to me in 1980 that the 1945 Constitution was less democratic than the 1950 Constitution. However, Siauw remained convinced that Baperki had to support the return to the 1945 Constitution. If Baperki had rejected it, Baperki would have been seen to be part of the Masyumi–PSI league which would jeopardise Baperki's position and reduce its effectiveness in defending the interests of the Chinese.

Yap Thiam Hien's resignation

Within Baperki there was a good deal of conflict about the transition to Guided Democracy and the return to the 1945 Constitution. Siauw's policies were openly challenged by a senior leader of Baperki. This was the first challenge after the split in 1955. This time, the opposition came from Yap Thiam Hien, Siauw's close political associate for a number of years.

Yap Thiam Hien had been active in Baperki since its formation in 1954. He had been its first vice-chairman since the second Baperki conference in late 1954. When several leaders associated with the PSI and Partai Katolik left Baperki in 1955, Yap Thiam Hien decided to remain active in the organisation. He was close to Siauw and often defended Siauw's position in meetings. When Auwyong Peng Koen attacked Siauw and accused him of being a communist in 1955, Yap defended Siauw and criticised Auwyong as opportunistic and politically dirty.

Yap admired Siauw's dedication and honesty. He recalled that when, in 1955, a group of Chinese rice millers gave Siauw a large sum of money as a sign of gratitude for his successful defence in parliament of their right to maintain their status as rice millers, Siauw refused to accept the money for himself and donated the whole amount to Baperki. In 1956, in one of Baperki's leadership meetings, Yap proposed that Baperki provide Siauw with regular wages and a driver. Yap argued that Siauw worked wholeheartedly for Baperki and his valuable services should be financially compensated. The meeting supported Yap's proposal but Siauw insisted that the proposal be dropped.[46]

Since 1957, Yap had been strongly opposed to the principles of Guided Democracy. In a number of Baperki meetings, he had frequently challenged Siauw's endorsement of Guided Democracy. Yap's most vehement objection to Siauw's policies was conveyed in the Baperki conference held between 12 and 14 December 1958.

Yap argued that the problems being experienced were not due to the failure of parliamentary democracy. He remained convinced that parliamentary democracy would ensure the realisation of a true democracy and that Guided Democracy would ultimately undermine the quality of democracy. Accordingly, Yap asserted that Siauw's opinion on Guided Democracy should not be regarded as Baperki's position and insisted that until the organisation fully accepted the principles of Guided Democracy, Siauw's view should be regarded as merely his own opinion.

In the same meeting, Yap argued that Baperki leaders should concentrate on citizenship issues. He was concerned that Baperki was becoming more and more involved in issues outside the scope of the organisation's charter. He did not want Baperki to align itself with left-wing forces. He questioned Siauw's decision in endorsing the government's action banning the Kuo Min Tang activities, following the crushing of the PRRI/

---

[46] Interview with Yap Thiam Hien, Melbourne, December 1988.

Permesta rebellions. He argued that Siauw's action was unwise as it would put Baperki in a dangerous position if the groups Siauw identified as reactionary were to come to power.

In his response, Siauw maintained that Baperki's activities were in line with its constitution. He argued that citizenship issues could not be divorced from broader political matters. The choice between parliamentary democracy and Guided Democracy was, according to him, linked to citizenship issues. Siauw further argued that parliamentary democracy had failed to expedite the settlement of dual nationality issues. He therefore hoped that the adoption and implementation of Guided Democracy principles would alter this situation in a positive way. With regard to the banning of Kuo Min Tang political activity in Indonesia, Siauw maintained that what he condemned was not the Kuo Min Tang's political orientation but its subversive activities designed to undermine the legal government of Indonesia.

All speakers in the meeting supported Siauw and rejected Yap's arguments. From the meeting minutes it is clear that Siauw's tolerance of Yap's insistence to keep on debating the issues frustrated many meeting participants. Siauw allowed two days of the three-day meeting to be devoted to the issues raised by Yap, with many speakers ridiculing Yap's position and behaviour in the meeting.[47] But Yap decided to remain in the organisation as vice-chairman and Siauw continued to tolerate Yap's persistent objections to a number of his policies. But as more and more left-wing members joined and led the organisation Yap became more and more uncomfortable and isolated. He was particularly displeased with Boejoeng Saleh, Go Gien Tjwan and Tan Foe Khiong.

When the question of the return to the 1945 Constitution was raised, Yap maintained his objection to Guided Democracy and indicated to Siauw and Oei Tjoe Tat that he would argue against the constitution in the Konstituante. Siauw respected Yap's position and agreed to let him express an opinion which was different to that of the Fraksi Baperki in the Konstituante.[48]

In March 1959, in a letter published in a number of newspapers in Jakarta, Yap openly challenged Siauw's endorsement of the Guided Democracy principles and the return to the 1945 Constitution. On 12 May 1959, Yap delivered his speech in the Konstituante arguing that the 1945 Constitution and the accompanying Guided Democracy principles did not

---

[47] Ibid.

[48] Interviews with Yap Thiam Hien in December 1988 and Oei Tjoe Tat in July 1993.

embody the essentials of democracy. He asserted that the 1945 Constitution included provisions that encouraged dictatorship based on greater presidential power. Under the 1945 Constitution, according to Yap, the President would play a major role in legislative, executive and judiciary functions and that his power would therefore be too great and would have dictatorial qualities. Accordingly, Yap rejected the 1945 Constitution and indicated his preference for the existing 1950 Provisional Constitution.[49]

After that, the relationship between Yap and the main group of Baperki leaders deteriorated. While Yap continued to be present at all leadership meetings, he frequently engaged in heated arguments with Go Gien Tjwan, Boejoeng Saleh, Liem Koen Seng and Tan Foe Khiong. On 3 August 1959, Yap wrote a letter to Baperki's secretariat criticising Siauw for endorsing the return to the 1945 Constitution which, according to Yap contained a racial discriminatory article (Article 6). He maintained that Guided Democracy would ultimately kill true democracy and criticised Siauw's leadership for aligning Baperki with left-wing forces.

The content of this letter was discussed in a leadership meeting of 27 August 1959 which was attended by both Yap and Siauw. All the meeting participants criticised Yap for challenging Siauw's policies. But Siauw calmed the meeting by indicating that Yap had the right to put forward his opinion. The atmosphere was not pleasant for Yap and he decided to leave the meeting. As soon as he left, Tan Foe Khiong proposed that Yap's position as vice-chairman be discussed and that he be replaced. Siauw disagreed and urged the members to allow Yap to express his opinion in Baperki's congress.[50]

The congress was held in Semarang between 24 and 26 December 1960. Yap attended this congress in his capacity as vice-chairman. On the agenda was Yap's motion of no-confidence in Siauw's leadership. This was quickly settled as Yap received no support from the meeting participants. Knowing that the battle was lost, Yap decided to leave the congress. As he was leaving the congress hall, many Baperki members yelled at and ridiculed him.[51]

After that, Yap did not appear at Baperki meetings and was removed from the vice-chairmanship. However, he later declared that he had not resigned from Baperki. He indicated to me that although he criticised Siauw, he had no feelings of resentment towards him. He left the

---

[49] *Risalah Perundingan, Konstituante*, 1959, Volume II, pp. 615–619.

[50] Baperki meeting minutes, 27 August 1959.

[51] Baperki meeting minutes, 24–26 December 1960; interview with Oei Tjoe Tat (July 1993), Go Gien Tjwan (December 1990) and Yap Thiam Hien (December 1988).

vice-chairmanship, he said, because he was no longer able to work with other Baperki leaders like Go Gien Tjwan, Boejoeng Saleh and Tan Foe Khiong. He maintained that he continued to respect Siauw and described him as one of the three people he respected most in his life.[52]

The feeling of respect was mutual. Siauw admired Yap as a highly principled man. Although he was often annoyed by Yap's stubbornness, he always allowed him to express his opinions. Although Siauw was in agreement with many of Yap's objections to Guided Democracy and the 1945 Constitution, he believed it would be fatal for Baperki to be aligned with the camp which rejected the 1945 Constitution. Quietly, Siauw regretted Yap's departure from Baperki[53]. Such a regret would have been based upon Siauw's understanding and respect of Yap's qualities.

Lev suggests that Siauw and Yap had a great deal in common. They were in agreement on a few fundamentals that set them apart from others, including close associates. Lev says:

> Both men were personally modest, unself-serving, serious and responsible – qualities they recognised and respected in one another. Siauw was probably more comfortable with a Chinese identity, whereas Yap, who did not regret being Chinese, nevertheless took it more lightly. But neither was naive or particularly chauvinistic about the peranakan minority in Indonesia nor given to justify the privileges many Chinese had gained in the colony and maintained thereafter. Both, indeed, tended to be censorious of bloated wealth, Chinese or other. They defended not Chinese commercial advantage, but Chinese minority rights.[54]

Like most socialists in that period, especially in third world countries, Siauw saw relatively few dangers in the centralisation of power 'as long as it was in the right hands'. He might well have thought that Lord Acton's dictum 'all power corrupts and absolute power corrupts absolutely' was excessively liberal. He was clearly attracted to the idea of a vanguard party, a progressive agent of change, which would overcome backwardness and create socialism. But he was also troubled by what the alliance of Soekarno and the army was doing to democratic and human rights values.[55]

---

52 Interview with Yap Thiam Hien, Melbourne, December 1988.
53 Siauw's own account in December 1980.
54 Lev, *Political Journey of Yap Thiam Hien*, p. 103.
55 Siauw's own account in December 1980.

Chapter 10

THE PERIOD OF GUIDED DEMOCRACY[1]

Having returned to the 1945 constitution in July 1959, Indonesia entered a period of Guided Democracy with Soekarno acting as the chief leader of both the government machinery and the political movement it claimed to speak for, which Soekarno termed the Indonesian revolution.

In the parliamentary period, Siauw was able to win significant support with arguments based on legal considerations and the fact that Indonesia would be flouting international conventions if it discriminated against one group of citizens on the basis of their race. In the period of Guided Democracy, Siauw's effectiveness was more to do with his success in bringing the mass of the Chinese community to a position of alignment with Soekarno, and hence against the army. In this second period legality carried much less weight, as Soekarno emphasised ideology and revolution and his political practice was one of radical transformation.

Although Siauw remained a member of the purged and reconstituted parliament, he was more effectively channelling his ideas and proposals as a member of the DPA and through personal connections with Soekarno and other powerful figures.

According to the 1945 Constitution, supreme state power was vested in the MPR. The president was answerable only to the MPR, not to the DPR (Dewan Perwakilan Rakyat – parliament). Thus the president was not dependent upon the DPR. He can be appointed and removed only by the MPR.

In the enactment of legislation, the president has to cooperate with the DPR. All legislation must be passed with the DPR's approval and state

---

[1] The information on the legislative and executive structure during the Guided Democracy period contained in this section is largely derived from Oey, *Indonesian Government and Press During Guided Democracy*, pp. 66–83 and Siauw's lecture notes, 1962.

budgets drawn up by the government must be approved by the DPR before implementation. The president can not dissolve the DPR, and all members of the DPR are automatically members of the MPR, providing the opportunity for the DPR, through the MPR to exercise supervision and control over the president's activities.

Under this constitution, ministers are appointed by the president and answerable to him. After 5 July 1959, Soekarno moved quickly to consolidate his power. Within days, he formed his first presidential cabinet, calling it the Work Cabinet, headed by himself as the prime minister, with Djuanda's role redefined as first minister.

In order to ensure that conflict between the government and political parties was not experienced as it had been in the parliamentary period, Soekarno demanded that all cabinet ministers renounce their political party affiliations before assuming their ministerial posts.

In August 1959 Soekarno established the DPA, with 43 members. Soekarno himself headed it, with Roeslan Abdulgani cooperating as his deputy chairman. The council consisted of leaders of the political parties and armed forces and representatives of the functional groups. Soekarno treated the DPA as the state's politburo. Many important government regulations, Soekarno's policies and contents of his speeches were proposed, debated and decided within the DPA. The PKI, PNI and NU were well represented in the council. Masyumi and PSI who had been discredited by their roles in the PRRI/Permesta rebellions were excluded. Siauw was its only peranakan member.

In the same month, Depernas was established, headed by Mohamad Yamin. The 77-member body included members of the PKI, PNI, NU and the Christian parties and many who were not party members. Economic plans for the country's development and construction were formulated in this institution.

In 1960, Soekarno dissolved the elected DPR and replaced it with the new DPRGR (DPR–Gotong Rotong or Mutual Assistance Parliament). The dissolution of the elected parliament came after it refused to pass the budget. The 283 member DPRGR was officially installed in June 1960. The new DPRGR, which included Siauw, consisted of representatives of the ten political parties which were allowed to exist after the banning of Masyumi and PSI in 1960. Like the old DPR, the DPRGR was dominated by the PNI, NU and PKI. It also included new members who were categorised as members of the Functional Group representing the armed forces, police, peasants, workers, women, youth and minority groups. The chairman of the

DPRGR was Aruji Kartawinata, leader of the PSII, assisted by four vice-chairmen, Subamia of the PNI, Achmad Sjaechu of the NU, Lukman of the PKI, and Naval Commander Mursalin of the Functional Group. Siauw, not being a party member, was said to represent the functional groups, as such, but not any particular group.

In August 1960, Soekarno created the MPRS. It was termed provisional, as its members were not elected but appointed by Soekarno. The 623-member MPRS consisted of all members of the DPRGR, 241 representatives of functional groups and 95 delegates from the regions. The chairman was Chaerul Saleh, who later became deputy prime minister. He was assisted by four vice-chairmen, Ali Sastroamidjojo of the PNI, Idham Chalid of the NU, Aidit of the PKI and Lt Colonel Wilujo Puspojudo representing a functional group. As a member of the DPRGR, Siauw automatically became a member of the MPRS, also belonging to the Functional Group.

In the same year Soekarno initiated the formation of the Front Nasional. Soekarno headed this body too, with Sudibjo of the PSII acting as its general secretary. The Front Nasional consisted of representatives of parties, functional groups, the government and the DPA. Its task was to mobilise the masses and to propagate Soekarno's political ideology. This body established branches at regional and local level, which stimulated mass support and enthusiasm for the West Irian and 'Crush Malaysia' campaigns. In the last years of the Guided Democracy period, the PKI's influence within the body became very strong. Siauw and many other Baperki members were active in this body.

The central ideas of Guided Democracy were summed up in a political manifesto, usually called Manipol USDEK (USDEK Political Manifesto), derived from Soekarno's 17 August speech in 1959. The five central themes were the 1945 Constitution (Undang), Indonesian socialism (Sosialisme), guided democracy (Demokrasi), guided economy (Ekonomi) and Indonesian identity (Kepribadian). All political parties and organisations had to declare their full support for the Manipol USDEK, and their leaders identified themselves as Manipolists.

Soekarno argued that the Indonesian revolution had been derailed by parliamentary democracy and that only with the adoption of Guided Democracy could the Indonesian revolution achieve its goals. The objectives of this revolution were defined to encompass:

1. the establishment of a democratic unitary state of Indonesia including West Irian
2. the establishment of 'Sosialisme à la Indonesia' i.e. a type of socialism which suited the character, psychology and culture of the Indonesian nation
3. the establishment of friendship with all countries that were anti-colonialist and anti-imperialist in order to achieve an international order free from imperialism and colonialism

A key aspect of the Manipol, which reflected the political orientation of Soekarno, was that it defined achieving socialism as the goal of the revolution. The left-wing forces, represented by the PKI, Partai Murba and their affiliated organisations as well as a large part of the PNI, were quick to accept this. Siauw and Baperki also fully supported it. Their political enemies, represented by the anti-communist organisations and institutions like the NU, the Christian parties and the army leaders, were forced to accept the concept, even though they were reluctant to endorse the term socialism.

Another important concept formulated by Soekarno was Nasakom (Nasionalis Agama dan Komunis – Nationalism, Religion and Communism). Soekarno had urged unity between nationalists, Muslims and communists in 1927, and in the Guided Democracy period, this slightly changed version became a key formulation of his strategy for political unity.

Through this formulation, Soekarno encouraged the political cooperation of the nationalists represented by the PNI, Partindo and Partai Murba; religious groups represented by the NU, PSII, Parkindo and Partai Katolik; and communists, represented by the PKI. In the later Guided Democracy period, mass organisations and government institutions were put under pressure to organise themselves in a way which expressed Nasakom representation. Their leadership boards were to include the representatives of nationalist, religious and communist organisations. Baperki was also 'Nasakomised', although by the end of the Guided Democracy period it was dominated by representatives of the left-wing forces.

This was a period of political slogans. Soekarno introduced a long series of ideological formulas like Berdikari (self-reliance); Maju terus, pantang mundur (ever onward, never retreat); Tavip (year of living dangerously); Resopim (revolution, socialism and leadership); and Trisakti (three holy precepts) – standing on one's own feet economically, being politically independent and being true to Indonesia's cultural identity. Most political leaders in this period, including Siauw, needed to repeat these political slogans to demonstrate their political support for and loyalty to Soekarno. Privately many of them ridiculed the situation of paying lip-service to Soekarno's slogans.

Siauw's responses

As we saw in the preceding chapter, Siauw welcomed Soekarno's call for Guided Democracy when it was first made. But Guided Democracy as implemented after the re-promulgation of the 1945 Constitution was a development he felt ambivalent about.

One of the first negative aspects of Soekarno's Guided Democracy was the elimination of minority representation when parliament was restructured and renamed. The new body, formed on 24 June 1960, had been purged of members of the outlawed Masyumi and PSI. Members appointed by Soekarno replaced these members and most of them belonged to the new Functional Group.

The composition of the new parliament was also significantly altered. The existing political factions, including Siauw's Fraksi Nasional Progresif, were dismantled. Under the new arrangement, there were five major factions. Four of these were the representatives of parties: the nationalist faction (consisting of the PNI, Partindo, IPKI and Partai Murba), the Muslim faction (the NU, PSII and Perti), the communist faction (the PKI) and the Christian faction (Parkindo and the Partai Katolik). These four together formed the 130-member Political Party Group, which was clearly dominated by the PNI (44 members), NU (36 members) and PKI (30 members). The fifth faction, the 153-member Functional Group faction, consisted of representatives of the armed forces, police, peasants, workers, women, youth and minority groups.

Under this new structure Ang Tjiang Liat, a Baperki member, lost his seat. Siauw retained his and was said to be representing the new Functional Group faction and was attached to its cooperatives section.

Siauw protested, though cautiously. He told the 1960 Baperki congress, 'It is difficult to define minority representatives as members of the Functional Group. Ethnic groups should have been treated like youth and women groups and identified as separate categories within the Functional Group'.[2]

---

[2] Siauw's speech, delivered to the Baperki Congress held in Semarang 25–28 December 1960.

In the same speech, Siauw further clarified:

> Looking only at the representation of Baperki in parliaments, both in central and regional bodies, one would get the impression that Baperki has failed to achieve its main political goals. But one must look at the reasons behind the restructuring of the parliaments. Baperki believes that the restructuring was done to expedite the realisation of a just and prosperous society, which will ultimately help realise Baperki's main political objectives. In this situation, Baperki accepts the restructuring as a positive and beneficial development.

The restructuring of the regional parliaments also resulted in the loss of many seats Baperki had gained in elections. On the other hand, many Baperki members who were businessmen, professionals, teachers, white-collar workers, labourers and tradesmen, were appointed as functional group representatives.[3]

Writing much later Siauw, was sharply critical of the deterioration of the democratic processes in the new parliament. In *Lima Jaman* he wrote:

> In practice, consensus did not work. The minority groups were forced to give in to the majority groups. As voting was not implemented, members of the minority groups had no incentive to fight for their positions. As a result, many of them became reluctant to voice their opinions and acted like bystanders. Many did not even come to parliamentary sessions. Deliberations therefore were only applicable to the majority groups.[4]

Siauw's disappointment was somewhat compensated for by the decision to include Baperki members in the DPA and the Depernas. Siauw himself was appointed as a member of the DPA by Soekarno as was Dr Ernst Utrecht, a senior member of Baperki and a lecturer at the Baperki University. Professor Tjan Tjoe Som, another senior member of Baperki and a dean at Baperki University, was appointed as a member of the Depernas.

As an experienced parliamentarian who respected and supported democratic principles, Siauw was not happy to see the apparent failure of the deliberative processes in achieving the country's political goals, and the way Soekarno and his political supporters manipulated the constitution. He was

---

[3] Ibid.
[4] Siauw, *Lima Jaman*, p. 291.

disturbed to experience a situation whereby DPRGR no longer constituted a check on executive roles and activities, the DPA became merely an advisory body and the handpicked MPRS never challenged executive actions. He was also concerned with the structure in which leaders of the DPRGR, MPRS and DPA became cabinet ministers and he was certainly not happy about the appointment of Soekarno, in 1963, as president for life.[5]

One regulation which particularly troubled Siauw was the Presidential Regulation 11 of 1963 which enabled the government to arrest people suspected of involvement in subversive activities. When the regulation was first tabled at the DPA, Siauw strongly objected to it, but he was later persuaded by fellow DPA members Aidit and Njoto, to endorse it to enable Soekarno to deal with his political enemies.[6]

Why, despite his objections to a number of regulations and policies that were introduced in the period did Siauw rarely challenged Soekarno's regime?

One reason for this was that he saw Soekarno as a fellow socialist. Another was that he saw it as important to help Soekarno to minimise the influence of the army leaders who were a major partner in his government in the Guided Democracy period. Thirdly, Siauw had little sympathy for the groups which protested most vigorously against the authoritarian trend, for these were mostly sympathetic to Masyumi and PSI, the parties which had expressed most sympathy for the Assaat movement and other expressions of anti-Chinese feeling.

Siauw also saw Soekarno's policies with respect to the position of the Chinese communities as highly positive, despite the political and economic disadvantages they created. As long as the quasi-dictatorship was Soekarno's and while Soekarno's policies remained advantageous to Baperki, Siauw was willing to compromise his own political principles.[7]

Siauw was particularly pleased with the assertion in Soekarno's 17 August speech in 1960 that the Indonesian revolution would proceed towards socialism in two stages. In the first phase, the goal was to create a national democratic society in which remnants of feudalism and imperialism would be eliminated, so that Indonesia could achieve full independence. Socialism, Indonesia-style, was to be achieved only in the second phase.

---

[5] Interviews with Go Gien Tjwan, Phoa Thoan Hian and Oei Tjoe Tat in 1993.
[6] Conveyed to the author by Hardojo, former chairman of CGMI, in April 1998.
[7] Interviews with Yap Thiam Hien in 1988, Oei Tjoe Tat, Phoa Thoan Hian, Go Gien Tjwan in 1992 and Utrecht in 1981.

Siauw saw this as recognising the positive contributions Chinese business could make to the movement towards socialism. He quoted Soekarno's speech delivered to the DPRGR in 1961: 'All forces and all funds which are proved to be progressive will be used to construct Indonesia. Thus, this includes forces and funds which belong to non-Indigenous groups of people, who have lived in Indonesia and who support the programs of the Work Cabinet'.[8]

Siauw interpreted this to refer to Chinese of foreign as well as Indonesian citizenship. Referring to Soekarno's 1961 speech to the DPRGR, he said, 'It is clear from this formulation that in the national-democratic revolutionary phase, capitalism is not the target of our revolution. Furthermore, domestic capital, including firms belonging to foreign citizens who live in Indonesia, have to be given the assistance to grow healthily as they can be used to expedite the achievement of our revolutionary goals'.[9]

Siauw also had reason to be pleased by the inclusion of his economic formulations as part of Soekarno's Manipol. A passage in the manifesto on the protection and enhancement of domestic capital clearly reflected the economic formulations that Siauw championed from the early 1950s.

Siauw had additional reasons to support Soekarno when he moved even closer to the People's Republic of China in 1963. Siauw clearly saw this as an opportunity to consolidate the Chinese position in Indonesia and to expedite the resolution of citizenship issues linked to the Dual Nationality Treaty.

Siauw's active support for Soekarno enabled him to exert political influence within the DPA. Many government decisions and regulations with respect to the Chinese issues were based on Siauw's formulations. A number of Soekarno's speeches reflected his acceptance of Siauw's proposals. Utrecht, who like Siauw was a member of the DPA, talks of how Siauw was able to convince Soekarno to adopt his economic formulations in his speeches.[10]

---

[8] Siauw's speech, titled 'Baperki Berdiri Bulat Tegak atas Rel Revolusi 1945' and delivered to Baperki's conference held in Jakarta on 29 July 1961. Judging from the terms used in Soekarno's speech, it is highly probable that the text was actually prepared by Siauw himself, as the use and the protection of domestic capital belonging to non-Indigenous businessmen had been part of Siauw's convictions since the early 1950s.

[9] Ibid.

[10] Interview with Ernst Utrecht. Many of Soekarno's speeches were in line with Siauw's convictions on racial issues.

Perhaps the clearest example of this can be found in Soekarno's 17 August speech in 1964, in which he declared:

> It is of primary importance to wipe out all traces of racialism. You all know that what I am always dreaming of is a harmony of Pancasila-ist manipolists among all the sukus [ethnic groups], the peoples of the nation. Harmony among all the sukus, including peoples of mixed descent or of foreign descent, whether Arab, European, Chinese, Indian, Pakistani or Jewish... It is impossible for us to eliminate the jaw of the Batak, or slanting eyes of the Chinese or the large nose of the Arab. Indeed this is not the problem! The problem is how to cultivate harmony, to cultivate unity, to build the Indonesian nation amongst all of us.[11]

The ban on rural retail traders

One major problem faced by the Chinese in the early stages of the Guided Democracy period was the regulation which banned aliens from retail trade in rural areas. The regulation, Peraturan Presiden 10 (PP-10 – Presidential Regulation no. 10) was introduced in November 1959.

PP-10 was partly the consolidation of a ministerial regulation issued by Rachmat Muljomiseno, the NU trade minister in the Djuanda cabinet, in May 1959 to abolish alien trade in rural areas.[12] Rachmat's regulation prohibited the involvement of aliens in retail trade and aliens' residence in rural areas. When this ministerial regulation was issued, Siauw strongly opposed it, calling it unconstitutional and arguing that a minister could not issue a regulation on this matter. He said that the Chinese traders had legitimate businesses and their rights as businessmen in Indonesia were protected by international law. Their absence from the industry would create a damaging vacuum as trade required experience and business networks which had been established by the existing traders for many years, he said.[13] Siauw's position was strongly supported by the PKI in parliament.

---

[11] Quoted from Soekarno's 17 August speech in 1964 in Legge, *Soekarno, A Political Biography*, p. 330.

[12] Muljomiseno, of NU, was a prominent leader of KENSI (All Indonesian National Economic Congress) which strongly promoted the Assaat Movement in the late 1950s.

[13] *Republik*, 21 May 1959.

The ministerial regulation was introduced when Soekarno was overseas. When he returned, he was apparently annoyed by it and decided not to include Rachmat in the cabinet formed after the 5 July presidential decree. In October, Foreign Minister Subandrio visited China and was apparently subjected to pressure by the Chinese leaders to withdraw the ban.[14] Although the Chinese Government had made clear to Subandrio its opposition to the ban, the joint communique between him and Foreign Minister Chen Yi did not reflect China's rejection of it.

Why Soekarno signed the PP-10 remains controversial. Siauw believed that he was under pressure from leaders of the army and Muslim parties to maintain the ban. Soekarno was not able to counter their argument that socialism required the transfer of foreign capital to the hands of national traders. Siauw himself was apparently called by Soekarno on a number of occasions to explain his opposition to it, but was unsuccessful in convincing him to withdraw it.[15]

Rural retail trade in many areas was largely in the hands of the Chinese. As the Dual Nationality Agreement had not been ratified by the time PP-10 was issued, its application affected not only the aliens but also many Chinese who were clearly Indonesian citizens. Baperki had to make frequent representations on behalf of Chinese of Indonesian citizenship whose shops were confiscated by local authorities. The main beneficiaries of this regulation were Asli traders who had ties with the Muslim parties.

PP-10 was perhaps the harshest anti-Chinese regulation since the founding of the republic in 1945. The total number of Chinese affected by the ban was estimated to be between 100 000 and 600 000. Also, about 25 000 businesses were affected by the ban.[16] In some areas, its implementation expanded to expulsion of Chinese from rural areas. The greatest impact appeared to have been experienced in West Java, where the influence of Islam was significant. In Central and East Java, many of the local authorities and local population did not force the Chinese to leave most rural areas. Of some 15 000 Chinese who were forced to leave the rural areas, almost 10 000 were from West Java. This regional variation was probably due to the way the Chinese had acculturated in Central and East Java and to the more tolerant Muslims. In West Java, there was a weaker acculturative

---

14   Siauw's account conveyed to author in December 1980.
15   Interview with Oey Hay Djoen in April 1998.
16   Somers, *Peranakan Chinese Politics*, p. 208.

pull of Sundanese culture and resentment against the Chinese which had developed since the colonial period.[17]

The impact on the livelihood of the Chinese and their confidence in Indonesia was severe. Many Chinese, both totoks and peranakans, believed that hopes of doing business in Indonesia would soon diminish, especially after rumours spread that the ban would be extended to urban areas and to all business sectors. When the Chinese government indicated that it would welcome the affected Chinese and sent its ships to transport them to China, many decided to leave for China – not only rural traders but also many urban people including students and some business people and professionals, peranakans as well as totoks. In 1960, approximately 136 000 Chinese had left Indonesia.[18]

Siauw and other Baperki officials tried hard to convince the peranakans that it would be unwise to go to China to live. They repeatedly indicated that Indonesia, not China, was their motherland and they should therefore remain in Indonesia. It is not clear how effective Baperki's campaigns were. But many of those who were affected by the PP-10, and others who remembered anti-Chinese rioting and persecution during the revolution period, decided to ignore Baperki's recommendations and went to China to settle. However, the number of people wanting to go to China dwindled over the course of 1960 after reports on hardship and poverty in China were publicised.

PP-10 strained relations with China. The Chinese ambassador to Indonesia, Huang Chen, repeatedly voiced his protests and resented the forced removal of the Chinese nationals from rural areas. Many Chinese in West Java refused to leave their premises and this had resulted in some violence against them. The crisis reached a climax when two Chinese women were shot dead and another two wounded by army troops who attempted to evict them by force from Cimahi, West Java, in July 1960. The incident prompted Soekarno to intervene and he issued instructions to military authorities to stop forcing the Chinese to leave the rural areas.[19] Soekarno's intervention ended the crisis and by the end of 1960 many Chinese who had not been moved from rural areas were able to remain there.

---

[17] J.A.C. Mackie, 'Anti-Chinese Outbreaks', in Mackie, *Chinese In Indonesia*, pp. 95–96; Somers, *Peranakan Chinese Politics*, p. 198.
[18] Ibid., p. 95.
[19] Ibid., p. 94.

PP-10 seriously disrupted rural trade in many areas. Lacking the experience and business connections, newcomers to business were not able to provide the services previously offered by the Chinese. Distribution of goods to and from rural areas stopped for some time. Availability of goods and dramatic price increases were some of the outcomes of the regulation. Many of the Chinese from rural areas could not get employment in cities and created additional burdens to their communities. Many of those left in rural areas had to face material hardships.

Dual nationality and citizenship

One of Siauw's significant achievements during this period was the resolution of the issue of dual nationality and the implementation of the citizenship laws of 1958.

As described earlier, the citizenship law of 1958 and the Dual Nationality Treaty, together with the Exchange of Notes, was something of a victory for Siauw. They included all the provisions he had long been fighting, including one affecting the children of 200 000 people who had repudiated Indonesian citizenship between December 1949 and December 1951. Despite the slowness of government apparatus in implementing this provision, Baperki was able to help process thousands of applications.

Baperki members, particularly in Java, were active in providing explanations about technical aspects of this legislation and urged people to avail themselves of the citizenship option. One reason for their success was that Chinese citizenship was becoming less attractive as news spread about the bad living conditions in China experienced by the 140 000 or so Indonesian Chinese who had gone there in 1960 because of PP-10, the regulation banning aliens from trading in rural areas. Many were sent to work in farms in China and news reached their relatives in Indonesia that they had regretted taking the path of 'Hwe Kuo' (returning to the home country).

Siauw's activities in the citizenship area were focused on settling the dual nationality issues. After much delay, the Dual Nationality Treaty and its associated Exchange of Notes, designed by Siauw, was finally ratified in parliament in 1959. In the same year, a committee was established to generate an implementation procedure led by Susanto Tirtoprodjo. Again, no agreement on how to implement the treaty could be reached. Siauw complained that the delays were mainly caused by the inability of the

Indonesian authorities to either propose a solution or accept the recommendations offered by the Chinese.[20]

On 22 November 1960, Susanto Tirtoprodjo submitted the committee proposal to the cabinet. The proposal contained a provision for Indonesian Chinese youths born in Indonesia between 27 December 1949 and 27 December 1951 and who became Chinese citizens because their parents had repudiated Indonesian citizenship to be given an opportunity to opt for Indonesian citizenship. A number of ministers in the cabinet rejected this proposal. They argued that it would enable young people who had been living in China and who might have been indoctrinated with communism to return to Indonesia as Indonesian citizens. The committee was therefore requested to structurally modify its proposal.

Soekarno, apparently annoyed by the slowness of the process, called Sukarni, then ambassador to China, a number of other ministers and the committee members to expedite the process. According to Siauw, Soekarno told them:

> The settlement of dual nationality issues is a political matter and is directly linked to our friendship with the People's Republic of China. We have to be positive and courageous and not get bogged down in details. Even if it is true that thousands of Chinese youths have been indoctrinated with communist ideologies, we do not have to be concerned. There are already more than eight million Indonesian citizens who are oriented to communism.[21]

Behind the scenes, Siauw was lobbying for a quick resolution which would contain provisions he had long been fighting for, namely that the maximum number of Indonesian Chinese should be exempt from the process of actively choosing Indonesian citizenship and that a simple process involving minimum cost should be available to Chinese required to opt for Indonesian citizenship.

Moreover, it was not only Baperki but the leaders of the totok communities and Huang Chen, then the Chinese ambassador to Indonesia, who were urging them to opt for Indonesian citizenship. In this period most Indonesian Chinese whose citizenship status was uncertain were keen to be accepted as Indonesian citizens. Indonesian citizenship was attractive also

---

20   Siauw's speech delivered to the Baperki congress in December 1960.
21   Ibid.

to totoks, because it made it easier to engage in business and professional work in Indonesia.

More importantly, Siauw's recommendation was fully understood and endorsed by the Chinese leaders, particularly Premier Chou En Lai and Foreign Minister Chen Yi. It was likely that due to Siauw's good relationship with Soekarno his recommendation was also endorsed by Soekarno.[22]

The agreement on how the treaty was to be implemented was finally reached in a meeting of Soekarno and Chen Yi on 24 December 1960. It provided that all Indonesian Chinese who had participated in elections for the central parliament or one of the regional ones were to be declared Indonesian citizens. They did not have to reconfirm their intention to become Indonesian citizens. Siauw believed that this group of people represented about 65 per cent of those affected by the dual nationality settlement. These people would be provided with statements from the Ministry of Justice that they had participated in elections. The statements were to be contained in a form called a D-form; Indonesian Chinese who worked as farmers were also to be confirmed as Indonesian citizens and were therefore exempted from the process. These people would be granted C-forms by the Ministry of Justice.[23]

Another important clause in the agreement provided for people with dual citizenship to send their confirmation rejecting Chinese citizenship by mail. They would not need to be physically present in various offices in capital cities. The period in which the choice was to be made was between 20 January 1961 and 20 January 1962.

Before this agreement was reached, many people classified as having dual nationality had found it almost impossible to become Indonesian citizens. To show that they had become Indonesian citizens, they had to prove that they were born in Indonesia and that their fathers were born in Indonesia. Documents required proving their birthplaces were often difficult to obtain. Many people born during the colonial period had not had their births registered. Others had lost their documents during the wars.

Siauw highlighted the importance of bureaucratic obstacles in this regard when he referred to the cases of two Indonesian Chinese badminton champions, Njoo Kim Bie and Tan King Gwan, who had to be assisted by government officials to gain their Indonesian citizenship in Jakarta so that

---

[22] Interviews with Go Gak Cho, Hong Kong, October 1994 and Chu Yi, Beijing, October 1994.

[23] Siauw's speech delivered to Baperki's conference on 29 July 1961.

they could represent Indonesia in the Thomas Cup championships overseas. Their citizenship was granted within one day. Siauw said, 'The process applied to these badminton champions should also be applied to the majority of Indonesian Chinese considered to have dual nationality. They too could provide significant contributions to the development of Indonesia'.[24]

Baperki's offices helped thousands of people fill in the various forms and obtain the necessary documents to prove their birthplaces. Baperki was also involved in defending applicants where there were disputes over documentation. Baperki members paid for documents to be made available for citizenship applications. They also provided legal services free of charge to citizenship applicants.[25]

The actual implementation of the agreement had disappointed Siauw. By February 1962 there were still thousands of people with dual nationality who had not formally opted for Indonesian citizenship. Siauw estimated this number to be about 20 000.[26] Mozingo's estimates were much higher. He argued that less than 30 per cent of dual nationals had made a choice on their citizenship, indicating that there were about 560 000 people who remained dual nationals by 1961 (assuming that there were 800 000 dual nationals).[27] The significant difference in these estimates was due to the interpretation of the way the treaty was to be implemented. Siauw had interpreted that people who were exempted from making a choice on their citizenship were already considered Indonesian citizens and hence no longer considered dual nationals. No action was therefore required from them to confirm their Indonesian citizenship. Mozingo seems not to have taken account of the effects of Regulation 20/1959 which exempted a large number of people.

Nevertheless, the number of people who had not opted for Indonesian citizenship by February 1962 was still considerable. Mozingo argues that there were two large groups of dual nationals. The first group was optimistic that the Soekarno government, having improved diplomatic relationships with China, would protect the interests of the Chinese. Hence, they could not see an advantage in becoming Indonesian citizens. The second group, the pessimistic ones, believed that it was more advantageous

---

24	Siauw's speech delivered to Baperki's conference on 29 July 1961.
25	Somers, *Peranakan Chinese Politics*, p. 246; Interviews with Phoa Thoan Hian, Oei Tjoe Tat and Yap Thiam Hien.
26	Siauw's speech, 22 February 1962.
27	Mozingo, *The Sino-Indonesian Dual Nationality Treaty*, p. 28.

to become Chinese nationals as they would be able to rely on the Chinese Embassy for protection should they become victims of anti-Chinese policies. If they were Indonesian citizens, this protection would no longer be available to them.

Siauw offered a more realistic argument. He believed that most of the dual nationals had not wanted to repudiate Indonesian citizenship, but were victims of bureaucratic obstruction. Despite the provision that options could be exercised through the mail, many people were still required to visit offices in provincial capitals. Many were still required to provide documents they could not produce or obtain. The release of d-Forms and c-Forms also was slow.[28]

There was certainly a difference between the situation faced by the Chinese in December 1951 and the situation in February 1962. In December 1951 the Indonesia-born Chinese had to actively repudiate Indonesian citizenship. Many did this because of the hardships they endured during the revolution period and the anti-Chinese attitudes of the Sukiman government. Most of these people were fully conscious in making their decision.

In February 1962, most dual nationals were exposed to a range of complicated regulations including the treaty, the Exchange of Notes, and various other implementation regulations as well as the citizenship law of 1959. These regulations required the production of documents which burdened most poor dual nationals. This, coupled with bureaucratic complexity, seems to have resulted in the large number of people failing to opt for Indonesian citizenship.

As a result of Baperki's push and protests, in late 1962 the Ministry of Justice finally agreed to allow a further group of people to become Indonesian citizens. In the case of people considered poor, statements from their Lurahs (heads of villages or low-level urban residential units) confirming their birthplace, would suffice.[29] By the end of 1963, almost all Indonesia-born Chinese were clearly in one of two groups, Indonesian citizens or aliens. A majority of them were Indonesian citizens.

---

[28] Siauw's speech, 22 February 1962.
[29] Siauw's speech delivered to the Baperki congress in March 1963.

The Guided Economy

Siauw was regarded as a man with skills in the area of economics. He often contributed to economic discussions in the DPA and, in 1963, he was appointed adviser to the minister for finance and economics. But, as Utrecht pointed out, a great number of Siauw's economic proposals were not accepted, or accepted but not implemented. Utrecht, who claimed to have supported many of Siauw's proposals in the DPA, blamed what he called the 'Subandrio–Chaerul Saleh–Leimena' group for this.[30]

In August 1961, Soekarno officially launched an eight-year plan for national construction. Prepared by Depernas, the plan was to become the basis of Guided Economy and cover the period 1961 to 1969. The plan encompassed a large number of projects covering the increase of production of industrial goods, foodstuffs, textile wares and medical supplies, as well as projects for the so-called 'mental construction' such as the development of the press. The capital required for these projects was to come from exports of oil, tin, aluminum, rubber, copra and timber as well as the expansion of fisheries and tourism.

It was a grandiose plan presented in 17 volumes, 8 parts and 1945 clauses, representing the day on which Indonesian independence was proclaimed, 17 August 1945. The fascination with symbols reflected in this labeling was also expressed in the government's concern to build prestigious projects. It put a lot of its resources into building luxurious hotels, large monuments and statues, government buildings, a multi-storey shopping complex and a large sports stadium to host the 1962 Asian Games.[31]

But problems were not limited to political symbolism and priorities. In fact, economic mismanagement was considered the main trait of the Guided Democracy period.

The economic problems were caused by a large number of factors. Significant economic decline began after Dutch firms were nationalised and their management was taken over by Indonesian managers, mostly army officers, in 1957 and 1958. A wide range of companies were brought into the hands of the state – most importantly, the hundreds of agricultural estates, large trading banks, trading companies, mines and factories (including textiles, paper, printing and electrical equipment).[32] The seizure was followed

---

[30] Interview with Ernst Utrecht, Amsterdam, November 1981.
[31] Feith, *Dynamics of Guided Democracy*, p. 384.
[32] Lance Castles. 'The Fate of the Private Entrepreneur' in T.K. Tan (ed.) *Sukarno's Guided Indonesia*, 1967, p. 76.

by the departure of 46 000 Dutch nationals from Indonesia.[33] A lack of management and industrial experience, as well as corruption, resulted in a severe decline in agricultural production, manufacturing outputs and exports. PP-10, as previously described, also resulted in a decline in economic performance and productivity.

The West Irian campaign, which involved costly military operations, further burdened the economy. Budget deficits and inflation grew dramatically as a result of the campaign which ended in 1962.[34] This was followed by the 'Crush Malaysia' campaign which had a much bigger impact on the economy, including the loss of $250 million of aid from the West in 1964 and a disruption in exports and trade. Trade with Malaysia and Singapore was cut off, which reduced imports due to the decline in exports, and in turn induced increased inflation and a huge budget deficit – in 1963 and 1964 the deficit equalled government revenues.[35]

Finally, corruption, over-regulation and ineffectiveness of legal control aggravated the economic conditions. Corruption involved private commissions, kickbacks and rackets that were found at various levels of the administration. Over-regulation involved forced price reductions, which significantly reduced incentives to produce, and the recruitment of a high number of secondary school graduates into the government service, which significantly increased costs and reduced productivity. The decline in the effectiveness of legal controls meant that government ministries and their staff were able to implement programs that deviated from budgetary plans and government priorities.[36]

In summary, the manifestations of these problems were huge budget deficits, declining production outputs, dwindling exports and foreign exchange reserves, and high inflation.

The Guided Economy was based on Article 33 of the 1945 Constitution which provides that the branches of production important to the Indonesian state and providing for the most essential needs of the majority of the people must be controlled by the state. Siauw often affirmed support for the idea of the Guided Economy but he also often criticised the way in which the government implemented its economic policies. Obviously aware of and

---

[33] Feith, *Dynamics of Guided Democracy*, p. 321.
[34] J.A.C Mackie, *Problems of the Indonesian Inflation*, Monograph Series, Cornell University, Ithaca, 1967, p. 32.
[35] J.A.C. Mackie, *Konfrontasi*, Oxford University Press, Kuala Lumpur, 1974, pp. 220–221.
[36] Feith, *Dynamics of Guided Democracy*, pp. 393–394.

disappointed by the deterioration of the economic conditions referred to above, he offered the following explanations and recommendations.[37]

Firstly, Siauw believed that the country lacked economic experts who were capable of managing free economic conditions, producing effective development plans, generating and implementing industrialisation plans, dealing with foreign countries to arrange mutually beneficial trade, and managing the circulation of money within Indonesia so that exchange rates could be fully controlled. The so-called experts who were running the economy, according to Siauw, were trained by the colonial regime and hence were only capable of running a colonial economy.

Secondly, Siauw argued that the government relied heavily on foreign aid but that the money was not used to strengthen the country's production capabilities and technical know-how. It was mainly used to bridge the gap between the ever-increasing import costs and the ever-declining export incomes. This, according Siauw, was a manifestation of neo-colonialism. The developed nations were happy to provide aid to enable Indonesia to buy expensive machinery from them for infrastructure projects, while keeping prices for raw materials exported by Indonesia low. Siauw alleged that the international markets were controlled by centres in London, New York, Amsterdam and Hamburg. He also referred to the People's Republic of China as a country from which Indonesia could learn about technology transfer and the appropriation of foreign expertise.

Thirdly, Siauw argued that racism was burdening the economy. Despite repeated calls from the top levels of the government to make effective use of domestic capital, there were still a large number of officials who practised discrimination – not only against the businesses of non-Asli citizens but also against businesses of Chinese citizens. Domestic capital, Siauw charged, continued to be wasted. An example of this was that many officials refused to let transportation companies owned by alien operators (Chinese) to distribute farmers' produce in rural areas. As a result, much of this produce rotted. The farmers, the transportation companies and people in general all ended up as losers.

Siauw also frequently complained about corruption and the lack of social control. Implementation costs were not properly monitored and controlled. Officials used government facilities for their personal use. Corruption within various government agencies was not effectively dealt with and, in some cases, Siauw charged, was accepted practice. He blamed capitalist

---

[37] Siauw's speech delivered to the Baperki congress on 12 November 1962.

bureaucrats for much of this, highlighting the way they often engaged 'Ali-Baba' practices, that is, putting the squeeze on Chinese business people. He sometimes put the blame directly on unqualified military officers who were running enterprises which had been taken over from the Dutch.

Lastly, Siauw criticised the way in which the government was attempting to combat inflation. He saw it as an error to force local industries to reduce their prices as this would destroy the incentive to create local industries.

In 1963, there were a number of key indicators which showed the troubles that were created by poor economic planning and mismanagement. Railway fares were increased by 300 per cent. Bus fares were doubled and airfares were increased by 500 per cent. Tariffs for public utilities like electricity, water and postage were increased by more than 400 per cent. The impact of these increases were soon felt in significant increases for all essential consumer goods like rice, eggs, fish, meat, sugar, oil and soap. Prices for imported goods rose by more than 100 per cent.[38]

To overcome the problems, First Minister Djuanda introduced, on 26 May 1963, a fairly comprehensive set of economic reforms in the form of 14 regulations. These regulations had been drawn up with the hope that they would be underwritten by IMF loans and they led to a lot of painful price increases. Djuanda had hoped that these 14 regulations would eventually result in a stabilisation of prices.

In July 1963, in a DPA meeting, Soekarno offered Siauw a cabinet post. Recognising Siauw's ability in formulating economic policies, Soekarno offered Siauw a post as either minister for social affairs or minister of state with a special task to reduce inflation. But Siauw rejected the offer and instead suggested that the offer be made to Oei Tjoe Tat, one of the vice-chairmen of Baperki who was by then also active in Partindo.

The reasons for Siauw's rejection were twofold. First, he felt that it would be impossible for him to control and check inflation if the economic programs were not structurally altered. Secondly, he was not prepared to join the group of leaders who were more interested in maintaining their executive roles than introducing and carrying out policies that would ultimately improve the situation. Siauw resented the behavior of political figures who abused their privileges and showed low-quality leadership. Six months later, Oei Tjoe Tat was appointed minister of state, tasked to assist Subandrio, Chaerul Saleh and Leimena.[39]

---

[38] Oey, *Indonesian Government and Press During Guided Democracy*, pp. 105–106.
[39] Siauw's own account in December 1980.

When Malaysia came into being in September 1963, Soekarno made it clear that he would not accept the newly formed state but rather intensified Indonesia's confrontation with it. Soekarno's approach and his refusal to back down on the 'confrontation' policy resulted in the suspension of the IMF loan and promised American aid. Efforts in the 'Crush Malaysia' campaign further damaged economic conditions. Inflation continued to rise sharply. Workers suffered a severe decline in real wages and in standards of consumption. The contrast between rich and poor increased. In addition, Indonesia's relations with the Western states deteriorated sharply and this forced Soekarno's government to turn to socialist governments, especially the People's Republic of China, further tilting the political pendulum to the left.

Siauw criticised the regulations of 26 May 1963 for putting too much emphasis on increasing exports, and he made similar criticism of a further set of regulations issued in April 1964. His main emphasis was on the need to create a self-reliant economy whereby the country's needs were met with minimum dependence on foreign markets or foreign aid. To achieve this, he urged the government to reduce unnecessary expenditure and increase the country's production capacities by encouraging growth and the use of all effective domestic capital.[40]

The anti-Chinese riots of 1963

A few days after Soekarno's participation in Baperki's congress on 13 March 1963, anti-Chinese riots flared up in Cirebon. The rioting was sparked by a court case in which an Indigenous boy, son of a medical doctor who was active in the PSI, was sentenced for killing a Chinese student in a traffic accident. Within hours of the court hearing, houses, shops and other properties of the Chinese in the city were ransacked by an angry mass.

The incident happened just before the visit of China's President Liu Sao Chi, which was to signify the improved relationship of Indonesia and the People's Republic of China. Liu was then the President of the People's Republic of China. It was the first visit by a head of the Chinese state to Indonesia. In the speech to welcome Liu, Soekarno thanked the Chinese Government for the help it had rendered to the Indonesian Government in crushing the PRRI rebellion.

Members of Baperki and Partindo who were sent to Cirebon to investigate the riot reported in early April that a group of influential activists of

---

[40] Siauw's speech, delivered to the Baperki congress in Surabaya on 27 August 1964.

the PSI and Masyumi were planning a much bigger riot in the weeks to come. They were reported to have used Soekarno's speech that the Chinese Government had assisted the crushing of the PRRI/Permesta rebellions as an indication that the Chinese were the enemies of all Muslims.[41]

A week after the Cirebon rioting there were anti-Chinese outbreaks in several smaller towns of Java.[42] The main outbreak of rioting erupted in Bandung on 10 May 1963. The May riots involved a large number of agitated demonstrators and represented one of the worst anti-Chinese riots ever experienced. Hundreds of houses, shops and cars were burned, looted and damaged. Some lives were also reported to have been lost. In the following days, the riots also spread to nearby Bogor, Cianjur, Garut, Cipayung and Sukabumi. In Jakarta, due to the presence of heavily armed troops around the Chinatown district and other shopping areas, riots did not break out. Students of the University of Indonesia had been warned by their rector against being involved in anti-Chinese riots.

On 19 May 1963, Soekarno condemned these riots, blaming the PSI, Masyumi and remnants of the PRRI–Permesta rebellions for them. He said that the aim of these disturbances was to undermine the reputation of the Indonesian Government and his own good name. These activities he declared, were designed to destroy the government's anti-imperialist policies, domestic and foreign.

Siauw was quick to issue statements condemning the riots and these were published in various newspapers. He labelled the instigators as counter-revolutionaries, but did not name any particular organisation, and demanded quick government action to squash anti-Chinese movements. The PKI was also quick to condemn the activities and, like Soekarno, they were more direct in accusing the PSI and Masyumi of being involved in the riots.

Baperki also got word of open letters blaming Chinese who refused to assimilate for this violence, and saw some evidence that members of the LPKB (Lembaga Pembinaan Kesatuan Bangsa – Institute for the Promotion of National Unity) were involved in spreading these. Various Baperki leaders alleged that the LPKB was responsible for the riots because it had been fanning mass anger.[43]

---

[41] These reports were written by a number of members of Baperki and Partindo and were submitted to Siauw and Oei in early April 1963.

[42] J.A.C. Mackie, 'Anti-Chinese Outbreaks in Indonesia, 1959–1968' in Mackie (ed.) *The Chinese in Indonesia: Five Essays* p. 98.

[43] Interviews with Go Gien Tjwan, Amsterdam, December 1993 and Oei Tjoe Tat, Jakarta, July 1993.

Anti-communists were very concerned in 1963 about the growing closeness of Indonesia to the People's Republic of China and Soekarno's apparent move towards the left. The general population was suffering from worsening economic conditions. The police and the army did not do much to curb the riots in the initial stages so the anti-Chinese rioting might be seen as a protest not only by Masyumi and PSI but by the right-wing forces as a whole.

Siauw's angry reaction to these incidents was quickly followed by an initiative to collect funds to assist the victims of the riots. Baperki formed the PPKKR (Panitia Penolong Korban Kontra Revolusi – Committee of Helpers of the Victims of the Counter-Revolutionaries) with the collaboration of the PKI and Partindo. Partindo's goodwill was especially welcomed by many of the Chinese and as a result, a large number of peranakans joined Partindo soon after the riots.[44]

The West Java riots sent shock waves through the Chinese community, highlighting once more how vulnerable the Chinese were in a situation of economic troubles. It is hard to be sure what the effect was on the community's willingness to support Baperki but there was widespread appreciation of the effectiveness of Siauw's political connections in getting support from Soekarno and other important political leaders who condemned the racial riots.

On the other hand, many Indonesian Chinese saw the riots as a sign that it was dangerous for the Chinese to identify themselves with left-wing forces and the People's Republic of China as anti-communist forces, supported by the army, could then retaliate against them.

Baperki's political alignments

Having sided with forces who supported Soekarno's Guided Democracy concept in the late 1950s, Siauw and Baperki remained aligned with the pro-Soekarno forces against Masyumi, PSI and some smaller parties like the Parkindo. As in the period before Guided Democracy, Siauw remained close to leaders of several parties – in particular, those of the PKI, PNI, Partindo, Partai Murba and PSII. By 1963, following in Soekarno's footsteps he was also becoming especially close to the PKI and Partindo.

---

[44] Interview with Oei Tjoe Tat, Jakarta, July 1994; Coppel, *Indonesian Chinese in Crisis*, p. 47.

How powerful was the PKI? The PKI was certainly growing. In terms of membership and the size of its affiliated mass organisations, such as the SOBSI, BTI and Pemuda Rakyat (People's Youth), it had the mass support of some seven million people. In the regional general elections of 1957–1958, the PKI was the only party which dramatically increased its share of the vote compared with 1955.

Soekarno, who had worked very closely with the army in dismantling the old parliamentary democracy system in the late 1950s, now needed an organisation that could counterbalance the new strength of the army. The army tried on numerous occasions to contain the growth of the PKI. Military restrictions were imposed on the PKI's political movements, particularly in the three strongly Muslim areas of South Kalimantan, South Celebes and South Sumatra. In 1959, army leaders even attempted to stop the PKI from holding its sixth congress. But Soekarno defeated that attempt and showed his support to the PKI by addressing the congress in person.[45]

By 1963, the position had changed and the PKI had become markedly stronger. The president was endorsing a great many of its ideological themes and some observers believed that he hoped the PKI would eventually become the dominant force in the country, perhaps after his death. On the other hand, the government apparatus remained in the hands of non-communists. Attempts to realise the formation of the Nasakom cabinet, in which the communists could be given executive roles, could not be implemented due to objections of the army. In 1963, Aidit and Lukman were included in the cabinet as coordinating ministers but were given no executive positions.

Siauw's decision to be close to Soekarno, in the end, brought him closer to the PKI. If during the parliamentary democracy period Siauw had often taken positions in conflict with those of the PKI, during the Guided Democracy period the growing PKI was always supportive of and sympathetic to Baperki's positions and requests. The PKI always supported Baperki in combating racism. Leaders of the PKI and Siauw often praised each other in public meetings and in the organisations' publications. When the army sponsored a rival organisation, the LPKB in 1962, the PKI joined Baperki in attacking it.

Many leaders of Baperki joined the PKI, and the PKI reciprocated by having some of its key members join Baperki. Liem Koen Seng and

---

[45] Ibid., p. 339.

Boejoeng Saleh, both important leaders of Baperki, were also members of the PKI. In the East Java branches of Baperki, most of the leaders were also members of the PKI. Many of the leaders of Baperki's youth organisations, the PPI (Permusyawaratan Pemuda Indonesia – Consultative Body of Indonesian Youths) and University student councils, also joined the mass organisations affiliated to the PKI, such as the Pemuda Rakyat, CGMI (Central Gerakan Mahasiswa Indonesia – Central Movement of Indonesian Students) and the Lekra (Lembaga Kebudayaan Rakyat – Institute of People's Culture).

But Siauw, being aware of the political implications and danger of being identified as affiliated to the PKI, remained cautious about such close relationships. Although he often encouraged members of Baperki to join parties appropriate to their own perspectives, he never urged them to choose the PKI. In the case of Liem Koen Seng, a member of Baperki's central leadership, Siauw in fact indicated his annoyance that Liem joined the PKI without consulting him.[46]

Siauw's attitude towards Partindo however was very different. Partindo members in parliament were part of Siauw's Fraksi Nasional Progresif during the parliamentary democracy period. Danu Asmoro and Winoto of the Partindo were close to Siauw, as were Partindo leaders Asmara Hadi and Armunanto. Winoto became a member of Baperki's board of leadership.

Siauw knew that Partindo's formation was prompted by Soekarno's initiative and hence considered it as Soekarno's favoured party. Partindo, as discussed earlier, joined Siauw's Fraksi Nasional Progresif in parliament. Because of this special connection, Siauw wanted to encourage members of Baperki who wished to pursue their political aspirations to join Partindo.

Discussions on how Baperki and Partindo could collaborate and how members of the two organisations might be strengthened took place in Jakarta a few months before the official birth of Guided Democracy on 5 July 1959. In this discussion, it was agreed that Oei Tjoe Tat would join Partindo as one of its vice-chairmen. Not long after that, Phoa Thoan Hian, another Baperki leader, joined Partindo and he too became one of its vice-chairmen. Partindo and Baperki worked closely together in many fields.[47]

---

[46] Siauw's account conveyed to author in prison, 1973; Interviews with Oei Tjoe Tat, July 1993 and Go Gien Tjwan, December 1990.

[47] Interview with Oei Tjoe Tat and Phoa Thoan Hian, Jakarta, July 1993.

When Baperki became Nasakomised, Siauw chose to link the organisation with the PKI for the communist element, with Partai Murba, Partindo and the left wing of the PNI for the nationalist element, and with Perti and PSII for the religious element. Leaders of these parties joined Baperki and were included in either the boards of leadership or advisory councils.

By the early 1960s, Siauw had changed his political strategy. Now that representation in parliament became less important than influence in other political spheres, Siauw was keen to have as many Baperki members as possible in various important institutions. He was of the opinion that it would be better for Baperki to focus on acting as a body which could voice the interests of the Chinese, and for its members to play influential roles in newspaper publications, parties, mass organisations and other institutions which had direct dealings with the Chinese.

Siauw was fortunate to have the support of a group of people with whom he had developed friendships in his earlier days in Surabaya, Semarang and Malang. Through this group of people, Baperki's programs were propagated in various fields. The Semarang group included Oei Tjoe Tat, a vice-chairman of Partindo and a state minister, and Tan Tjwan Hwie, an executive of the Semarang *Sin Min* daily. The Malang group included Go Gien Tjwan, an executive of the government-run Antara; Tan Hwie Kiat, an executive of the popular and influential daily *Warta Bhakti* (formerly *Sin Po*); Oey Hay Djoen, secretary general of Lekra; and Ong Hwie Yang, director of the transport ministry. The Surabaya group included Tan Ling Djie, a veteran of the PKI leadership; Tjoa Sik Ien, an influential figure in Surabaya; and Tjoo Tik Tjoen, a member of parliament representing the PKI.

Apart from this group of people, Siauw also relied upon the support of prominent figures in Jakarta like Ang Jang Goan, Thio Thiam Tjong, Tan Eng Tie and Liem Koen Seng. Totok leaders like Go Gak Cho, Kho Nay Tjong and Kho Ie Sioe also helped organise enormous financial assistance for Baperki.

The diminished importance of parliament meant that Siauw had to rely heavily on the support of individual leaders who had influential positions within executive and legislative bodies. The people he relied on included Chaerul Saleh, chairman of the MPRS and a Partai Murba sympathiser; Sartono, deputy chairman of the DPA and a member of the PNI; Aruji Kartawinata, chairman of the DPRGR and a member of the PSII; Soedibyo secretary of the Front Nasional and a member of the PSII; Prijono, education minister and a member of the Partai Murba; Jusuf Muda Dalam, finance minister and a PKI sympathiser, and others. Through these connections, Siauw was able to gain various political concessions for Baperki and the Chinese in Indonesia.

Siauw's personal connections with these leaders also enabled him to get them involved in various committees or bodies that dealt with Chinese issues. For example, Aruji Kartawinata became chairman of the Indonesian-Chinese Friendship Committee. Soedibyo was always prepared to go with Siauw to functions organised by Baperki or Chinese associations.[48]

With such a situation, one must see Siauw's closeness to the leaders of the political parties more from the perspective of personal relationship than his commitment to certain political ideologies. Siauw was to maintain that what he always advocated was an adherence to Soekarno's political direction, not that of the PKI or any other party.

On the other hand, Siauw was often in conflict with the right-wing forces, particularly the army. To pursue his goals, from time to time he had to follow the PKI's line in attacking the army and sometimes also the NU and the Christian parties (although he remained personally close to Tambunan of Parkindo and Kasimo of the Partai Katolik). Thus, Siauw made himself and Baperki vulnerable to the attacks from the right-wing political forces. Until the end of September 1965, due to the support and protection from Soekarno and the left-wing political forces, the advantages this policy provided outweighed the risks it involved, although the possibility of a right-wing backlash was worrying to many.

Within the Chinese community, Siauw's policies were becoming more controversial as the polarisation between right and left grew even sharper in the years after 1963. As Coppel says:

> Siauw Giok Tjhan's policies succeeded in making him an unprecedentedly successful leader of the Chinese in Indonesia. But they were too pro-communist and too China-minded for some sections of the community. His concern for alien Chinese interests (other than those of the Chinese who favoured the Kuo Min Tang), his campaign to have Indonesian citizenship available to the largest possible number of Indonesian Chinese in the easiest way possible, and the fact that one of his own children was sent to China for schooling aroused suspicions not only among many Indigenous Indonesians, but also among WNI (Warga Negara Indonesia – Indonesian citizens) Chinese who

---

[48] Interviews with Oei Tjoe Tat, Go Gien Tjwan and Phoa Thoan Hian in 1993.

were anti-communist, or advocates of assimilation or unsympathetic to the interests and orientation of totoks.[49]

But this group was a minority during the Guided Democracy. Most people, who were associated with Baperki or benefited from Baperki's achievements were convinced that Siauw's decision to align himself and Baperki with Soekarno was sensible. Somers sums up the situation by saying:

> Significantly, many older generation peranakans, although dissatisfied with Baperki because of political and personal disagreements with its leadership, nevertheless remain inactive, nominal members of the organisation. They regard Baperki as a necessary weapon to defend the special interests of the peranakan Chinese against either discrimination or forced change by the Indonesian government.[50]

Under Siauw, Baperki set itself apart from other Chinese organisations in Indonesia in that its presence in Indonesian society encouraged a large number of Chinese, throughout the archipelago but particularly in Java, to adopt Indonesia-oriented politics and hence to regard Indonesia as their motherland. During the Guided Democracy period Baperki was most successful in providing political education to the Chinese in Indonesia, both peranakans and totoks.

---

[49] Charles Coppel, 'Patterns of Chinese Political Activity in Indonesia' in Mackie (ed.) *The Chinese in Indonesia: Five Essays* p. 50.
[50] Somers, *Peranakan Chinese Politics*, p. 263.

Chapter 11

BAPERKI'S EDUCATIONAL, CULTURAL AND YOUTH PROGRAMS

In the years after 1957, Baperki came to operate a large number of schools and a university with branches in various cities. These were open to all Indonesian citizens but a great majority of their students were Chinese, most of them peranakans. Baperki also accepted alien Chinese who had difficulty in studying in national schools and state universities. Because of this policy, and the high standard of education offered, the majority of the Indonesian Chinese supported Baperki. Baperki was able to rely on a large number of Chinese businessmen, peranakan and totok, for generous financial support to build and equip their school and university buildings. Baperki's university, established in 1958, became the largest private university in Indonesia. It had modern and advanced facilities, matching those offered by the University of Indonesia and the Bandung Institute of Technology.

In fact, towards the end of the Guided Democracy period, Baperki was better known for its educational institutions than as a political organisation. In this sense it paralleled the THHK but, whereas the THHK educational bodies emphasised Chinese nationalism and Confucianism, Baperki ones placed importance on Indonesian nationalism and the integration of the Chinese and other Indonesian citizens into Indonesian society.

Siauw established Baperki's Foundation for Education and Culture (Yayasan Pendidikan dan Kebudayaan Baperki) in 1958 and became its chairman. Under his leadership, students of Baperki's senior secondary schools and university were exposed to topics relevant to Siauw's long political journey, including citizenship and dual nationality issues, nation building and the national economy. The Baperki university encouraged its students to be involved in building their own facilities, a unique program which received wide support from the community.

Despite attempts to attract Asli students, over 90 per cent of the students in Baperki's institutions were Chinese. Because of this, their opponents were able to label these institutions as exclusive. But such criticisms did not reduce Baperki's popularity within the Chinese communities. Baperki's decision to establish schools in many cities and towns in Indonesia had strengthened its claims to speak on behalf of these communities.

Siauw believed that political awareness should be fostered among young children. He urged Baperki schools to form student unions whose activities included cultural performances, political discussions and the publication of political journals. He also initiated the formation of a youth organisation, the PPI, led by Baperki students and coordinated by Baperki. The PPI was involved in promoting Indonesian culture and Siauw's ideas of natural integration.

This chapter outlines how Baperki became involved in providing education and how its educational bodies functioned.

Before World War II most Chinese students went to Chinese-language schools, mainly run by the THHK. Those who were financially successful sent their children to Dutch-language schools. Only a small number of peranakans went to Indonesian-language schools. During the Japanese occupation, Dutch schools were closed and the Chinese were not allowed to go to Indonesian-language schools. Because of this, they had no alternative but to go to Chinese-language schools.

After 1945, peranakans established schools in some cities with Dutch curricula. These schools, known as the Tjing Iems, accommodated thousands of peranakans who wished to resume their Dutch education, often hoping to go on to study in Holland. The Angkatan Muda Tionghoa (AMT or Chinese Youth Movement), established by Siauw in Malang in 1945, provided Dutch-language education for hundreds of peranakans in Malang until 1948. However, a majority of the peranakans continued to send their children to Chinese-language schools whose academic standards and facilities were considered high.[1]

The fact that a large number of Chinese of Indonesian citizenship were studying in Chinese schools in the 1950s generated controversy. Early in 1954, Sutan Takdir Alisjahbana, a famous writer and member of Jakarta Regional Parliament representing the PSI, moved a motion in that

---

[1] According to Siauw in some of his speeches in 1954, a large number of Asli parents, acknowledging the superiority of the Chinese schools, also sent their children to Chinese schools.

parliament demanding the exclusion of some 200 000 Indonesian citizens from alien schools, and the conversion of alien schools into national schools if over 25 per cent of their students were Indonesian citizens. Takdir acknowledged that there were insufficient numbers of national schools to accommodate the displaced students but argued that the peranakan Chinese were rich enough to organise their own national schools. This motion was finally passed by the regional parliament.[2]

Siauw criticised the motion. In a statement published in *Berita Baperki* in July 1954, Siauw argued that until the government established enough schools for all citizens, the peranakan Chinese should be given freedom to send their children to any school. Because national schools were not able to accommodate Chinese students, Siauw added, their parents were forced to send their children to Chinese-language schools. This action, he said, should not be understood as the unwillingness of the Chinese to send their children to Indonesian-language schools. Furthermore, he argued that many national schools in Indonesia rejected Chinese pupils. He referred to cases where peranakan students who wanted to enrol in national secondary schools were rejected because they were not able to prove their citizenship or because these schools were not willing to accept them.

To defuse the criticism, Siauw invited Takdir to meet with a group of Baperki leaders, including Go Gien Tjwan, Oei Tjoe Tat and Sie Boen Lian, on 4 August 1954 in Jakarta. In this meeting, Siauw said that it was erroneous to assume that the peranakans were rich and were capable of setting up their own national schools. Siauw added that Chinese-language schools were run by alien Chinese associations whose members were businessmen. The peranakans did not have such associations.[3]

In response to Siauw's remarks, Takdir conceded that it would be unwise to force students to leave alien schools unless alternative placements in national schools were available. However, he remained convinced that it was wrong to have Indonesian citizens studying in Chinese-language schools. The meeting failed to reach a workable conclusion.

In March 1955, the government began to establish experimental schools (Sekolah Rakyat Percobaan – Experimental Elementary Schools), specifically for Indonesian citizens of Chinese descent. Within Baperki, there were mixed reactions to the establishment of such schools. Some, like Auwyong

---

[2] *Berita Baperki*, 26 July 1954.
[3] Baperki meeting minutes, 4 August 1954.

Peng Koen, supported the idea while others, like Siauw, rejected it. Siauw argued that these schools would maintain the isolation of the Chinese.[4]

In May 1955, Baperki organised a conference on education and culture which came out against the experimental elementary schools. It urged the government to expedite increasing the number of state schools and to improve the quality of text books. It protested against discriminatory measures against the Chinese in the field of education. It also urged the government to abolish the experimental schools on the grounds that the system would reinstitute divisions in society. Moreover, it confirmed Baperki's intention to establish its own schools with a national curriculum which would be open to all citizens.

Calls for Baperki to set up its own schools were made repeatedly in the following years but Baperki's preoccupation with citizenship issues and the 1955 elections delayed serious efforts to collect funds for that purpose.

Baperki schools

The issue of Indonesian citizens going to Chinese-language schools run by foreign citizens was resurrected in 1957. Following the introduction of martial law in March 1957, a number of military authorities in various regions, motivated by their anti-communist convictions, started closing alien schools and prohibiting Indonesian citizens from attending those alien schools which were still allowed to operate. This activity began in West Nusa Tenggara in May 1957. All Chinese language schools in the region were closed. Within a number of months, military authorities in other cities followed suit. In November 1957, a similar policy was implemented in Jakarta.

Not all Chinese language schools were closed. A significantly reduced number of schools were allowed to continue. Regulations were also issued to streamline national schools. For schools to qualify as national schools, they had to be operated by Indonesian citizens and all of their teachers had to be Indonesian citizens.[5] In the same year, the authorities imposed further restrictions. School directors and teachers in Chinese language schools had to pass an examination in writing and speaking Indonesian. The number of new foreign teachers teaching in these schools was also to be severely limited.

---

[4] Baperki meeting minutes, June 1955.
[5] Somers, *Peranakan Chinese Politics in Indonesia*, p. 164.

By July 1958, the number of Chinese language schools had been reduced from 2000 to 850 and the number of students attending them from 425 000 to 150 000. The majority of the 250 000 displaced students were Chinese of Indonesian citizenship. The situation encouraged Baperki to establish more schools to accommodate the displaced students. At the end of 1956, it had been running schools in Jakarta, Ciputat, Garut, Tanggerang, Cilamaya, Kudus and Kediri, in Java, and Bagan Siapi Api, in Sumatra, but there was pressure to establish many more.[6]

Baperki's Foundation for Education and Culture was established early in 1958 in order to more effectively collect funds for the schools. The foundation was also charged with managing and running of the schools.[7]

Through Siauw's connections with leaders of the Chinese-language oriented CHTH, Sito Chang, Go Gak Cho, Kho Nai Chong and Kho Ie Sioe, Baperki was able to closely cooperate with directors of Chinese-language schools and leaders of Chinese associations who ran the schools, to quickly establish schools and accommodate the students who were displaced by closures and regulations during 1957 and 1958. By 1960, Baperki owned and ran 96 Indonesian-language schools, mainly primary and junior secondary schools.

In many cases, Baperki took over the buildings of the closed alien schools. In some cases, the schools were divided into two parts, one for the alien students, with Chinese as the language of instruction, and the other for Indonesian citizens using a national curriculum. There were also school buildings which were still owned by the Chinese Associations but were made available to Baperki free of charge.

In all cases, the Chinese associations provided Baperki with the initial funds to establish and run the schools. Siauw was able to convince leaders of the Chinese associations that these schools, built during the colonial period, were the culmination of efforts of all Chinese, then Dutch subjects. Siauw therefore argued that it would be fair if parts of these schools were transferred to Baperki to accommodate the displaced Chinese students.[8]

Many of the students affected by the school closures were from the totok communities. So leaders of the Chinese associations had a strong incentive

---

[6] Somers, *Peranakan Chinese Politics in Indonesia*, p. 166; Willmott, *The National Status of the Chinese in Indonesia*, p. 87; *Berita Baperki*, 15 October 1956.

[7] Laporan Secretariat Yayasan Pendidikan Dan Kebudayaan Baperki, 29–30 July 1961.

[8] Interviews with Go Gak Cho and Kho Nai Chong, Hong Kong, December 1990; Siauw, *Lima Jaman*, p. 253.

to assist Baperki. They did not need much convincing and readily accepted Siauw's recommendations.[9]

Baperki's serious involvement in the educational field and its ownership of schools were debated at a leadership meeting, held on 8 February 1958, in which the formation of Baperki's Foundation of Education and Culture was formalised. Vice-Chairman Yap Thiam Hien questioned Siauw's decision to allow Baperki to become an education provider and owner of a large number of schools. Yap argued that it would be better for Baperki to fight against the implementation of the military regulations on alien schools and students of Indonesian citizenship than to become an education provider. Yap was concerned that Baperki was not well equipped to operate educational institutions.[10]

In response to Yap's objection, Siauw maintained that Baperki's direct involvement in providing education would attract moral and material support from the communities. Such support, Siauw added, was crucial for Baperki. He was confident of being able to collect sufficient funds to properly operate the educational institutions. Yap was overwhelmingly defeated.[11] Although Yap initially objected to the decision, he remained involved in supporting Baperki's activities in education.[12]

Lev, however, learned from Yap that he, in fact, fiercely objected to the establishment of Baperki University on the grounds that its establishment would endanger Baperki schools, and peranakan interests in general, by association.[13] Go Gien Tjwan however recalls that once the decision to establish the university had been made, Yap supported it.

Funding was largely raised from the students. While well-to-do parents were requested to provide significant financial contributions, poor parents were often exempt from paying fees. In addition to school fees, Baperki was able to rely on contributions from its sympathisers, both for budget support and to construct additional class rooms and sporting facilities.[14]

The number of Baperki schools grew steadily. By 1961 it had 107 schools: 27 in Jakarta, 17 in West Java, 12 in Central Java, 33 in East Java,

---

[9] Interviews with Go Gak Cho and Kho Nai Chong, Hong Kong, December 1990.
[10] Baperki meeting minutes, 8 February 1958.
[11] Ibid.
[12] Interview with Go Gien Tjwan, Amsterdam, December 1990.
[13] Daniel Lev, *Becoming an Orang Indonesia Sejati: The Political Journey of Yap Thiam Hien*, p. 105.
[14] Interviews with Mrs Lie Tjwan Sien, Go Gien Tjwan and Siauw Giok Bie, Amsterdam, December 1990.

four in South Sumatra, ten in North Sumatra, one in Bali and two in Sulawesi. Seventeen of these schools were junior secondary schools and three were senior high schools.[15]

In large capital cities like Jakarta, Baperki's schools were very popular. Their standard was known to be better than that of most state schools and was considered comparable with that offered by elite Catholic and Protestant private schools. Many teachers who taught at these private schools also taught at Baperki schools. The schools' pass rates usually exceeded 90 per cent.

Baperki's university

Having established large senior secondary schools, Baperki was confronted with the issue of where their graduates might continue their studies. At that time, there were very few private universities. Places in state universities were limited and a quota of ten per cent was informally applied to students of Chinese descent.

In 1958, a number of peranakan students who obtained the highest marks in their government-run secondary school examinations failed to gain entry to the University of Indonesia. Although no public explanation of their failure to enter the university was ever given, it was assumed that they were rejected because they were Chinese. The situation prompted a discussion within Baperki. Siauw was urged to initiate the establishment of Baperki's university. After several discussions Baperki decided to establish its own tertiary education institution.[16]

The first step was to establish an academy of physics and mathematics specifically designed to train secondary teachers. When Siauw was able to secure funding from the Chinese associations, Baperki decided to establish courses which were popular, such as medicine, dentistry and engineering courses.[17]

In September 1959, a dentistry faculty was established. In November 1959, the engineering faculty was set up, covering mechanical, civil and electrical engineering courses. These were later followed by the establishment of the medical and arts faculties in 1962.

---

[15] Laporan Tentang Keadaan Pendidikan di Sekolah Baperki, Desember 1960 s/d Juli 1961.

[16] Interviews with Go Gien Tjwan and Mrs Lie Tjwan Sien, Amsterdam, December 1993.

[17] Laporan Sekretariat Yayasan Pendidikan and Kebudayaan Baperki, 29–30 July 1961.

Siauw's approach to university education was expressed when the engineering faculty was inaugurated:

> The Peoples' Republic of China, which was one of the most underdeveloped nations in the world, has shown that with technological know-how developed within the nation and its people, and within a short period of time, it has significantly increased its people's standard of living. This experience indicates that if people can master high technology, their productivity will be significantly increased and this will ultimately improve prosperity of the people. Based on this experience, Baperki has decided to prioritise the commencement of an engineering faculty, with three separate courses, over the medical faculty. Baperki's engineering faculty would set up laboratories and workshops which would not be run purely for academic reasons but would also provide services to the community at large. Students would be trained to be practical and to run practical businesses while conducting academic experiments.[18]

Siauw's admiration for China's technological advancement was evident from both his speeches and private statements. He was convinced that China's technological drive would make it one of the most technologically advanced states. Such a positive impression had resulted in him encouraging all his children to improve their Mandarin by taking extra lessons at home. He believed that by mastering the language, people could access China's technology more readily. He also sent three of his children to China for their tertiary education – the first left for China in 1957 to do an engineering course, the second in 1960 to do medicine and the last in 1965 also to do engineering. Two of them travelled on Indonesian Government scholarships.

In the same speech, Siauw said:

> The decision to set up tertiary institutions was not to compete with state universities by merely accommodating people who were racially discriminated against by these state universities. The decision is based on our desire to provide opportunities to Indonesian students who deserve to be accommodated in university programs so that people whose average examination marks exceed 8 and 8.5 no longer have to accept the fact that, because they belong to a particular ethnic group, they can not continue their studies.

---

[18] Siauw's speech on 10 November 1959 to formalise the establishment of the engineering faculty.

Success with the engineering and dentistry faculties in 1960 prompted Baperki to formalise the establishment of the university. Symbolically, Baperki chose 28 October 1960, which is Hari Sumpah Pemuda (Youth Pledge Day) to do this.

While Siauw failed to attract a large number of prominent Asli and other ethnic figures to join the leadership of Baperki, he was successful in convincing a number of non-Chinese academics to accept senior posts in Baperki's university. On the inauguration day, Siauw announced the formation of three faculties, dentistry, under Bie Wie Tjoen, engineering, under Pudjono Hardjo Prakoso and the new faculty of social studies under Ernst Utrecht.[19]

Ferdinand Lumban Tobing became the first rector. He was a medical doctor, of Batak origin, a former minister and a member of Siauw's Fraksi Nasional Progresif in parliament. In his inauguration speech, Siauw pointed to Tobing being from outside Java as a happy reflection of the state's motto, Bhineka Tunggal Ika.[20]

Within months of the university's opening, Tan Kah Kee, the Singaporean Chinese leader who had been in hiding in Malang during the Japanese occupation, offered Siauw a large of block of land in West Jakarta for the university. However, that land required a significant amount of work before buildings could be constructed so Siauw reluctantly declined the offer.[21] Siauw managed to gain support from the Governor of Jakarta, Sumarno, who provided Baperki with a large block of land in a better location in Jakarta.[22]

By 1962, three large buildings, covering 4200 square metres, had been constructed for the dentistry and engineering faculties and an additional 2400 square metre building was being constructed. In the same year, three more faculties were established, a medical faculty, under Goedadi Wreksoatmodjo, a law faculty, under Professor Lie Oen Hock, and a faculty of letters, under Professor Tjan Tjoe Siem.[23] The social studies faculty was

---

19   Be Wie Tjoen was chairman of the Persatuan Dokter Gigi Indonesia – PDGI (Association of Dentists of Indonesia). Ernst Utrecht, an Indo-European, was a member of DPA (Dewan Pertimbangan Agung – Supreme Advisory Council), like Siauw. He was also a professor of law.

20   Siauw's Speech in the inauguration of Baperki University, 28 October 1960.

21   Siauw told this story to author in 1978 while driving near the land that was to be Tan Kah Kee's contribution to Baperki.

22   Interviews with Go Gien Tjwan and Mrs Lie Tjwan Sien, Amsterdam, December 1993. Sumarno, a medical doctor, was assisted by Siauw to gain employment in Jakarta in the early 1950s.

23   Goedadi Wreksoatmodjo, was a prominent medical doctor in Jakarta. Lie Oen Hock was a professor in the University of Indonesia and was head of the High Court of

reorganised and named the economics faculty, though it remained under the leadership of Ernst Utrecht. The engineering faculty was also expanded to include pharmacy courses.

By 1962, the Baperki university had also established a branch in Surabaya, offering engineering, law and pharmacy courses. The Surabaya branch was headed by Professor Gondowardojo who was also rector of Airlangga University, the leading government university in Surabaya. The number of students jumped dramatically. By 1962, the Jakarta branch had 2490 students while the Surabaya branch had 592 students. As a result, by 1962, some three years after its establishment, the total number of students enrolled in the Baperki university was more than 3000.[24]

When Rector Tobing died in 1962, Siauw decided that his successor should be a woman, Indonesia's first woman rector. Siauw respected and admired women in public life. He had proposed Mrs Ratu Aminah Hidayat to be one of the vice-chairpersons of the Konstituante. In 1962 he had appointed Mrs Lie Tjwan Sien to be the general secretary of Baperki. As rector, he chose Mrs Utami Suryadarma, a political activist and the wife of the air force's chief of staff, Commodore Suryadarma.[25]

In the same year, Siauw proposed that the name of the university be changed. Initially, the university was to be named Bhineka Tunggal Ika, but after some discussions, Siauw agreed to name it Respublica University (URECA), based on the title of one of Soekarno's speeches to the Konstituante 'Respublica, sekali lagi Respublica' (Respublica, once again Respublica).

In 1964, the Ministry of Education ruled that URECA's bachelor degree graduates (sarjana muda) in dentistry, engineering, economics and law were of equal standard to holders of similar degrees from state universities.[26] In 1965, URECA passed another significant milestone – it was also accredited to produce fully qualified dentists and engineers. By 1964, the number of students increased to almost 4000 and the prediction was that

---

Jakarta. Professor Tjan Tjoe Siem, a well known expert on Javanese literature, was also of the University of Indonesia.

24 Laporan Pendidikan Pada Konperensi Pleno Pusat Baperki di Jakarta, 10–12 November 1962.

25 Siauw, *Lima Jaman*, p. 259.

26 Laporan Rektor Universitas Respublica on 27 April 1964; in Indonesia at that time, bachelor degree, translated as Sarjana Muda, was not a full professional qualification. Normally the bachelor's degree could be completed within three years. To obtain full professional qualifications, the students need to do an additional two years for science and social studies and three years for medical studies.

this would rise by at least 1000 students per year. Out of these students, there were more than 300 bachelor degree holders.

But the university had serious financial problems. Its expansion programs could not be funded by student fees and, by 1964, its deficit had grown to almost 19 million rupiah. Siauw was opposed to increasing student fees – instead he asked students and lecturers to work together in designing and managing the construction of new buildings and other facilities. This program resulted in savings of up to 30 per cent in some cases. He also urged students to volunteer as construction workers.[27]

The university was unconventional in its student orientation program. There was to be no 'hazing' as in most state universities where new students were subjected to harsh and humiliating treatments by their seniors. Orientation programs required new students to work on productive projects. To show that Baperki was grateful to the Chinese businessmen who provided significant contributions to the university, some URECA students were directed to work in Glodok, Jakarta's Chinatown, to upgrade the quality of its roads. Others were required to help their senior fellow students to construct university buildings and lecture theatres.[28]

Siauw was concerned that Chinese of Chinese citizenship should be allowed to study in the university, especially as he hoped that they would eventually become Indonesian citizens. This attitude helped the university to raise money from the totok communities. Some very rich totoks sent their children overseas for university education, to Singapore, Taiwan, Hongkong, China, Australia, the US or Europe. For people who were not so rich, URECA was an attractive alternative.

To counter accusations that URECA was set up only for the Chinese, Siauw tried to encourage Asli students to enter the university. By 1965, he had initiated a scholarship program to enable graduates of Taman Siswa secondary schools to attend URECA free of charge. The number of graduates under this program was limited to five per faculty. In addition, URECA's good academic reputation meant that it attracted a number of Asli students who had been admitted to University of Indonesia. Some of Siauw's colleagues in parliament also sought his help to have their children accepted into URECA.[29]

---

[27] Siauw's speech delivered to Baperki's conference held in Bandung on 13 May 1965; Siauw, *Lima Jaman*, p. 256.
[28] Siauw, *Lima Jaman*, p. 256–257.
[29] Ibid., p. 256.

But the efforts to increase the number of Asli students failed to significantly alter the ratio of Chinese to Asli students. The great majority of the students at URECA continued to be Chinese and this had made it difficult for Baperki to counter the LPKB's accusation that the institution was established exclusively for the Chinese. Siauw, however, frequently stated that the Catholic and Protestant universities had the same problem. They too accommodated largely students of Chinese extraction. Siauw argued that this was due to the educational situation – most Chinese students were not able to enter state universities.

Later, when Baperki was dissolved in 1966 and the management of URECA was taken over (with some members of the new management team being LPKB members), the university, now renamed Trisakti University, did not significantly change in the composition of students. The great majority of the students, now having to pay relatively high university entrance fees, continued to be Chinese. Writing much later, Siauw asserted, 'In the 1970s, it became apparent that the charges against Baperki based on its "exclusivism" were politically motivated. Organisations whose leaders accused Baperki of being exclusive are now running educational institutions such as Atma Jaya University whose students are mostly Chinese'.[30]

By May 1965 branches of URECA had been established in other cities. In Medan, economics and education faculties were established. In Semarang, a medical course was commenced. In Yogyakarta, an economics faculty was set up[31], and work had commenced towards opening faculties in Malang, Solo, Cirebon and Bandung.[32]

Political activities in Baperki schools and university

Like Soekarno, Siauw believed in the efficacy of idealistic rhetoric and statements of goals to be pursued. Soekarno's definition of a true patriot was related to five aspects. A true patriot was said to be:[33]

1. a person who loves true independence with sovereignty in the hands of Indonesian people
2. a person who loves an independent national economy

---

[30] Siauw, *Lima Jaman*, p. 258.
[31] Siauw's speech delivered in Bandung on 13 May 1965.
[32] Interviews with Siauw Giok Bie and Mrs Lie Tjwan Sien, Amsterdam, December 1993.
[33] Siauw's lecture notes, 1964.

3. a person who loves his own culture
4. a person who fights hard for the realisation of a socialistic society à la Indonesia
5. a person who is opposed to racism and chauvinism.

In 1960, Siauw responded by devising a similar set of five principles, the Five Loves – Panca Cinta:[34]

1. Love the motherland and the Indonesian people.
2. Love humanity and peace.
3. Love knowledge and culture.
4. Love work.
5. Love your parents.

The Baperki education program was endorsed by Prijono, then education minister. Soekarno, in his 'year of living dangerously' speech delivered in 1964, also confirmed that he viewed Panca Cinta as in line with the direction of educational programs stipulated in the DPA's formulation.

From the commencement of the university programs in 1959, the Baperki university had made Panca Sila and civics a compulsory subject in all courses. All students were required to pass this before they could gain a pass in their full academic year. Siauw himself was the main lecturer for this subject.

Siauw produced comprehensive lecture materials on the subject. Through this subject, Siauw attempted to highlight the experiences the Chinese in Indonesia had through history. Issues related to citizenship, natural integration, Soekarno's concepts of Indonesian socialism, guided democracy and national economy were the main themes of Siauw's lectures. Like Soekarno, Siauw stressed that university education should not be narrowly academic and that it should not be too 'textbookish'. Much of Siauw's lecture materials for his university courses were also used in Baperki secondary schools.

In the context of preparing students for employment in Indonesia, Baperki's programs were different to those run by Chinese-language schools.[35] In Chinese-language schools most of the materials were from China. The curriculum was structured so that graduates from these schools

---

[34] In some of the PKI documents, Panca Cinta was also described as part of the party's educational programs. It is not clear whether the concept was originated by Siauw or Baperki. Refer to Siauw's lecture notes, 1964.

[35] Siauw's lecture notes, 1961.

were able to continue their studies in China. Their cultural programs were also largely linked to China. Pro-Mao Chinese-language schools provided political education to their students. They relied on materials that promoted Chinese nationalism and detailed achievements of Mao's revolution. Most of their students were admirers of Mao and his teachings. But they would have had little or no exposure to Indonesian culture and political development.

Baperki-run schools used the curricula of the Ministry of Education. In addition, the schools introduced their students to Indonesian culture and to Baperki programs. This had 'peranakanised' the students from totok backgrounds. Because of Baperki's programs, most of the totok students, particularly those in secondary schools, adopted Indonesia-oriented thinking.

Most of the leaders of student organisations, in both secondary schools and URECA, were in fact from the totok community. This was partly due to the fact that the totok students came from poor families and were therefore more attracted to leftist policies. Also, many had previously attended Chinese-language schools in which they had learned of Mao's revolution. In general, they were more political than their fellow peranakan students.[36]

In 1959 Siauw initiated the formation of the PPI in Jakarta, coordinated by Baperki's youth section. Membership included both students and other young people. Most members were peranakans from Baperki schools and URECA. The organisation was charged with the dissemination of Baperki's programs and the promotion of Indonesian culture. Its members were encouraged to learn the traditional and folk dances of various ethnic communities.

In the early 1960s, the PPI was known for the high level of performances of its dances. Lekra, a body closely linked with the PKI, often asked the PPI dancing group to perform for it on big occasions. Soekarno often asked them to perform at state functions.[37]

The organisation of PPI was assisted by the ikatan pelajar (student unions), established in all Baperki secondary schools, and dewan mahasiswa (student councils) in Baperki's university campuses. These student unions published their own school journals which included political discussions and analysis. Agricultural programs were also encouraged in Baperki's schools. Some time in 1964, all available land in some of the schools in Jakarta were cultivated to grow corn. In 1965 URECA engineering students produced

---

[36] Interviews with former students of Baperki schools and Universitas Respublica.
[37] Interview with Tan Swie Ling, a leader of the PPI in 1960, Jakarta, December 1994.

agricultural tools and basic machines in their workshops. A program with the BTI was developed which was designed to exchange information and to conduct research on how agricultural techniques could be improved.[38]

Political activities in Baperki schools became more intense in 1964. Baperki's congress in August 1964 supported the suggestion that Baperki school students should automatically be members of an association for secondary school students, the IPPI (Ikatan Pemuda Pelajar Indonesia – Association of Indonesian Student and Youth). Not long after that, Siauw declared that some 6000 students of Baperki schools were members of the IPPI. Many leaders in Baperki's student unions were also leaders of the IPPI.

Initially only the PPI was active in Baperki's university but by 1962 there were also others. The most popular body was Perhimi (Perhimpunan Mahasiswa Indonesia – Association of Indonesian Students), formerly called Ta Hsueh Hsueh Sheng Hui (Association of University Students), a university student body whose members were predominantly peranakan students. Others included the PMKRI (Persatuan Mahasiswa Katolik Indonesia – Association of Indonesian Catholic Students) and the CGMI.

By 1965, many leaders among Baperki's students were actively involved in the Pemuda Rakyat or CGMI, both bodies being closely linked to the PKI. CGMI and Pemuda Rakyat parades and shows of force frequently depended on Baperki students' coordination and actual participation. Tensions which developed between Baperki and PKI organisations will be discussed in Chapter 13.

Siauw's initiatives in establishing the educational institutions had helped Baperki to attract both financial and moral support from the Chinese communities. His drive in providing political education in Baperki's schools and university had peranakanised students from totok backgrounds and had significantly increased student awareness of Indonesian politics. It had also encouraged student participation in various student and youth organisations like the Pemuda Rakyat, CGMI, PMKRI and Perhimi.

---

[38] *Harian Rakyat*, 14 March 1965.

Chapter 12

THE ASSIMILATION-INTEGRATION DEBATE

Through being close to President Soekarno, Siauw was able to consolidate Baperki's position in the political arena during the period of Guided Democracy. However, in the early 1960s the positions of Siauw and Baperki were challenged by a group of peranakans who advocated assimilation as the solution to minority problems and who came to enjoy the patronage of an important group of army leaders. The assimilationists included people who had left Baperki in 1955. In 1963, this group established the LPKB to counter Baperki's influence in the peranakan community.

While the LPKB's leaders were mostly members who were sympathetic to right-wing political orientation and Baperki was more closely associated with left-wing political forces, the fundamental difference between these two organisations lay in their position on how the minority problems should be solved. Siauw rejected the concept of assimilation and advocated a principle he referred to as the 'natural integration principle' which was adopted and endorsed by Baperki. Thus, in the early 1960s, a public debate on integration versus assimilation began.

The implementation of the PP-10 of 1959 was a major blow against the Chinese community. It not only upset the alien Chinese but also deeply concerned many peranakans. Many began to consider emigrating, including to China. The popular term used by the Chinese, peranakans and totoks, in the early 1960s was 'Hwe Kuok' (literally, 'going home' – that is, to China).

In this situation of anger, anxiety and confusion, a group of peranakans launched a new debate on assimilation. In early 1960, they published articles in *Star Weekly* to popularise the assimilation concept and invited reaction from the peranakan communities. One of their key arguments was that the problems the Chinese peranakans experienced were due to the way they behaved in society. Thus the assimilation movement was born.

There are a number of theories about how this movement was initiated and later developed. According to Suryadinata, the assimilation movement developed as a response to Baperki's integrationist approach.[1] However, the background to the movement was more complicated than a mere response to Baperki's proposed solution to Chinese problems.

Somers links the movement to the aftermath of the implementation of PP-10. She argues that the hardship experienced by the Chinese, mainly alien Chinese, gave the assimilationists reasons to endorse their concept. They, Somers says, had urged the peranakans to disassociate themselves from alien Chinese and remove barriers to Asli Indonesians by changing their names and inter-marrying with Asli Indonesians.[2]

Coppel's account of the movement's origins is detailed. According to him, the assimilation group consisted of people 'who were either anti-communist, or advocates of assimilation or unsympathetic to the interests and orientation of totoks'. He further suggests, 'The roots of the movement were various and were not confined either to the Chinese community or to those who were principled advocates of assimilation'.[3] He goes on to describe that the assimilation approach was aired by individuals well before 1960. There was already a school of thought within the peranakan community which favoured assimilation, before the formation of Baperki in 1954. In April 1958, Copel says, the army's General Nasution, urged all citizens of foreign descent 'not to mix with aliens but ally themselves with Indigenous Indonesian groups and organisations'.[4] The birth of the movement, he says, was also made possible by former Baperki leaders, mostly Catholics and young idealistic students, who had good personal relations with Asli students and saw exclusive communal associations as old-fashioned and products of colonial days.

Coppel links the birth of the assimilation concept to the aftermath of the implementation of PP-10 in 1959–1960 which led many peranakans to see the need to look for ways of protecting themselves and distance themselves from alien Chinese. The assimilationists, he says, were divided into three main groups. The more conservative supporters were against communal organisations and particularly Baperki. Most of these were willing

---

[1] Suryadinata, *Pribumi Indonesians, the Chinese Minority and China*, p. 70.
[2] Somers, *Peranakan Chinese Politics*, p. 258.
[3] Charles Coppel, 'Patterns of Chinese Political Activity in Indonesia', in Mackie *The Chinese in Indonesia: Five Essays*, pp. 50–51.
[4] Ibid.

to initially sign their names in support of the movement but did nothing after that. The more radical supporters actively promoted the assimilation concept and urged the peranakans to adhere to it. The extremists went further – they condemned Confucianism and peranakan customs and argued that name-changing to Indonesian-sounding names be made compulsory for all Chinese of Indonesian citizenship.

It is clear that there was also a strong political motivation against Baperki when the assimilationist group was formed. Somers supports this view by saying, 'Although peranakan leaders of the assimilationists have consistently denied that they wish to fight Baperki, they cannot escape the implication of their stand. Nor does the fact that many of them came from Catholic, Protestant, and other right-wing elements in the peranakan community make more convincing their argument that they are free of political motives'.[5]

In his speeches and writings of the 1960s, Siauw did not publicise his interpretation of how the movement was born and developed. However, privately he connected it (and the later formation of the LPKB), to the army's deliberate attempt to establish an organisation to counter and, ultimately, destroy Baperki. The army, he said, was agitated because Baperki had openly challenged and obstructed their anti-Chinese programs manifested in the implementation of PP-10 and various other regional regulations designed to jeopardise Chinese businesses.[6] This assertion is in line with what he wrote in his memoir, although he was less explicit on the army's involvement. Siauw gave a detailed account of how Baperki successfully made invalid a regulation issued by a governor of West Java in the early 1960s. The governor, a military man, introduced a regulation requiring 50 per cent of rice mills' shares to be owned by Asli Indonesians. At Baperki's insistence, the central government had invalidated the governor's instruction. Siauw wrote in his memoir, 'Since Baperki was constantly fighting against regulations in the economic field produced by the policies of discrimination, it naturally fell foul of those who hoped to make quick profits for themselves by these regulations. These people, therefore, tried to create a counter-organisation which would diminish the effectiveness of Baperki.'[7]

---

[5] Somers, *Peranakan Chinese Politics*, p. 260.
[6] Interviews with Oei Tjoe Tat and Phoa Thoan Hian, Jakarta, December 1993.
[7] Peter Burns (ed.), *Siauw Giok Tjhan Remembers*, pp. 60–61; Siauw, *Suatu Renungan*, p. 124.

Junus Jahja has admitted that the army was involved in encouraging the assimilationists to form an organisation. He says:

> When I returned from the Netherlands in 1959, I often went to the *Star Weekly* office in Jalan Pintu Besar, Jakarta, to read papers, journals and exchange views (with like-minded people). From there, the assimilation concept was developed. In that office, we were contacted by Lt. Col Soeparman from the army headquarters to form the Panitia Penyuluhan Assimilasi [Committee for the Promotion of Assimilation]... Then came a young leader, Ong Tjong Hay, who would later be better known as K Sindhunatha.[8]

It is however difficult to verify Siauw's assertion that the early motivation in 1960 by the group and the army was to reduce Baperki's effectiveness.

It is equally difficult to quantify the number of people who supported the assimilation movement. The group which later formed the LPKB did not intend to make it a mass organisation. Its membership was therefore small. However, as the political polarisation developed in the period, many anti-communist intellectuals who were not strongly committed to assimilation chose to support the assimilationists.[9]

The assimilation theory was defined by people in the group in various ways. Ong Hok Ham, a history student at the University of Indonesia argued that assimilation had been successful in eliminating minority groups in the Indonesian society. He referred to historical data which confirmed that a large number of Chinese who went to Indonesia in the 18th and 19th centuries had descendants who were now regarded as Indigenous Indonesians. These Chinese had assimilated by marrying local people and often by becoming Muslims and their offspring had become accepted as Asli. Ong stressed:

> The only way to remove conflicts between the majority and minority groups is for the Chinese to totally assimilate with the majority and to become Asli Indonesians. Assimilation means the disappearance of minority identities. Name-changing is only one of the means to

---

[8] H. Junus Jahja, *Catatan Seorang WNI – Kenangan, Renungan dan Harapan*, Yayasan Tunas Bangsa, Cetakan ke II, 1989, p. 98.

[9] Interview, Jakarta, July 1998. The person interviewed was an active participant of the LPKB who later regretted that choice. According to him (a student of the Institute of Technology of Bandung in the 1960s) there were quite a number of students, mostly Catholics, who followed his suit.

achieve assimilation. Name-changing has to be followed by integration in the economic and political spheres. In short, the exclusiveness of the minority groups has to be totally eliminated.[10]

In another *Star Weekly* article, Ong argued:

> The failure of a minority to be absorbed is also often the fault of the minority itself, which maintains its group identity. In Indonesia the obstructions created by the majority are few. The greater difficulty is caused by the minority… The problem now is that the minority has to realise that they can not remain here as Indonesian citizens and continue to behave like foreigners. They must realise that absorption into the society is the only road for them.[11]

In some other *Star Weekly* articles, Ong further endorsed the correctness of the assimilation theory by highlighting the success of assimilation of the Chinese in the Philippines.

In an article published in *Star Weekly* on 26 March 1960, the assimilationists argued that the Indonesian national motto, Bhineka Tunggal Ika, should not be used as a justification to reject the assimilation theory. They stressed that the motto was designed to promote unity but it was never intended to stop the natural process of the attrition of ethnic groups in Indonesia. They asserted that the intermarriages of people from different sukus would eventually eliminate ethnic barriers and Indonesia would only know an Indonesian nation. This principle, they argued, was endorsed by President Soekarno and should accordingly be applied to the peranakans. They should be prepared to marry Indigenous Indonesians. If the peranakans maintained their cultural identity and existed exclusively in the society, they would not be accepted by the majority of Indonesians and would always be discriminated against.[12]

On 24 March 1960, a group of ten peranakans issued a statement on natural assimilation. The statement criticised Siauw's rejection of the assimilation theory and fully endorsed the assimilation principle as the only solution to the minority problems. The statement also referred to President Soekarno's speech delivered in Yogyakarta on 22 December 1959. In this speech, Soekarno encouraged intermarriages among all Indonesian ethnic

---

[10] Star *Weekly*, 27 February 1960.
[11] Star *Weekly*, 2 April 1960.
[12] Star *Weekly*, 26 March 1960.

groups. The group had viewed this speech as Soekarno's blessing on the assimilation concept. The group of ten included people like Injo Beng Goat, Kwee Hwat Djien and Auwyong Peng Koen who had helped form Baperki in 1954 but left the organisation in 1955 for reasons connected with their anti-communist convictions.

The *Star Weekly* articles invited mixed reactions from both the peranakan and Indigenous communities. Most Indigenous respondents supported the movement, although some indicated their doubts over the sincerity of the peranakans to assimilate. Some peranakans welcomed the assimilation idea, while others opposed it.

On 2 April, Siauw responded in the pages of *Star Weekly*. He argued that cultural and biogical assimilation would not guarantee that minority problems and racial discrimination could be eliminated. He indicated that the only way of achieving an effective solution to the minority problems was by working together with all Indonesians to realise a just and prosperous society where the need to exploit people was eliminated. He agreed that natural processes involving changing name and religion and mixed marriages could not and should not be stopped. But he was concerned that the promotion of the assimilation argument would result in processes to force changes in names and religions, mixed marriages and overall elimination of ethnic identity and tradition. Accordingly, he said, he preferred to adopt an integration process whereby various ethnic groups could coexist harmoniously, feel that they share the same problems and share a determination to consolidate national unity and full independence.[13]

The term assimilation (assimilasi) associated with the Chinese in Indonesia was, perhaps, first publicly addressed by Kwee Hing Tjiat, one of Siauw's mentors, in August 1934. Kwee wrote an article in the first edition of *Mata Hari*, published on 1 August 1934, titled 'Baba Dewasa' (Mature Peranakans). In this article, Kwee urged the peranakans to become Indonesian sons and hence to undertake responsibilities identical with those of people who consider Indonesia as their motherland.

Although Kwee did suggest that the peranakans be assimilated into Indigenous communities, he did not elaborate on how they should be assimilated. No reference was made to changing name or religion.[14] Kwee used the term assimilation to express his view that eventually the Indonesian Chinese would be absorbed – assimilated – into the Indonesian population,

---

[13] *Star Weekly*, 2 April 1960.
[14] *Mata Hari*, 1 August 1934.

like the Chinese in the Philippines, Thailand and other places.[15] Siauw argued that what Kwee advocated was political and cultural assimilation for the Chinese to develop the sense of belonging to Indonesia, not China.[16]

The assimilationists however tended to refer to Liem Koen Hian, of the PTI, as the father of assimilation.[17] What Liem advocated was political assimilation. He urged the Chinese in Indonesia to work side by side with Indonesians and participate in local politics. Junus Jahja (Lauw Chuan To, a leader of the LPKB) has argued that Siauw himself was an advocate of assimilation in his PTI days.[18] He is right in the sense that Siauw wanted to be part of Indonesian national politics.

Yap Thiam Hien, who had just resigned as vice-chairman from Baperki, also rejected the assimilation theory. Yap argued that a nation-building process could be achieved by the cooperation of various ethnic groups. He also argued that assimilation could only be effective if the dominant group of Indigenous Indonesians was ready to accept the Chinese minority. The current climate, according to Yap, was not conducive for this. He endorsed the integration approach, prioritising the upholding of the rule of law and elimination of racial prejudice. But he distinguished his position from Siauw's, which he branded communist.[19] Siauw was quick to point out that his policies with respect to the creation of a just and prosperous society were not those of the communists, as they reflected policies which were endorsed by Soekarno and supported by all major political parties.[20]

Star Weekly editorials ridiculed the solutions offered by both Siauw and Yap, emphasising that it was dangerous to maintain the existence of Chinatowns and exclusive patterns of Chinese social life. They also ridiculed the concept that the peranakans belonged to a suku. They argued that the sukus have territorial bases while the peranakans did not have a territory in Indonesia. Their ancestors came from various parts of China. They also argued that the adoption of solutions offered by Siauw and Yap would mean that the peranakans would never break their ties with China.

---

[15] *Djawa Tengah Review*, August 1934.
[16] Siauw, *Lima Jaman*, pp. 53–54.
[17] Leo Suryadinata, *Political Thinking of the Indonesian Chinese, 1900–1977*, Institute of South East Asian Studies, 1979, p. 134.
[18] Interview with Junus Jahja, Melbourne, August 1989.
[19] *Star Weekly*, 16 April, 20 April and 17 May 1960.
[20] *Star Weekly*, 23 April 1960.

In January 1961, the assimilationist group organised a conference on national awareness which was attended by 30 participants, mainly peranakans, and issued a charter on assimilation. Among those who signed the charter were Kwik Hway Goan, one of Baperki's founders who had argued for inclusion of the word 'Tionghoa' at Baperki's inaugural meeting, and Tjoa Tjie Liang, Siauw's former colleague at *Mata Hari* in Semarang.

In 1962, the assimilitionists were successful in attracting support from a number of senior army officials including Colonel Soetjipto and General Nasution. They were also able to assemble Indigenous politicians oriented to the right wing to join and support them. A new organisation, the Body for Nation Building (Organisasi Pembinaan Kesatuan Bangsa) was formed, which operated under the protection of a new army-organised umbrella organisation, the Body for the Development of Functional Potentials (Badan Pembina Potensi Karya).[21]

In 1962, the assimilationists further defined what they meant by assimilation. Their assimilation program involved assimilation in five fields which were to be accomplished simultaneously. The fields concerned were political assimilation, cultural assimilation, economic assimilation, social assimilation and family (marriage) assimilation. In the political field, they urged the abolition of organisations whose membership was limited to Chinese. To them, forming a political group which was solely focused on Chinese concerns endangered national unity and would jeopardise the positions of the peranakan Chinese. They also believed that peranakan issues could not be divorced from national issues. Accordingly, they believed that the peranakans should participate in national organisations to achieve their goals.

In other fields, they believed that the peranakans had to be courageous in confronting the majority so that all efforts which were designed to settle specific majority and minority issues were put aside and replaced by those designed to find national solutions.

Their emphasis however was on social assimilation. They urged the peranakans to start mixing with majority Indonesians in their daily activities. They encouraged them to take their children out of schools established and run specifically for the peranakans. They also encouraged the peranakans to stop being part of organisations that were established exclusively for the Chinese or peranakans. They argued that by doing this, the peranakans would develop a sense of belonging to Indonesia.

---

[21] Somers, *Peranakans Chinese Politics in Indonesia*, pp. 260–261; Coppel, *Indonesian Chinese in Crisis*, p. 45.

But many people were unclear about how assimilation was to be achieved. Suryadinata and Coppel are generally in agreement on the assimilationists' lack of definitive details on how to achieve their programs. Suryadinata sums this up by saying:

> While advocating assimilation, they did not discuss whether or not the Chinese minority should be assimilated into Indigenous ethnic groups first, prior to their absorption into the Indonesian nation. They failed to examine the position of the Chinese in the areas where Islamic culture is extremely strong. They did not advocate the conversion of the Chinese to Islam because many of the LPKB leaders were Christians. They neglected to discuss the position of the Chinese in areas where they lived in isolation or where they constituted the majority. The assimilationist group was rooted in urban areas where ethnic Chinese problems were generally acute. They did not have strong and feasible programs to implement their ideas.[22]

Siauw himself often used what appeared to be a contradiction in the assimilationists' argument to attack the concept. He asserted that while the assimilationists pushed for the disappearance of the traits which distinguished the peranakans as an ethnic minority, they resisted giving up their own religious identity – also a minority in Indonesia – by saying that a move to force them to give up their religious identity was a violation of human rights. He argued that forcing people to change names and inter-marry was also a violation of human rights.

In 1963, the group was able to attract a new level of government support. Supported by a group of senior army officers, they formed the LPKB. This organisation worked out of an office of the army. In July 1963, it was able to create formal links with a government ministry. It became a government body called LPKB under the Ministry of Information. Its chairman was Lieutenant Sindhunatha who changed his name from Ong Tjong Hay.[23]

Integration as an alternative to assimilation

The formulation of the concept of assimilation prompted Siauw to develop his theme of integration. Siauw began to frequently use the term

---

22   Suryadinata, *Pribumi Indonesians, the Chinese Minority and China*, pp. 71–72; Coppel, 'Patterns Of Chinese Political Activity In Indonesia', p. 60; Coppel, *Indonesian Chinese In Crisis*, p. 54.
23   Coppel, *Indonesian Chinese In Crisis*, pp. 46–47.

'integration' after 1960[24]; however, the basis of his concept of integration was consistent with what he and other Baperki's leaders had promoted since the birth of Baperki in 1954.

Siauw's approach was one which stressed the importance of the Bhineka Tunggal Ika concept. He proposed that the minorities of Chinese, European and Arab origin be integrated into Indonesian society without losing their cultural distinctiveness. In 1957, he argued repeatedly that the Indonesian constitution had no provision for the disappearance of ethnic identities reflected in their names, traditions and culture.

It was in that year, a time when regional protest heightened awareness of the country's ethnic diversity as a source of political conflict, that Siauw began to popularise the idea that the peranakan Chinese should be considered as one of the Indonesian sukus. Hence, the acceptance of the peranakan suku would be totally in line with the Bhineka Tunggal Ika concept.

The term Suku Tionghoa (Chinese ethnic group) was often used in Siauw's unwritten speeches and lectures. But there were indeed written references in some of his speeches and lecture notes.[25]

A Soekarno message read at Baperki's fourth anniversary conference in Solo, in 1958, supported several aspects of Siauw's position. According to Soekarno:[26]

> The Indonesian nation consists of many sukus. The effort to expedite the integration process to achieve a nation which is free from racial prejudice and free from fear of being treated as stepchildren requires time and commitments. We are now working toward the creation of a just and prosperous society which would guarantee the realisation of a nation which ensures that every citizen is free from racial prejudice, free from fear of being treated as a stepchild and free from want. From this point of view, the solution to minority problems is related to the effort to eliminate underdevelopment and to achieve full employment.

---

[24] Although in a Baperki conference held in 1957 Boejoeng Saleh and Siauw used the term 'integrasi' loosely, Siauw and Baperki did not use the term in his speeches or Baperki documents until the beginning of the 1960s.

[25] Siauw's lecture notes, 'Ceramah Siauw Giok Tjhan, Dokumen Baperki nomor 53/Stn/58 (Stensilan Baperki nomor 53 tahun 1958)', 1958. Siauw's lecture notes, 'Stensilan Baperki no 65 tahun 1961', 1961. Siauw's lecture notes, 1962.

[26] A number of Baperki leaders were aware that this, Soekarno's written message, was in fact written by Siauw. It is indeed easy to recognise Siauw's language in the text. I have found the original text of the message that was typed with Siauw's typewriter.

Therefore, the solution will not be achieved by carrying out racial discrimination or the implementation of Asli policies, but by developing the country using all available resources including technical know-how, managerial skills and capital, which are also available from the minority groups in Indonesia. The emphasis is on how to achieve a fair distribution of prosperity.[27]

This speech became the basis of Baperki's program in 1958.

The increasing use of socialist language by President Soekarno made Siauw's position easier in 1959, after the presidential decree of 5 July 1959 and the introduction of the Manipol in August 1959. The term 'just and prosperous society' was replaced by 'a socialistic society, free from exploitation of man by man'. Socialism à la Indonesia was one of the key principles of the Manipol.

From then on, Siauw argued that once a socialistic society was achieved and the exploitation of one by another was ended, racial prejudice would also end and the need for racial discriminatory measures would disappear. He indicated that in socialist countries like the People's Republic of China and the Soviet Union minority issues were successfully and satisfactorily settled such that almost no racial riots or disturbances were reported. In contrast to this, countries like the USA were continuously disturbed by racial prejudice and racial discrimination.

Siauw was always careful, however, to insist that his formulation was not that of the communists. He indicated that the socialistic society he referred to was the society Soekarno and his followers pursued. He was therefore able to gain full support from Soekarno himself and other political leaders who were close to him, not only Aidit of the PKI, but also Ali Sastroamidjojo of the PNI and various leaders of smaller parties.

By 1960, to counter the term assimilation, as previously described, Siauw began to popularise the term integration. Siauw was convinced that having an Indonesian-sounding name, or following a particular religion or seeming to be Indonesian by physical experience would not guarantee one's loyalty to the state and instil a sense of belonging. Siauw indicated that it would be better to have a situation whereby people with Chinese names felt that they belonged in Indonesia and were committed to working for a better Indonesia.

---

[27] The speech was written by Siauw. It was done, according to Go Gien Tjwan, with the approval of Soekarno himself.

Siauw was able to pick up on the idea of mental retooling which Soekarno popularised from 1959. Soekarno called repeatedly for mental retooling so that every citizen, regardless of their ethnic and religious backgrounds, became committed to the creation of a socialistic society. This, according to Siauw, could only be achieved by encouraging all Indonesian Chinese to integrate into Indonesian society and work and live closely with the Indonesian majority so that their aspirations became the same as each other.

Siauw criticised the idea that biological assimilation would eliminate the biological identity of an ethnic group. In this context, he referred to the statement drafted by world experts engaged by the United Nations in which they stated:[28]

> National, religious, geographic, linguistic and cultural groups do not necessarily coincide with racial groups and the cultural traits of such groups have not demonstrated genetic connection with racial traits... For all practical social purpose, "race" is not so much biological phenomena as a social myth. The myth of "race" has created an enormous amount of human and social damage.

Siauw often referred to his own family experiences. He indicated that two of his children had curly hair, similar to that of the Ambonese. It was possible, he said, that he in fact had Ambonese ancestry. He asserted that the elimination of ethnic identities by force was a violation of human rights and an act of genocide which should be stopped and condemned.[29]

Siauw was also concerned with people's confusion over the terms 'race', 'nation', and 'ethnic'. In Indonesian, all of these terms were translated as 'bangsa'. He was therefore concerned that many who suggested and accepted assimilation as a solution to the minority problems did not understand the differences between these terms. Race, Siauw argued, is linked to biological or genetic conditions, while ethnic identity is linked to cultural background, geography and language. To Siauw, 'nation' is a political term that defines a group of people united by political needs. Indonesia is a multi-racial and multi-ethnic nation. However, there is no Indonesian race, nor was it possible or desirable to have a homogeneous Indonesian nation. The formation of the Indonesian nation, to Siauw, was a process involving

---

[28] Leo Kuper (ed.), *Race, Science and Society*, The UNECSO Press and George Allen & Unwin, Paris and London, 1975, pp. 344 –5; Siauw's lecture notes, 1962.

[29] Siauw's lecture notes, 1962.

the integration of groups with various ethnic identities, including culture, traditions and languages.[30]

Siauw was consistent in fighting the assimilation movement. He did however accept that voluntary assimilation should not be stopped. On this, there appears to be some misinterpretation of what he said. Somers and Suryadinata conclude that many Baperki members, including Siauw, saw total assimilation as possible in a socialist state and wanted the assimilation process to be postponed until Indonesia became a socialist state.[31] This is incorrect; Siauw did not see total assimilation as necessary to strengthen Indonesian nationhood. What he repeatedly argued was that in a socialist Indonesia, there would not be exploitation and that this would resolve ethnic problems.

The assimilationists ridiculed Siauw's integrationist approach. In various publications, they indicated that what Baperki wanted was to maintain a colonial structure in which various ethnic groups existed separately and exclusively. They charged that Baperki wanted to overcome ethnic problems by following structures of countries based on federalism.[32] They also argued that Baperki's deliberate attempt to retard the process of assimilation meant that it was promoting exclusivism, which would ultimately aggravate anti-Chinese feeling and work against the true interest of its own members.[33]

Siauw's suggestion that the Indonesian Chinese be accepted as a suku prompted debates. Somers argues that Siauw derived the suku concept from the models he saw and admired in the USSR and China. Summing up the arguments against this theory, she states:

> While his (Siauw's) argument is essentially one for cultural autonomy and equality of treatment for the peranakans, the analogy is hardly appropriate, for the national minorities in China and the Soviet Union (like the Asli Indonesian sukus) occupy a territory of their own, something the peranakan Chinese in Indonesia neither have nor would conceivably want. Furthermore, the problem of these national minorities is not complicated by the presence of resident aliens who

---

30 Siauw's lecture notes, November, 1962.
31 Somers, *Peranakan Chinese Politics*, p. 256; Suryadinata, *Pribumi Indonesians, The Chinese Minority and China*, p. 73.
32 Riyanto D. Wahono (ed.), *70 Tahun Junus Jahja: Pribumi Kuat Kunci Pembauran*, PT Bina Rena Pariwara, p. 324–325.
33 Somers, *Peranakan Chinese Politics*, p. 276.

are also members of the minority group, as is that of the peranakan Chinese community in Indonesia. More than half of the persons of Chinese descent in Indonesia, including many peranakans, are citizens of China and not Indonesia.[34]

Siauw responded to arguments like these by saying that there was no real definition of a suku in Indonesia. If territory or location was to be used as the basis of the definition, there were numerous locations in Indonesia in which Chinese people had lived for many generations as majority communities. If number of generations was used as the basis, he argued, there were also a large number of Chinese who had lived in Indonesia for more than 100 years. If lifestyle or standard of living was used as the basis, again he argued, there were millions of Chinese who lived as poor peasants and labourers, like their Asli counterparts. The main thing, he said, was that the great majority of the Chinese of Indonesian citizenship regarded Indonesia, not China, as their home.[35]

While Siauw had difficulty in convincing many people to accept the concept, it became widely used after 1963, the year in which Soekarno officially endorsed it. More on this is described below.

The LPKB challenge

When the assimilationist concept was first launched in 1960 through *Star Weekly*, Baperki did not officially respond. But when the group, which was later called the Panitia Penjuluhan Assimilasi (Committee of Assimilation Promoters), began to publicise their activities and attacked Baperki in 1961, Baperki's officials responded through their publications such as *Republik* and other newspapers.

In 1961 the assimilationists urged peranakans in other parts of Indonesia to form regional Panitia Penjuluhan Assimilasi. The assimilationists argued that the assimilation idea was first introduced by the PTI and its leader, Liem Koen Hian.

Baperki disputed this assertion. In its newsletter of 26 July 1961 it highlighted the fact that in October 1934 the PTI had supported the formation of the PAI implying that it was not against ethnic parties. The PTI did indeed use the term 'assimilation', but what it implied was social

---

[34] Ibid., p. 257.
[35] Siauw's lecture notes, 1962; Siauw, *Lima Jaman*, pp. 203–204.

assimilation, not biological assimilation. Baperki stressed that the term social assimilation as used in the 1930s meant something like integration. Various one-time leaders of the PTI like Tjoa Sik Ien, Ko Kwat Tiong and Siauw Giok Tjhan did not join the assimilationist group, but were instead leading Baperki.

The assimilationists accused Baperki of being an exclusive organisation because most of its members were Chinese. Baperki was similar to the Chinese organisation established by the Japanese Kakyo Shokai and its successor in the late 1940s, the CHTH. They also alleged that it was a pro-communist organisation and that it supported the People's Republic of China.

Baperki responded by declaring that it supported the revolution led by Soekarno and ridiculed the assimilationists for being anti-China, with whom Soekarno wanted to establish good relations. On name-changing, Baperki referred to the situation experienced by the African Americans in the USA. Most of them, it indicated, had Anglo-Saxon names but they continued to be discriminated against. Similarly many German Jews had German names, but they too had been persecuted by Hitler's government.

The debate over assimilation and integration reached a point of high tension in 1963. Knowing that Baperki and Siauw continued to be close to Soekarno and major political parties, the assimilationists decided to gain wider support from various other political forces. They were also concerned that the end of martial law in May 1963 would weaken their position.

An assimilationist-sponsored conference on national unity, held in Jakarta from 10 to 12 March 1963, attracted attention and support from many major political figures including Roeslan Abdulgani, information minister; Chaerul Saleh, chairman of the MPRS; Muljadi Djojomartono, Minister of Social Affairs; Ipik Gandamana, Minister of Public Works, and General Nasution, chief of the armed forces. Most of these figures sent their written speech supporting the conference. Also received was a speech from Sunario, Siauw's long time adversary on the passive system of Indonesian citizenship.

The conference highlighted Soekarno's clarification of Bhineka Tunggal Ika, which had been delivered to the assimilationists in February 1963. Soekarno had said then that bhineka (diversity) was das Sein (the present [in German]), and tunggal ika (unity) was das Sollen (the future [in German]), and that a nation with a minority group is not a nation.

The assimilationists interpreted this clarification as an indication that the ultimate goal was to create one nation without minorities. But when the minority solutions were discussed, many of the written speeches did not categorically support what was advocated by the assimilationists. Some, like those of Chaerul Saleh and Ipik Gandamana, proposed schemes which were more in line with what Siauw and Baperki advocated.[36]

At the end of this conference, on 12 March 1963, one day before Baperki's ninth anniversary, the LPKB was established. The organisation was to be structured like Baperki with a central leadership and regional branches. But its headquarters was still located at one of the army's major offices.[37]

By 1963, Soekarno was in a situation of tremendous personal power. Organisations of many kinds tried to get his blessing. The ability of an organisation to carry out its programs often depended on how fully Soekarno endorsed it. In this context, it was very important to have Soekarno appearing at an organisation's political meetings and to have him delivering speeches with blessings and political directions contained within it.

Two days after the LPKB was formed, on 14 March 1963, Soekarno attended Baperki's 9th anniversary celebration. His long speech was a blow to the assimilationists, with Soekarno reconfirming that he was in agreement with Siauw and Baperki to call the peranakan group one of the sukus of the Indonesian nation. Soekarno indicated:

> I will not say that this suku is a minority, or that suku is a minority, the suku Dayak a minority, the suku Irian Barat a minority, the suku Tionghoa a minority. No! There is no minority, only sukus, because if there is a minority group then there is also a majority group. Usually, if there is a majority, then the minority group will be exploited by the majority group. Sukus are legs. The Indonesian nation has many legs, a Javanese leg, a Sundanese leg, a Dayak leg, a Balinese leg, a Chinese leg. All these legs belong to one body, the Indonesian nation.

Furthermore, with regard to assimilation, he said:

> Brother Siauw urged us not to promote assimilation. All right, brother Siauw, I will not dwell on assimilation, I personally do not recognise

---

[36] The speeches are compiled in *Assimilasi*, Jajasan Pembinaan Kesatuan Bangsa, published by the Department of Information in 1964.

[37] Coppel, *Indonesian Chinese in Crisis*, p. 46.

racial differences. My name is Soekarno. Is that an Asli Indonesian name? No! It is a Sanskrit name. Abdulgani is an Arab name. Ali Sastroamidjaja is a mixed name. Ali is Arab, Sastroamidjaja is Sanskrit. He is of mixed ancestry. To me personally, what is in a name? If you want to be an Indonesian, you don't have to change your name. I will not demand of anyone who wants to be a citizen of Indonesia to change their name. No. That is a private matter. What I will request is that you, my brothers, become real Indonesians, become good Indonesian citizens. The lady over there, a very capable dancer. What is your name? Tan Tian Ie. Brothers, this Tan Tian Ie performs Sundanese dances, brothers, and performs these dances better than many Sundanese ladies. Have I ever asked you to change your name? No! Continue to use Tan Tian Ie.

Why have I come to the Baperki congress? Because Baperki is a good organisation. Baperki is solidly based on Panca Sila. Baperki clearly supports the implementation of the Message of the People's Suffering. Baperki decisively stands on Manipol USDEK. Baperki is one of the fighters of the Indonesian Revolution. Baperki shares Bung Karno's feelings.

This speech clearly demonstrated Soekarno's support for Baperki and Siauw's formulation on integration. But Soekarno needed to maintain balance between competing groups. He was careful not to go too far in antagonising the army and the right-wing political elements.

So, in July 1963, Soekarno blessed the formation of a new LPKB which would be part of the Department of Information under Minister Roeslan Abdulgani. In his written speech on 18 July 1963, he endorsed the effort to implement assimilation as a process of nation building, and the removal of exclusiveness and Asli and non-Asli boundaries. He was careful in formulating his support. He did not refer to name changing. He was also careful to avoid discussion of the necessity to eliminate ethnic identities in the creation of an Indonesian nation.

Siauw, faced with a damage-limitation problem, argued that the acceptance of the LPKB as part of the Department of Information did not imply that Soekarno supported the concept of total assimilation. He indicated that natural assimilation could only be achieved if Indonesia had become a socialist state and that integration would still be the correct process preceding it. With regard to the LPKB, Siauw indicated that the organisation was anti-Nasakom, as there were no communists in it.

In his 17 August speech in 1963, Soekarno made a reference to the formation of the LPKB but he did not raise the issue of assimilation or exclusiveness. As if responding to Siauw's call for the LPKB to be Nasakomised, he demanded that Roeslan Abdulgani ensure that the LPKB was free of 'communist-phobia'.

The LPKB defended its composition by indicating that it was a government body and as such did not have the obligation to be Nasakomised. It remained able to exclude communist elements from its organisational activities and structures.[38]

In November 1963, the LPKB went onto the attack. Its chairman, Sindhunatha, sent a letter to a number of cabinet ministers requesting that Baperki's position be reviewed. He said that Baperki was an exclusive organisation which served primarily the needs of the Chinese and rejected the assimilation concept and would therefore jeopardise the promotion of national unity.[39]

But Baperki's position was too strong for this to have much effect. Prior to receiving the LPKB letter, Soekarno had offered Siauw a cabinet position as described in the preceding chapter. And in December 1963 he appointed Oei Tjoe Tat as minister of state.

The strongest support for Baperki was demonstrated in Soekarno's 17 August speech in 1964. Soekarno indicated that although he accepted both the assimilation and integration concepts, he re-emphasised his preference to call the peranakan group a suku Tionghoa. He also indicated:

> It is impossible to eliminate ethnic identities in one or two generations, even in ten generations. We cannot eliminate the Batak Jaw, the Chinese slant eyes, the Arab's sharp noses, the tongues of the Balinese, the yellow skins of the Menadonese or the frizzy hair of the Irianese. This is not the issue. The issue is how to foster unity, promote nationhood so that each suku contributes positively and each suku accepts contributions from other sukus. In other words, all sukus must integrate to the great family of the Indonesian nation. Bhineka Tunggal Ika must be understood as a dialectic unity.

What hit the LPKB most was Soekarno's statement in the same speech that the LPKB had to be Nasakomised and cleansed of communist-phobia. Siauw lost no time in endorsing Soekarno's direction to restructure the LPKB.

---

[38] Coppel, 'Patterns of Chinese Political Activity in Indonesia', p. 58.
[39] Ibid., p. 59. Siauw, *Lima Jaman*, p. 311.

In his speech delivered in Surabaya on 27 August 1964, he indicated that Soekarno's statement on the LPKB was a reaction to its attempts to have the Nasakom's forces accept their total assimilation concept. Siauw referred to the conference organised by the LPKB in July 1964, in which representatives from all Nasakom streams were invited. The conference, according to Siauw, had failed to achieve the LPKB's goals. Most of the conference attendees did not endorse what Siauw called the 'total assimilation concept'.

In this speech, Siauw indicated that people who supported the assimilation concept were unconsciously supporting racism. He argued that people's loyalty and commitment should not be judged by the way they look or names by which they are called. Thus, to support the idea that people could be real Indonesians only if they assimilated to Asli Indonesian society was erroneous and was an act of racism. He proposed that the LPKB be reorganised and run under the guidance of the cabinet. Under this pressure, the LPKB agreed to accept a formula which said that integration was one of the three stages of assimilation, namely adaptation, integration and identification.[40]

Although the LPKB did not become a mass organisation, the concept advocated by its leaders attracted young peranakan intellectuals and university students. The organisation also received support from anti-communist peranakans and peranakans with no sympathy for totoks. As the country shifted more to the left in the later part of the period, the fear that Baperki was too close to the PKI and too China-minded prompted more peranakans to sympathise with the LPKB position.

Somers appears to be in agreement with many Chinese in the period saying:

> For Baperki's leadership, interest in mainland Chinese affairs is as much motivated by their political sympathy with China's present political system as by desire to revive (or in some aspects, introduce) Chinese culture among peranakans. For most members, interest in China as their ancestral land probably overshadows admiration of mainland's China's achievements under communist rule. But in practice, for both the leadership and the mass, the two considerations tend to reinforce one another.

She also argues that excessive emphasis on mainland Chinese culture could jeopardise Baperki's promotion of Indonesia-oriented thinking.[41]

---

[40] Coppel, 'Patterns of Chinese Political Activity in Indonesia', p. 59.
[41] Somers, *Peranakan Chinese Politics*, p. 253.

If such coverage of Chinese culture had not been accompanied by political programs, Somers' assertion would have validity. However, Siauw's speeches and numerous Baperki documents suggested that what Baperki intended to do was to develop awareness of one's Chineseness and to stimulate a comfortable feeling that it was acceptable to maintain one's Chineseness as an Indonesian citizen. On the promotion of Chinese language in Baperki schools and university, Siauw, admiring Chinese technological advancement, believed that by mastering Mandarin Baperki students would be able to read books on science and medicine written in Chinese.[42] In this context, Baperki's promotion of Chinese culture, language and technology was not excessive and could be said to complement Siauw's integration approach.

Many people also misunderstood Siauw's push for pluralism. The LPKB leaders, in particular, attempted to describe Siauw's preference for pluralism as maintaining ethnic groups within the society and hence rejecting the need for social interactions. Somers, supporting this argument suggests:

> Baperki inhibits social interaction by its separate organisation of peranakans. Most important in this respect is its separate school system, the great majority of whose students are of Chinese origin. It would seem that Baperki holds to the third alternative as an accommodation for peranakans. That Baperki appears to be moving toward the second alternative course demonstrates a recognition that absolute pluralism cannot provide the basis for the peranakans' acceptance into Indonesian society.[43]

But the discussion above indicates that what Siauw meant by pluralism was not a mere segregation of the Chinese group from Indonesian society. He wanted the realisation of a Bhineka Tunggal Ika society – a plural society – in which the Chinese group co-existed along with other sukus and worked together with the other sukus to better the living condition of the society. He clearly wanted the 'Suku Tionghoa' – the Chinese ethnic group – to have maximum and effective social and political interaction with the other sukus. The implementation of this concept was demonstrated in the way in which members of Baperki were encouraged to join Partindo, the IPPI,

---

[42] Siauw also encouraged all his children to learn Mandarin at home.
[43] Somers, *Peranakan Chinese Politics*, p. 289. Somers suggests that there are three alternative solutions to the Chinese problems: total assimilation, social interaction with the Indigenous communities and pluralism.

Pemuda Rakyat, the CGMI and other organisations, and their youths to appreciate Indonesian culture.

By the last months of 1963, Baperki had the upper hand due to President Soekarno's support. The Baperki leadership after 1964, as Coppel observes, was preoccupied with general political issues. The political power of the LPKB had been neutralised, at least until October 1965. Coppel further suggests:

> On issues affecting the Chinese as Chinese, this situation favoured Baperki since it was the LPKB that was urging changes in the status quo. But Baperki's advantage was precarious; should things turn against Soekarno and the PKI, the LPKB was still there lying dormant, as it were, but ready to erupt with the backing of its military sponsors, not to speak of other anti-communist forces with an axe to grind against the Chinese.[44]

Baperki leaders, particularly Siauw, as discussed in the next chapter, were aware of this potential danger but unable to control the situation which was dramatically affected by the country's political upheavals.

Thus, a situation developed where the arguments between Baperki and the LPKB had less to do with integration versus assimilation than with their attitudes to the leftward trend. The LPKB was attractive both to people who were afraid of communism and to others who feared a situation in which the army would come out on top and punish Chinese people for Baperki's leftism. But to some Chinese, the closeness of the LPKB to the army was also seen as a threat. While some thought that it was advantageous for the organisation to have the army's backing, they also believed that the Chinese had to be cautious of the army which in the past had carried out anti-Chinese programs and had many leaders with anti-Chinese prejudices.[45]

---

[44] Coppel, 'Patterns of Chinese Political Activity in Indonesia', p. 50.
[45] Interviews with former LPKB members in Jakarta and Surabaya, 1994.

PART IV

1965–1981

Chapter 13

BAPERKI'S LAST MONTHS

Having successfully built a close relationship with Soekarno and the forces around him in the later part of the Guided Democracy period, Siauw was able to have a number of Baperki's main political goals and objectives included in Soekarno's speeches and hence formally announced as state policies.

By 1965, Siauw had built Baperki into a large and active organisation. Although Baperki remained focused on citizenship and racial discrimination issues, it also had wider political concerns.

Many Baperki leaders joined and became leaders of either the PKI or Partindo. Many Baperki students joined and became leaders of the PKI-aligned Pemuda Rakyat, Perhimi and the CGMI.

To Siauw's disappointment, towards September 1965 many of these Baperki activists and members, particularly the young and militant ones, regarded Baperki's goals as secondary to those of the PKI and its associated mass organisations. Siauw attempted to contain this trend, but with limited success.

This chapter outlines Siauw's activities in the last few months of Baperki's life, the risks to which he exposed both himself and Baperki and the conflict which developed within Baperki in this last phase of the Guided Democracy period.

By early 1965, political polarisation between the left and the right had become extreme. Soekarno and the PKI had become closer to and dependent upon each other. Because of Soekarno's popularity and his domination of the political arena, the left-wing forces appeared to have the upper hand. On the other hand, the army and other right-wing political forces, mainly represented by the NU and Christian parties, had no choice but to temporarily accept the situation.

Although Soekarno did not accept all of the PKI's demands, he did not conceal his political bias towards the party. In most cases of conflict between the PKI and its adversaries, he sided with the PKI.

Following the ongoing pressure from the PKI to crush one of its main political rivals, the Partai Murba party, Soekarno agreed to suspend the Partai Murba party in January 1965. Many of the newspapers that had supported the Partai Murba-led BPS (Badan Pendukung Soekarnoisme – Body for Upholding Soekarnoism) were closed down. This was a blow to the PKI's opponents as it signalled Soekarno's bias towards the PKI. The BPS movement was also supported by the army. Not long after this, Adam Malik, leader of the Partai Murba and a senior cabinet minister, and Chaerul Saleh, a Partai Murba–sympathiser, who was chairman of the MPRS as well as a senior deputy prime minister, were also attacked by the PKI as anti-Soekarnoists. In March 1965, they were demoted in a cabinet reshuffle.[1] In September, the Partai Murba was officially banned and a number of its leaders, including the party chairman, Sukarni, were jailed.

After the attack on the Partai Murba, the PKI began to mount pressure on the Islamic groups, namely the NU and the HMI (Himpunan Mahasiswa Islam – Muslim Students' Association). In March 1965, there were demonstrations in Jakarta and East Java organised by the CGMI and Pemuda Rakyat demanding the banning of the HMI. Although Soekarno on a number of occasions warned the Islamic forces that they should be free of 'communist-phobia', he was reluctant to ban the organisation. By the time the PKI was destroyed in 1965, Soekarno had not had the opportunity to purge anti-communist members from those organisations and reorganise them. But it was clear from the media in that period that they were on the defensive.

The PKI continued to show political strength in its control and influence of large numbers of people. In May 1965, celebrating its forty-fifth anniversary, it claimed to have three million members and some twenty million members of its affiliated mass organisations[2], making it the third largest communist party in the world.

The PKI's main challenge was to shake its most powerful adversary, the army. Early in 1965, the PKI increased its attacks on corrupt and bureaucratic capitalists, pointing at army officers involved in running large business enterprises – mainly ones taken over from their Dutch owners in 1957 and 1958. The PKI also accused the army and its publications of engaging in anti-communist propaganda and thereby sabotaging the president's call for the unity of all Nasakom elements. In August 1965, Soekarno

---

[1] *Harian Rakyat*, 1 April 1965.
[2] *Harian Rakyat*, 14 May 1965.

himself began to criticise high-ranking army leaders for luxurious living and reactionary attitudes.³

The battle between the PKI and the army was further fuelled by PKI demands that the Front Nasional should be named a 'fifth force' that was to be manned by workers and peasants. The PKI's justification for the fifth armed force was to have the workers and peasants trained and armed to defend the nation against imperialist attacks. Again, Soekarno endorsed the plan. In August 1965, in his capacity as Supreme Commander of the Armed Forces, he urged leaders of the armed forces to seriously consider and make the necessary plans to form the 'fifth force'. This endorsement received support from the commanders of the air force and naval force, but the army opposed it. General Yani openly declared his opposition to the idea on 27 September 1965, a few days before the abortive coup.⁴

While the army and the right-wing forces appeared to be on the defensive, the PKI's real strength as measured by control over the government's machinery was very limited. The army leaders, Nasution and Yani, had been successful in preventing Soekarno from forming a Nasakom cabinet with substantial PKI representation. Aidit, Lukman and Njoto were state ministers. But they had no portfolios so could not exercise executive control. The army's representation in the cabinet was much more substantial. In provincial governments the army–PKI imbalance was even clearer. While there was no PKI governor, there were army governors in 12 of 24 provinces.

This situation improved slightly for the PKI towards the later part of 1965. In May 1965, Setiadi Reksoprodjo, leader of the Pemuda Rakyat, was appointed minister for electricity and energy. Njoto was also becoming more influential as he became one of Soekarno's trusted aides. Many of Soekarno's important speeches in the later part of the Guided Democracy period, including the 17 August speeches, were apparently prepared and written by Njoto.⁵

Economic mismanagement was an evident part of the Guided Democracy period. The deficits of the time were a key measure of the health of the economy. In 1962 the deficit was 12.8 billion rupiah with revenue of 19.4 billion rupiah. In 1963 and 1964, while revenue declined (18.9 billion rupiah and 8.5 billion rupiah respectively), the deficits became a much

---

3   Mortimer, *Indonesian Communism Under Soekarno*, pp. 383–384.
4   Ibid., p. 385.
5   Siauw, *For a Brighter Future*, p. 179; Interviews with Oey Hay Djoen, Jusuf Isak and Oey Tjoe Tat, July 1995.

larger per cent of revenues, 103 per cent in 1963 and 113 per cent in 1964.[6] By the end of 1965 the deficit was 3000 per cent of the total revenue.[7]

The large deficits were partly due to the government's inability to control inflation. The reduction in exports resulted in the fall in imports of production materials and capital goods, which in turn resulted in inflation. An example of the effects of this was in transportation: by 1962, only 50 per cent of all buses and trucks in Java were on the roads due to a shortage of spare parts. Another example relates to production in the agricultural sector, which ran at only 25 to 35 per cent of its capacity.[8]

Inflation reduced domestic production and hence exports were reduced. The reduction of exports and imports also reduced tax revenues, hence the large deficits. The problem was compounded by the 'Crush Malaysia' programs which required large expenditure.

In the last quarter of 1964, prices of most commodities doubled. The value of the rupiah on the black market fell from about 3000 rupiah per US dollar in September to over 8000 in December.[9] By 1965, general prices rose 500 per cent with rice prices rising 900 per cent.[10]

The pressure to find donors to help improve the country's economic situation forced Soekarno's government to turn to the communist world, particularly the People's Republic of China.

In his 17 August speech in 1965, Soekarno spoke of an anti-imperialist axis between Jakarta, Phnom Penh, Hanoi, Peking and Pyongyang. Indonesia also continued to take initiatives towards holding the large Conference of the New Emerging Forces to be held in Jakarta in early 1966.

The army leadership of General Yani, a Javanese, was careful to avoid publicly opposing Soekarno's policy of moving closer to China. But quietly and secretly they were ignoring and indeed sabotaging many of Soekarno's programs. The supporters of Soekarno's Konfrontasi programs which included the air and naval forces were often frustrated by the army's refusal to act and their deliberate attempts to obstruct the effective implementation of the Konfrontasi policies. During 1964 and 1965 a group of army leaders conducted secret discussions with Malaysia's senior leaders. The purpose of these was to convince the Malaysian leaders that the Indonesian army

---

6   Mackie, *Problems of the Indonesian Inflation*, p. 8.
7   Bruce Grant, *Indonesia*, Melbourne University Press, Second Edition, 1966, p. 97.
8   Ibid., p. 90.
9   Mackie, *Problems of the Indonesian Inflation*, p. 42.
10 Grant, *Indonesia*, p. 97.

was looking for a way of disengaging from the Konfrontasi policies and to reduce the possibility of serious warfare between the two countries.[11]

But the army itself was divided. Although it was clearly dominated by anti-communist figures, there were a number of high-ranking officers who were sympathetic to Soekarno and the PKI.

Relationship with Soekarno

The country's shift to the left and the closeness of Soekarno to the People's Republic of China further advantaged Siauw's political position and hence that of Baperki. Baperki's campaigns to eliminate racial discrimination were openly supported by Soekarno and the PKI.

Siauw's relationship with Soekarno grew even closer. Siauw was often invited to Soekarno's breakfast meetings in which important issues were discussed and major decisions were made. Siauw also frequently went to Soekarno's private accommodation to discuss various issues. He often went in and out of the Merdeka Palace in casual clothes and wearing sandals instead of shoes.[12] According to Siauw's own account, sometimes Siauw discussed matters with Soekarno in his bedroom at the palace.

Politically, Siauw continued to fully support Soekarno. In exchange for this, Soekarno gave Siauw and Baperki protection and incorporated a number of Siauw's main proposals in his speeches and decisions made by MPRS and DPA.

Siauw's speeches in 1965 were full of quotations from Soekarno's speeches and writings, particularly those which were close to Siauw's heart – namely the liquidation of the colonial economy, the use of domestic capital (hence Indonesian Chinese capital), the acceptance of peranakan Chinese as Suku Tionghoa and the realisation of socialism à la Indonesia.

As discussed before, Siauw had reasons to be pleased with the inclusion of an economic formulation which he advocated in the 1950s in Soekarno's important speeches and Manipol. One of the speeches that included his formulation was titled 'Banting stir untuk berdikari' ('Change of direction to be self-reliant'), which was read before the MPRS meeting on 11 April 1965. The inclusion of this formulation was apparently discussed in one of

---

[11] Crouch, *The Army and Politics in Indonesia*, Cornell University Press, Ithaca, 1978, pp. 74–76.

[12] Interviews with Oei Tjoe Tat, Jakarta, July 1994 and Fransisca Fanggidaej, Amsterdam, November 1987.

the DPA meetings and Siauw's suggestion that the president adopt the formulation in his speech was accepted.¹³

Soekarno declared:

> Why do we have to banting stir? ... Because there is a reformist disease which obstructs the efforts of creating a situation whereby the government dominates the economy and obstructs the full implementation of land reform. There is also a disease which tries to stop the inclusion of private and domestic capital for development and this disease attempts to "nationalise" all enterprises. These two errors are dangerous and can severely jeopardise our struggle.

Furthermore, Soekarno stated:

> I urge all my assistants, MPRS and DPRGR and other institutions, to think and work hard to overcome the inflation problems and to liquidate colonial and semi-colonial regulations which have tied our own hands and feet... I urge you to introduce regulations and measures with national characteristics which simplify our tasks.

Reinforcing his anti-racism position, Soekarno further stated:

> The utilisation of funds and forces outlined in Manipol and Dekon is not limited to the mere registration of capital investment, but it involves the creation of a favourable economic climate which maximises productivity without any kind of discrimination.¹⁴

Soekarno's speeches in the later part of the Guided Democracy period were often quoted by political figures and when they touched on subjects considered important their contents were treated as state policies. In this regard, the 'Banting stir' speech was reinforced by MPRS Regulation No. VI/1965, Clause 13 which called for:

1. the effective utilisation of progressive private funds and forces including national and domestic funds in the production fields
2. the creation of a favourable economic environment which eliminates regulations which delay the issuing of important licences and facilities for productive activities.

---

13 Interview with Utrecht, Amsterdam, November 1981.
14 Soekarno, 'Banting Stir Untuk Berdikari', 11 April 1965.

These formulations represented a significant achievement for Siauw. Having argued and debated these issues in various political arenas for more than ten years, Siauw was satisfied with the outcome. In his speech delivered to Baperki's congress in May 1965, Siauw said:

> The liquidation of colonial and semi-colonial regulations, which have indeed tied our hands and feet, has in the past been only one of the resolutions passed in Baperki conferences. We are indeed glad to acknowledge that President Soekarno has now instructed all his assistants to adopt that as policy. This is a significant improvement which brings hopes that many of the regulations which are essentially in conflict with the political manifesto and the economic declaration will soon be scrapped.[15]

In the same speech, Siauw indicated that the formulation had to be followed with an effective plan and determination which would encourage private enterprises to be really involved in constructing a self-reliant national economy. He criticised practices that reduced the confidence of Chinese businessmen in the national program.

Siauw also supported the decisions of 1964 and 1965 to take over the ownership and management of large corporations from British and American companies. But he criticised what he called 'capitalist bureaucrats' ('kapitalis birokrat' or kabir), the term commonly used to describe corrupt army officers who became managers and directors of these corporations. Siauw stated:

> It is difficult to accept the fact that these large corporations, when run by foreign monopolies, were able to transfer significant profits to foreign countries. But now, after being taken over by the country and run by the so-called kabirs, they have failed to reduce our people's suffering.

Siauw therefore urged the government to be committed and tough in retooling corporations' management resources and in ensuring the implementation of proper cost control and cost accounting.

Siauw supported Soekarno's foreign policy. He praised Soekarno for having the vision and determination to fight imperialism represented by

---

[15] Siauw's speech: Melaksanakan 'Banting Stir Untuk Berdikari' di Bidang Ekonomi, May 1965.

the American and British governments. Supporting Soekarno's decision to withdraw from the United Nations, Siauw said:

> The United Nations is fully dominated by the United States of America. The USA's activities in Vietnam and other countries have remained unchallenged and not condemned by the United Nations… It is therefore appropriate for Asian and African countries to consider the formation of a new type of United Nations which would be capable of ensuring the end of exploitation of man by man. The proposed holding of a Conference of New Emerging Forces in Algeria in the coming June is a good step towards the formation of such a new United Nations body.[16]

Naturally, Siauw welcomed Soekarno's decision to bring the country to be even closer to the People's Republic of China. Siauw was hopeful that this would help expedite the settlement of the continuing dual nationality issues. Siauw complained that six years after the 1959 dual nationality agreement there were still deliberate attempts by government officials to ignore the agreement.

Siauw stated that many people had difficulty obtaining proof of Indonesian citizenship although, by law, they were already Indonesian citizens. Siauw said:

> Many regional courts rejected people's applications to obtain Indonesian citizenship on the grounds that they do not have proper supporting documents which include birth certificates. For those who do have the birth certificates, if their names are incorrectly spelled in these documents their applications will still be rejected. Also there are many people whose applications are rejected because they had registered an intention to leave Indonesia for China at the time of Government Regulation 10 of 1959 [PP–10 against aliens trading in rural areas]. These registrations of intention are seen by local courts as repudiations of Indonesian citizenship. There are 270 heads of families in Sumbawa, 200 in Bali and about 700 in Jakarta who are experiencing this problem.

---

[16] Siauw's speech: Melaksanakan 'Banting Stir Untuk Berdikari' di Bidang Ekonomi, May 1965.

Siauw therefore urged the government to adhere to the spirit of the axis between Jakarta, Phnom Penh, Hanoi, Peking and Pyongyang by expediting the resolution of the dual nationality issues.

Siauw continued to pressure both governments to reconvene the meetings between Indonesia China to quickly settle and resolve the matter of dual nationality so that as many Indonesian Chinese as possible could become Indonesian citizens.

Because of Siauw's good relationship with Soekarno and the Chinese ambassador to Indonesia, Yao Chung Ming, Siauw was able to gain assurance that his ongoing requests as to how these issues would be solved would be granted. However, his hopes were shattered when the political situation changed dramatically in October 1965.[17]

As a politician who was always critical of how leaders of political parties and military forces abused privileges for their own comfort and greed, Siauw was critical of Soekarno's sultan-like lifestyle. He was particularly concerned about the way in which money was spent on prestige projects in Jakarta. Siauw also disliked the attitudes and lifestyles of many leaders who were close to Soekarno. Their luxurious bourgeois existence, womanising habits and hunger for power and position disgusted Siauw.[18] However, as long as they provided the necessary leadership and political direction which aligned with Baperki's political objectives, Siauw was able to tolerate their weaknesses.

To him, the economic problems experienced were caused by a lack of commitment from the country's executives towards achieving socialism. He declared:

> It is necessary for us to develop a realistic plan and economic policies which ensure that waste and corruption are eliminated. The emphasis has to be on improving our production capabilities. For this to be achieved, imports of luxury goods which are not needed to improve the country's economy and people's conditions should be limited or replaced by production machinery and spare-parts... It is depressing to see that we continue to increase the imports of new cars while many trucks and buses have to be idle because there are no spare parts to repair and maintain them... It is also sad to see that our textile industry runs only at 30 per cent of its total production

---

[17] Interview with Go Gak Cho, Hong Kong, December 1990.
[18] The ringleaders surrounding Soekarno referred to by Siauw in this context were Subandrio and Chaerul Saleh.

capacity because many of the manufacturers' facilities cannot be run due to spare-part shortages...[19]

Relationship with the PKI

In order to achieve his political gains, particularly those required to protect the interests of the Chinese, Siauw was compelled to become even closer to Soekarno and rely heavily on his protection and wisdom. In this he was like leaders of the PKI and other left-wing political parties but, in doing so, Siauw brought Baperki into the political camp of Soekarno and the PKI.

The PKI continued to support Baperki in various ways. The PKI daily *Harian Rakyat* frequently reported Baperki's achievements and quoted Siauw's speeches. Aidit also frequently declared that with respect to minority issues the PKI fully supported Siauw's opinions.[20] In his speech delivered to the Baperki conference held on 12 May 1965, Aidit stated:

> Baperki is an organisation which I know will not sit on the fence in facing current political developments and the revolutionary period. Baperki, as I indicated on your 11th anniversary, is not an exclusive organisation as alleged by some people. Baperki is a useful tool for the revolution, particularly in integrating the Chinese minority into the revolutionary masses of Indonesia.

Most scholars are in agreement that Baperki found the PKI a reliable ally. Suryadinata for example suggests that under Siauw, 'Baperki became pro-communist and pro-Soekarno from whom it obtained protection'.[21] McVey is more definitive in saying, 'Siauw's continuing personal association with the far left, coupled with the fact that the PKI was the only major party to take a firm stand against anti-Chinese discrimination, tended to identify the Baperki in the popular mind as leftist'.[22] Somers, however, views the special relationship between the PKI and Baperki more critically, saying, 'The PKI's aid to the Baperki in the assimilation controversy was partly influenced by domestic political considerations, for military

---

[19] Siauw's speech, *Melaksanakan 'Banting Stir Untuk Berdikari' di Bidang Ekonomi*.

[20] Interview with Njoo King Ming, member of the PKI's CDB of East Java, Melbourne, June 1990.

[21] Suryadinata, *Pribumi Indonesians, The Chinese Minority and China*, p. 66.

[22] McVey, 'Indonesian Communism and China', p. 363 in Tang Tsou (ed.), *China's Policies in Asia and America's Alternatives*, Volume 2, The University of Chicago Press.

personnel who were extremely unsympathetic to the PKI were on the side of the assimilationists. The PKI is most pro-Chinese when those who are anti-Chinese are anti-communists'.[23] If the alliance was found too dangerous to the PKI's position or was not going to be popularly accepted by its members, Somers argues, then the party would not be as enthusiastic in publicly defending Baperki. Baperki leaders, Somers indicates, were also cautious not to give the impression that they were too close to the PKI.

In the last phase of Guided Democracy there were, in fact, important conflicts between Siauw and leaders of the PKI, especially Aidit.

In 1965 the PKI intensified its campaigns in the streets. Demonstrations and rallies involving thousands of people, especially students and other young people, were often organised in Jakarta and other large cities. These rallies and demonstrations required funds, trucks and buses and, most importantly, participating students. For these, the PKI organisers turned to Baperki. A number of Chinese public transport operators who were members of Baperki were asked to provide free transportation. Students of the Baperki schools and university were also urged to participate in these demonstrations and rallies. Baperki's school and university buildings in Jakarta were often used to provide free accommodation for PKI members arriving in the capital for conferences and other meetings.

When the PKI and its affiliated organisations organised military training for their members, many Baperki youths took part. Some Baperki students were also involved in the last phase of military training held in the Lubang Buaya area, on the edge of Jakarta, in which the six army generals were to be buried on 1 October 1965.

Arrangements for these PKI-initiated activities were often made by leaders of Baperki who were also members of the PKI or its associated organisations such as Lekra, Pemuda Rakyat and the CGMI. Many were made without Siauw's knowledge, which Siauw resented. He ridiculed the PKI's claims that all the people involved in their public demonstrations and rallies were PKI members, as many of them were in fact from Baperki. He frequently argued that Baperki was not an affiliate of the PKI and that the PKI leaders should not take it for granted that Baperki members were at their full disposal.

His anger was directed not only at the PKI leadership but also and especially at Baperki members who put their loyalty to the PKI above their loyalty to the Baperki leadership. In March 1965, a number of student leaders at URECA proposed to mobilise a large number of their followers for a

---

[23] Somers, *Peranakan Chinese Politics*, p. 273.

PKI-led demonstration against American movies. The demonstration was planned for 13 March but Baperki was due to celebrate its 11th anniversary on that day and Siauw wanted large numbers of URECA students to attend that. Through Go Gien Tjwan, Siauw ordered the students to cancel the arrangements they had made and they bowed to his authority.

Siauw's criticism of the PKI leadership was often conveyed to Aidit himself. Sometime in September 1965 Aidit promised Siauw that PKI members would be instructed not to take advantage of Baperki's facilities and members. PKI members who disobeyed his instructions would be disciplined.[24]

Partly in response to government pressure on organisations to Nasakomise themselves, a number of key leaders of Baperki joined the PKI. Liem Koen Seng, secretary of Baperki's Education and Culture Foundation, and Njoo King Ming, vice-chairman of East Java's Baperki, became members of the PKI in late 1964 and represented the PKI in regional parliaments in Jakarta and East Java respectively. Many other members in the regional branches also joined the PKI. Furthermore, many Baperki students, as outlined in the previous chapter, became leaders of the Pemuda Rakyat and CGMI. These youths were highly militant. When Siauw indicated that Baperki was not subordinated to the PKI and should remain organisationally independent, some of these PKI members were disappointed and viewed Siauw as conservative or even reactionary.[25]

Although Siauw never publicly criticised the leaders of the PKI, he spoke very critically of them to a number of his close associates. As he saw it, the PKI had become a party of the petty bourgeoisie. Its leaders had become more interested in gaining positions in the cabinet, DPRGR, MPRS, regional councils and other important government institutions than in pursuing the party's goals. If pro-PKI members of Baperki depicted Siauw and his immediate associates as conservative for wanting to maintain Baperki's organisational independence, Siauw retaliated by describing the Aidit group as out of touch with their membership.

Many PKI members of legislative bodies, Siauw said, were too interested in exercising their right to obtain and enjoy the facilities, benefits and privileges of the positions offered to them. On the day the PKI celebrated its 45th anniversary in May 1965, which turned out to be a day of huge celebration,

---

[24] Interview with Go Gien Tjwan, Amsterdam, December 1990.
[25] Interviews with Go Gien Tjwan, Oei Tjoe Tat, Tan Tjin Siang and a number of former Baperki activists in 1993.

Siauw reportedly told Aidit, 'You are the chairman of the party. You are not here as a state minister. It is silly for you to attend this function in a ministerial uniform'. Aidit was apparently angered by Siauw's comments, but he refrained from replying.[26]

The more annoyed Siauw became with the PKI's actions, the more resistant he became to the PKI using Baperki's facilities and members for its own activities. Within Baperki there were frequent conflicts between those who were also members of the PKI and those, like Siauw, who wanted to maintain Baperki's separate identity.

In some regional branches, like East Java, most Baperki office bearers were members of the PKI. But Siauw, highly respected by the organisation's rank and file, was still able to contain the drive which would have made Baperki another of the PKI's mass organisations. Siauw maintained that what he advocated was to fully support Soekarno. If there was a conflict between Soekarno and the PKI, Baperki should support Soekarno's position.

There were people who criticised Baperki for being too close to the PKI. Siauw rebutted by saying that Baperki supported Soekarno's policies and these policies were also supported not only by the PKI but also by all other political parties in Indonesia and leaders of the armed forces. Baperki, he said, was an independent mass organisation unlike such affiliated bodies as the Pemuda Rakyat, CGMI or Gerwani (Gerakan Wanita Indonesia – Indonesian Women's Movement).

In the months before 1 October rumours developed within Baperki that Aidit was urging Liem Koen Seng to mount pressure within the organisation to replace Siauw. But Liem himself respected Siauw. Not being a good public speaker, he would also have had difficulty in gaining support from senior members for a challenge to Siauw. Towards October 1965 it was apparent to most Baperki leaders that they should stick with Siauw.[27]

While it is clear that Siauw's relationship with Aidit worsened in the last few months of the Guided Democracy period, he remained close to Njoto and Lukman. Njoto in particular visited Siauw's place frequently.

One major aspect of Siauw's political stance in the late Guided Democracy period was that he maintained good relations with a number of leaders of the Partai Murba party, the PKI's long-time rival. He was in frequent

---

[26] Siauw's own account and verified by Oei Tjoe Tat in July 1990.

[27] Interviews with Tan Tjin Siang in December 1988, Go Gien Tjwan in December 1990 and Mrs Lie Tjwan Sien in December 1990.

contact with Adam Malik, Sukarni and Pandu even after the Partai Murba party had been suspended at Soekarno's behest. Siauw refused to follow the PKI's lead in condemning the Partai Murba and its leaders. He never criticised the activities of the BPS or the Partai Murba party. Adam Malik remained a member of Baperki's Advisory Council. Siauw's decision not to break with Malik when he and his group were in trouble helped reduce his suffering as a political prisoner after November 1965.

Baperki had particularly close relations with the small leftist party, Partindo. Oei Tjoe Tat and Phoa Thoan Hian of Baperki were chairmen in Partindo. Good relationships with other small Islamic parties like Perti and PSII were also maintained. Nja Diwan, leader of Perti, joined the Baperki advisory council. Sudibjo, leader of the PSII and general secretary of the Front Nasional, frequently came to Baperki's functions.

The coup attempt

By September 1965 the PKI still had very little foothold in the government machinery. Its political strength was derived from its capability to mobilise large numbers for street demonstrations and, of course, from the active support it received from the president. It enjoyed support from the leaders of the air force, to a lesser extent the navy, and from a minority of army officers at various levels. But its campaign to have a 'fifth force' established was meeting strong resistance.

In the middle of 1965, there were rumours in Jakarta that a council of generals was preparing to oust Soekarno, and these grew stronger after the president's health seemed to be faltering in August. In September, there was talk of a coup to be staged by the army on Armed Forces Day, 5 October 1965, and indeed troops were being moved to Jakarta in preparation for a huge celebration of the 20th anniversary of the armed forces on that day.

It is generally believed that leaders of the PKI were alarmed by Soekarno's illness and that this had prompted Aidit and his assistant Sjam to take action to remove the anti-communist generals of the army. The so-called G30S movement (Gerakan 30 September – 30th September Movement) was then formed, led by Lieutenant Colonel Untung, a member of the Cakrabirawa Corps (Soekarno's bodyguards).

In the early morning of 1 October 1965 troops of the G30S movement entered the houses of seven top generals. They were successful in kidnapping all of these except General Nasution, who managed to escape. Three, including Chief of Staff Yani, were killed in the process. Their bodies and those who were captured alive were taken to the Halim Air Force Base, the coup group's headquarters. Those still alive were then killed and all the bodies dumped in an unused well.

The movement's troops also occupied radio and telecommunication centres and surrounded the Merdeka Palace. At 7.15 am on 1 October, a special announcement was read announcing that the movement had successfully arrested members of a council of generals who were plotting to overthrow the president. It also stated that President Soekarno was safe and under the protection of the G30S movement.

At 11 am on the same day another announcement was made. This time the G30S movement declared that a revolutionary council had been established to carry out the day-to-day management of the government until elections could be held. The cabinet was then placed in a decommissioned status. At 2 pm the names of the 45 members of the revolutionary council were announced, including deputy prime ministers Subandrio and Leimena and some twenty senior members of the armed forces. Siauw was on the list too, though he had not been consulted prior to the inclusion of his name, as was the case with many of those on the list. He was the only Chinese on the list.

Siauw first heard of the movement around 7.30 am from Sunito, a Partindo activist who dropped by. He went to parliament in the morning as usual but was unable to find out much about what was happening. In the afternoon, he gave a lecture to the staff of Kotoe (Komando Tertinggi Operasi Ekonomi – Supreme Command of Economic Operations) finishing around 7 pm. By 9 pm that evening, he knew from the radio and other sources that General Soeharto, the head of the army's strategic reserve, had outmaneuvered the G30S movement and that its leaders were on the run.

Siauw saw the involvement of the PKI leadership in the coup attempt as major and a disastrous mistake. He believed that it was totally unnecessary for the PKI to take the initiative to attack the army. In his view, the political atmosphere in the country and in the international arena was favourable for the Soekarno–PKI alliance. Politically, the army was on the defensive. He was critical of the masterminds of the movement for being ill prepared for the situation and for leaving their troops without giving proper direction.[28]

Within weeks of the coup's defeat, Soeharto was very much in command of the country. While Soekarno still remained president of the republic, he

---

[28] Siauw's own account conveyed to author in the military prison, 1972.

quickly lost control of the real power. The battle between the army and the PKI had been completely won by the army and in October 1965 Soeharto, as the new commander of the army, began to slowly but surely take over the government and its machinery.

Siauw's lack of prior knowledge of the coup attempt was evident in his delayed response or reaction to it. Leaders of the PKI who were closely involved in the planning had made arrangements for the party's mouthpiece, *Harian Rakyat*, to publish an editorial supporting the G30S movement on 2 October. It was apparently too late for them to alter this piece to reflect what had taken place on the evening of 1 October.

Siauw waited until Soekarno made his first announcement on his health and his command on 3 October. On the following day, Baperki issued a statement to say that Siauw had no involvement in the G30S movement and did not know why his name was listed in the revolutionary council. Although Siauw believed that the movement was instigated by Aidit and Sjam, following Soekarno's stance, Baperki referred to the incident as an internal affair within the army. Siauw was convinced that the PKI as a party was not involved in masterminding the movement.

The aftermath of the coup attempt

On 4 October 1965 the bodies of the six generals who had been killed were discovered in the Lubang Buaya area. The discovery was televised and widely publicised, accompanied with stories on how the bodies were mutilated prior to the dumping in the unused well, highlighting the cruelty of the members of the Pemuda Rakyat and Gerwani who participated in the G30S movement. On 5 October they were given a state heroes' burial which was televised and widely publicised. With this background, Soeharto, backed by Nasution, quickly moved to destroy the PKI.

The disappearance of Yani and his close associates, who before the coup attempt tended to avoid confrontation with Soekarno, meant that Soekarno now had to deal with army leaders who were willing to challenge his policies directly. On 2 October Soeharto and his group refused to accept Soekarno's instruction to install General Pranoto as the new army chief.

Soeharto's most blatant insubordination was apparent in relation to the PKI. His forces moved quickly in Jakarta and other parts of Java to arrest leaders and members of the PKI and its mass organisations. The PKI's headquarters and its buildings were ransacked and burned down by angry anti-communist demonstrators. The army also encouraged members of the anti-communist political parties and organisations, namely the NU, HMI and Partai Katolik to clean society of communist elements. This encouragement, coupled with military assistance organised by Soeharto's subordinate Colonel Sarwo Edie with his RPKAD troops (Resimen Para Komando Angkatan Darat – Regiment of Army Command), induced mass killings in Central Java, East Java, Bali and Aceh. The number of people, communists and their sympathisers, who were brutally massacred by this organised movement was estimated to be between 500 000 and 1 million. PKI members, deprived of their leadership and virtually unarmed, were in no position to resist.

The anti-communist organisations which demanded the dissolution of the PKI were quick to extend that demand to Baperki, which they defined as a financier of the PKI. It was easy to point to evidence that Baperki had provided assistance to the PKI in many pre-coup demonstrations and public rallies. To these anti-communist organisations, Baperki was no different to the Pemuda Rakyat, CGMI and BTI. Moreover, Baperki was easily identified as a pro-China organisation at a time when the anti-communist press was asserting that the People's Republic of China was behind both the G30S movement and the PKI.

In this situation, the LPKB campaigned actively for the dissolution of Baperki. The LPKB argued that Baperki had failed to condemn the G30S movement and had not offered condolences to the army for the killed generals. They urged the Indonesian Chinese to abandon Baperki quickly, as it was clearly an ally of the PKI and the People's Republic of China. People supporting Baperki would expose the community to the same disaster that had befallen the communists. LPKB leaders provided newspapers with material to spread their strategy. Supported by regional army administrations, they moved quickly in encouraging the dissolution of Baperki branches. By 3 December 1965, 25 Baperki branches throughout the country had dissolved themselves.[29]

On 15 October anti-communist demonstrators attacked Baperki's URECA buildings in Jakarta. When Baperki leaders were tipped off that the demonstrators were moving towards the university, they quickly requested the police to protect the buildings. According to Siauw, such protection was provided half-heartedly. When the demonstrators did arrive, the police did nothing to stop the demonstrators from attacking the buildings. Baperki students attempted to defend the buildings but they were outnumbered. After three hours of clashes, most of the university buildings

---

[29] Coppel, *Indonesian Chinese in Crisis*, pp. 56–57.

were burned down. Siauw attempted to initiate Soekarno's intervention by visiting him at the palace. Together with Siauw, Soekarno briefly witnessed the burning of the university from a helicopter, but he was powerless to stop the action. He did however send troops to protect Siauw's house from being burned down. They blocked the street in which Siauw's house was situated.[30]

Siauw was emotionally affected by the burning of the university campus. Standing on the ruins of the buildings, surrounded by hundreds of his students, he wept and pledged to rebuild the campus. But the move against Baperki did not stop there. Outside Jakarta, many Baperki members were arrested. Those who were members of the PKI, Pemuda Rakyat and CGMI were arrested first. Large numbers of Baperki members and sympathisers who were not arrested were subjected to extortion by military authorities.

Leaders of Baperki had a number of meetings in Jakarta to review the situation. Some suggested that leaders of Baperki, including Siauw, should go into hiding to avoid arrest, following in the steps of leaders of the PKI and its mass organisations. But Siauw was determined not to go into hiding. Always something of a legalist, he urged his fellow Baperki leaders to stay put and provide as much protection and direction as possible to the members of the organisation who were in trouble. He sent his brother Giok Bie back to East Java to make arrangements with its military commander General Sumitro, whom he knew well, in an attempt to reduce hostility towards Baperki.

Siauw repeatedly stated that leaders of Baperki should not run away and that they should defend the organisation and protect its members. He argued that Baperki was not guilty of any crimes. He did, however urge Baperki members to avoid arrest at all costs.[31] Go Gien Tjwan recalls that there were a number of leaders who disagreed with Siauw and did go into hiding.

Siauw also rejected offers by Baperki students who had received military training, and were thus armed, to act as his bodyguards. In the first two weeks of October, he continued to appear at DPRGR offices, at public functions and carried out his duties as a guest lecturer of the Kotoe. His house was attacked and ransacked by KAMI and KAPPI[32] students more

---

30   Siauw's own account, military prison, 1972.
31   Interviews with Go Gien Tjwan, Siauw Giok Bie and Tan Tjin Siang in December 1990.
32   KAMI (Kesatuan Aksi Mahasiswa Indonesia – Indonesian Students Action Forum) and KAPPI (Kesatuan Aksi Pemudan Pelajar Indonesia – Indonesian Student Youth

than three times. In one of these attacks, Siauw was at home. The agitated demonstrators intended to burn the house. But Siauw was somehow able to talk the leader of the demonstrators out of it. The house was not damaged, though it was painted with large graffiti saying 'Crush Baperki! Hang Siauw Giok Tjhan! Baperki is PKI's Financier!'[33] The KAMI/KAPPI students also ransacked the houses of other Baperki leaders like Go Gien Tjwan and Liem Koen Seng. But none of their houses were burned down.

In the middle of October 1965 Siauw and Go Gien Tjwan visited Subandrio, Chaerul Saleh, Adam Malik and other senior ministers to try to save Baperki. They demanded that the government move to protect Baperki and give Siauw an opportunity to show in court that Baperki had no involvement with the G30S movement and to rebut accusations that it was the PKI's financier.[34] However, these demands fell on deaf ears. The country was in turmoil and the balance of power had already been tipped. Soeharto and his army machinery were driving the new political agenda. The existing apparatus led by Subandrio had lost its executive powers.

Siauw was also powerless to do anything to defend the Chinese. Anti-Chinese feeling was developing rapidly. Although the number of Chinese who were killed in the waves of killing in Java and Sumatra was comparatively low, violence against them in the form of property burning (including shops, houses, schools, factories, buses and cars), ransacking, looting and physical torture was experienced in many places.

The worst violence against the Chinese occurred in Makassar and Medan in late October. In Makasar, shops and houses of some 2000 households were damaged, ransacked and burnt, causing the bankruptcy of some 1000 families. In Medan, apart from a large number of properties being damaged, some 200 Chinese were killed.[35]

On 4 November 1965, a group of army officers arrived at Siauw's place to arrest him, which they did after searching the house in a way that created great havoc. Their pretext was that they wished to safeguard him from the anger of the masses. In January 1966, he was honourably discharged from DPRGR, MPRS and DPA.

Action Unit).

[33] An article in *Harian Angkatan Bersenjata* on 17 October 1965 indicated that Siauw's house, unlike houses of other leaders of the PKI and mass organisations, was left intact. It is not clear whether the article was intended to encourage KAMI/KAPPI to damage Siauw's house.

[34] Interview with Go Gien Tjwan.

[35] Coppel, *Indonesian Chinese in Crisis*, pp. 60–61.

Soekarno desperately tried to re-establish the status quo. For months after the attempted coup, he struggled to contain Soeharto's movements. But with the PKI largely destroyed, Soekarno was isolated and politically crippled. However, he stubbornly refused to condemn and disband the PKI. He continued to argue that Nasakom principles should be upheld, hence the need to have a communist element in the country.

By January 1966, the streets of Jakarta and Bandung were controlled by students and youths influenced by the right-wing forces who continued to demand the dissolution of the PKI and the sacking of Subandrio and other left-wing ministers. Soekarno continued to protect the PKI and left-wing leaders. General Supardjo, who was involved in masterminding the G30S movement, was protected in Soekarno's Bogor palace in the first few weeks of October 1965. Omar Dhani was also protected in the same manner. In one of the cabinet meetings of December 1965, Soekarno was said to have instructed Soeharto to release Siauw Giok Tjhan from prison.[36]

On 21 February 1966, Soekarno announced a cabinet reshuffle which included the removal of Nasution and a number of other anti-communist figures from the cabinet. In contrast to this, senior left-wing ministers, including Subandrio, Omar Dhani, Setiadi Reksoprodjo and Oei Tjoe Tat were retained in the cabinet. In addition to this, Soekarno also added a number of military figures considered loyal to him, including General Mursid, General Hartono, Air Marshall Herlambang and Commodore Mulyadi. Soeharto's position as chief of army; however, was retained. The new cabinet showed Soekarno's intention to confront the army and its allies but he was fighting a losing battle.

On 11 March 1966 the army was successful in forcing Soekarno to transfer real executive power to the hands of Soeharto. Soekarno's instruction affirming this was better known as the Supersemar (Surat Perintah Sebelas Maret – Instruction of Eleventh of March). On 12 March, Soeharto issued instructions to dissolve the PKI and a number of mass organisations. Baperki was included in the list of organisations to be dissolved. A few days later, left-wing ministers including Subandrio, Omar Dhani, Chaerul Saleh, Setiadi, Sumardjo and Oei Tjoe Tat were arrested. Thus ended the legal existence of Nasakom in Indonesian politics.

By then, Baperki had been totally dissolved. Its senior members were either jailed or politically inactive. Baperki's URECA was taken over by

---

[36] Interview with Oei Tjoe Tat in July 1993. Siauw himself heard of this when he was in the Nirbaya Prison together with Sumardjo, one of the jailed ministers.

a management group and renamed Trisakti University. Coordinated and encouraged by the LPKB, the management of Baperki schools was transferred to the Department of Education. These schools became state schools and Asli students were encouraged to enter them. Left-wing lecturers and teachers were purged and replaced by staff with right-wing orientations. Most peranakan teachers were replaced by Asli staff.

Oei Tjoe Tat and Tan Tjin Siang recalled that Siauw, keen to protect Baperki and its members from persecution and mass arrest, issued instructions to leaders of Baperki to always state that he, Siauw Giok Tjhan, was solely responsible for all Baperki's policies and was the only person to blame for all their consequences. But this did not stop the persecution and Siauw himself remained in prison for the next twelve long years.

Was Siauw responsible for the anti-Chinese violence?

We have seen in this chapter how Siauw made numerous political gains by being close to Soekarno. Siauw's political position enabled him to expand Baperki, influence the issuing of regulations that protected the economic position of the Chinese and diminish the political influence of Baperki's political opponent the LPKB. Under Siauw, Baperki became the largest mass organisation involving the Chinese with definitive Indonesia-oriented politics. Many Chinese, influenced by Baperki, joined various leftist political organisations and played major roles in them. Lea Williams has described this as an effective political assimilation. The effectiveness is to be judged by how successful the political assimilation was in providing protection to the Chinese community and having its members develop the political awareness to regard Indonesia as their home.

In this context, Siauw had proved that Chinese involvement in politics at the highest level and having a mass organisation and educational institutions as large as Baperki helped protect the Chinese interest prior to the end of the Guided Democracy period.

But the anti-Chinese violence which immediately followed the G30S movement in October 1965 raised questions about how responsible Baperki, and for that matter Siauw, was for the hardships the Chinese were forced to endure in the 1965–1967 period.

LPKB leaders were quick to allege that Baperki's policies and Siauw's communism were largely responsible for the violence. They stated that Baperki, established on Chinese ethnicity, was involved in political activities. This, according to them, was dangerous because the Chinese group as a whole could be identified with Baperki. If the political situation changed, they argued, the whole group would then be exposed. They further argued that most members of Baperki were not political. They became members because they were attracted to Baperki's social and educational programs. But these people, they said, were deceived by the Baperki leaders' political direction and brought into a damaging and disastrous situation.[37] Writing much later, Junus Jahja repeatedly states that it was the LPKB who improved the situation in the months after October 1965 and helped bring the Chinese out of a dangerous position by taking initiatives in disbanding Baperki offices and reorganising the management and structure of Baperki schools and university.[38]

The role of the LPKB in saving the Chinese in the months following G30S remains a debatable issue. The good relationship LPKB leadership had with leaders of the army was indeed helpful in making LPKB leaders welcome in the anti-communist movement led by General Soeharto. Coppel suggests that this close relationship might have assisted in reducing anti-Chinese violence in that period:

> Their (LPKB's) previous association with the army and any other anti-communist Indonesians had been a valuable demonstration to their partners that there were "good" Chinese who were neither pawns of Peking nor camp followers of the PKI. By pressing the rank and file membership of Baperki to dissolve their branches in the months after the coup attempt, the LPKB probably moderated the extent of anti-Chinese violence at that time. They were able to present the Baperki mass following as a non-political one which had been duped by a leftist leadership.[39]

But while some of the activities of the LPKB may have had this moderating effect, others possibly worked in the opposite way. It is in fact highly probable that LPKB loyalty rallies held in April 1966 by WNI Chinese, in which they appealed to the people of Indonesia to direct their anti-Chinese hostilities against alien Chinese and China, further encouraged anti-Chinese violence as it would be extremely difficult for people involved in the violence to distinguish between WNI Chinese and alien Chinese. Furthermore, the LPKB leaders' enthusiasm in promoting their assimilation programs

---

[37] Wahono (ed.) *70 Tahun Junus Jahja*, pp. 364–365.
[38] Ibid., p. 365; Jahja, *Catatan Seorang WNI*, pp. 46–47.
[39] Coppel, *Indonesian Chinese in Crisis*, p. 174.

resulted in a series of anti-Chinese governmental regulations being issues which were much resented by the Chinese communities, both WNI and alien. These regulations included prohibition of using Chinese characters, celebrating Chinese New Year and holding lion dance performances. Also included were regulations which encouraged name-changing and formalised the term Cina, a term found to be insulting by most Chinese at that time.[40]

The strongest accusation from the LPKB that Baperki was guilty came from its former chairman, K Sindhunata, who declared, 'The most sinful act of Oei Tjoe Tat and Baperki was to give the impression that the whole peranakan Chinese community had become communists, such that when the G30S–PKI movement was crushed, there were a high number of (Chinese) victims'.[41]

Similar opinions were also expressed by Yap Thiam Hien. Yap had voiced his objection to Baperki becoming a leftist organisation in the late 1950s. In various Baperki meetings, particularly those held in 1959, he had repeatedly stated that it was dangerous for Baperki to take sides in politics. Lev sums up his concern: 'For Yap, though his own ideological biases naturally made a difference, the primary consideration was that the Chinese minority must not risk taking ideological sides. To do so would split the community more than it was already and envelop it in political danger'.[42] Based on this conviction, Yap maintained that Baperki and Siauw Giok Tjhan had adopted an erroneous path. In a public meeting held in Amsterdam in July 1980, in which Yap and Siauw were present, Yap apparently said, 'Baperki was an effective organisation and had provided good services to the nation. However, it had backed the "wrong horse" and as such it had brought the Chinese community to disaster'.[43]

Coppel's analysis seems to concur with this view. He writes:

> The combination of Baperki's unprecedented mobilisation of WNI into political life, coupled with the leftist orientation of its leadership, helped to identify the Chinese in the minds of many Indonesians (not

---

[40] Interviews with leaders of INTI (Indonesia Chinese Association) established in April 1999, who had a meeting with former LPKB leaders including Sindhunatha. In that meeting, held in May 1999, Sindhunatha claimed that most of the anti-Chinese regulations were the result of the LPKB's work in 1966.

[41] *Gatra*, 14 October 1995.

[42] Lev, *Political Journey of Yap Thiam Hien*, p. 105.

[43] Siauw's letter to author, 27 July 1980.

least sections of the military) with communism. So long as the PKI was riding high, Soekarno almost deified, and relations with mainland China close, this identification could even be beneficial. But these conditions were to prove short-lived; in a situation in which an anti-communist campaign against the PKI and China could rage with Soekarno powerless to check it, the identification was bound to be dangerous.[44]

However, to counter this position, a strong argument could be mounted that the disaster and subsequent hardship experienced by the Chinese was produced by forces far more influential than the political position of Baperki or Siauw Giok Tjhan. The anti-Chinese violence was part of a dramatic change in the whole political environment, involving the interests of the superpowers – particularly those of the USA – and the power struggle between the PKI and the army. Soekarno's leftward shift towards the end of the Guided Democracy period, which had brought Indonesia close to People's Republic of China and upset the Western world, led to a showdown in which the Soekarno–Left alliance was defeated, and the anti-Chinese violence was a result of that defeat. The violence would exist regardless of whether Baperki or, for that matter, Siauw Giok Tjhan, was on the left or right side of politics.

Many Baperki members, particularly those who suffered political persecution, came to the conclusion that Baperki had gone too far in supporting Soekarno and the PKI. On the other hand many remained convinced that Siauw did not have a choice and hence continued to endorse what he stood for.[45]

---

[44] Coppel, *Indonesian Chinese in Crisis*, pp. 50–51.
[45] Interviews with Go Gien Tjwan, Oei Tjoe Tat, Tan Tjin Siang, Phoa Thoan Hian and many other ex-Baperki members in 1993.

Chapter 14

IMPRISONMENT AND RELEASE

For six months after 4 November 1965, Siauw was detained in a series of very crowded camps in Jakarta. These camps, which were mostly offices of the PKI and its affiliated organisations, houses of PKI leaders or army barracks, were quickly established by the military authorities to function as detention centres for the very large number of political prisoners. In the first 12 months after the abortive coup of October 1965, the authorities had arrested between 600 000 and 750 000 political prisoners, mostly members of the PKI and its affiliated organisations.[1]

The conditions in these ill-equipped camps were poor. Most of them did not have appropriate facilities and the rooms were so crowded that prisoners had to take turns to sleep. In some camps, prisoners were forced to take shifts for shelter. There was a great shortage of food and that which the authorities provided was severely lacking in nourishment. Most of the prisoners were subjected to torture and were deprived of books and other reading material. Meetings with their family members were difficult to arrange and were closely supervised. Most of these temporary camps were demolished when the number of prisoners reduced towards the end of 1966.

In May 1966 Siauw was transferred to Jakarta's largest jail, Salemba. It had been built by the Dutch in the 1920s to accommodate less than 1000 prisoners but when Siauw was transferred to it there were more than 4000 political prisoners in it. Cells designed for one prisoner were occupied by four prisoners and some were so cramped that the inmates had to take turns to sleep.

In the meetings I had with Siauw in various prisons, he described the suffering that inmates had to endure. Food was a major problem for tapols (tahanan politik – political prisoners), especially in the early years. The authorities provided very little and tapols had to rely heavily on food sent

---

[1] Amnesty International Report, *Indonesia, sebuah laporan Amnesti Internasional*, 1977, pp. 47–48.

in by their families. Between 1966 and 1970 prisoners like Siauw, who received food regularly from their families, often had to share it with up to eight others. Prisoners cultivated unused land within the prison compounds, planting vegetables and cassava, but the prisoners' determination to feed themselves encouraged the authorities to reduce the amount of food they provided. By 1968, thousands of inmates of Salemba and other prisons had reportedly died of starvation and malnutrition.[2]

The tapols were often subjected to interrogations, which involved torture. Many had to be hospitalised after the torture. Many became crippled and died. Siauw was relatively fortunate for, while he was often interrogated, he was never tortured and most of the investigators treated him with respect.[3]

The authorities did not provide clothing or sleeping mats – these were supplied by churches and inmates' families. The church organisations often sent additional food, medicine and other basic necessities like towels and soap to the prisons. Because of this, a large number of Muslim inmates were attracted to Christianity and wished to convert to it. Initially, mass baptism took place; however, when the number of people being baptised continued to increase the authorities disallowed the conversion and, in some cases, forced the baptised inmates to declare their loyalty to Islam. Interestingly, inmates who wished to become Muslims did not experience the same level of discouragement.

Many of the political leaders whom Siauw resented during the Guided Democracy period – particularly those who were members of the PKI and its affiliated organisations – were also jailed. Siauw described how most of these figures behaved poorly and humiliated themselves in jail. Many of them were not able to bear hardship and torture. They provided the authorities with information regarding their organisations and the whereabouts of members and people who had helped the organisations. For the sake of a few cigarettes, they were willing to betray and jeopardise their colleagues. Some of these figures became informants and interrogators. Obviously amazed and disgusted by the behaviour of some of these figures, Siauw often said that the PKI and its affiliated organisations were in fact destroyed by elements of these organisations.

If many of the prominent figures disappointed Siauw, the majority of the inmates, particularly those from the grassroots, impressed him. They showed determination to survive and refused to betray their political aspirations.

---

[2] The actual number who died cannot be confirmed.

[3] Interviews with a number of former fellow prisoners in Jakarta, July 1992.

Siauw was grouped with leaders of the PKI and its affiliated organisations, as well as intellectuals, in prison blocks designated as blocks Q and R. Many tapols in these blocks, including Siauw, were spared from the routine hard labour most tapols from other blocks had to perform.

Tapols were not allowed to read newspapers or listen to radios. Their reading material was limited to religious material. One way in which Siauw kept himself busy was by teaching English, German, Dutch and French to fellow tapols. He often used this opportunity to carry out political discussions and exchange information, which were forbidden activities in prison. In 1969, an informant reported to the authorities that Siauw had conducted political discussions. The authorities punished Siauw by putting him in the block reserved for criminals for six months. During this period, he was not allowed to see his family. Tapols sent into the criminal block usually suffered as they were often robbed and bullied by fellow prisoners. But Siauw was fortunate. He was able to develop a good relationship with one of the 'heavyweight' criminals who provided him with protection.[4]

In August 1971 Siauw was transferred to the RTM (rumah tahanan militer – military prison) located in the centre of Jakarta. He was informed that he would be tried and would need to be questioned thoroughly at that prison before the trial. From his discussions with his interrogators, he understood that the Ministry of Justice had been asked to put a Chinese prisoner on trial for involvement in the G30S movement. Siauw would have been the first Chinese to be put on trial in connection with the G30S movement.

Although Siauw was not subjected to physical torture, the 18-month interrogation process itself was a psychological torture. Siauw was subjected to long hours of interrogations, most of which were in the evenings but some that went on for more than 24 hours at a stretch. Siauw's would-be witnesses were often subjected to torture in his presence. He himself was interrogated heavily for a period of three months and then left alone for six months before the next round of interrogations.

The interrogators' main objectives were to prove that Siauw was a member of the PKI and that he was directly involved in the preparation work that preceded the G30S movement. But their 18-month interrogations failed to confirm either of these. In February 1973, the interrogations stopped and he was transferred to the Nirbaya prison located near the Halim Air Force base outside Jakarta. Nirbaya was specially set up to detain ex-cabinet ministers

---

[4] Siauw's own account, verified by former tapols in 1992.

and senior military officers. Conditions there were far better than in Salemba or the RTM and contact with family members was allowed on a weekly basis. Together with Siauw in this camp were Omar Dhani (former air force chief), General Pranoto (whom Soekarno had tried to appoint as chief of the army), Setiadi (former electricity minister), Astrawinata (former justice minister) and many other prominent players in Soekarno's regime. In September 1973 Siauw was transferred back to Salemba.

The tens of thousands of tapols were categorised into three major groups. People to be put on trial for their involvement in the abortive coup attempt were categorised as being in group A. Group B contained members of the PKI and its affiliated organisations whom the government did not intend to try but wanted to keep as prisoners on a long-term basis. The majority of the tapols belonged to group C and were classified as communist sympathisers.

The categorisation, however, was neither final nor rigid. Most tapols were not informed of their categories and had to make their own assumptions. A tapol who assumed that he was a group C prisoner could be treated as one of group A if the military authority had information on his direct involvement in the coup. The categorisation became clearer between 1969 and 1971. Over this period 10 000 tapols were sent in staggered groups to Buru Island in the eastern part of Indonesia. The tapols were given a few hours warning to prepare for the long trip to Buru and their families were never informed prior to their departure. The government classified them as group B prisoners.

In 1967 Siauw was informed that he was a group C prisoner but in November 1970 his wife was tipped off by a friend that his name was on the list of tapols to be sent to Buru. She went to see Adam Malik, then minister for foreign affairs, and Mursalin, transportation minister and also an old friend of Siauw, to seek their intervention. They promised to intervene. It is not clear whether they did indeed intervene, though Siauw believed that Malik did. Not long after Mrs Siauw's visit to Malik, Siauw was sent to the army hospital in Jakarta for a general check-up. The doctor who conducted this informed him that he was instructed by Malik to make sure that he received proper medical treatment.[5]

The family members of tapols also suffered. Most of them had no income and due to their association with tapols had difficulty in getting employment. By the end of 1965 all government institutions and many private ones required employees and job applicants to produce 'free of G30S involvement' certificates. People whose relatives were tapols or ex-tapols would

---

[5] Siauw's own account in 1972.

have difficulty getting these certificates. Thus, unless they had friends and relatives who were willing to help, they faced material hardship.

Siauw's family was comparatively fortunate. A group of totok businessmen who were admirers of Siauw collected regular donations for his family. Additionally, Mrs Siauw received financial support from her brothers and sister. The financial support, which was maintained until the end of 1978, enabled her to send food to prison regularly and to pay the family's living expenses including the children's school fees.

In September 1975, Siauw was allowed to leave prison and put under house arrest. He was required to report to the authorities on a weekly basis and had to seek permission to leave the house. But Siauw decided not to comply with the restriction. Weeks after he was returned home, he visited friends who helped him while he was in prison, including Adam Malik, Mursalin, Sudibyo and Sultan Hamengku Buwono. He also started to attend functions organised by the Angkatan 45 (1945 Generation) at which contact with a large number of old political figures was re-established. Siauw had been a member of the Angkatan 1945 leadership board in the early 60s.

But Siauw was still isolated from society at large. People who visited him at home were largely former tapols and family members. Many of his other friends from before 1965 were still afraid of visiting him.

In August 1978 Siauw was officially released. By then, his health had deteriorated, prompting his daughter, who had recently established an acupuncture clinic in Amsterdam, to sponsor him and his wife to go to Holland for medical treatment. Siauw and his wife left for Amsterdam in September 1978.

In Holland, Siauw ignored the advice of his doctors to rest. He was excited by his new freedom to express his views and organise activities. He established contacts with Indonesians who had been living in Europe as political refugees. He began to campaign for the release of tapols and for funds to assist the released tapols and their families. He also gave lectures on Indonesia to Indonesian students and exiled Indonesians in a number of European cities. In these lectures he affirmed that he would stick to the principles he had held for decades and that the achievement of a democratic Indonesia would speed up the elimination of racism.

But by this time Siauw's thinking about socialism and China had changed. He saw the failure of socialist countries to become prosperous. He was also disappointed to learn that the countries he had admired before he was jailed, particularly China, had failed to become democratic. In a 1976 letter he said:

> Socialism without democracy and economic prosperity is not what people want. The most important fundamental of socialism is in fact the upholding of democratic values. If leaders start oppressing their people and ignoring democratic values, they will quickly lose people's trust. Chairman Mao appears to have lost control and the people around him have begun to exercise dictatorial power. The Chinese leaders should now concentrate on building the country and making it prosperous. They should not be busily arresting people.[6]

Reflecting this view, he modified his approach to the minority problems in Indonesia. He now emphasised the importance of realising democracy in achieving the solution to the minority problems. In September 1981, two months before his death, he wrote:

> The solution to the minority problems has to be associated with efforts involving the commitment and determination of each Indonesian to implement the 1945 Constitution and to achieve a national unity based on democracy. The realisation of a democratic society which respects and protects basic human rights will ensure that racial differences as well as differences in ideology and religions will be tolerated. It is also important that the Bandung spirit of 1955 should be upheld to ensure that foreign intervention does not jeopardise Indonesia's drive to create such a society.[7]

On the question of whether Baperki was guilty for the anti-Chinese violence, Siauw said that the anti-Chinese pogroms from 1965 to 1967 were, in fact, caused by the two superpowers who were keen to see the end of Peking's influence in Indonesia. Siauw collected information from his fellow prisoners and summed up their stories and recollections by saying:

> The USSR was not pleased with the closeness of the PKI leadership to Peking. A number of PKI leaders were warned by a Russian leader that the Soviet Union was capable of replacing the PKI leadership with one more sympathetic to itself. The USA obviously resented the popularity of China in Indonesia. Hence, these two superpowers had a common interest in encouraging anti-Chinese pogroms. The Indonesian Chinese

---

[6] Siauw's letter, 15 March 1976.
[7] Siauw, *Menuju Indonesia yang Baik dengan Terrealisasinya Bhineka Tunggal Ika*, PPI Amsterdam, September 1981, p. 49.

could not have avoided this situation and Baperki cannot be blamed for the anti-Chinese violence which took place after the G30S movement.[8]

On 20 November 1981, a few minutes before he was to deliver a speech on the failure of Indonesian democracy before a group of Indonesianists at the University of Leiden, Siauw suddenly collapsed and died of a heart attack.

---

[8] Siauw's letter, 25 February 1977.

Chapter 15

A HIGHLY SUCCESSFUL CHINESE LEADER

Siauw was a political figure with a number of objectives. Paramount to him was the elimination of racism against the Chinese minority. He was convinced that solutions to issues affecting minority groups form part of the solution to national problems. Hence, to Siauw, effective participation in national politics was mandatory.

Siauw's participation in politics set him apart from the majority of Chinese who were stereotyped as non-political and business-minded. From his school days, Siauw was always keen to be involved in organisational work. When he was in secondary school, he joined and became a leader of the boy scout organisation run by the THHK (Tiong Hoa Hwee Kwan – Chinese Association). He maintained his involvement with the boy Scouts even after he left school and worked as a journalist in Semarang.

Siauw's comfortable existence as a wealthy peranakan enjoying a Dutch education ended abruptly with the sudden death of his parents in 1932. Unable to pursue the earlier plans to go to the Netherlands for his tertiary education, Siauw became associated with Liem Koen Hian, then in his early 30s and a key leader of the new Indonesia-oriented political stream of peranakan politics. Impressed by Liem's ability to express his political views and exert influence through articles in newspapers, Siauw decided to follow Liem's footsteps and joined the daily newspaper, *Sin Tit Po*, as a young journalist.

Through his association with Liem Koen Hian, Siauw was also introduced to the Surabaya study club, led by Soetomo, where he met many other nationalist activists. In 1934, he was recruited by another influential Indonesia-oriented peranakan, Kwee Hing Tjiat, to work as a journalist in a Semarang-based daily called *Mata Hari*. In this capacity, he was introduced to exiled political leaders like Tjipto Mangunkusumo, Soekarno and Hatta. Kwee gave him the task of establishing and maintaining regular contact with a number of these exiled leaders whose articles were published in *Mata Hari*.

From the beginning of his career, Siauw was sympathetic and committed to the struggle to achieve Indonesia Merdeka – an Indonesia free from Dutch colonialism. Like Liem Koen Hian and a small number of like-minded peranakan leaders, Siauw was going against the overwhelming majority of peranakans who at that time preferred to support either China-oriented politics or the colonial status quo.

Siauw's political training was further enhanced by Tan Ling Djie, some 13 years older, who returned to Indonesia from Holland in 1936. Tan, well known for his in-depth knowledge of Marxism and Leninism, was highly respected by many of the freedom fighters. After independence, Tan was one of the most senior leaders in the Partai Sosialis and the PKI. When Tan returned to Surabaya, Siauw was also in Surabaya heading the local branch of *Mata Hari*. Tan introduced Siauw to Marxism and influenced him to be sympathetic towards Mao Tse Tung's leadership in China.

Siauw had been publishing anti-Japanese articles for years in *Mata Hari*. So when the Japanese arrived in Indonesia in 1942 he decided to leave Semarang and go into hiding in Malang. He remained there throughout the Japanese occupation.

Siauw's ability to provide leadership and direction was first shown in Malang during the occupation period. Together with Han Kang Hoen, some 15 years older than himself, Siauw provided leadership to the Chinese community in Malang. The Japanese administration recognised this and, in 1944, Siauw was appointed as a leader of the local Kebotai, the local branch of the Japanese-established Chinese militia. Most Chinese community leaders given a position like this represented their communities at a social level but played the role more politically to protect their welfare, business and education programs.

By this time Siauw was convinced that the Japanese would lose the war and that the Indonesians should get themselves ready for an armed movement to achieve independence. He also believed that the Chinese would benefit from independence. He therefore urged his close peranakan associates to actively take part in the independence movement. He also had secret contacts with leaders of paramilitary units whose members were mainly Indigenous Indonesians – the Seinendan (Youth Corps) and Keibodan (Vigilance Corps) – to ensure that coordination work between the Chinese and Indonesian units could develop in the event of armed uprising, either against the Japanese or the Dutch if they attempted to return.

When independence was imminent in 1945, Siauw, together with Tan Ling Djie, Tjoa Sik Ien and Liem Koen Hian, helped formulate a position reflecting the concerns of the Chinese in Indonesia in the new independent state. This formulation was then presented by Liem Koen Hian in the famous meeting of the Panitia Persiapan Kemerdekaan Indonesia (Preparatory Committee for Indonesian Independence) on 1 June 1945, the birth date of Pancasila.

Siauw's activities in the first few years after independence were devoted to convincing the Chinese in Indonesia to support the newly established republic against the efforts of the Dutch to re-establish their control. That was an uphill battle. Following racial violence against the Chinese in late 1945 and early 1946, the number of peranakans who supported Indonesian nationalism declined dramatically. Most peranakans believed that they would be better off if the Dutch administration was fully restored. Siauw worked hard to restore their confidence in the new republic by indicating that, while racial outbreaks were to be condemned, they represented unfortunate excesses of revolution and would accordingly end with the consolidation of independence. However, this remained a minority opinion within the peranakan community.

In December 1945 Siauw decided to join the party that was in control of the government, the Partai Sosialis. Its leaders then included two men he greatly respected, Amir Sjarifuddin and Tan Ling Djie. He was quickly given a leadership position, being charged with the coordination of youth movements and the dissemination of the party's political programs.

Siauw's political activities during the Japanese occupation and in the first few months after independence resulted in him being known and respected by many Indigenous leaders including Soekarno. The young government needed to have effective representation from the Chinese community so that support for the republic could be mobilised and, in April 1946, Soekarno appointed Siauw as a member of the KNIP, the Republic's new legislative body. In 1947, he was elected by the KNIP to become a member of its Badan Pekerja, as the only Chinese representative.

In July 1947 Prime Minister Amir Sjarifudin appointed Siauw as minister for minority affairs. Very soon after his appointment as minister, the Dutch launched a major attack on the republic and occupying major towns in West and East Java. In fighting against the Dutch, the Indonesian armed units treated the Chinese badly. Many of the Chinese were forced to leave their homes and were detained in concentration camps and their houses and property were looted. Siauw, assisted by close friends like Soemarsono and

Mustopo who were in command of Indonesian military units, was able to get most of the detained peranakans released quickly. He organised temporary accommodation for them in Chinese schools and buildings owned by Chinese associations.

Although the Chinese victims had reason to be grateful to Siauw for what he did in saving their lives and property, they remained resentful towards the people who had caused them such harm. Many ridiculed Siauw for being blindly loyal to the republic when he urged them to treat those who had fought against the Dutch as their local brothers and sisters.

With the demise of Amir's cabinet in 1948, Siauw joined the newly formed opposition group, the FDR, led by Amir. Upon Musso's return to Indonesia later in 1948, the FDR, of which the Partai Sosialis was part, was transformed into the larger PKI under the leadership of Musso and Tan Ling Djie. With the disappearance of the Partai Sosialis, Siauw decided to continue his parliamentary role without being a member of any political party.

Following the Madiun Affair in September 1948, which gave the Hatta government a pretext for crushing the PKI and its affiliated organisations, Siauw was arrested, along with thousands of others. He was sent to the Wirogunan prison in Yogyakarta. This imprisonment was cut short by the Dutch capture of Yogyakarta in December 1948. However, within days of this, Siauw was recaptured by the Dutch and was jailed in the same prison. The times spent at the Wirogunan consolidated Siauw's relationship with influential politicians who were to play important roles in future governments. Among those imprisoned by the Dutch with Siauw were Yamin, Iwa Kusumasumantri, Aruji Kartawinata, Anwar Tjokroaminoto and Wilopo. Yamin and Iwa Kusumasumantri were leaders oriented to the 'national communist' political party, the Partai Murba. Aruji Kartawinata and Anwar Tjokroaminoto were leaders of the PSII and Wilopo was a leader of the PNI. Good relationships with these people contributed to Siauw's political achievements in the 1950s and 60s.

Minimising racial discrimination

The political experiences he gained and personal contacts he established during the revolution years enabled Siauw to be much more effective in his parliamentary career in the 1950s. During the period of parliamentary democracy, Siauw was one of the most prominent and respected peranakan parliamentarians. He was chairman of the Fraksi Nasional Progresif, a fairly influential faction involving small political parties and individuals.

Perhaps the key thing about Siauw's politics was that he was an eclectic figure, a man who could relate well to a large number of people. Most of these people were leftists but there were also quite a few people on the right of politics, like Tambunan of the Christian Party, Kasimo of the Partai Katolik and Zainul Arifin of the NU.

His main achievements in this period were related to the containment of racially discriminatory measures introduced by ministers in various cabinets. Racial discrimination in the 1950s was closely linked to the rising number of Indigenous politicians who became interested in being involved in lucrative businesses, many of which had been run by the Chinese in the colonial period. In the name of building a national economy, those in power and those who had connections to power were keen to introduce and implement measures which involved displacing Chinese businessmen from a number of business sectors. In combating these trends, Siauw was able to rely on his faction members and others so that many of the measures were either dropped or their impact minimised.

To Siauw, building a national economy meant undoing the colonial economic structure and making effective use of domestic capital. He argued for developing the country's production capacities and taking over management of ventures dominated by multinational corporations. He also stressed that all Indonesian citizens should be treated equally.

One important consequence of Siauw's success in containing the discriminatory measures was to increase the determination of some influential government leaders to make as many Chinese in Indonesia as possible into foreigners. Citizenship bills were prepared in 1953 to nullify the earlier citizenship laws which had made most Indonesia-born Chinese Indonesian citizens.

Up to this point, Siauw was not affiliated to any political organisation. A number of peranakan political organisations existed but they were ineffective. Their leaders were mostly Dutch-educated peranakans who had not fully supported the republic during the revolution years. Some of them had been actively pro-Dutch. Because of this, leaders of the government and political parties did not trust or respect them. Under such circumstances, they could not effectively represent and defend the interests of the peranakan community.

In this situation, Siauw Giok Tjhan's credentials as a long-time supporter of Indonesian nationalism acquired a new relevance. Leaders of the peranakan organisations concluded that Siauw was the most suitable person to represent the peranakan community and lead a new organisation to combat racism and resolve the citizenship issues.

The efforts of these leaders led, in 1954, to the formation of Baperki with Siauw elected as its general chairman. Within a short period of time, Baperki became the largest and best-mobilised organisation in the history of the Indonesian Chinese. Widespread support from the peranakan community for Baperki was reflected in the results of the general elections for parliament and the Konstituante in 1955. About 70 per cent of the peranakan vote went to Baperki.

One of Siauw's most important contributions, and perhaps his most important political legacy, was concerned with Indonesian citizenship. Without Siauw and Baperki, many of the Chinese in Indonesia would not be Indonesian citizens.

Siauw's political manoeuvering in the 1950s brought about, in 1955, the signing of the Dual Nationality Agreement by the governments of Indonesia and China and this significantly reduced the numbers of Chinese who lost Indonesian citizenship. Siauw was able to convince both Prime Minister Ali Sastroamidjojo and Premier Chou En Lai to alter the agreement so that only a limited number of Chinese in Indonesia were denied the opportunity to enjoy Indonesian citizenship. The final citizenship law passed by parliament in 1958 contained provisions for which Siauw had fought for many years and achieved a compromise with those who wished to make many Chinese in Indonesia become foreigners.

Like the THHK in the colonial period, Baperki was involved in providing education, but on a much bigger scale. Baperki's education programs spanned kindergarten to the tertiary level. More than 100 000 Chinese students were accommodated in Baperki's schools. Unlike the THHK, which had propagated Chinese nationalism in its schools, Baperki schools promoted Indonesian nationalism.

The most important aspect of Siauw's solution to the problems faced by ethnic minorities was the way the Chinese in Indonesia were to be integrated into the Indonesian society. Siauw believed that the most effective way of minimising racial disturbances and racial prejudices was for the minority groups to integrate both socially and politically into the majority world. He argued that if the Chinese were integrated into Indonesian society, their aspirations would be the same as those of the majority of the Indonesians. But he believed that such integration should be achieved in a way that avoided forcing people to deny their cultural heritage.

From the late 1950s, Siauw argued that the Chinese in Indonesia should be treated as one of the sukus (ethnic groups) of Indonesia. Knowing that he did not have a strong case to defend this assertion, he continued to use the word sukus in his speeches and numerous discussions. To him, accepting the peranakans as one of the sukus would strongly justify his integration solution.

Siauw's view was challenged by a number of young peranakans, mainly Catholic, who in 1962 formed the LPKB. This group advocated a solution based on assimilation. They argued that if the Chinese of Indonesian citizenship continued to identify themselves with alien Chinese and China, the prejudices of Indigenous Indonesians against them would prevail. They believed that to gain acceptance in Indonesian society, the peranakans should cease to be culturally different and should disassociate themselves from Chinese traditions. Some of them opted to change their own names to Indonesian-sounding names and asked other Chinese to follow their example. They also suggested that the Chinese should become more positive about intermarriage between themselves and Indigenous Indonesians.

In a situation of increasingly sharp polarisation between right and left, the LKPB leaders depicted Siauw's solution to the minority problem as being the same as that of the communists, and encouraged the peranakans to disassociate themselves from it. The political orientation of the LPKB also appealed to right-wing elements of the peranakan population.

In 1959, the parliamentary democracy period was succeeded by a new period which was known as the Guided Democracy period. Under the 1945 constitution, re-promulgated by presidential decree in July 1959, parliament ceased to have control over government actions and the president became the most powerful agent in the country. For Siauw, this dramatic change created problems of principle.

Although Siauw highly valued the implementation of parliamentary democracy, he was concerned about the frequent changes of government, which had resulted in delays in passing various important bills, and in the use of ministerial regulations which ignored articles of the constitution. These negative outcomes that resulted from the parliamentary system led to Siauw being one of the first politicians to support Soekarno's move to kill off parliamentary democracy when the idea was first introduced in 1957.

Siauw's reasons for supporting the concept of Guided Democracy were partly based on his conviction that Soekarno was impressed by the models developed in China and the USSR. As a Marxist and socialist, Siauw was sympathetic to the systems established in these two countries. He hoped that Soekarno's new system would accelerate the achievement of a solution to the problems facing minority groups.

Siauw's close relationship to Soekarno was further consolidated in the Guided Democracy period. This helped him to forestall and countervail various racially discriminatory measures. Siauw was able to play major roles in formulating government guidelines and regulations relating to Chinese matters. This situation, coupled with Soekarno's good relationship with leaders of the Peoples' Republic of China, gave considerable protection to the Chinese in Indonesia.

But Siauw was not entirely happy with the situation. He resented the way in which the Soekarno regime betrayed democratic values and destroyed the economy. Although he was careful not to directly criticise Soekarno, his messages against the violations of human rights, economic conventions and democratic values were loud and clear. However, for the survival of the Chinese in Indonesia, Siauw continued to publicly support Soekarno and his regime.

Siauw's role as a peranakan leader dramatically changed in this period. In the parliamentary democracy period, Siauw gained a lot of mileage from legal arguments that Indonesia would be flouting international conventions if it allowed racism to prevail. In the Guided Democracy period, his effectiveness was more to do with his success in changing the attitude and behaviour of many Chinese. He encouraged a large number of Chinese in Indonesia to participate in politics and regard Indonesia as their motherland as well as bringing the Chinese community to a position of alignment with Soekarno after 1963. It was a conscious decision to belong to the left-wing political camp in the country. In this period, Siauw also encouraged Baperki to be an effective educational institution, providing a comprehensive education platform for the Chinese.

In the Guided Democracy period the country's politics were highly polarised. On the one hand, the Muslim and Christian political parties, supported by leaders of the army, represented the right-wing political camp. On the other hand, the PKI, supported by its affiliated mass organisations and nationalistic political parties, represented the left-wing camp. President Soekarno initially acted as a balancer between these two forces but from 1963 was inclined to support the left-wing forces.

With the events of 1 October 1965 – the attempt of the so-called G30S movement to install a revolutionary government and its defeat by Major General Soeharto – the balance of power which Soekarno was able to maintain throughout the Guided Democracy period collapsed. Under the leadership of General Soeharto, the army, supported by right-wing political parties and student movements, quickly crushed the PKI and members of the left-wing forces. Soekarno himself finally became the target of Soeharto-led activities and was virtually removed from the presidency on 11 March 1966.

When Soekarno's regime collapsed and the right-wing groups took over power in October 1965, Siauw and Baperki were exposed to attacks and left without effective defenders. Baperki was branded as the financier of the PKI. Within weeks, its schools were taken over by the government and its university buildings were burnt down by army-backed demonstrators. Baperki's branches were dismantled and many of its members were arrested or purged. Siauw's desperate attempts to save the organisation failed. He himself was arrested on 4 November 1965 and jailed for the next 12 years. Baperki was banned on 12 March 1966.

A long-term struggle

Throughout his political career, Siauw had to deal with two major obstacles, the nature and patterns of which varied according to both the Indonesian and the international political environments. The first obstacle was that of a major political school of thought which saw discrimination against the Chinese as necessary to achieve its political and economic goals. During the revolution, leaders of the Pemuda groups (organised armed Indonesian youths looking to achieve and maintain independence) saw the Chinese as allies of the Dutch and treated them as enemies. They also targeted the Chinese in their attempts to defend independence. The political mainstream became strongly anti-Chinese when most parties embraced the politics of Indonesianisation in the 1950s. The strength of these schools of thought declined during the Guided Democracy period, especially after Soekarno turned to the People's Republic of China for financial and other assistance in the later part of the period.

Siauw's other obstacle concerned the responses of the Chinese communities to the various political actions and measures which were directed towards them. During the revolutionary period, Siauw encountered reluctance from the Chinese communities to support the newly formed republic because they had been subjected to harsh treatment by the Pemuda units and they saw China or the Netherlands as more reliable forces to associate with. Such resistance to the republic declined when it became obvious that the Dutch would no longer rule Indonesia and that China was not going to become an international power. Chinese communities increased their support for Siauw and his policies after Baperki was formed, especially during the Guided Democracy period when Baperki effectively defended the Chinese and provided high quality and accessible education. Still, Siauw had be careful to maintain Baperki's independence from the PKI to avoid creating anxieties among apolitical Chinese.

Siauw always had to juggle his priorities and objectives. Whenever the position of the Chinese minority was threatened by actions and policies of governments and parties he was always ready to oppose them, even if this required compromising his own political principles. His opposition to the PKI's calls to liquidate private enterprises in the early 1950s and his acceptance of Soekarno's Guided Democracy reflected the conflicts between the interests of the Chinese and his own principles.

Despite these difficulties, Siauw became one of the most successful Chinese leaders in Indonesia and managed to achieve some outstanding results. A key factor that made Siauw such an effective leader for the Chinese community was clearly his upbringing and educational background. Siauw was brought up by three strong personalities. His father, a Westernised peranakan, enrolled him at prestigious Dutch schools. His maternal grandfather, a China-oriented totok and a businessman, however, wanted him to maintain a strong Chinese identity. His mother introduced him to Indonesian customs practised by many peranakan women in the 1920s. Such a background enabled Siauw to relate well to the totok as well as peranakan communities. Though primarily a peranakan, he was at ease with leaders of the totok communities and was always able to secure financial contributions for his organisational projects. Siauw's admiration of Mao's China brought him closer to China-oriented totoks. This relationship enabled him to attract the totoks to participate as leaders in Baperki's activities.

Another factor that helped Siauw was the personal capital he brought to his role as a political leader in Jakarta in the 1950s and 1960s. This included his circle of close associates from the groups he established in Semarang, Surabaya and Malang, his ability to call on financial support from a range of businessmen and his many friendships with Asli (Indigenous) politicians of a wide range of positions – especially those friendships formed during his periods in the Badan Pekerja and while in Wirogunan prison.

Siauw also faced a number of obstacles that forced him into actions inconsistent with some of his principles. His commitment to the agreement he made, in 1945, with former leaders of the PTI to not form a communal organisation resulted in him joining the Partai Sosialis in the same year. But as the Chinese problem escalated and the Partai Sosialis was absorbed into the larger PKI in 1948, Siauw decided to leave the party. He was disillusioned by the fact that as a member of a political party he would be constrained by party discipline which could be in conflict with minority interests.

Siauw remained an independent member of parliament until a group of peranakan leaders invited him to join them in forming a mass organisation in 1954. It had been intended that this be a Chinese organisation, but Siauw was able to convince the founders to call it Baperki, a name which did not incorporate any reference to the Chinese. He was elected as chairman and had every intention of making Baperki a national organisation that involved and embraced Asli individuals. This was demonstrated by the appointment of his Asli parliamentarian colleagues to head the organisation's Jakarta branch.

However, as the organisation was pre-occupied with the defence of Chinese interests – fighting against racial discrimination and settling issues associated with citizenship and dual nationality in their favour – most Baperki members were Chinese. The organisation's decision to represent the Chinese in the 1955 and 1957 elections further confirmed Baperki's existence as a Chinese organisation and Siauw as a leader of the Chinese community. Baperki quickly grew because of support from the Chinese communities and, in return, Baperki provided effective solutions to problems in the spheres of Indonesian citizenship, economic protection and education. Such services were made possible by Baperki's leaders' effective involvement in government, educational and cultural institutions as well as newspapers.

However, under Siauw, Baperki differed from other Chinese organisations because Baperki's political orientation was clearly towards Indonesia. One of the organisation's aims was to make as many as possible of the Indonesian Chinese into Indonesian citizens. More importantly, it also encouraged the Indonesian Chinese to treat Indonesia as their home.

The organisation however had two major weaknesses. Firstly, it remained a Chinese organisation. No matter how useful its major political and economic programs were to the country, they were seen as a means to defend the interests of the Chinese minority rather than the nation as a whole. Secondly, the political polarisation in the later part of the Guided Democracy period forced Siauw to abandon his unaligned political position and associate himself and Baperki with Soekarno's political direction. This positioned Siauw and Baperki, as elements of the left camp, directly against the army and anti-communist forces.

Siauw's support for Soekarno and Guided Democracy was based on a number of factors. Firstly, Siauw viewed Soekarno as a fellow socialist who was committed to the creation of socialism à la Indonesia. Siauw viewed Soekarno's accommodation of policies and parties of right-wing political orientation, before September 1963, as primarily tactical moves. My discussions with Siauw in 1980 and his writings on Soekarno suggest that Siauw did not share the view of Western scholars who saw Soekarno as a conservative figure who was primarily motivated by maintaining power, who sought to protect his own position by using Nasakom as a mere tactical device.

Siauw was convinced that Soekarno's decision to ally himself with the PKI and left-wing forces domestically and to align Indonesia with communist countries was motivated by his desire to expedite the achievement of socialism. When looking back on the pre-1965 period in later years, Siauw remained convinced that 'socialism à la Indonesia' could have been achieved if the imperialist forces of the world and their local partners had not opposed and defeated the attempt.

Siauw's interpretation was like that of Hauswedell:

> It seems to me that we have placed Soekarno too much among the elite and too little among the masses. His decided shift to the left in the late period of Guided Democracy represents a conscious shift to a new social reference group. There was a conflict rising between him and the rest of the elite who wanted to sabotage the leftist interpretation of the revolution. Soekarno seemed intent on cutting the umbilical cord to the 'hypocritical' and 'reactionary' leaders who used revolutionary vocabulary merely for self-enrichment. He tried to live up to his claim to be a social revolutionist in addition to being an anti-imperialist, and attempted to establish his revolutionary-progressive credentials and a distinctively new social identity.[1]

Secondly, Siauw could rely on Soekarno's protection for the position of the Chinese in general and Baperki in particular. Siauw had direct access to Soekarno and was able to convince Soekarno to state various formulations in his speeches which defended the position of the Chinese. Baperki's economic policies for using Chinese capital (of both aliens and Indonesian citizens), which were articulated by Siauw, were included in Soekarno's

---

[1] Peter Christian Hauswedell, 'Soekarno, Radical or Conservative? Indonesian Politics 1964–5', *Indonesia*, Cornell University, December 1972, p. 113.

speeches and his political manifesto. These policies were also included in governmental guidelines introduced between 1960 and 1965 by the MPRS.

Moreover, Siauw was able to capitalise on the closeness of Soekarno to the People's Republic of China after 1963 to achieve more concessions and protection for the Chinese. But Siauw's closeness to Soekarno, the PKI and the People's Republic of China had created concerns among some peranakans.

When Soekarno's regime collapsed and right-wing groups took over power in October 1965, Siauw and Baperki were exposed to attacks and left without effective defenders. This quickly led to their demise.

The aftermath of the abortive coup of October 1965 was extremely harsh for a large section of the Chinese community and especially for people associated with Baperki. Anti-Chinese feelings were promoted by the new military regime. Because the People's Republic of China was accused of being involved in supporting the G30S movement, the Indonesian Chinese became targets of the anti-communist movement led by General Soeharto. By early 1966, Baperki was totally dissolved. Many of its leaders were arrested and some were kept in jail for many years. A large number of its members lost their jobs as a result of the administrative purges. Many who were also members of the PKI were victims of the massacres which took place between October 1965 and 1968.

To what extent Siauw was responsible for the destruction of Baperki and the suffering of its members and the Chinese community in general continues to be controversial.

The LPKB leaders and others like Yap Thiam Hien often blamed Siauw for the destruction of Baperki in October and November 1965. They argued that Siauw's political stance and his decision to ally Baperki with Soekarno and the PKI were the main reasons for the demise of Baperki and the suffering of the Chinese.

Siauw himself was burdened by the situation in which Baperki was destroyed and the Chinese were attacked by anti-communist forces. In the interrogations, he consistently stated that he alone was responsible for the formulation of Baperki's policies and for the decision to ally the organisation with Soekarno. When he was about to be released from prison, he indicated to the authorities that other members of Baperki should also be released with him. On the very day in September 1975 that he was discharged into house arrest from the Salemba prison, Siauw urged the head of the prison to change the status of his closest associates who were also at

Salemba, Lie Tjwan Sien and Phoa Thoan Hian, to the extent that his discharge was delayed by more than five hours.

When Oei Tjoe Tat, one of Baperki's vice-chairmen and a former state minister in Sukarno's last cabinet, was brought to trial in 1976, Siauw wrote to me in the July of that year and said, '...I have to help Oei Tjoe Tat to be released as soon as possible. No matter what, I am responsible for the suffering he has to endure. It is not right for Oei to remain in prison...'. Siauw then helped Oei prepare his defence speech delivered in court.

There is no doubt that Siauw's political strategy during the Guided Democracy period of staying close to President Soekarno was risky, and the risk grew greater in 1963 when Soekarno moved into closer cooperation with the PKI and the People's Republic of China. If the largest Chinese community organisation in the country had been led by people of anti-communist outlook, the organisation arguably might not have been hit as hard by the army backlash against Soekarno and his left-wing allies.

Siauw himself remained convinced that he had no choice but to go down Soekarno's political path. In order to be effective in gaining concessions for Baperki and the Chinese, Siauw said, Baperki had to be closely associated with Soekarno during the period of Guided Democracy. He further argued that even if Baperki had not been close to Soekarno, the manifestation of Soeharto's anti-communist and anti-Chinese movements would still have crushed the organisation.

But it should at least be said in Siauw's defence that he persistently kept good relations with leaders of various non-communist parties, including the Partai Murba and PSII, and that he fought hard for Baperki's autonomy at a time when PKI members of the organisation were trying to push it towards fuller alignment with the PKI.

It is even more difficult to measure how relevant Siauw's policies were to the pogroms experienced by the Chinese in the immediate aftermath of the abortive coup. It was clear that there were powerful international forces at work, most importantly the China-containment policy of the USA, which greatly influenced Soeharto's military and political strategies. These, arguably, had much greater impact on the treatment of the Chinese than Siauw's policies and his affiliation with Soekarno and the left-wing forces.

What Siauw left behind was a possible solution to the problems faced by minority groups in Indonesia: the integration solution which encourages the Chinese in Indonesia to be treated as members of the 'Suku Tionghoa' (Chinese ethnic group) and be integrated harmoniously into the Indonesian nation without having to forfeit their cultural heritage and ethnic identity. Siauw argued that if Soekarno succeeded in creating socialism à la Indonesia, integration would take place and racial prejudice would be eliminated from Indonesia. The effectiveness of such a solution is yet to be tested.

The fall of Soeharto in May 1998 brought about a dramatic change to Indonesia's political situation. The new era Indonesia has entered provides an opportunity for Siauw's proposed solution to be tested. The post-Soeharto era has witnessed more freedom of expression and this has encouraged people to discuss issues and matters which had been considered taboo for more than 32 years. Many people can now discuss Baperki and its activities more objectively, and freely assess how Siauw contributed to resolving ethnic minorities' problems in Indonesia. I am also aware of a group of peranakans who are attempting to establish a political organisation whose platforms would be similar to those of Baperki.

I agree with Coppel's argument that the Chinese could never determine their own fate; that external influences involving political stability in Indonesia, policies the government has adopted toward the Chinese minority and the nature of relations with China play an overpowering role, and that total political association with forces in power is dangerous. However, the absence of effective political representation in executive and legislative bodies, and the lack of a mass organisation which can effectively voice Chinese interests – as was the case for 32 years – left the Chinese totally unprotected and vulnerable to political and racial attacks. This suggests that there must be effective representation of the Chinese in the highest level of legislative and executive bodies. There must also be organisations capable of representing the interests of the Chinese in various political arenas. In the interests of community security however, such organisations, should maintain political neutrality.

After Soeharto's downfall in May 1998, the political atmosphere in Indonesia dramatically changed. Numerous Chinese organisations were established in that year; most prominent of all were the two organisations, Persatuan Marga Tionghoa Seluruh Indonesia (PMTSI – Association of Chinese Clans of Indonesia) and Perhimpunan Indonesia Tionghoa (INTI – Chinese Indonesia Association), established in Jakarta in 1998 and 1999 respectively.

Interestingly the people who instigated the formation of many of the Chinese-based organisations were people who went to Baperki's schools and university. It seems apparent that political training as part of their education played a major part. Benny Setiono, Tan Swie Ling and Nancy

Wijaya were among the prominent public figures who attended Baperki's educational institutions.

It is equally interesting to note that the Chinese who were part of the Catholic youth organisations, notably PMKRI (Persatuan Mahasiswa Katolik Republik Indonesia – Association of Catholic Students of Republic of Indonesia) were able to work with those of Baperki in leading the organisations.

The racial riots of May 1998 were seen by many who supported the assimilation concept as manifestations of the concept's failure. Those Chinese who were victims of the mass attacks had changed their names from Chinese names to non-Chinese names. Some had in fact become Muslims.

Many also observed that the adoption of the assimilation concept by the Soeharto Government had resulted in the introduction and implementation of anti-Chinese policies. Most resented of all were the prohibition of public Chinese New Year celebrations, the use of Chinese languages in public and the restrictions of Chinese in government universities and government institutions.

By the early 2000s what was advocated by Siauw and Baperki appeared to have received widespread support. More so as developed nations like the USA, Australia and Canada formally endorsed multiculturalism which offers the same basis as that of integration.

Abdurrahman Wahid's presidency from 1999 to 2002 established a welcoming path to the integrationists. His pluralism was continued during the presidencies of Megawati, Susili Bambang Yudhoyono and Joko Widodo.

What Siauw and Baperki fiercely fought for, the outlawing of racism, was achieved in the presidencies above. The 1945 Constitution has been amended to the extent that the president of Indonesia can now be a non-Asli Indonesian. This was one of the concerns that Siauw had as the old article gave justification for the continuing differentiation between Indigenous and non-Indigenous Indonesians, which to him was destructive to nation building.

Siauw was right. The elimination of racism was indeed conducive to nation building. Many Chinese, particularly those of the younger generation today have no qualms in treating Indonesia as their homeland. Many Chinese are involved in politics and social organisations. As encouraged by Baperki in the 1960s, many are actively involved in politics, most notably the former Jakarta governor, Ahok.

In view of recent developments in Indonesia, I believe that the study of Siauw's ideas and experiences gain new relevance to contemporary

Indonesia. While the Chinese today no longer face legal discrimination, one can argue that racism and anti-Chinese feelings remain in existence in social circles. The upheavals against Governor Ahok reflect anti-Chinese sentiments which are manifestations of the situation Siauw maintained would take generations to achieve: '…menghilangkan rasialisme adalah sebuah perjuangan yang akan memakan waktu panjang…' (the elimination of racism is a long-term struggle).

GLOSSARY

'abdi negara'	'servants of the state' (Siauw Giok Tjhan proposed that this term be used to replace the term 'pemerintah', which literally means people who give orders and instructions)
Acoma	Angkatan Communis Muda – Communist Youth League
AMT	Angkatan Muda Tionghoa – Chinese Youth Movement (established by Siauw Giok Tjhan in Malang in 1945)
Asli	the term used to describe Indigenous Indonesians
Badan Pekerja	Working Committee of the Central National Committee of Indonesia or KNIP (functioned as the parliament during the revolution)
Baperki	Badan Permusyawaratan Kewarganegaraan Indonesia – Consultative Body For Indonesian Citizenship
Baperwatt	Badan Permusyawaratan Warga Negara Turunan Tionghoa – Consultative Body of Citizens of Chinese Descent (the name initially proposed by the founding members of Baperki)
'berdikari'	'self-reliance' (a popular term during the Guided Democracy period, derived from one of Soekarno's speeches in 1963)
Berita Baperki	Baperki's monthly bulletin
BFO	Bijeenkomst voor Federaal Overleg – Federal Consultative Assembly (Dutch controlled administration)
Bhineka Tunggal Ika	the Indonesian national motto (meaning 'unity in diversity')
Bintang Merah	*Red Star*, journal published by the Indonesian Communist Party (PKI)
BKPRI	Badan Kongres Pemuda Republik Indonesia – Congress of the Organisation of Youth of the Republic of Indonesia
BKR	Badan Keamanan Rakyat – Body for People's Security
Boen Bio	Confucian Temple in Surabaya

BPKI	Panitia Persiapan Kemerdekaan Indonesia – Preparatory Committee for Indonesian Independence
BPRI	Barisan Pembrontak Rakyat Indonesia – Insurgent Corps of the Indonesian People
BPS	Badan Pendukung Soekarnoisme – Body for Upholding Soekarnoism
BTI	Barisan Tani Indonesia – Indonesian Peasant Front
Cap Go Meh	the 15th day after the Chinese New Year
CGMI	Central Gerakan Mahasiswa Indonesia – Central Movement of Indonesian Students
CHHN	Chung Hua Hui Netherlands – Chinese Association Netherlands
CHTH	Chung Hua Tsung Hui – Chinese General Association
Chung Hua Hui	Chinese Association (a political party)
Conefo	Conference of the New Emerging Forces
cukong	financier (the term used to describe rich Chinese businessmen)
Cungkup	a holy Muslim grave
dasar negara	state philosophy
Depernas	Dewan Perancang Nasional – National Planning Agency
Dewan Mahasiswa	Student Councils
Dewan Nasional	National Council
DPA	Dewan Pertimbangan Agung – Supreme Advisory Council
DPR	Dewan Perwakilan Rakyat – Parliament
DPRGR	Dewan Perwakilan Rakyat Gotong Royong – Mutual Assistance Parliament
DPRS	Dewan Perwakilan Rakyat Sementara – Provisional People's Representative Council
ELS	Europese Lagere School – European Elementary School

Glossary

FDR	Front Demokrasi Rakyat – People's Democratic Front
Fraksi Nasional Progresif	National Progressive Faction (a faction led by Siauw Giok Tjhan during the Parliamentary Democracy period)
Front Nasional	National Front (a body, headed by Soekarno, set up to mobilise the masses and to propagate Soekarno's political ideology)
G30S	Gerakan 30 September – 30th September Movement
Gerindo	Gerakan Rakyat Indonesia – Indonesian People's Movement
Gerwani	Gerakan Wanita Indonesia – Indonesian Women's Movement
GIKI	Gabungan Indo untuk Kesatuan Indonesia – Association of Indo-Europeans for Indonesian Unity
Golongan Tani	Peasant Group
Hari Sumpah Pemuda	Youth Pledge Day
Harian Rakyat	*People's Daily* (a paper that Siauw Giok Tjan established in 1951 and directed until it was sold to the PKI in 1953)
HBS	Hogere Burgerschool – Dutch Secondary School
HCS	Hollandsch Chineesche School – Dutch Chinese School
HCTNH	Hua Chiao Tsing Nien Hui – Chinese Youth Organisation (associated with the THHK)
HMI	Himpunan Mahasiswa Islam – Muslim Students' Association
Hua Chiao Tsung Hui	Overseas Chinese Federation (formed by the Japanese during the occupation)
Indische Partij	Indies Party
IPKI	Partai Ikatan Pendukung Kemerdekaan Indonesia – League of Supporters of Indonesian Independence
IPPI	Ikatan Pemuda Pelajar Indonesia – Association of Indonesian Students and Youth, an association for secondary school students
Kabupaten	Regencies

Kakyo Shokai	Overseas Chinese Federation or Hua Chiao Tsung Hui (formed by the Japanese during the occupation)
Kebotai	Chinese Vigilance Corps (a Chinese militia set up by the Japanese during the occupation)
Keibodan	Vigilance Corps
KNIP	Komite Nasional Indonesia Pusat – Central Indonesian National Committee
Konstituante	Constituent Assembly
Kotoe	Komando Tertinggi Operasi Ekonomi – Supreme Command of Economic Operations
Kun Chan Tang	Chinese Communist Party
Kuo Min Tang	Chinese Nationalist Party
Kuo Yu	National Language – Mandarin
Lekra	Lembaga Kebudayaan Rakyat – Institute of People's Culture
Lima Jaman	*Five Periods*, Siauw Giok Tjhan's memoir
LPKB	Lembaga Pembina Kesatuan Bangsa – Institute for the Promotion of National Unity
'Maju terus, pantang mundur'	'Ever onward, never retreat' (a popular slogan during the Guided Democracy period)
Manipol USDEK	Political manifesto based on five major themes, the 1945 Constitution (Undang-Undang Dasar 1945), Indonesian socialism (Sosialisme a la Indonesia), Guided Democracy (Demokrasi Terpimpin), Guided Economy (Ekonomi Terpimpin) and Indonesian identity (Kepribadian Indonesia) – USDEK
Mata Hari	*The Sun*, daily newspaper in Semarang
MPR	Majelis Permusyawaratan Rakyat – People's Consultative Assembly
MPRS	Majelis Permusyawaratan Rakyat Sementara – Provisional People's Consultative Assembly
mufakat	consensus (the term often used in achieving resolutions)

Glossary

MULO	Meer Uitgebreid Lager Onderwijs – Dutch Junior Secondary School
musyawarah	deliberations
Nasakom	Nasional Agama Komunis – Union of Nationalists, Religious groups and Communists developed by Soekarno
Naspro	another name for the Fraksi Nasional Progresif – National Progressive Faction (a faction led by Siauw Giok Tjhan during the Parliamentary Democracy period)
negara boneka	puppet states
Nirbaya	a camp specially established in 1966 to detain former ministers and senior military officers, located in Jakarta
NU	Nahdatul Ulama – Religious Scholars League
PAI	Partai Arab Indonesia – Indonesian Arab Party
Palang Biru	Blue Cross, an organisation established by Siauw Giok Tjhan in Malang in 1945 to assist the Red Cross
Panitia Permusyawaratan	Consultative Committee (a working committee of the parliament in 1950)
Panitia Rumah Tangga	Management Committee (a working committee of the parliament in 1950)
Paras	Partai Rakyat Sosialis – Socialist People's Party
Parkindo	Partai Kristen Indonesia – Indonesian Christian Party
Parsi	Partai Sosialis Indonesia (or PSI) – Indonesian Socialist Party
Partai Buruh	Labour Party
Partai Murba	A 'national communist' political party
Partai Rakyat Jelata	Party for Poor People
Partai Sosialis	Socialist Party (formed by the fusion of the PSI and PARAS)
Partindo	Partai Indonesia – Indonesian Party
PBI	Partai Bangsa Indonesia – Indonesian Nation Party

PDTI	Partai Demokrat Tionghoa Indonesia – Party of Indonesian Chinese Democrats (formerly the PT)
pecinan	Chinese quarter (area established by the Dutch specifically for the Chinese)
Pedoman Baru	New Guidelines Bill (regulations introduced by Djuanda in the 1950s)
pegawai negeri	state officers
Pemuda Rakyat	People's Youth
peranakan Chinese	an Indonesia-born Chinese of mixed ancestry
Perdi	Persatuan Djurnalis Indonesia – Indonesian Journalists' Association
Perhimi	Perhimpunan Mahasiswa Indonesia – Association of Indonesian Students
Persatuan	Unity, the name of the printing company led by Siauw Giok Tjhan in the 1950s
Persatuan Marhaen Indonesia	Union of Indonesian Marhaens
Persatuan Perjuangan	Union of Struggle
Perti	Perhimpunan Tarbiyah Islamiyah – Islamic Educators Association
Pertip	Perserikatan Tionghoa Peranakan – Union of Indonesian Chinese
Perwanit	Persatuan Warganegara Indonesia Tionghoa – Union of Chinese of Indonesian Citizenship
Perwari	Persatuan Wanita Republik Indonesia – Union of Indonesian Women
Perwitt	Persatuan Warga Indonesia Turunan Tionghoa – Union of Indonesian Citizens of Chinese Descent
Pesindo	Pemuda Sosialis Indonesia – Indonesian Socialist Youth

Glossary

Peta	Pembela Tanah Air – Defenders of the Motherland
Pewarta Surabaya	*Surabaya News*, daily newspaper in Surabaya
PI	Perhimpunan Indonesia – Indonesian Association
PIR	Persatuan Indonesia Raya – Greater Indonesian Union
PKI	Partai Komunis Indonesia – Indonesian Communist Party
PKR	Partai Kedaulatan Rakyat – People Sovereignty Party
PMKRI	Persatuan Mahasiswa Katolik Republik Indonesia – Association of Indonesian Catholic Students
PNI	Partai Nasional Indonesia – Indonesian National Party
PP-10	Peraturan Presiden 10 – Presidential Regulation no. 10 (introduced in November 1959 and banned aliens from retail trade in rural areas)
PPI	Permusyawaratan Pemuda Indonesia – Consultative Body of Indonesian Youths (Baperki's Youth Organisation)
PPKKR	Panitia Penolong Korban Kontra Revolusi – Committee of Helpers of the Victims of the Counter-Revolutionaries
PRN	Partai Rakyat Nasional – National People's Party
PRRI	Pemerintah Revolusioner Republik Indonesia – Indonesian Revolutionary Government
PSI	Partai Sosialis Indonesia (or Parsi) – Indonesian Socialist Party
PSII	Partai Serikat Islam Indonesia – Islamic Association Party of Indonesia
PT	Persatuan Tionghoa – Chinese Union Party (became the PDTI in 1950)
PTI	Partai Tionghoa Indonesia – Indonesian Chinese Party
Putera	Pusat Tenaga Rakyat – Centre of People's Power
PWI	Persatuan Wartawan Indonesia – Association of Indonesian Journalists

Resopim	Revolusi, Sosialisme dan Pimpinan – Revolution, Socialism and Leadership (one of Soekarno's slogans)
RI	Republik Indonesia (part of the federation that made up the Republik Indonesia Serikat after independence)
RIS	Republik Indonesia Serikat – Republic of the United States of Indonesia (RUSI)
RTC	Round Table Conference
RTM	rumah tahanan militer – military prison
RUSI	Republic of the United States of Indonesia (also Republik Indonesia Serikat or RIS)
Sayap Kiri	Left Wing (a coalition of groups that supported the Partai Sosialis)
Seinendan	Youth Corps (paramilitary unit formed by the Japanese during the occupation)
Serba Serbi Parlemen	Parliamentary News (regular column Siauw Giok Tjhan wrote in the weekly newspaper *Sunday Courier*)
sin keh	newcomers (the term used to describe Chinese people who have recently arrived in Indonesia)
Sin Po	a daily newspaper, published in Jakarta (one of a number of papers published in Malay or Sino–Malay for Chinese readers)
SKI	Serikat Kerakyatan Indonesia – Indonesian People's Association
SMH	Sin Ming Hui – Association of New Light
Soe Poe Sia	Chinese Reading Club
SPS	Serikat Perusahaan Surat Kabar – Association of Newspaper Enterprises
SPTI	Sarekat Peranakan Tionghoa Indonesia – Union of Peranakan Chinese of Indonesia
STKI	Surat Tanda Kewarganegaraan Indonesia – Proof of Indonesian Citizenship
Suara Ibu Kota	*Voice of the Capital City* (the mouthpiece of the Partai Sosialis in Surabaya)

Glossary

Suara Rakyat	*People's Voice* (a weekly paper that became the daily *Harian Rakyat*)
Suara Tapa	*Voice of the Hermits* (newsletter published by Siauw Giok Tjan while in Wirogunan prison in 1949)
Suatu Renungan	*A Reflection*, a book written by Siauw Giok Tjhan
suku	ethnic group
Ta Hsueh Hsueh Sheng Hui	Association of University Students
tapol	tahanan politik – political prisoner
Tavip	Tahun 'vivere pericoloso' – The Year of Living Dangerously (one of Soekarno's political slogans)
THHK	Tiong Hoa Hwee Kwan – Chinese Association
Tiong Hoa Siang Hwees	Chinese Chambers of Commerce
Tjin Tjay Hwee	a movement that raised funds to help China fight against the Japanese
Toapekong	a shrine god
totok Chinese	a Chinese person, either China-born or Indonesia-born, who continues to maintain Chinese culture and tradition in their way of life
Trisakti	Three Holy Precepts – standing on one's own feet economically, being politically independent and being true to Indonesia's cultural identity (one of Soekarno's political slogans)
URECA	Universitas Respublica – Baperki's University (was renamed Trisakti University after Baperki was dissolved in 1966)
Volksraad	People's Council
wayang kulit	shadow puppet
WNI	Warga Negara Indonesia – Indonesian citizens
Yayasan Kebudayaan Sadar	Foundation of Cultural Awakening (publishing firm led by Siauw Giok Tjhan in the 1960s)

SELECT BIBLIOGRAPHY

(Baperki documentation and transcripts of Siauw Giok Tjhan's speeches are held in the Asian Collections, Monash University Library [SIAUW Collections], Clayton, Australia.)

Alisjahbana, S. Takdir. 'Kedudukan Bahasa Melaju-Tionghoa'. In *Dari Perdjuangan dan Pertumbuhan Bahasa Indonesia*, Djakarta: Pustaka Rakyat, 1957: 55–61.
Amnesty International. *Indonesia, sebuah laporan Amnesti Internasional*. London: Amnesty International, 1977.
Ananta Toer, Pramoedya. *Hoa Kiau di Indonesia*. Djakarta: Bintang, 1960.
Anderson, Benedict. 'In Memoriam: Soe Hok Gie'. *Indonesia*, no. 9 (1970): 225–27.
Anderson, Benedict. *Java, In Time of Revolution*. Ithaca: Cornell University Press, 1972.
Anderson, Benedict. 'Old State, New Society: Indonesia's New Order in Comparative Historical Perspective'. *Journal of Asian Studies*, 42 (1983): 477–96.
Anonymous. *Hari Ulang ke-50 Tiong Hoa Kwee Koan Djakarta* (3 Juni 1900 – 3 Juni 1950). Djakarta, 1950.
Assaat. *Perlindungan Chusus bagi Usa Nasional*. Djakarta, 1956.
Bachtiar, Harsja W. 'Masalah Integrasi Nasional di Indonesia'. *Prisma* 5, no. 8 (1976): 3–13.
Badan Pekerdja KENSI Pusat. *KENSI Berdjuang*. Djakarta: Djambatan, 1956.
Bakom-PKB Pusat. *Assimilasi dan Islam*. Jakarta: Bakom-PKB, 1981.
Bakom-PKB Pusat. *Wawasan Kebangsaan Indonesia, Gagasan dan pemikiran Badan Komunikasi Penghayatan Kesatuan Bangsa*. Jakarta: Bakom PKB Pusat, 1987.
Baladas, Ghoshal. *Indonesian Politics, 1955–1959. The Emergence of Guided Democracy*. Calcutta: K.P. Bagchi, 1982.
Baperki. *Pedoman Kampanje Perdjoangan Badan Permusjawaratan Kewarganegaraan Indonesia (Baperki) dalam Pemilihan Umum*, Djakarta: Baperki, 1955.
Baperki. *Simposion Baperki tentang Sumbangsih Apakah jang Dapat Diberikan oleh Warganegara² Indonesia Keturunan Asing Kepada Pembangunan Kebudajaan Nasional Indonesia*, Djakarta: Baperki, 1957.
Baperki. *Segala Sesuatu tentang Kewarganegaraan RI*, Djakarta: Baperki, 1960.
Barnett, A. Doak. *A Choice of Nationality: Overseas Chinese in Indonesia – Problems and Issues Raised by the Sino-Indonesian Agreement on the Issue of Dual nationality*. American Universities Field Staff, May 28, 1955.
Brown, Colin and Cribb, Robert. *Modern Indonesia: A History since 1945*. London, New York: Longman, 1995.
Budiardjo, Carmel. 'In Memory of Siauw Giok Tjhan'. *Tapol Bulletin*, no. 48, 1981: 11.

Budiardjo, Carmel. *Surviving Indonesia's Gulag: A Western Woman Tells Her Story*. Cassell, London, 1996.

Siauw, Giok Tjhan, Hering, B. B. (Bob Berthy), Burns, Peter, and James Cook University of North Queensland. *Siauw Giok Tjhan Remembers*, Centre for Southeast Asian Studies, James Cook University of North Queensland, Townsville, Qld, 1982.

Castles, Lance. 'The Fate of the Private Entrepreneur' in *Sukarno's Guided Indonesia*. Edited by T.K. Tan. Brisbane: Jacaranda, 1967.

Castles, Lance. 'The Ethnic Profile of Djakarta', *Indonesia*, no. 3 (1967): 153–204.

Cator, W.J. *The Economic Position of the Chinese in the Netherlands Indies*. Oxford: Blackwell, 1936.

Clark, Marilyn W. *Overseas Chinese Education in Indonesia*. US Government Printing Office, 1965.

Coppel, Charles A. 'Indonesia: Freezing Relations with China'. *Australia's Neighbours*, 4th series, March-April, 1968.

Coppel, Charles A. 'The National Status of the Chinese in Indonesia'. *Papers on Far Eastern History*, no.1 (1973): 115–39.

Coppel, Charles A. 'Mapping the Peranakan Chinese in Indonesia'. *Papers on Far Eastern History*, no. 8 (1975): 143–67.

Coppel, Charles A. 'The Indonesian Chinese in the Sixties: A Study of an Ethnic Minority in a Period of Turbulent Political Change'. Ph.D. thesis, Monash University, 1976.

Coppel, Charles A. 'Patterns of Chinese Political Activity in Indonesia'. In Mackie (1976): 19–76.

Coppel, Charles A. 'Select Bibliography on the Indonesian Chinese'. In Mackie (1976): 251–70.

Coppel, Charles A. 'The Chinese Minority: Politics or Culture'. In *People and Society in Indonesia: A Biographical Approach*, edited by Leonard Y. Andaya et al. Clayton, Victoria: Monash University, 1976: 12–30.

Coppel, Charles A. 'Studying the Chinese Minorities: A Review. *Indonesia* no. 24 (1977): 175–83.

Coppel, Charles A. 'Arab and Chinese Minority Groups in Java'. *Southeast Asia Ethnicity and Development Newsletter* 3, no. 2 (1977).

Coppel, Charles A. 'Contemporary Confucianism in Indonesia'. In Proceedings of the Seventh IAHA Conference, held in Bangkok, 22–26 August 1977, Bangkok: Chulalongkorn University Press, 1979: 739–52.

Coppel, Charles A. 'China and the Ethnic Chinese'. In *Indonesia: Australian Perspectives*. Edited by J.J. Fox et al., Canberra: Research School of Pacific Studies, Australian National University, 1980: 729–34.

Coppel, Charles A. 'The Origins of Confucianism as an Organised Religion in Java, 1900–1923'. *Journal of Southeast Asian Studies*, 12 (1) 1980: 179–96.

Coppel, Charles A. 'The Position of the Chinese in the Philippines, Malaysia and Indonesia'. In *The Chinese in Indonesia, the Philippines and Malaysia*, London: Minority Rights Group. 1972: 2–9.

Coppel, Charles A. *Indonesian Chinese in Crisis*. Kuala Lumpur: Oxford University Press, 1983.

Coppel, Charles A. and Leo Suryadinata. 'The Use of the Terms "Tjina" and "Tionghoa" in Indonesia: An Historical Survey'. *Papers on Far Eastern History*, no. 2 (1970): 97–118.

Coppel, Charles A. 'The Class of '59: Indonesian Chinese Identity in Hong Kong'. Paper presented at the Symposium on Changing Identities of the Southeast Asian Chinese since World War II. Australian National University, Canberra, 1985.

Crouch, Harold. 'Another Look at the Indonesian "coup"'. *Indonesia* 15 (April 1973): 1–20.

Crouch, Harold. *The Army and Politics in Indonesia*. Ithaca: Cornell University Press, 1978.

Dahm, Bernard, *History of Indonesia in the Twentieth Century*. Pall Mall Press. London, 1971.

Feith, Herbert. *The Indonesian Elections of 1955*. Interim Reports series, Southeast Asia Program, Ithaca, N.Y.: Cornell University, 1956.

Feith, Herbert. *The Decline of Constitutional Democracy in Indonesia*, Ithaca, N.Y.: Cornell University Press, 1962.

Feith, Herbert. 'Dynamics of Guided Democracy' In Ruth T. McVey (ed.), *Indonesia*. New Haven, Conn.: Southeast Asia Studies, Yale University, by arrangement with HRAF Press, 1963.

Feith, Herbert. 'President Soekarno, the Army and the Communists: The Triangle Changes Shape' *Asian Survey*, 4, 8 (August 1964).

Feith, Herbert. 'Dayak Legacy'. *Far Eastern Economic Review*, 25 January 1968.

FitzGerald, C.P. *The Third China*. Melbourne: Cheshire, 1965.

Friedson, Anthony M. (ed). *New directions in biography*. Biographical Research Center by the University Press of Hawaii, 1981.

Gani, M. *Surat kabar Indonesia pada Tiga Zaman*. Djakarta: Departemen Penerangan, 1978.

Go Gien Tjw. 'In Memoriam: Siauw Giok Tjhan (1914–1981)'. *Indonesia*, no. 33 (1982): 123–26.

Gouw Giok Siong. *Tafsiran Undang-undang Kewarganegaraan R.I.* Djakarta: Keng Po, 1960.

Grant, Bruce. *Indonesia*, Carlton, Vic.: Melbourne University Press, 1966.

Hauswedell, Peter Christian. 'Soekarno, Radical or Conservative? Indonesian Politics 1964–5' *Indonesia*. Ithaca, N.Y.: Cornell University, Volume 15 (April 1973), 109–143.

Hering, Bob (ed). *Siauw Giok Tjhan Remembers: A Peranakan-Chinese and the Quest for Indonesian Nationhood. JCUNQ SE Asia Monograph* 11, James Cook University of North Queensland, 1982.

Hindley, Donald, *The Communist Party of Indonesia 1951–1963*. Berkeley & Los Angeles: University of California Press, 1970.

Hughes, John. *The End of Sukarno*. London: Angus and Robertson, 1968.

Hwang Wuu Wen. *Masalah Minoritet Tionghoa di-Indonesia*. Yogyakarta: Skripsi, 1960.

Ibrahim, Harmaili. *Pemilihan Umum di Indonesia 1955, 1971 dan 1977*. Jakarta: CV Alhidayah, 1978.

Jahja, Junus. *Catatan Seorang WNI – Kenangan, Renungan dan Harapan*. Jakarta: Yayasan Tunas Bangsa, 1988.

Jahja Junus (ed.) *Nonpri dimata pribumi/pemikiran Bung Karno*. Jakarta: Yayasan Tunas Bangsa, 1991.

Kahin, George McT. *Nationalism and Revolution in Indonesia*. Ithaca, N.Y.; Cornell University Press, 1952.

Kroef, Justus M. van der. 'Social Conflict and Minority Aspirations in Indonesia'. *American Journal of Sociology* 55 (1949–50), pp. 450–63.

Kroef, Justus M. van der. 'Chinese Assimilation in Indonesia'. *Social Research* 20 (1953): 445–72.

Kroef, Justus M. van der. 'Problems of Chinese Assimilation' In *Indonesia in the Modern World*. Bandung: Masa Baru. Vol. I, pt. 1 (1954): 216–49.

Kroef, Justus M. van der. 'Minority Problems in Indonesia'. *Far Eastern Survey*, 24 (1955): 165–171.

Kroef, Justus M. van der. 'Indonesia's Economic Dilemma'. *Far Eastern Survey* 29, no. 4 (1960): 49–63.

Kroef, Justus M. van der. 'The Sino-Indonesian Rupture'. *China Quarterly*, no. 33 (1968): 17–46.

Kroef, Justus M. van der. 'Before the Thaw: Recent Indonesian Attitudes towards People's China'. *Asian Survey* 13, no. 5 (1973): 513–30.

Kroef, Justus M. van der. 'Normalizing Relations with China: Indonesia's Policies and Perceptions'. *Asian Survey* 26, no. 8 (1986): 909–34.

Kwee Kek Beng. *Doea Poeloe Lima Tahon sebagi Wartawan*, Batavia: Kuo, 1948.

Kwee Tek Hoay. *The Origins of the Modern Chinese Movement in Indonesia*. Trans. & Ed. Lea E. Williams. Modern Indonesia Project. Ithaca, N.Y.: Cornell University, 1969.

Leclerc, Jacque. 'Amir Sjarifuddin, Between State and The revolution' in *In Search of Cross-cultural Understanding*, edited by Angus McIntyre, Clayton, Vic: Monash Papers on South East Asia, 1993.

Legge, J.D. *Sukarno*. Penguin, Harmondsworth, 1973.

Legge, J.D. *Intellectuals and nationalism in Indonesia: A study of the following recruited by Sutan Sjahrir in Occupation Jakarta*. Ithaca, N.Y.; Cornell Modern Indonesia Project Publications, 1988.

Lev, Daniel S. *The Transition to Guided Democracy: Indonesian Politics 1957–1959*. Modern Indonesia Project. Cornell University, Ithaca, 1966.

Lev, Daniel S. 'Becoming an Orang Indonesia Sejati: The Political Journey of Yap Thiam Hien', Symposium on The Role of the Indonesian Chinese in Shaping Modern Indonesian Life, Cornell University, 1991.

Liauw Kian Djoe (Suryadinata, Leo). *Pers Indonesia-Tionghoa dan Pergerakan Kemerdekaan, 1901–1942 Sebuah Pengantar*. Djakarta Universiti Indonesia, Fakultas Sastra, Djurusan Sedjarah, 1965.

Lie Tek Tjeng. *Masalah Tionghoa dalam Rangka Stabilisasi Politik: Prasaran jang Diadjukan dalam Seminar AD ke.II/1966*. Djakarta: LRKN-MIPI, Bagian Asia Timur, 1966.

Lie Tek Tjeng. *Tentang Asimilasi*. Djakarta. LRKN_MIPI, Bagian Asia Timur, 1967.

Lie Tek Tjeng. *Tentang Aspek Sosial-Budaja 'Masalah Tionghoa'*. Djakarta: LRKN-MIPI, Bagian Asia Timur, 1967.

Lie Tek Tjeng. 'The Chinese Problem in Indonesia Following the September 30 Movement: A Personal View'. *Internationale Spectator* 24, no. 12 (1969): 1145–14.

Lie Tek Tjeng. *Masalah WNI dan Masalah Huakiau di Indonesia*. Djakarta: LRKN-LIPI, 1971.

Liem Thian Joe. 'Pengaroeh Tionghoa di Java', *Jade* 12, no. 2, 1948.

Mackie, J.A.C. *Problems of the Indonesian Inflation*. Modern Indonesia Project, Ithaca: Cornell University, 1967.

Mackie, J.A.C. *Konfrontasi: The Indonesia-Malaysia Dispute 1963–1966*, Kuala Lumpur.: Oxford University Press, 1974.

Mackie, J.A.C. (ed). *The Chinese in Indonesia: Five Essays*. Melbourne: Nelson, 1976.

Mackie, J.A.C. 'Anti-Chinese Outbreaks in Indonesia, 1959-68'. In Mackie *The Chinese in Indonesia: Five Essays*. Melbourne: Nelson, 1976: 77–138.

Maxwell John R. *Soe Hok Gie – A Biography of a Young Indonesian Intellectual*, Unpublished PhD Thesis, Australian National University, Canberra, 1997.

McDonald, Hamish. *Suharto's Indonesia*, Melbourne: Fontana, 1980.

McIntyre, Angus (ed). *Indonesian political biography: In Search of Cross-Cultural Understanding*, Clayton, Vic: Centre of Southeast Asian Studies, Monash University, 1993.

McVey, Ruth. *The Development of Indonesian Communist Party*, Center for International Studies, MIT, 1954.

McVey, Ruth (ed). *Indonesia*, New Haven, Conn, Southeast Asia Studies, Yale University, by arrangement with HRAF Press, 1963.

McVey, Ruth. 'Indonesian Communism and China' in *China's Policies in Asia and America's Alternatives*. Edited by Tang Tsou, Volume 2. Chicago: The University of Chicago Press, 1968.

Ministry of Information. *Act No. 62 of the Year 1958 Concerning Republic of Indonesia Citizenship*. Djakarta, 1958.

Mortimer, Rex. *Indonesian Communism under Sukarno*. Ithaca: Cornell University Press, 1974.

Mozingo, David. 'The Sino-Indonesian Dual Nationality Treaty', *Asian Survey* I, no. 10: 25–31, 1961.

Mozingo, David, 'New Development in China's Relations with Indonesia', *Current Scene* 1, 1962.

Mozingo, David. *Sino-Indonesian Relations: An Overview, 1956–1965*. Santa Monica, Calif.: The Rand Corporation, 1965.

Mozingo, David. 'Chinese Policy in Indonesia', Ph.D. thesis, University of California, 1973.

Mozingo, David. *Chinese Policy towards Indonesia. 1949–1967*. Ithaca, N.Y.: Cornell University Press, 1976.

Muaja, A.J. *The Chinese Problem in Indonesia*, Djakarta: New Nusantara, 1960

Nasution, Adnan Buyung. *The Aspiration for Constitutional Government in Indonesia: A Socio-legal Study of the Indonesia Konstituante 1956–1959*. Jakarta: Pustaka Sinar Harapan, 1992.

Niel, Robert van. *The Emergence of the Modern Indonesian Elite.* The Hague and Bandung: Van Hoeve, 1960.
Oei Tjoe Tat. *Memoar Oei Tjoe Tat - Pembantu Presiden Soekarno.* Jakarta: Hasta Mitra, 1995.
Oey Hong Lee. *Indonesian Government and Press during Guided Democracy.* University of Hull, Hull monographs on South-East Asia; no. 4, 1976.
Onghokham. 'The Peranakan Officers' Families in Nineteenth Century Java' In *Historiography of Indonesia and the Middleman in Indonesian History: papers presented at the Third Dutch-Indonesian Historical Congress*, Lage Vuurche, The Netherlands, June 23 – June 27, Lage Vuursche, 1980.
Pigeaud, Th. *Javanese Volksvertoningen.* Batavia, 1938.
Purcell, Victor. *The Chinese in Southeast Asia*, 2nd ed. London: Oxford University Press, 1965.
Ray, J.K. *Transfer of Power in Indonesia (1942–1949)*, Bombay, Manaktals, 1967.
Robison, Richard. 'Capitalism and the Bureaucratic State in Indonesia: 1965–1975'. Ph.D. thesis, University of Sydney, 1977.
Saleh, Boejoeng. *Kata Pengantar Sdr. Boejoeng Saleh.* Djakarta: Baperki, 1957.
Siauw Giok Tjhan. *Membina Bangsa Jang Bulat Bersatu.* Djakarta: Baperki, 1957.
Siauw Giok Tjhan. *Pantja Sila Anti-rasialisme.* Djakarta: Baperki, 1962.
Siauw Giok Tjhan. *Gotong Rojong Nasakom Untuk Melaksanakan Ampera*, Djakarta, Baperki, 1963.
Siauw Giok Tjhan. *Lima Jaman, Perwujudan Integrasi Wajar.* Jakarta: Yayasan Teratai, 1981.
Siauw Giok Tjhan. *Menuju Indonesia Yang Baik Dengan Terrealisasinya Bhineka Tunggal Ika.* PPI, Amsterdam, 1981.
Siauw Tiong Djin. 'Siauw Giok Tjhan: The Making of a Peranakan Leader' in Angus McIntyre (ed.), *Indonesian Political Biography: In Search of Cross-cultural Understanding*, Clayton, Vic: Centre of Southeast Studies, Monash University, 1993.
Siauw Tiong Djin. *Siauw Giok Tjhan, Perjuangan Seorang Patriot Membangun Nasion Indonesia dan Masyarakat Bhineka Tunggal Ika.* Jakarta: Hasta Mitra, 1999.
Skinner, G. William. 'The Chinese of Java'. In *Colloquium on Overseas Chinese.* Edited by Morton H. Fried, New York: Institute of Pacific Relations, 1958: 1–10.
Skinner, G. William. 'Java's Chinese Minority: Continuity and Change'. *Journal of Asian Studies*, 20, no. 3 (1961): 353–62.
Soebagiyo, I.N. *SK Trimurti: Wanita Pengabdi Bangsa.* Jakarta: Gunung Agung, 1982.
Somers Heidhues, Mary F. 'Questions Concerning The Chinese in Indonesia Since the Chou-Sunarjo Treaty', unpublished, April, 1960.
Somers Heidhues, Mary F. *Peranakan Chinese Politics in Indonesia.* Ithaca, N.Y.: Cornell University Southeast Asia Program, 1964.
Somers Heidhues, Mary F. 'Peranakan Chinese Politics in Indonesia'. Ph.D. thesis, Cornell University, 1965.
Somers Heidhues, Mary F. 'Peking and the Overseas Chinese: the Malaysian Dispute'. *Asian Survey* 6, no. 5 (1966): 276–87.

Somers Heidhues, Mary F. *Southeast Asia's Chinese Minorities*. Melbourne: Longman, 1974.
Staf Umum Angkatan Darat. 'Masalah Tionghoa di Indonesia'. Djakarta, 1961.
Suryadinata, Leo. 'A Brief Historical Survey of the Peranakan Chinese Press in Java (1900–1942)'. *Journal of Southeast Asian Research* 5 (1969): 160–62.
Suryadinata, Leo. 'Indonesian Policies Towards the Chinese Minority under the New Order.' *Asian Survey* 16, no. 8 (1976): 770–87.
Suryadinata, Leo. 'The Search for National Identity of an Indonesian Chinese: A Political Biography of Liem Koen Hian'. *Archipel*, no. 14 (1977): 43–69.
Suryadinata, Leo. *The Chinese Minority in Indonesia: Seven Papers*. Singapore: Chopmen. 1978.
Suryadinata, Leo. *Pribumi Indonesians, the Chinese Minority and China*. Singapore: Heinemann Asia. 1978.
Suryadinata, Leo. *Political Thinking of the Indonesian Chinese, 1900–1977*. Singapore: Singapore University Press, 1979.
Suryadinata, Leo. *Eminent Indonesian Chinese: Biographical Sketches*. Revised ed. Singapore: Gunung Agung, 1981.
Suryadinata, Leo. *Peranakan Chinese Politics in Java, 1917–1942*. Revised ed. Singapore: Singapore University Press. 1981.
Sutter, J.O. *Indonesianisasi: Politics in a Changing Economy, 1940–1955*. 4 vols. Ithaca, N.Y.: Cornell University Southeast Asia Program, 1959.
Swift, Ann. *The Road to Madiun: The Indonesian Communist Uprising of 1948*. Ithaca, N.Y.: Cornell Modern Indonesia Project, Southeast Asia Program, Cornell University, 1989.
Tan, Kah Kee. *The Making of an Overseas Chinese Legend*. Singapore: Oxford University Press, 1987.
Tarmizi, Taher. *Masyarakat Cina, Ketahanan Nasional, dan Integrasi Bangsa di Indonesia*. Jakarta: Pusat Pengkajian Islam dan Masyarakat, 1997.
Tjokrosisworo, Soedarjo (S.Tj.S). *Sedjarah Pers Sebangsa*. Djakarta: SPS, 1958.
van Niel, R. *The Emergence of the Modern Indonesian Elite*. The Hague–Bandung: W. van Hoeve, 1959.
Wahono, Riyanto D (ed). *70 Tahun Junus Jahya: Pribumi Kuat Kunci Pembauran*, Jakarta: Bina Rena Pariwara, 1997.
Wellem, Frederick Djara. *Amir Sjarifoeddin, Pergumulan Imannya dalam Perjuangan Kemerdekaan*. Jakarta: Sinar Harapan, 1984.
Williams, Lea E. and Massachusetts Institute of Technology. Center for International Studies. *Overseas Chinese Nationalism: The Genesis of the Pan-Chinese Movement in Indonesia, 1900–1916*. Free Press Glencoe, Ill, 1960.
Willmott, Donald E. 'Sociocultural Change Among the Chinese of Semarang, Indonesia'. PhD thesis, Cornell University, 1958.
Willmott, Donald E. *The Chinese of Semarang: A Changing Minority Community in Indonesia*. Ithaca, N.Y.: Cornell University Press, 1960.
Willmott, Donald E. *The National Status of the Chinese in Indonesia, 1900–1958*. Revised edition. Ithaca, N.Y.: Cornell University Southeast Asia Program, 1961.

Yap Tjwan Bing. *Meretas Jalan Kemerdekaan: Otobiografi Seorang Pejuang Kemerdekaan*. Jakarta: Gramedia, 1910.

Yasni, Z. *Bung Hatta Menjawab*. Jakarta: Gunung Agung, 1978.

Yong. C.F. *Tan Kah Kee: The Making of an Overseas Chinese Legend*. Singapore, Oxford University Press, 1987: 280–291.

INDEX

A note about the indexing of personal names

To accommodate cultural variations in the placement of family names, where two names are given the index entry is alphabetised by the first name.

30th September Movement *See* G30S

A

Abdul Halim 79
Abdulmadjid 19, 49, 50, 60, 66, 70, 71, 73
Abdurrahman Wahid 321
Acoma (Angkatan Communis Muda, Communist Youth League) 84, 130, 186, 192
Adam Malik xx, xxi, 53, 74, 76, 81, 93, 201, 276, 288, 293, 302, 303
Agus Salim 58, 59, 74
Aidit, DN *See* DN Aidit
Ali Sastroamidjojo 58, 59, 76, 81, 104, 105, 122, 148, 160, 185, 186, 210, 261, 311
   cabinet of 84, 103, 113, 125, 132, 136, 142, 143, 156, 163, 165, 171, 185, 190
Alimin 20, 43, 89, 98
Amir Sjarifuddin 21, 24, 48, 49–55, 67–71, 73, 76, 308
   cabinet of 48, 59–67, 75, 85, 93, 105, 309
   relationship with Siauw Giok Thjan xix, 25, 37, 47, 90, 94, 116, 137
AMT (Angkatan Muda Tionghoa, Chinese Youth Movement) 40–42, 237
Ang Jang Goan 85, 98, 111, 119, 121, 233
Ang Tjiang Liat 143, 144, 212
Angkatan Communis Muda *See* Acoma
Angkatan Muda Tionghoa *See* AMT
Anwar Tjokroaminoto 74, 309
armed youth organisations *See* Pemuda
Aruji Kartawinata xx, 74, 80, 87, 105, 210, 233, 234, 309
Asian–African Conference 156, 194

Assaat 173, 180, 181, 182
Association of Chinese Clans of Indonesia *See* PMTSI
Association of Indo-Europeans for Indonesian Unity *See* GIKI
Association of Indonesian Catholic Students *See* PMKRI
Association of Indonesian Journalists *See* PWI
Association of Indonesian Students and Youth *See* IPPI
Association of Indonesian Students *See* Perhimi
Association of New Light *See* Sin Ming Hui
Association of Newspaper Enterprises *See* SPS
Auwyong Peng Koen 112, 114, 115, 119, 125, 131–135, 138, 139, 204, 256

B

Badan Pekerja xix, 48, 53, 55, 58, 69, 75, 76, 80, 106
Badan Permusyawaratan Kewarganegaraan Indonesia *See* Baperki
Badan Permusyawaratan Warga Negara Turunan Tionghoa *See* Baperwatt
Baperki (Badan Permusyawaratan Kewarganegaraan Indonesia, Consultative Body for Indonesian Citizenship) xx–xxii, 295, 311, 315, 316, 321
   1963 anti-Chinese riots 228–230
   birth of 117–122
   Chinese minority representatives 141–144

challenge from assimilationists 251–254, 264–267
   the integration approach 260–264
citizenship legislation 146, 148, 149, 151–153, 156, 157, 160, 163, 166, 219, 220, 222, 223
economic conference 177, 179
educational programs 236–250, 311, 313
   curricula and political education 247–250, 320
dissolution 290–295, 314, 318
founders 114, 115
Guided Democracy 186, 189
   Manipol USDEK 211
   opposition from Yap Thiam Hien 203–207
   parliamentary restructure 213
leadership 116, 121, 122, 130
LPKB attack 268–271, 295–297
national constitution 191, 198, 203
participation in 1955 general elections 125–131
   cooperation with other parties 132, 133
   election guidelines and campaign 134–137
   internal tension 137–139
   votes polled 140
participation in 1957 regional elections 144, 145
political alliances 230–235, 297, 298, 316, 319
   PKI 284–287
   Soekarno 268, 279, 317
response to 'Assaat movement' 181
youth organisation *See* PPI
Baperwatt (Badan Permusyawaratan Warga Negara Turunan Tionghoa, Consultative Body of Citizens of Chinese Descent) 116, 120
Barisan Banteng 68, 72, 73
Barisan Pembrontak Rakyat Indonesia *See* BPRI
Barisan Tani Indonesia *See* BTI
Bhineka Tunggal Ika 245, 255, 265, 268
BPRI (Barisan Pembrontak Rakyat Indonesia, Insurgent Corps of the Indonesian People) 41, 42

BTI (Barisan Tani Indonesia, Indonesian Peasant Front) 68, 103, 104, 250, 291
Bung Tomo *See* Soetomo

C

Catholic Party *See* Partai Katolik
Central Electoral Committee *See* Panitia Pemilihan Indonesia
Central Gerakan Mahasiswa Indonesia *See* CGMI
Central Movement of Indonesian Students *See* CGMI
Central National Committee of Indonesia *See* KNIP
CGMI (Central Gerakan Mahasiswa Indonesia, Central Movement of Indonesian Students) 232, 250, 275, 276, 285, 286, 287, 292
Chaerul Saleh 53, 55, 210, 233, 265, 266, 276, 293, 294
Charles Coppel xxv, 24, 94, 95, 234, 252, 271, 296, 297
Chinese Association *See* THHK
Chinese Association (political party) *See* Chung Hua Hui
Chinese General Association *See* CHTH
Chinese Nationalist Party *See* Kuo Min Tang
Chinese Union Party *See* PT
Chinese Youth Movement *See* AMT
Chou En Lai 146, 153–156, 160, 161, 221, 311
CHTH (Chung Hua Tsung Hui, Chinese General Association) 62, 110, 112, 240, 265
Chung Hua Hui xxxi, 14, 18, 22, 23, 111l
Chung Hua Tsung Hui *See* CHTH
citizenship system (passive/active) 56, 65, 75, 104–107, 110, 146–150, 154, 156, 157, 159, 162
   Act of 1946 56, 106, 156
   Act of 1958 166, 219, 311
   Bill of 1946 56
   Bill of 1953 114, 146, 152, 310
Communist Youth League *See* Acoma
Constituent Assembly *See* Konstituante
Constitution
   1945 Constitution xxii, 184, 192, 197–201, 203, 205–208, 225, 312, 321

INDEX

Article 6 198
Article 33 79, 192, 199, 225
1950 Constitution 194, 203
Article 38 192, 193
Consultative Body for Indonesian Citizenship *See* Baperki
Consultative Body of Citizens of Chinese Descent *See* Baperwatt
Consultative Body of Indonesian Youths *See* PPI
Coppel, Charles *See* Charles Coppel
Council of Indonesian Islamic Associations *See* Masyumi

D

Dan Lev 95, 96, 130, 177, 202, 297
David Mozingo 154, 155, 164, 165, 222
Depernas (Dewan Perancang Nasional, National Planning Agency) 201, 209, 213, 224
Dewan Nasional 188–190, 195, 196
Dewan Perancang Nasional *See* Depernas
Dewan Pertimbangan Agung *See* DPA
Dewan Perwakilan Rakyat Gotong Royong *See* DPRGR
Diapari, DS *See* DS Diapari
Djody Gondokusumo xxxiii, 83, 84, 105, 137, 148, 200
Djohan Sjahroezah 51, 67, 97
Djuanda 152, 168, 171, 174, 175, 199, 201, 209, 227
   cabinet of 163, 165, 190, 216
DN Aidit 43, 65, 88–91, 94, 96, 98, 188, 200, 210, 214, 231, 261, 277, 284–288, 290
DPA (Dewan Pertimbangan Agung, Supreme Advisory Council) 198, 200, 201, 209, 213, 214, 280
DPRGR (Dewan Perwakilan Rakyat Gotong Royong, Mutual Assistance Parliament) 209, 210, 214
DS Diapari 81, 82, 87, 118, 122, 159, 170, 175
Dual Nationality Treaty 146, 156, 161, 162, 165, 166, 215, 219
   Exchange of Notes 160–162, 164, 219, 223
Dutch East India Company 24, 28

F

FDR (Front Demokrasi Rakyat, People's Democratic Front) 68–71, 309
Feith, Herbert *See* Herbert Feith
Fraksi Nasional Progresif 77, 82, 83, 118, 186, 188, 189, 201, 212, 309
Front Demokrasi Rakyat *See* FDR
Front Nasional 196, 210, 277
functional groups 188, 195–198, 209, 210
   Functional Group faction 196, 197, 209

G

G30S (Gerakan 30 September, 30th September Movement) 288–291, 293, 294, 302, 305, 313
   aftermath of 295, 296, 297, 301, 318
Gabungan Indo untuk Kesatuan Indonesia *See* GIKI
George Kahin 60, 70, 72
Gerakan 30 September *See* G30S
Gerakan Rakyat Indonesia *See* Gerindo
Gerindo 21, 24
GIKI (Gabungan Indo untuk Kesatuan Indonesia, Association of Indo-Europeans for Indonesian Unity) 141
Go Gak Cho 91, 233, 240
Go Gien Tjwan 20, 32, 41–43, 51, 75, 88, 118, 119, 121, 128, 130–132, 134, 135, 137–139, 143, 144, 151, 160, 174, 191, 205–207, 233, 238, 241, 286, 292, 293
Greater Indonesian Union *See* PIR
Guided Democracy 182, 186–188, 195, 197, 201, 208, 210–212, 224, 277, 312, 313
   political manifesto (Manipol USDEK) 210, 211, 215, 261, 267, 279
   support for 184, 203, 312, 317, 319

H

Han Kang Hoen 32–35, 38, 39, 307
Harian Rakyat (*People's Daily*) 88, 90, 94, 196, 284, 290
Hatta xxxii, 19, 25, 30, 33, 37, 48, 49, 53, 55, 57, 66, 67, 69, 72–75, 77, 79, 169, 185, 309

Heidhues, Mary. *See* Mary Somers
Herbert Feith 81, 84, 108, 201, 202
Hua Chiao Tsung Hui *See* Kakyo Shokai
Huang Chen 154, 160, 218, 220

I

IJ Kasimo *See* Kasimo, IJ
Ikatan Pemuda Pelajar Indonesia *See* IPPI
Indonesian Christian Party *See* Parkindo
Indonesian Chinese Party *See* PTI
Indonesian Communist Party *See* PKI
Indonesian National Party *See* PNI
Indonesian Party *See* Partindo
Indonesian Peasant Front *See* BTI
Indonesian People's Movement *See* Gerindo
Indonesian People's Association *See* SKI
Indonesian Revolutionary Government *See* PRRI
Indonesian Socialist Party *See* PSI
Indonesian Socialist Youth *See* Pesindo
Indonesian Study Club 12
Injo Beng Goat 54, 85, 86, 111, 114, 115, 137, 256
Institute for the Promotion of National Unity *See* LPKB
Insurgent Corps of the Indonesian People *See* BPRI
Inter-Asian Relations Conference 58
IPKI (Partai Ikatan Pendukung Kemerdekaan Indonesia, League of Supporters of Indonesian Independence) 198, 200, 212
IPPI (Ikatan Pemuda Pelajar Indonesia, Association of Indonesian Students and Youth) 250, 270
Iskaq (Tjokroadisurjo) 108, 109, 136, 170–173, 176
Islamic Association Party of Indonesia *See* PSII
Iwa Kusumasumantri xxxiii, 53, 54, 76, 84, 97, 99, 103, 105, 170, 175, 195, 309

J

John Legge 52, 203
Junus Jahja 254, 257, 296

K

Kahin, George *See* George Kahin
Kakyo Shokai 33–35, 39, 110, 265
Kasimo, IJ 87, 170, 234, 310
Kebotai 35–37, 39
Keibodan 35, 307
Khoe Woen Sioe 111, 114–116, 119, 121, 132, 137
KNIP (Komite Nasional Indonesia Pusat, Central National Committee of Indonesia) xxxii, 47, 48, 52, 54, 55, 57, 58, 75, 106
Komite Nasional Indonesia Pusat *See* KNIP
Konstituante 124, 139, 143, 144, 191–195, 197, 198–200
  and Baperki 125, 126, 131, 134, 140, 311
Kuo Min Tang 24, 65, 104, 155, 204, 205
Kwee Hing Tjiat 16–19, 24, 25, 27, 28, 306
Kwee Hwat Djien 125, 133, 256

L

Labour Party *See* Partai Buruh
Lauw Chuan To *See* Junus Jahja
League of Supporters of Indonesian Independence *See* IPKI
Legge, John *See* John Legge
Lembaga Pembinaan Kesatuan Bangsa *See* LPKB
Leo Suryadinata 24, 94, 252, 259, 263, 284
Lev, Dan *See* Dan Lev
Lie Kiat Teng 105, 113, 148
Lie Tjwan Sien 145, 245, 319
Liem Koen Hian xix, 12, 15, 16, 17, 19, 24, 28, 31, 32, 34, 37, 38, 54, 81, 98, 99, 127, 257, 264, 306–308
Liem Koen Seng 112, 144, 145, 206, 231–233, 286, 287
Liem Tjiong Hian 119, 121, 131, 143
Linggadjati Agreement 57, 58
LPKB (Lembaga Pembinaan Kesatuan Bangsa, Institute for the Promotion of National Unity) 229, 231, 247, 251, 253, 254, 259, 266, 267–271, 291, 295, 297, 312

Partindo 84, 186, 212, 230, 232, 233, 288
Party of Indonesian Chinese Democrats *See* PDTI
PDTI (Partai Demokrat Tionghoa Indonesia, Party of Indonesian Chinese Democrats) 110–121
Pemerintah Revolusioner Republik Indonesia *See* PRRI
Pemuda xxxii, 39–41, 48, 54, 56, 62, 63, 75, 76, 314
Pemuda Rakyat 231, 232, 250, 275, 276, 286, 287, 290, 292
Pemuda Sosialis Indonesia *See* Pesindo
People's Consultative Assembly *See* MPR
People's Council *See* Volksraad
People's Daily See Harian Rakyat
People's Democratic Front *See* FDR
People's Youth *See* Pemuda Rakyat
peranakan Chinese
    definition and distinction from totok Chinese xxv–xxxii
    publications 4, 11, 13, 15–18, 22, 26, 29, 38, 43, 85–88
    student organisations 14, 40, 43, 249, 250 (*See* also AMT, Perhimi, PPI)
Peraturan Presiden 10 *See* PP-10
Perhimi 250, 275
Perhimpunan Indonesia *See* PI
Perhimpunan Mahasiswa Indonesia *See* Perhimi
Permesta (Pemerintah Revolusioner Republik Indonesia, Indonesian Revolutionary Government) *See* PRRI
Permusyawaratan Pemuda Indonesia *See* PPI
Persatuan Indonesia Raya *See* PIR
Persatuan Mahasiswa Katolik Republik Indonesia *See* PMKRI
Persatuan Marga Tionghoa Seluruh Indonesia *See* PMTSI
Persatuan Perdjuangan 54, 55, 57
Persatuan Tionghoa *See* PT
Persatuan Wartawan Indonesia *See* PWI
Pesindo 52, 68, 69, 72
Phoa Thoan Hian 232, 288, 319
PIR (Persatuan Indonesia Raya, Greater Indonesian Union) 83, 140, 144

PKI (Partai Komunis Indonesia, Indonesian Communist Party) 20, 21, 48, 49, 68, 70–73, 78, 82, 89–99, 103, 104, 132, 140–145, 157, 163, 175, 181, 182, 184–189, 192, 196, 197, 200–202, 209, 212, 216, 229–234, 249, 250, 269, 277, 279, 284–294, 298, 299, 302, 304, 309, 313, 319
PMKRI (Persatuan Mahasiswa Katolik Republik Indonesia, Association of Indonesian Catholic Students) 250, 321
PMTSI (Persatuan Marga Tionghoa Seluruh Indonesia, Association of Chinese Clans of Indonesia) 320
PNI (Partai Nasional Indonesia, Indonesian National Party) 16, 48, 49, 55, 60, 61, 66–69, 83, 97, 108, 126, 127, 136, 144, 149, 156, 157, 163, 164, 167, 172, 181, 182, 184, 186, 189, 192, 197, 200, 202, 209–212, 233
political manifesto USDEK *See* Guided Democracy – political manifesto
political prisoners *See* tapols
PP-10 (Peraturan Presiden 10, Presidential Regulation no. 10) 216–219, 225, 251–253
PPI (Permusyawaratan Pemuda Indonesia, Association of Indonesian Students and Youth) 232, 237, 249, 250
Presidential Regulation no. 10 *See* PP-10
PRN (Partai Rakyat Nasional, National People's Party) 82, 83, 132, 140, 149, 168, 186
proof of Indonesian citizenship *See* STKI
Provisional People's Consultative Assembly *See* MPRS
PRRI (Pemerintah Revolusioner Republik Indonesia, Indonesian Revolutionary Government) 186, 191, 204, 209, 228
PSI (Partai Sosialis Indonesia, Indonesian Socialist Party) 49, 52, 67, 83, 84, 96, 99, 103, 119, 126, 127, 132, 136, 137, 138, 140, 149, 159, 162, 181, 182, 185, 191, 209, 212, 214, 229, 230
PSII (Partai Serikat Islam Indonesia, Islamic Association Party of Indonesia) 61, 144, 212, 233

PT (Partai Persatuan Tionghoa, Chinese Union Party) 110, 111
PTI (Partai Tionghoa Indonesia, Indonesian Chinese Party) xxxi, 12, 13, 18, 19, 21–25, 128, 264
PWI (Persatuan Wartawan Indonesia, Association of Indonesian Journalists) 18, 77, 92, 93, 122, 138

R

Religious Scholars League *See* NU
Renville Agreement 69–70, 72, 74
Republic of the United States of Indonesia *See* RIS
Republic of Indonesia *See* RI
Republik Indonesia *See* RI
Republik Indonesia Serikat *See* RIS
Respublica University *See* URECA
RI (Republik Indonesia, Republic of Indonesia) 57, 77, 79, 80, 146, 182, 193
RIS (Republik Indonesia Serikat, Republic of the United States of Indonesia) 75, 77–79
Roeslan Abdulgani 8, 37, 209, 265, 267, 268
Roosseno 173, 179
Round Table Conference Agreement *See* RTC Agreement
RTC Agreement 75, 150, 155, 166, 167, 178

S

Sakirman 64, 91, 142, 170, 175
Sartono 24, 76, 80, 81, 97, 98, 201, 233
Seinendan 35, 37, 39, 307
Serikat Kerakyatan Indonesia *See* SKI
Serikat Perusahaan Surat Kabar *See* SPS
Setiadi Reksoprodjo 52, 66, 277, 294, 302
Siauw Giok Bie 6, 8, 9–11, 22, 31–33, 40–42, 130, 292
Sin Ming Hui 111
Sindhunatha 254, 259, 268
Sjahrir 30, 48–55, 57, 58, 59–61, 67, 68, 74, 76
SKI (Serikat Kerakyatan Indonesia, Indonesian People's Association) 82, 118, 140, 186

Skinner xxvi, xxvii, 164
Socialist Party *See* Partai Sosialis
Soeharto 289, 290, 293, 294, 296, 313, 314, 318, 319, 320
Soekarno 16, 20, 24, 30–34, 37–39, 42, 48, 53, 55, 57, 63, 66, 67, 69, 73, 74, 124, 182, 184–191, 195–203, 208–218, 220–222, 224–234, 245, 247–249, 255–257, 260–262, 264–269, 275–280, 288–290, 294, 298
    relationship with Siauw Giok Tjhan xix, xx, xxxii, 12, 18, 27, 93, 141, 183, 207, 221, 227, 230, 231, 261, 268, 271, 275, 279, 281–284, 287, 290, 292, 294, 295, 298, 306, 308, 312–320
Soemarsono 37, 41, 52, 54, 62, 64, 69, 72, 73, 308
Soetomo xix, xxxii, 12, 27, 29, 41, 64, 142, 186, 306
Somers, Mary *See* Mary Somers (Heidhues)
SPS (Serikat Perusahaan Surat Kabar) 77, 92, 122
STKI (Surat Tanda Kewarganegaraan Indonesia, Proof of Indonesian Citizenship) 150, 151, 152
Subadio Sastrosatomo 67, 132, 170
Subandrio 58, 163, 217, 289, 293, 294
Subardjo 19, 74, 99
Sudarjo Tjokrosiswor0 18, 43, 92, 122
Sudibjo 105, 210, 288
Sudirman (General) 54, 64, 74
Sukarni 53, 55, 81, 159, 220, 276, 288
Sukiman (Wirjosandjojo) 48, 67, 84, 97, 98, 99, 107, 169, 223
Sumitro Djojohadikusumo 136, 170
Sunario 106, 107, 110, 146, 148, 156, 160, 265
Supreme Advisory Council *See* DPA
Surat Tanda Kewarganegaraan Indonesia *See* STKI
Suripno 58, 69
Suryadinata, Leo *See* Leo Suryadinata

T

tahanan politik *See* tapols
Tambunan 58, 80, 81, 99, 170, 234, 310
Tan Boen An 57, 78, 111

Tan Eng Tie 114, 115, 119, 145, 233
Tan Hwie Kiat 90, 93, 233
Tan Kah Kee 36, 58, 244
Tan Ling Djie 19–21, 22, 31, 38, 49, 50, 51, 54, 55–58, 60, 69, 70, 73, 74, 75, 81, 86, 89, 98, 106, 118, 127, 144, 233, 308, 309
  relationship with Siauw Giok Thjan 24, 27, 28, 61, 71, 90, 94–96, 137, 138, 307
Tan Malaka 53–55
Tan Po Goan 56, 57, 61, 67, 76, 81, 97, 99, 111, 112, 119, 127, 131, 137, 175
Tan Siang Lian 119, 121, 131
tapols 299–303
Teng Tjin Leng 20, 78, 130, 131, 138, 141, 143, 144
THHK (Tiong Hoa Hwee Kwan, Chinese Association) xxix, xxx, 5, 6, 17, 34, 236
Thio Thiam Tjong 110, 111, 112, 114, 115, 118, 119, 121, 233
Tiong Hoa Hwee Kwan *See* THHK
Tjan Tjoe Som 195, 213
Tjin Tjay Hwee movement 22, 24, 29
Tjipto Mangunkusumo xix, xxxii, 15, 18, 19, 27, 29, 86, 306
Tjoa Sie Hwie 8, 111, 126
Tjoa Sik Ien 19, 20, 21, 27, 31, 32, 38, 65, 76, 81, 111, 118, 127–129, 233, 265, 308
Tjoa Tjie Liang 18, 31, 258
Tjokronegoro 61, 66
Tjoo Tik Tjoen 141–143, 233
Tjung Tin Yan 111, 112, 127, 172
Tobing, Dr FL 105, 118, 244, 245
totok Chinese – definition and distinction from peranakan Chinese xxv–xxxii
Tumakaka 195, 201

U

Union of Struggle *See* Persatuan Perdjuangan
Unity in Diversity *See* Bhineka Tunggal Ika
Universitas Respublica *See* URECA
URECA (Universitas Respublica) 245–247, 249, 285, 291, 294
  Trisakti University 247, 295

USDEK Political Manifesto *See* Guided Democracy – political manifesto
Utrecht 201, 213, 215, 224, 244, 245

V

Vigilance Corps *See* Keibodan
Volksraad xxxi, 12, 14, 23

W

Wikana 60, 66, 68, 70, 71
Willmott 154, 159, 164
Wilopo 74, 99, 124, 125, 171, 175, 191, 309
Wirogunan prison 73–76, 81, 309, 315
Working Committee of the Central National Committee of Indonesia *See* Badan Pekerja
Working Committee on Indonesian Citizenship *See* Panitia Kerja Kewarganegaraan Indonesia

Y

Yamin *See* Mohamad Yamin
Yani (General) 277, 278, 288, 290
Yap Thiam Hien 112, 114, 115, 119–121, 125, 130–135, 138, 139, 142–144, 159, 177, 193, 203, 204, 241, 257, 297, 318
Yap Tjwan Bing 33, 34, 37, 54, 78, 81, 111, 126
Youth Corps *See* Seinenden

ABOUT THE HERB FEITH TRANSLATION SERIES

The Herb Feith Translation Series publishes high-quality non-fiction manuscripts not previously available in English, which enhance scholarship and teaching about Indonesia. Published by the Herb Feith Foundation in conjunction with Monash University, the books are available in print and online.

The Herb Feith Foundation was established in 2003 to commemorate the life and work of Herb Feith (1930–2001), volunteer, scholar, teacher and peace activist. Its mission is to promote and support work of the kind to which Feith devoted his life, including the study of Indonesia, through a range of educational activities including research and teaching and in the publication and promotion of such work.

'Healing and reconciliation after conflict' is the first mini-series of publications, co-ordinated by Dr Kate McGregor and Dr Jemma Purdey, focused on the mass violence in Indonesia in 1965–66. Until recently there have been very few accounts available in Indonesian or English of the mass violence as told by witnesses, survivors or perpetrators. Today, an increasing number of memoirs and short testimony collections are available in Indonesian; however, very few are yet available in English. This has prevented a greater understanding outside Indonesia of how this violence continues to impact on Indonesians and of how they now understand this traumatic period in their nation's history.

These translated works are valuable resources for all who seek to understand Indonesia today, and especially for undergraduate students of Asian history and the history of mass violence and genocide.

The following pages list Herb Feith Translation Series titles available from Monash University Publishing.

Basudara Stories of Peace from Maluku
Working Together for Reconciliation

Edited by Jacky Manuputty, Zairin Salampessy, Ihsan Ali-Fauzi and Irsyad Rafsadi
Translated by Hilary Syaranamual
Published January 2017

Between early 1999 and early 2002, in the Maluku Islands archipelago in Indonesia, Christian and Muslim communities engaged in a bloody conflict.

Various causes of this prolonged ethno-religious violence have been put forward. In this book, for the first time, participants in and victims of what happened speak variously of what they did and saw, of the effects of the violence on them, as individuals and members of families and communities, at the time and after, and of how they have sought to build bridges of peace.

'Basudara', a word evoking kith and kin showing care for each other, touches the central concern of the writers – the bearers of eyewitness testimony in this book – who pray for the growth of this caring spirit.

How, they reflect, can this idea be put into practice? How can such conflict be avoided in the future? What can the world learn from their experiences of violent upheaval?

Basudara Stories of Peace from Maluku is affecting, instructive and inspiring, and sheds a unique light on the world of Indonesia's Maluku Islands.

For more information see
www.publishing.monash.edu/books/bspm-9781925495140.html

About the Herb Feith Translation Series

Breaking the Silence
Survivors Speak about 1965–66 Violence in Indonesia

Edited by Putu Oka Sukanta
Translated by Jennifer Lindsay
Published March 2014

Edited by former political prisoner Putu Oka Sukanta, this is a collection of accounts from people around the archipelago who experienced the 1965 violence in Indonesia. Fifteen witnesses from Medan, Palu, Kendari, Yogyakarta, Jakarta, Bali, Kupang and Sabu Island share their stories of how they navigated this horrifying period of Indonesian history and how they have lived with this past. The book is based on life history interviews with ordinary people who worked as teachers, artists, women's activists and policemen, whose lives were turned upside down when the attack on those considered to be supporters of the Indonesian Communist Party began. These accounts, including one from a perpetrator who is now tormented by guilt and survivors who still feel isolated and rejected by society, show how the violence continues to influence Indonesian society. The book will be a valuable resource for students of history, of Indonesia and for people wanting to understand the impact of this violence.

For more information see
www.publishing.monash.edu/books/bs-9781922235121.html

Bridges of Friendship
Reflections on Indonesia's Early Independence and Australia's Volunteer Graduate Scheme

Includes writings from Betty Feith and Kurnianingrat Ali Sastroamijoyo
Edited by Ann McCarthy and Ailsa Thomson Zainuddin
Published April 2017

Bridges of Friendship unveils personal ties between Indonesians and Australians in the early days of the Indonesian Republic. At the same time it reveals an important chapter in the history of international development and volunteering, and provides insight into Indonesian–Australian relations.

Betty Feith, co-founder of the Volunteer Graduate Scheme (VGS) in Indonesia – an initiative under which Australian graduates were employed in the Indonesian civil service – draws on both first-hand experience and an array of archival documents to narrate a history of the Scheme from 1950 to 1963. The VGS pioneered the concept of international volunteering as we understand it today. Feith's nuanced and insightful narrative demonstrates the ideals of equality and support for the newly formed Indonesian Republic that were at the heart of the Scheme.

The reminiscences of Kurnianingrat Ali Sastroamijoyo – an educator who worked extensively in English language teaching and training, and who took an active part in the Indonesian Revolution – include a fascinating and moving account of daily life in occupied Yogyakarta during the struggle for independence against the Dutch. Kurnianingrat illuminates Indonesian social and cultural history at this critical time for the nation.

A common thread across these two accounts is the friendship of Kurnianingrat and Harumani Rudolph-Sudirdjo with Australian volunteer graduates Feith and Ailsa Thomson Zainuddin: all four women worked together at the English Language Inspectorate in Jakarta in the mid-1950s. Extracts from correspondence, in a final section, illustrate the mutual interests and lasting connections and commitments of this circle of friends.

Taken as a whole, *Bridges of Friendship* suggests the depth of human connection between Australia and Indonesia, fostered by the international spirit common to both the Indonesian Revolution and the Volunteer Graduate Scheme.

For more information see
http://publishing.monash.edu/books/bf-9781925495225.html

About the Herb Feith Translation Series

Forbidden Memories
Women's Experiences of 1965 in Eastern Indonesia

Edited by Mery Kolimon, Liliya Wetangterah and Karen Campbell-Nelson
Translated by Karen Campbell-Nelson
Published October 2015

This is the first book to consider the experiences of women survivors of 1965 anti-communist violence in the majority Christian province Eastern Indonesia. So far, most studies of the 1965 violence have focused on the Muslim majority population of Java and Hindu majority population of Bali. The book presents stories from across the regions of Sumba, Sabu, Alor, Kupang and other parts of West Timor of women who were imprisoned and tortured or whose husbands were murdered. The book is a critical examination of the role of the Protestant Church at the time of the violence and in its aftermath, including ongoing sanctions and political purges against those considered to be supporters of the Indonesian Communist Party. Themes include the impact of the violence on women teachers, members of the women's organisation Gerwani and the fracturing of social and religious communities. The writers critique the role of religious and state institutions for failing to care for this vulnerable community in the face of state terrorism and a culture of fear. The editors and research team hope this publication will create a safe and peaceful environment for survivors to tell their stories and for society to acknowledge their suffering and to struggle with them to restore their rights.

For more information see
http://www.publishing.monash.edu/books/fm-9781922235909.html

Truth Will Out
Indonesian Accounts of the 1965 Mass Violence

Edited by Dr. Baskara T. Wardaya SJ
Translated by Jennifer Lindsay
Published August 2013

This striking compilation of essays surveys a variety of views about the 1965 mass violence in Indonesia and current efforts to understand it. The book is the product of an oral history project involving senior and young researchers from Yogyakarta. The accounts it presents include a military man who continues to see the violence as justified and refuses survivors the status of victim, two Muslims who believe that the Communist were and continue to remain a threat to society, and a Catholic activist who reflects on how they were manipulated to support the violence. These accounts are complemented by the views of survivors of the violence, some of whom see this as a national problem that goes far beyond individual suffering. This book provides a valuable window into why this past remains contested today and some of the obstacles to reconciliation and full rehabilitation of survivors.

For more information see
http://www.publishing.monash.edu/books/two-9781922235145.html

Lukman 56, 88–90, 98, 210, 231, 277
Lukman Hakim 56, 106

M

Madiun Affair 68, 72, 73, 78, 309
Majelis Permusyawaratan Rakyat *See* MPR
Majelis Permusyawaratan Rakyat Sementara *See* MPRS
Mary Somers (Heidhues) xxvi, 20, 24, 94, 164, 165, 235, 252, 253, 263, 269, 270, 284, 285
Masyumi 48, 60, 61, 66, 69, 78, 83, 84, 97, 103, 149, 163, 173, 180–182, 184, 185, 189, 191, 197, 199, 201–203, 209, 229, 230
McVey 94, 284
Mohamad Yamin xxxii, 24, 53, 55, 78, 81, 83, 84, 105, 143, 170, 186, 198, 209
Mozingo, David *See* David Mozingo
MPR (Majelis Permusyawaratan Rakyat, People's Consultative Assembly) 198, 199, 208, 209
MPRS (Majelis Permusyawaratan Rakyat Sementara, Provisional People's Consultative Assembly) 200, 201, 210, 214, 279, 280, 318
Musso 20, 21, 49, 70–73, 309
Mutual Assistance Parliament *See* DPRGR

N

Nahdatul Ulama *See* NU
Nasakom 211, 231, 233, 267, 268, 277, 294, 317
Naspro *See* Fraksi Nasional Progresif
Nasution (General) 186, 190, 196, 197, 200, 252, 258, 277, 288, 290, 294
National Council *See* Dewan Nasional
National Front *See* Front Nasional
National People's Party *See* PRN
National Planning Agency *See* Depernas
National Progressive Faction *See* Fraksi Nasional Progresif
Natsir 60, 169
Njoto 65, 88–90, 93, 98, 214, 277, 287
NU (Nahdatul Ulama, Religious Scholars League) 140, 144, 164, 184, 185, 189, 197, 199, 209, 210, 212, 275, 276, 291

O

Oei Gee Hwat 21, 24, 49, 50, 51, 58, 69, 75
Oei Tiang Tjioe 34, 86, 87
Oei Tjoe Tat 25, 112, 115, 118–121, 130, 131, 134, 135, 138, 139, 144, 191, 193, 227, 232, 233, 238, 268, 288, 294, 295, 297, 319
Oey Hay Djoen 144, 233
Omar Dhani 294, 302
Ong Eng Die 76, 87, 105, 113, 148
Ong Tjong Hay *See* Sindhunatha
Overseas Chinese Federation *See* Kakyo Shokai

P

Panitia Pemilihan Indonesia 125, 133
Panitia Kerja Kewarganegaraan Indonesia 112, 115, 121
Parkindo 142, 144, 149, 159, 182, 185, 212
Partai Buruh 48, 60, 61, 68, 70, 98, 198
Partai Demokrat Tionghoa Indonesia *See* PDTI
Partai Ikatan Pendukung Kemerdekaan Indonesia *See* IPKI
Partai Indonesia *See* Partindo
Partai Katolik 119, 126, 127, 137, 142, 144, 149, 159, 163, 170, 182, 185, 198, 212, 291
Partai Komunis Indonesia *See* PKI
Partai Kristen Indonesia *See* Parkindo
Partai Majelis Syuro Muslimin Indonesia *See* Masyumi
Partai Murba 82, 83, 140, 182, 186, 188, 198, 211, 212, 233, 276, 288, 309
Partai Nasional Indonesia *See* PNI
Partai Persatuan Tionghoa *See* PT
Partai Rakyat Nasional *See* PRN
Partai Serikat Islam Indonesia *See* PSII
Partai Sosialis xxxii, 44, 48, 49, 51, 53, 55, 58, 60, 61, 65, 67, 68, 70, 71, 75, 76, 106, 308, 309
Partai Sosialis Indonesia *See* PSI
Partai Tionghoa Indonesia *See* PTI